ORSON WELLES *in Italy*

ORSON WELLES

in

Italy

Alberto Anile
Translated by Marcus Perryman

INDIANA UNIVERSITY PRESS   *Bloomington & Indianapolis*

This book is a publication of

INDIANA UNIVERSITY PRESS
Office of Scholarly Publishing
Herman B Wells Library 350
1320 East 10th Street
Bloomington, Indiana 47405 USA

iupress.indiana.edu

Telephone orders 800-842-6796
Fax orders 812-855-7931

Orson Welles in Italia by Alberto Anile
Published by arrangement with Editrice Il Castoro Viale Abruzzi
72 20131 Milano (Italia)

Manufactured in the United States of America

Anile, Alberto.
 [Orson Welles in Italia. English]
 Orson Welles in Italy / Alberto Anile ; translated by Marcus Perryman.
   pages cm
 Includes bibliographical references and index.
 ISBN 978-0-253-01041-4 (cloth : alk. paper) — ISBN 978-0-253-01048-3 (pbk. : alk.
paper) 1. Welles, Orson, 1915–1985—Homes and haunts—Italy. 2. Motion picture
producers and directors—United States—Biography. 3. Actors—United States—
Biography. I. Title.
 PN1998.3.W45A6513 2006
 791.4302′33092—dc23
 [B]

2013016446

1 2 3 4 5 18 17 16 15 14 13

CONTENTS

TRANSLATOR'S PREFACE

This book describes Welles's personal and professional life in Italy, his adopted country from late 1947 to 1953, and deals extensively with Italy's reaction to Welles and his films, notably *Macbeth* and *Othello*. Below are brief biographies of the leading film critics whose reviews are quoted throughout the book, and with whom English-speaking readers may not be familiar. I have included a note on André Bazin, a brief gloss on neo-realism, in defense of which the critics attacked Welles, and a summary of this book in relation to contemporary Welles studies.

THE FILM CRITICS AND THEORISTS

Luigi Chiarini (1900–1975)

Filmmaker, screenwriter, critic, and theorist Luigi Chiarini was the co-founder (in 1935) of the Centro Sperimentale di Cinematografia (the Italian National Film School), located near Cinecittà in Rome, which he directed for fifteen years. The school rapidly attained world prominence; its students included the future neorealists Rossellini, Antonioni, De Santis, Zampa, and Germi; the films of Eisenstein and Pudovkin were influential. From 1937 to 1951, Chiarini edited *Bianco e Nero*, the school's theoretically oriented in-house journal. In one of its first issues he expressed his lifelong belief that film is art, and cinema is industry.[1] Together with *Cinema*, edited after 1938 by Vittorio Mussolini, this journal provided a forum for filmmakers to discuss their ideas. *Cinema* became particularly associated with *verismo* in films, a commitment to contemporary social issues that would later morph into neorealism. In the 1940s, Chiarini directed five films—most based on literary works—that were characterized by a high degree of formalism. His last film, *Patto col diavolo* (*Pact with the Devil*, 1949) appears to be in polemical opposition to neorealism, an aesthetic and moral position he supported in all his critical writings. He regarded neorealism as the dialectic between war and peace, civilization and barbarism, and reaction and progress. For Chiarini, neorealism was a critique of social systems, although he warned against film espousing the viewpoint of any political party.

His colleague at the Centro Sperimentale, contributor to *Bianco e Nero*, and translator of Russian film theory Umberto Barbaro (1902–1959) saw film as a form of social and political action—to be modeled on the Soviet school—and urged filmmakers to be active in the political debate. Barbaro frowned on Zavattini's form of documentary neorealism, criticized Visconti for his lack of political commitment, and was intolerant of Rossellini's, Fellini's, and Antonioni's experiments in neorealism during the 1950s. Together Chiarini and Barbaro gave a strong imprint to the film culture of the postwar period.

Chiarini wrote many film scripts in this period, including, in 1953, the screenplay for De Sica's *Stazione termini* (*Indiscretion of an American Wife*), based on a story by Cesare Zavattini and with contributions by Truman Capote. The film ran into production difficulties immediately, with co-producer David O. Selznick firing off daily complaints to De Sica, who read no English.

Chiarini's seven books are a mixture of militant criticism and film theory, the last of them, *Cinema e film* (The film industry and films, 1972), anthologized his lectures at the University of Urbino, where he taught from 1967 until his death. He and Guido Aristarco were the first film critics and theorists to be appointed to full-time academic posts in Italy. In 1969, he published the pamphlet *Un leone e altri animali* (A lion and other animals), dedicated to his years running the Venice Film Festival (1963–1968), including the 1968 challenge to his direction—which came, paradoxically, from the left.

Initially a supporter of Fascism and follower of Giovanni Gentile, in the postwar period he was a Marxist intellectual with a tendency toward moralism. He persuaded the philosopher Benedetto Croce to publicly endorse his unpopular position on film as an art form. He was an influential thinker and, for many years, a driving force in the Italian film industry.

The National Film School he co-founded is now significantly involved in the restoration of films from the 1940s and 1950s, which might otherwise have been lost.

Guido Aristarco (1918–1996)

Guido Aristarco was a Marxist film critic and theorist influenced by Gramsci and Georg Lukacs.[2] He founded *Cinema Nuovo* in 1952 and edited the journal for over forty years. In 1946, he scripted the Aldo Vergano film *Il sole sorge ancora* (The sun also rises—not an adaptation of the Hemingway novel—released in the United States as *Outcry*). In 1953, he and Renzo Renzi co-wrote the script *L'armata s'agapò* (The "I love you" army) on the Italian occupation in Greece; he was imprisoned for forty-five days following its publication and was successfully sued for slander by the Italian Army. In the ensuing scandal, the press accused the military tribunal of being little more than a firing squad. In 1954, Aristarco's former employer *Cinema* was acquired by the parliamentarian and future minister of culture Egidio Ariosto. In 1969, Aristarco and Luigi Chiarini were awarded the first chair in film history in Italy. Aristarco's lessons were based on his close relationships with the protagonists of the Italian film industry—notably Cesare Zavattini, the most rigorous theorist and practitioner of neorealism. Aristarco is considered a leading expert on the films of Luchino Visconti and the Taviani brothers. In May 1943, the war still raging, he had praised Visconti's *Ossessione* for its "intimate fusion of style and human values" as opposed to the easy—and sometimes sleazy—entertainment of the Fascist era. After viewing the film, Vittorio Mussolini stormed out of the cinema, crying, "This is not Italy!" Aristarco also praised Visconti's *Senso* (1954), where Chiarini and others had criticized it, for embodying a form of historical realism he called revolutionary. In his view, the film moved neorealism into critical realism. According to Mark Shiel, "Aristarco argued that, rather than rely on the simple interaction of camera and environment, realist cinema should rely on the creative intervention of the film maker applied to the adaptation of historic novels whose detailed reconstructions of the past could enlighten viewers on the possibility of a better collective future."[3] In the 1950s, after savaging *La strada* (1954), Aristarco began to accept the new cinema of Fellini and Antonioni as they moved away from neorealism. His influential books include *L'arte del film* (The art of film), *Storia delle teoriche del film* (The history of film theory), *Il dissolvimento della ragione: Discorso sul cinema* (The fading of reason: An essay on film), as well as works on Marx and the cinema, neorealism, Visconti, Antonioni, and the film industry under Fascism. In 2007, Falsopiano published a volume edited by Lorenzo Pellizzari and dedicated to Aristarco's work as a film critic: *Il mestiere del critico* (The critic's profession); it included many of his reviews.

Aristarco's prescriptive, rather than descriptive, review style can be seen in his analysis of Steno and Monicelli's *Le infedeli* (*The Unfaithfuls*):

> The world of the rich, of the upper bourgeoisie, is often so absurd and ridiculous that those who fail to go deeply into it, in other words those who fail to get to its roots, instead of giving a critical judgment, end up becoming absurd and ridiculous themselves. This is what happens in the first part of Steno and Monicelli's *Le infedeli* (1952). It would be interesting to investigate why Italian realist film has yet to produce an important document on the upper bourgeoisie in Italy. For example, in Vergano's *Il sole sorge ancora*[4] the least successful portion of the film—the most schematic—deals with the countess and her world. Even Michelangelo Antonioni in *Cronaca di un amore* did not entirely manage to portray precise human conflicts. Concerned as he was to understand Paola, the wife of the industrialist, he limits the depiction of the psychologies of the two protagonists, virtually isolating them in time and space; and they end up not telling us as much as they should have about the world they come from. . . .
>
> . . . *Le infedeli* is worth seeing. But Italian realist cinema is still without a true document of the upper bourgeoisie and its so-called beautiful people.[5]

It should be noted that Welles's Hollywood films did offer a critique of the American upper bourgeoisie. Italian films needed to go beyond neorealism to provide what Aristarco appears to be asking for. One evident example is Fellini's *La dolce vita* (1960), a film Aristarco praised (presciently comparing it to Petronius's *Satyricon*) while trying to define it as belonging to a now superseded neorealism by virtue of its episodic narrative structure—what Fellini called "filmed newspaper" or "illustrated newspaper on film."

Gian Luigi Rondi (b. 1921)

A film critic, screenwriter, and prolific author and director, Gian Luigi Rondi has been the head of the David di Donatello Institute since 1981.

Originally a theater critic, Rondi became the film critic for *il Tempo* in 1947 and for the film journal *La Rivista del Cinematografico* and the Italian edition of *Le Figaro* in 1948. From 1948 to 1954 he taught cinema history and aesthetics at the Pro Deo International University in Rome (today LUISS). He was part of the Jury at the tenth, eleventh and twelfth Venice Film Festivals (1949–1951) and presented a program of film criticism on radio from 1950 until 1995. He has been on the jury of the film festivals in Cannes, Berlin, and Rio de Janeiro.

In 1951, he edited *Il Neorealismo Italiano,* published by the Organizers of the Venice Film Festival. His publications include *Vent'anni di cinema a Venezia* (as editor, 1952) and *Cinema italiano, oggi* (1952) with a preface by Cesare Zavattini and contributions by Alessandro Blasetti. He began writing for the prestigious film journal *Bianco e Nero* in 1952. He has directed innumerable documentaries in the fields of art, music, and contemporary history, and collaborated with G. W. Pabst on the script for *La voce del silenzio* (*Voice of Silence*). In 1954, he co-scripted *La contessa scalza* (*The Barefoot Contessa*) with J. L. Mankiewicz and was one of the script writers for the French film *Obsession,* based on the story *Silent as the Grave* by Cornell Woolrich. The following year he worked with director Ladislao Vajda on the Italian dialogue for the Spanish film *Marcellino pane e vino* (*The Miracle of Marcellino*).

In 1959, he reviewed Bolognini's *La notte brava* (*The Big Night*), the film adaptation of Pasolini's novel *Ragazzi di vita* (1955): "If you go and see it, do so as an analyst examining something under a microscope. You will find in it the whole gamut of wretched creatures that are undermining the moral health (and perhaps not only the moral health) of our cinema. It was written by P. P. Pasolini who, notoriously, in his books, gives expression only to the lowest dregs of society in Rome."[6] Three years later, Pasolini's "La ricotta" (one of the short films in *RoGoPaG*) was praised by Moravia and numerous other reviewers. The years immediately following the decline of neorealism were ones of renewal not only for Italian cinema but also, perhaps, for its film criticism.

In 1962 Rondi was asked by Ingmar Bergman to oversee the Italian dubbing of *Winter Light*. He is Italy's elder statesman of film criticism and theory.

Arturo Lanocita (1904–1983)

Arturo Lanocita was a rookie reporter for *Corriere della Sera,* which he joined during the Fascist era (he offered to resign when his anti-Fascist sympathies became known), who worked his way up to film critic, veteran journalist, and senior editor. He published three books while still in his twenties. During the immediate postwar period he collaborated in numerous ventures narrating the lives of interns in prison camps in Switzerland, an experience he shared with his publisher. Although best known as a writer of mystery and crime novels, characterized by a droll, ironic narrative voice, he had a long and distinguished career as a film critic. Preferring a cinema of the imagination, he had been unimpressed with Visconti's neorealist film *La terra trema* (The Earth shakes, 1948). He was a member of the jury at the Venice Film Festival in 1948 and again in 1962. He championed the films of Billy Wilder. Tullio Kezich called him "a gruff and conscientious film critic." His 1950 publication *Cinema: Fabbrica di sogni* (The cinema: Dream factory), in its insistence on film as entertainment, ran contrary to prevailing tastes. His biography of Sofia Loren appeared in 1966. In 1991, Andrea Napoli published a collection of his film writings entitled *Cinema '50: Pagine scelte di un critico militante* (Films of the '50s: Selected reviews by a militant critic).

André Bazin (1918–1958)

Co-founder in 1951 of the influential *Cahiers du cinéma,* Bazin was a pioneering film theorist who broke with traditions based on silent movies to argue the inherent realism of film through continuity (rather than montage), deep-focus photography, and wide angles. His four-volume *Qu'est-ce que le cinéma? (What Is Cinema?)* was published posthumously between 1958 and 1962; two of the volumes were translated into English in the 1970s. Bazin was a liberal Catholic who was influenced by existentialism and the surrealist reading of film noir in the United States. Naremore comments,

Many of the basic tenets of his theoretical writing resemble Sartre's arguments about literature, minus any traces of Marxism. On the grounds of "realism," for example, Sartre wanted to do away with both omniscient narration and temporal ellipsis; modern narratives he argued, should resemble *Ulysses,* employing multiple perspectives and detailed renditions of a day, an hour, or even a minute. For his part, Bazin argues that cinema should provide relatively passive observation rather than intrusive commentary and should make greater use of long takes or *temps morts,* such as the coffee-making sequence in De Sica's *Umberto D.* In place of Sartre's neutral or ambiguous literary narrators, however, Bazin valorized the camera, which he regarded as a phenomenology machine that could preserve ambiguous reality without the tendentious intervention of the human hand.[7]

In his review of De Sica's *Ladri di biciclette* (*Bicycle Thieves,* 1948) Bazin proclaimed a new cinematic form: "No more actors, no more stories, no more sets, which is to say that in the perfect aesthetic illusion of reality, there is no more cinema."[8] In this film, De Sica indicates the gulf between neorealism and Hollywood by showing Antonio putting up a poster of Rita Hayworth at the moment that his bicycle is stolen.

In relation to Welles, it has been argued that Bazin's theoretical framework enabled the first proper criticism of his work. In 1972, V. F. Perkins wrote, "Bazin's work provided an inestimable service by blasting a way through the orthodox impasse. Important artistic procedures which established theory had dismissed now became open to serious discussion. An appreciation of Stroheim, Renoir and Welles, among others, was given a rational basis."[9]

Bazin was also capable of doing what seemed beyond Italian film critics: appreciating both neorealism and Welles, albeit as different steps in the direction of realism in film. In an essay collected in *What Is Cinema?* Bazin wrote,

> Recent years have brought a noticeable evolution of the aesthetic of cinema in the direction of realism. The two most significant events in this evolution in the history of the cinema since 1940 are *Citizen Kane* and *Paisà.* Both mark a decisive step in the direction of realism but by different paths. . . . Orson Welles restored to cinematic illusion a fundamental quality of reality—its continuity. . . .
>
> . . . [He] started a revolution by systematically employing a depth of focus that had so far not been used. Whereas the camera lens, classically, had focused successively on different parts of the scene, the camera of Orson Welles takes in with equal sharpness the whole field of vision contained simultaneously within

the dramatic field. It is no longer the editing that selects what we see, thus giving it an *a priori* significance, it is the mind of the spectator that is forced to discern as in a sort of parallelepiped of reality with the screen as its cross-section. . . . Thanks to the depth of focus of the lens, Welles restored to reality its visible continuity.[10]

NEOREALISM

Neorealism was a highly influential way of filmmaking in Italy, based on a documentary style, location filming, often using nonprofessional actors, natural lighting, loose storylines, and discreet directorial guidance. The masterpieces of neorealism are generally considered to be Rossellini's postwar trilogy *Roma città aperta* (*Rome, Open City,* 1945), *Paisà* (*Paisan,* 1946), and *Germania anno zero* (*Germany Year Zero,* 1947); De Sica's *Sciuscià* (*Shoeshine,* 1946), *Ladri di biciclette,* and *Umberto D.* (1951); and Luchino Visconti's *La terra trema* (1948)—all released in a period of just five years.

However, in its broadest definition, neorealism spanned the years from the mid-1940s to the end of the 1950s, a period corresponding roughly to the era of American noir, with which Welles has been associated (but should not be identified) by virtue of *The Stranger, The Lady from Shanghai,* and *Touch of Evil.* According to Robert Sklar, even *Macbeth* would qualify:

> The hallmark of the *film noir* is the sense of people trapped—trapped in webs of paranoia and fear, unable to tell guilt from innocence, true identity from false. Its villains are attractive and sympathetic, masking greed, misanthropy, malevolence. Its heroes and heroines are weak, confused, susceptible to false impressions. The environment is murky and close, the setting vaguely oppressive. In the end, evil is exposed, though often just barely, and the survival of good remains troubled and ambiguous.[11]

Thematically, neorealism and noir explored the shifting roles in society after the war. In one instance, the two genres settled on the same story: Visconti's *Ossessione* (1943) was based on James Cain's *The Postman Always Rings Twice* and predated the first Hollywood version by three years. There may be some noir influence reflected in the portrayal of the treacherous Marina in *Roma città aperta* and in the use of black for evil and mirrors to indicate duplicity. Rossellini's *La paura* (*Fear,* 1954), was rather Hitchcockian, with atmospheric shadow and chiaroscuro, a clearly symbolic use of objects, dream and nightmare sequences influenced by expressionism, and jarring sounds.

Borde and Chaumeton briefly discuss the influence of noir on Italian neorealism:

> In Italy, more readily than in France, realism takes the form of a social commentary and occasionally reworks the style of Soviet films. Few of its details echo the noir series, even in the more disenchanted works. Nevertheless, Giuseppe De Santis has handled certain sequences in *Riso amaro* (1949) in the style of American films: the settling of scores in the butcher's shop, amid the sides of beef, the scene in the silo, or the thrashing Vittorio Gassman gives his mistress. In *Anna* (1951), Silvana Mangano performs a dance number and an exotic song that are meant to recall those in *Gilda*. In this uneven film there is, furthermore, a fight to the death in the cellars of a watermill inspired by the Hollywood tradition, some of whose dramatic devices the director, Alberto Lattuada, has managed to assimilate. *Senza pietà* (1948) is another example of this. More to our liking, Fernando Cerchio's *Il bivio* (1951) with its police inspector-cum-gang boss, would be more reliant on the gangster film.[12]

The first films to be called noir were the French prewar poetic realist films made by Duvivier, Renoir, Carné, Chenal, and others. Many of the Italian neorealists, most notably Luchino Visconti, worked with poetic realist filmmakers before starting their own independent careers. When the French used the term noir in reference to Hollywood pictures, they recalled something that they had seen in their own films, which had elements of realism that were utilized by Italian filmmakers but that critics were less able to spot. In Italy, critics noted the expressionist, rather than realist, effects of noir, and this may have contributed to their perception of Welles as an out-and-out expressionist.

Like American noir, neorealism was not a single philosophy or method of filmmaking, as the three different approaches to the genre by leading exponents, cited below, indicate. Vittorio De Sica described it as "an overwhelming desire to throw out of the window the old stories of the Italian cinema, to place the camera into the mainstream of real life, of everything that struck our horrified eyes,"[13] and wondered,

> What is the point of going off to seek extraordinary adventures when what happens under our very noses, to the least fortunate among us, is itself so full of genuine anxiety? Some time ago, literature discovered this modern dimension

based on minimal things, states of mind that are considered too common. A camera is the best way to capture this reality. Its sensibility is of this kind, and that is how I think of realism, which is not a documentary.[14]

Rossellini described his filmmaking at the time of *Roma città aperta* in a way that suggests psychological urgency, technical virtuosity, and a relentless investigation of the subject:

> I need a depth of perspective that perhaps only the cinema can give; to see people and things from all sides; and to be able to cut, leave out, dissolve and use interior monologue. Not, you understand, in the way of Joyce—more like Dos Passos. To put some things in and leave others out, to include what takes place around a given event that may, perhaps, however distantly, have given rise to it. I will be able to place the camera according to my abilities and the characters will be followed and obsessed by it: today's anguish comes precisely from this inability to escape the implacable eye of the camera.[15]

Rossellini was to pursue these aims into the fifties, adopting experimental techniques with sequencing, montage, and lengthy close-ups on faces, particularly that of his wife, Ingrid Bergman. Opposed to this auteurist stance was Zavattini's idea of neorealism as an almost directorless record of history unfolding, a pure documentary style. In a 1951 interview Zavattini told Pasquale Festa Campanile,

> Let's take a character, say Umberto D. Of course the character was taken from reality; it didn't start out as an intellectual exercise. I think that instead of telling the story of Umberto D. we should tell the story of a real person who has retired, with him as the protagonist. That doesn't mean that, right from the start, the cinema forgoes the ability to tell a story in a way that moves an audience. But I'd say even more. The kind of cinema I'm interested in doesn't tell the story of something that happened, of a real event, with the actual people involved playing themselves. No, I think the cinema should show what *is happening*. The camera should look at what is in front of it.[16]

Neorealism reflected the complex relations in postwar Italy between progressive politics and Catholic charity. The demilitarized, yet hardening, political polarization in the country created an atmosphere in which the evident but nuanced moral and ideological content of neorealism was subjected to the harsher, often overly simplistic, rival claims of the left and right. Visconti was championed by the former; Rossellini was thought to favor the center-right.

In 1951 Giulio Andreotti, an influential ministerial undersecretary
and later prime minister in a succession of governments, criticized De
Sica's *Umberto D.* for giving a false and negative view of Italy. As a result
distributors withdrew the film, the Cannes Film Festival was instructed
not to give it recognition, and few people actually saw it. The industry
took note, and proponents of the narrow definition of neorealism point
to this moment as the effective end of the movement.[17]

Despite Italian critics' fierce defense of neorealism (and dismissal
of other genres), it would be wrong to suppose that Italian filmgoers in
the postwar period appreciated nothing else. Many were surreptitiously
drawn to American films, as Tullio Kezich has written of his generation,
born around 1930:

> For many of us, Bogart was an idol. We kept a private space to enjoy films as they
> needed to be enjoyed, without having a ready answer for everything, without
> necessarily having to award political points to everything we saw. Maybe the
> following day at the local cinema club we would present *Non c'è pace fra gli ulivi*,
> in the presence of the director. We would have loved to organize a debate on
> Humphrey Bogart. Instead, we talked about rice pickers.[18]

This supports Naremore's intuition about the attraction of noir:
"[T]he themes of isolation, ambiguity, and uncertainty must have ex-
erted a strong appeal to anyone who was wary of collective politics and
inclined to treat social issues in terms of personal ethics."[19] The Italian
critics who attacked Welles espoused collective politics, outside which
personal ethics made little sense.

After the heyday of neorealism, Pasolini indicated its tacit assumptions and the need for a new form of realism:

> In neo-realist films, day-to-day reality is seen from a crepuscular, intimistic,
> credulous and above all naturalistic point of view. . . . [I]n neo-realism, things
> are described with a certain detachment, with human warmth mixed with
> irony—characteristics which I do not have. Compared with neo-realism, I
> think I have introduced a certain realism, but it would be rather hard to define
> it exactly.[20]

Federico Fellini[21]—a filmmaker with impeccable neorealist creden-
tials who was to display a certain baroque taste in the 1960s, when the
"economic miracle" had changed the social and economic complexion
of Italy—was able to say what would never have been forgiven of Welles:

"Why should people go to the movies if films show reality only through a very cold and objective eye? It would be better just to walk around in the street."[22] Ironically, in this context, Benamou has suggested that Welles was actually a forerunner of Italian neorealism:

> First [in *It's All True*] . . . Welles chose to work with nonprofessional actors in key roles to provide texture to the depiction of stories based on lived experience. Second, through the focus on ritualized activity shown in both reenacted and directly documented form . . . he rejoins the "fictionalized individual" to the social and national collectivity, thereby increasing the synecdochal value of the characters and the symbolic reach of the plot.
>
> These moves echo the fictional experiments in Mexico of Fred Zinnemann in *Redes* (*The Wave,* 1934) and of Herbert Kline in *The Forgotten Village,* while anticipating the work of Italian neorealists such as Luchino Visconti (*La terra trema*) and of Latin American filmmakers who adopted neorealist strategies in their fictional films in the fifties and early sixties.[23]

This may further help to explain the acrimonious standoff between Welles and Italian critics, for whom neorealism was wholly a product of Italian ingenuity that rose out of the ashes of war and bore the stamp of a moral and ethical authenticity deemed to be beyond the reach of a filmmaker such as Welles.

ORSON WELLES IN ITALY AND WELLES STUDIES

English and American readers of this book will perhaps recognize the tone and content of specific criticisms leveled at Welles by the Italian reviewers of *Macbeth* and *Othello;* at times they are strikingly similar to the films' reception in the English-speaking world. Indeed, the American reviews were often fiercer: for example, in *The New Republic,* Robert Hatch wondered if audiences viewing *Macbeth* might think the film had been "made in the Carlsbad Caverns by a company of Mongolian yak herders."[24] Readers may also be familiar with the numerous biographies of Welles and related works, which Jonathan Rosenbaum grouped thus: "One attitude, predominantly American, sees his life and career chiefly in terms of failure and regards the chief question to be why he never lived up to his promise—his 'promise' almost invariably being tied up with the achievement of *Citizen Kane.* . . . The other attitude—less monolithic and less tied to any particular nationality, or to the expectations aroused by any single work—views his life and career more sympathetically as well as inquisitively."[25] In the first group Rosenbaum includes Charles Higham, Robert Carringer, Pauline Kael, David Thomson, and—to a lesser extent—Simon Callow. In the second he places Bazin, Berthomé, Brady, Juan Cobos, Peter Cowie, Barbara Leaming, Joseph McBride, James Naremore, Esteve Riambau, and Peter Bogdanovich. He does not mention Peter Noble's 1956 biography of Welles, and in an aside, cites Laura Mulvey as not belonging to either category. Robert Garis would presumably fit into the first group; Clinton Heylin (mostly), Peter Conrad, and Irving Singer belong to the second,[26] captained by Catherine Benamou. Alberto Anile's analysis of Welles's reception in Italy and the failed attempts by the filmmaker to win over Italian critics is sympathetic to Welles's lifestyle and art. It is critical of the ideological stance of the reviewers, some of whom considered it their duty not so much to comment on films as to influence, if not determine, their content and style—for the good of society. Several were also exponents of filmmaking. Their aesthetics were influenced by the philosophy of Benedetto Croce, who had vigorously opposed the revaluation of the baroque in European culture, which he regarded as a symptom of chronic political and moral weakness. However, these critics also considered Croce's brand of idealist aesthetics complicit in the rise of Fascism in Italy, so their antagonism toward the baroque appears to have been motivated by its remoteness from the pressing concerns of the day. In other words, they took it as an affront. Anile points to the virtual cultural hegemony of Marxist critics in the important film journals and newspapers of the era as another reason for Welles's hostile reception in the country. Like Eisenstein in the Soviet Union, with whom he was compared, Welles was accused of formalism. In Eisenstein's case the fault was supposed to lie in an excessive interest in camera angles, montage, and technicalities at the expense of socialist realism. The Italian critique of Welles was not dissimilar.[27] Bazin, on the other hand, saw the two filmmakers quite differently. In his essay "The Evolution of the Language of Cinema," written in the early 1950s, he suggested that Welles's long takes and deep focus were fundamentally realist, whereas Eisenstein's technique of montage was not. Alone among critics, Bazin saw Welles and neorealism as giving back to the cinema "a sense of the ambiguity of reality."[28] The Italian critics did their utmost to exclude from the minds of their readers any association of Welles with realism, let alone neorealism.

This book gives the first detailed account of the proceedings—some might say machinations—of the Venice Film Festival in 1948, which set Welles up for a heavy tumble. It describes the events surrounding the no-show of *Othello* at the festival in 1951. Running through the narrative is Welles's frustration with Italy and his bluff manner that estranged sympathies. Equally evident, at times, is the seething resentment of his hosts. Listed as a Communist sympathizer by the Californian Committee on Un-American Activities chaired by State Senator Jack Tenney,[29] in Italy Welles was derided by Marxist critics for making films that failed to engage socially and politically in a way that was recognizable and acceptable to them. Having left Hollywood to make films independently, Welles found his reputation in Italy was tarnished by the Hollywood films he needed to act in to finance his own projects. Un-American in America, too American in Italy; a Communist sympathizer at home, the proponent of an aesthetics implicated with Fascism abroad.

Some observers saw in *Othello* something of Welles's relationship to Italy (and Europe)—he in the role of the Moor, the outsider and brash doer; Italy as Iago, the cunning, treacherous underminer. Peter William Evans recounts that when Welles was desperately looking for funds for *Othello*, Alexander Korda reneged on a promise to cast him as Willems in Reed's follow-up to *The Third Man*, the Conrad adaptation *Outcast of the Islands*.[30] Welles had been counting on a large paycheck, but the part went to another member of the cast from *The Third Man*, Trevor Howard, whose gaunt look may have been considered more suitable. Given Welles's interest in Conrad, it would have been interesting to see how he would have handled the role of Willems, an overreacher, exiled geographically and from himself. Evans cites psychoanalytical sources to trace the trajectory of the migrant's search for knowledge coupled with a tendency to put obstacles in his own way;[31] the migrant's experience follows a pattern of "migration–exile–expulsion," which Evans likens to Willems's trajectory. Anile reveals that Welles's unused script, *The Emperor*, based on Pirandello's *Enrico IV*, dealt with similar concerns and perhaps reflected Welles's awareness of his own "inner exile" and an intuition of his future "expulsion" from a country that had begun to ridicule and belittle him.

Anile presents firsthand testimony of the crew of *Othello*, which includes intriguing shooting details provided by the cameraman Oberdan Troiani and eyewitness accounts of Welles's working practices, his reactions to criticism, and his personal life. The subtext throws up insights into the political battle raging in Italy at the time of Welles's arrival, after the referendum abolishing the monarchy but before the first general election of the republic, a period in which it was unclear whether Italy would seek to remain within the American sphere of influence or elect a Communist government with links to the Soviet Union. At this delicate moment, on the eve of a general strike, Welles met the head of the Italian Communist Party, Palmiro Togliatti. The book intriguingly eavesdrops on their conversation and suggests that Togliatti sought political capital by publicizing their meeting under his strict supervision. The political battle included a fight for control of the film industry within Italy and with the United States, by the creation of a bureaucracy to ensure that money made in Italy was recirculated in the Italian economy. On numerous occasions Welles became ensnared within this bureaucracy. The book itemizes all expenses associated with *Othello* and provides, for the first time, a complete list of its cast and crew. No account of Welles's life has had as much to say about the crucial years between 1947 and 1953, when Welles made his first fully independent film.

Since Alberto Anile completed *Orson Welles in Italia* in 2006, several important books have touched on these years or the issues discussed by the author. They are listed chronologically below, with references to pages that also treat the concerns of this book:

Joseph McBride, *What Ever Happened to Orson Welles?* (Lexington: University Press of Kentucky, 2006): Reasons for Welles's exile in Europe and his relations with the IRS, FBI, and HUAC, 48–54, 106–108; *Othello*, 111–14; Hedda Hopper, 96; departure for Europe, 97–99; theme of betrayal, 192

Simon Callow, *Hello Americans* (London: Vintage, 2007): Welles and the Black Dahlia case, 377–79; Welles's interference with Ratoff on *Black Magic*, 415; *Macbeth* (including U.S. and UK reviews), 414–41; *Othello*, 441

Jonathan Rosenbaum, *Discovering Orson Welles* (Berkeley and Los Angeles: California University Press, 2007): Welles and *The Third Man*, 261–68; 1992 "restored" version of Othello, 163–74; American reaction to *Macbeth*, 167–68

Catherine L. Benamou, *It's All True: Orson Welles's Pan-American Odyssey* (Berkeley, Los Angeles, and London: University of California Press, 2007): Welles as *auteur*, 146–52; *Macbeth* and *Othello*, 177–78, 185–87; Welles's baroque sensibility, 184; Welles, documentary, and fiction, 167–72, 206–10
Chris Welles Feder, *In My Father's Shadow* (Edinburgh and London: Mainstream, 2010): Making *Macbeth*, 28–35; Olivier's tribute to Welles, 110

In 2007, Milan-based Il castoro published the papers presented at a February 2–4, 2006, Welles conference held in Udine, Italy, under the title *My Name Is Orson Welles: Media, forme, linguaggi*, edited by Giorgio Placereani and Luca Giuliani (translations from French by Giorgio Placereani and from English and Spanish by Giorgio Placereani and Valentina Cordelli). The book includes contributions by Alberto Anile (on Welles and his Italian critics), Carlos Aguilar (on Welles and European genre cinema), Jean-Pierre Berthomé (on Welles and the dream of total creative independence), Jean-Loup Bourget (Welles as White Elephant?), Peter Conrad (on Welles in Venice), Giorgio Cremonini (Welles the comedian), Elena Dagrada (from *Heart of Darkness* to *F for Fake*), Maurizio Del Ministro (on utopia in Welles's poetics), Gianfranco Giagni (on Welles, the voice, words), Loretta Guerrini (on Welles and the paternal and maternal archetype), Nuccio Lodato (on Welles, an outsider in Washington), Roy Menarini (on *F for Fake* and the strange falsity of cinema), Mariapaola Pierini (on aborigines and men with film cameras) Giorgio Placereani (on Welles, reader of *Dracula*), Roberto Pugliese (on the music of *Citizen Kane*), Ángel Quintana (on *F for Fake* and the boundary lines of the contemporary documentary), Esteve Riambou (on the impossible *Quixote2*), Jonathan Rosenbaum (on methodological observations on Wellesian research), Paolo Spaziani (on Deleuze, metamorphosis, and Welles), François Thomas (on voiceover narration), Micaela Veronesi (on Welles's prefaces), Peter von Bagh (on Welles and TV) and Santos Zunzunegui (on melancholy, incompletion, mannerism, and DIY in Welles).

For details of the correspondence between Welles, Republic, and others about the initial editing and subsequent relooping of *Macbeth*, see Catherine L. Benamou, "'Everybody's Orson Welles': Treasures from the Special Collections Library at the University of Michigan," *Michigan Quarterly Review* 48, no. 2 (Spring 2009): 187–97. The effects of the relooping of the soundtrack of *Macbeth* are described by Michael Anderegg in *Orson Welles, Shakespeare and Popular Culture* (New York: Columbia University Press, 1999), 91–93.

André Bazin's biography and criticism of Welles was translated into English by Jonathan Rosenbaum and others as *Orson Welles, A Critical View* (Los Angeles: Acrobat, 1991). (See "André Bazin and the Politics of Sound in *Touch of Evil*," in Rosenbaum, *Discovering Orson Welles*, 62–66). Rosenbaum's translation is the version I consulted.

In the notes, I have translated titles of newspaper, journal and magazine articles, and books that are not self-explanatory. In the text, I have translated excerpts from articles written by Welles and others, published in Italian, for which there are no traceable originals in English.

ORSON WELLES *in Italy*

Introduction

I pray you, in your letters,
When you shall these unlucky deeds relate,
Speak of me as I am; nothing extenuate,
Nor set down aught in malice.

—*Othello*

Welles's Italian exile began and ended with escape. Welles fled Hollywood for Rome, to act in Ratoff's swashbuckler *Black Magic* (1947); a few years later he quit the set of Steno's *L'uomo, la bestia e la virtù* (1953), being shot on the Amalfi coast, and headed back to America. These are the most adventurous and uncertain years of Welles's film career, characterized by continuous roaming in Italy, Europe, and North Africa. With *The Lady from Shanghai*, Welles had made his last attempt at a career in Hollywood on his own terms. In his nearly six years in Italy he worked on numerous projects but turned only one into a film. Meanwhile, the myth of the histrionic, unreliable Welles, an exile of his own genius, began to take shape.

Welles arrived in Italy on a cold autumn evening, leaving behind him a Hollywood that did not understand him. He sought new stimuli in a country brought to its knees by war, with which he had perhaps only one thing in common: the wish to shake off the dust of the past and start afresh. Straight away it was an idyll: Welles said the Eternal City had adopted him; he rented a house in Frascati, made agreements with production companies large and small, courted Italian actresses, and said Italy was "an adorable country."

But Italy spurned Welles. After a few months of curiosity, high society in Rome's Via Veneto considered him one of the great disappointments of the postwar period. Producers began to go back on what they had promised, the most influential film critics called his films presumptuous, horrible, and messy; at least one actress turned down a proposal of marriage and others left him. For six years Welles lived in or near Rome—through some ups and many downs—until he finally called it quits and left. He then married an Italian actress—only to live in France, Spain, and America, and return to Italy only once in a while to shoot commercials or appear in films such as Pasolini's short "La ricotta." His wife, Paola Mori, had a villa in Fregene, a seaside resort outside Rome. Gradually—inevitably—he fell out of love with Italy and became more detached and cynical about the country that had never shown him much respect.

In all of Welles's career, the period from autumn 1947 to the spring of 1953 is the one that has been investigated least. Most biographies skip through the period—making only a few references to the films in which he acted, details of the one film he made, and a few anecdotes, sometimes with misspelled Italian names. This is not surprising, perhaps; certainly a biographer who knew no Italian would find it very difficult to write about the period. But the fact that no Italian has ever tried to tell the story of Welles's reception in Italy is at least strange; one might even say it is suspicious. No Italian academic has attempted a detailed analysis of Welles's career in Italy and no Italian writer has filled in the gap in the biographies. The reason is essentially guilt: Italian film criticism—the schematic or priestly variety—first welcomed Welles's films, then heaped scorn upon them and ended up insulting their creator. The clash reached such levels of bad faith and pettiness that most critics subsequently had no wish to recall their previous comments, preferring not to disturb the veil of dust that had settled on their words.

In Welles's wandering life, six years in one country is a record. It is hard to imagine him, had his reception been warmer, actually settling in Italy. Nevertheless, the hostility he faced there almost certainly cut his sojourn short; he was admired in France and given a warm welcome in Spain. Welles left Italy not because of rumored debts or to take on new creative challenges, but because his talents went unrecognized in his adopted country and none of his films—not even *Citizen Kane*—was given a dispassionate appraisal.

The aversion of Italian film critics to Welles should be viewed in light of several factors: the influence of the propaganda of the American media machine, which depicted him as an overexcited narcissist and buffoon, and the conviction held by many critics that serious artists and filmmakers were shyly retiring, spiritually elevated people who shunned the limelight. Yet these would not have been enough to make Welles a persona non grata in Italy. Certainly his character—proud and ingenuous, aggressive and fatalistic—played into the hands of the supporters of neorealism and their ideological objections to Welles's art. Frustrated and irritated, Welles responded by increasingly appealing to an absolute artistic freedom, which took him down the road of independent filmmaking with all the risks and dangers, delays, fast footwork, and double-talk that this ambition involved. For this courageous—some might say foolhardy—act, he was given no credit at all in his adopted country. Even given bad luck and the accidents that befell him and his films, the hostility Welles faced in Italy—the persistent aversion and obstinacy of its leading film critics and the ostracism that was decreed, justified, and prolonged—is hard to understand, unless one considers these critics to have been immature and provincial. The face-off led to animosity and misunderstandings on both sides.

This book aims to show the conflict between Welles and Italy, his unrequited love affair with the country he chose to make his home, and his relations with its film industry and culture. It describes the meeting of Welles with Palmiro Togliatti, head of the Italian Communist Party; and a lawsuit brought by Welles against one of Italy's leading film critics. The book includes episodes in Welles's Italian life previously unknown to the English-speaking world; some of the eyewitness accounts herein were at risk of becoming lost forever. In biographical terms the focus is on the making of *Othello*, the only film Welles completed film during his Italian years, from the initial interest of producer Michele Scalera to the final editing of the various versions. The middle chapters include previously unpublished information about the production of the film, its cost and financing, cinematic techniques, and shooting, with explanations and remarks from several crewmembers. The final chapters of the book are dedicated to the filmmaker's numerous returns to Italy after 1953.

Analysis of Italian film reviews and newspaper articles from 1947 to 1953 was fundamental to the writing of this book. Many of the authors are no longer with us, and all that remains of their testimony are their reviews and reports of Welles's daily life. I have consulted both film journals and newspapers, since these sources contributed equally to public opinion about Welles in Italy as they reflected and reinforced each other. Most of the quotations in this book are from articles and reviews written during this period. Film journals and magazines such as *Bianco e Nero*, *Film*, *Cinema*, *Cinema Nuovo*, *Fotogrammi*, *Hollywood*, *Cine Illustrato*, *La Settimana Incom*—their contents ranging from sophisticated film theory to celebrity gossip—are quoted extensively, and *Oggi* and *Tempo* are among the sources of news about Welles's life in Italy.

Research was carried out in the Rome National Library, the Luigi Chiarini Library at the National Film School near Cinecittà in Rome, the Sormani Civic Library in Milan, and the State Archives in Rome. I would like to thank Maria Paola Scollo of the archive of *il Messaggero;* the Marciana Library of Venice (special thanks to Mirco Toso); Luciana Spina of the Mario Gromo Library of the Turin Cinema Museum; Cesare Ballardini and Anna Fiaccarini of the Bologna Cineteca; the Arnoldo and Alberto Mondadori Foundation and its president, Cristina Mondadori; and the staff of the Mondadori Documentation Center in Corso Europa, Milan, and at corporate headquarters in Segrate. At the Rome National Cineteca I was able to watch a splendid Italian version of *Othello* and material not included in the film, the so-called *Othello Doubles,* a selection from the two thousand meters of unused film from the final months of shooting in Morocco (January–March 1950) that was found in 1994.

Three studies were particularly useful for the critical appreciation of Welles in Italy: Gaetano Strazzulla, "Orson Welles e la critica italiana" (Orson Welles and Italian criticism), *Inquadrature* 12 (Autumn 1964): 19–28; Guido Fink, "Rapporto confidenziale su Orson Welles e la critica italiana"(Confidential report on Orson Welles and Italian criticism), *Bianco e Nero* (January–March 1986): 6–29; and Nuccio Lodato, "Sciangai, Shangai, Shanghai: Welles e la critica italiana" (Sciangai, Shangai, Shanghai: Welles and Italian criticism), in *Nelle terre di Orson Welles* (In the lands of Orson Welles), ed. Toni D'Angela (Alessandria: Falsopiano, 2004), 215–36. Although they declare themselves to be incomplete, they provided a wealth of information.

I presented portions of this book (before its publication) at an international conference in Udine organized by Giorgio Placereani and Luca Giuliani. The papers were collected and published as *My Name Is Orson Welles* (Milan: Il castoro, 2007).

I owe a debt of gratitude to Gianfranco Giagni and Ciro Giorgini's 1993 documentary *Rosabella, la storia italiana di Orson Welles* (Rosebud, the Italian story of Orson Welles). The film inspired me to write this book.

I would like to thank these friends and colleagues for their help in researching the book, for material they provided, and for their advice: Giovanni Austoni, Roberta Avolio, Andrea Barzini, Jean-Pierre Berthomé, Paola Cogotti, Cristina D'Osualdo, Elena Dagrada, Angelo Draicchio, Fabio Ferzetti, Goffredo Fofi, Tag Gallagher, Gianfranco Giagni, Ciro Giorgini, Alessandro Giorgio, Tullio Kezich, Mauro Marchesini, Francesco Marchetti, Miguel Victor Morano, Paolo Piccioli, Pier Luigi Raffaelli, Simone Riberto, Tatti Sanguineti, Ciro Scognamiglio, Daniele Terzoli, François Thomas, Sergio Toffetti, Massimiliano Troiani, and Micaela Veronesi. Those who amiably agreed to return to distant memories included Franca Faldini, Tullio Kezich once more, Gina Lollobrigida, Alvaro Mancori, Patrizia Mori, Giancarlo Nicotra, Gian Luigi Rondi, Gisella Sofio, Sergio Sollima, Alfredo Todisco, and the much-missed Oberdan Troiani—with whom I had the opportunity to speak only once, by phone, and who is now "on the other side, giving Orson Welles the blackest eye you ever saw."

This book is dedicated to M. Gabriella—my lady from Shanghai, my Dulcinea, my Desdemona.

1

Arrival

On December 25 an aeroplane was sighted off
the coast of Barcelona. It was flying empty.
—*Mr. Arkadin*

The weather had been fair over France; a clear autumn sun provided good visibility and a perfectly comfortable ride. The flight was on schedule.

The tiny cockpit of the twin-engine plane was occupied by just two people, Orson Welles and an expressionless English pilot. The two sat beside each other at the controls; behind them was a nacelle full of baggage. The journey was long and tedious: the American passenger spent his time admiring the view, reading, and—when needed—taking over the airplane controls.

Above the Alps, the weather suddenly worsened. The plane hit thick fog; when it was spotted over the Mediterranean it was about to be swallowed by clouds. The pilot stuck to the south-southeast course, but there were no visible landmarks. He lost his way and began to circle, hoping to get out of the mist. Radio contact was lost, a sign that the small Consul was off course.

In a few short hours, every possible landing spot was counted out. A red light came on in the cockpit: fuel was low. Welles closed his book and for the first time looked at the pilot, perplexed. His glance was met by a still-expressionless face.

Daylight was fading; the sky went dim, then red, then black. Above them, stars flickered in and out of the clouds.

They were almost out of fuel; there was no hope of a routine landing. The image of a tiny plane hitting the water, leaving a trail of smoke and oil, came into the two men's minds. They looked down and saw a runway of lights.

"I fear that is Rome," said the pilot, almost apologetically.

When Orson Welles left America for Italy, he was thirty-two years old and already had a reputation as a burned-out talent.

His departure from Hollywood seemed premature. It looked like he was running away. Rumor had it that Welles was somehow involved in the famous Black Dahlia case, the murder of aspiring actress Elizabeth Short in Los Angeles a few months earlier.[1] This was scandal-mongering, of course. The immediate reason behind his flight was a rather shabby cloak-and-dagger film called *Black Magic*, aka *Cagliostro*, to be shot in the Scalera Film Studios. But the deeper reasons were artistic, economic, and political.

Welles had always been a supporter of Roosevelt and the New Deal. He had never officially gone into politics, but he had been involved in electioneering and had written some presidential speeches. He had been friendly with Roosevelt himself and had often angered the president's wife by keeping him up until the small hours with his blarney.

Once, Welles had been on the point of running for the Senate: Roosevelt was willing to support him, but it seems that California democrats thought he didn't lean far enough left and considered his chances of winning rather poor—even in his home state of Wisconsin, which went, ironically, to the fervent anti-Communist Republican Joseph McCarthy.

Although Welles never belonged to any party, he was clearly thought of by society at large as a left-wing intellectual. It was enough to look at his work in the theater, starting with *Voodoo Macbeth* (1936), a transposition of the Shakespeare tragedy to tribal Haiti that featured a cast largely of black, unemployed, amateur actors. The following year he had staged *The Cradle Will Rock*, a musical supporting the working class, followed by a gloomy, black-shirted *Julius Caesar*, clearly a statement about Hitler and Mussolini, before the invasion of Poland.[2]

Anxiety about the coming war had played an important role in his hoax CBS radio broadcast, *The War of the Worlds*, an adaptation of the

H. G. Wells novel, which had fooled millions of Americans into believing in an ongoing extraterrestrial invasion. Venerated for his radio and theater work, Welles had got the best deal ever struck in Hollywood—a totally free hand—to make *Citizen Kane*, evidently and controversially modeled on the life of the newspaper tycoon William Randolph Hearst.

Then troubles began. Hearst wielded his influence, paid hacks and friends in Hollywood and the theater to try to block the film's release. He ordered his film reviewers to trash *Native Son*, a play Welles had based on a novel by Richard Wright, in which a black man kills a white woman. Hearst's newspapers spoke openly of propaganda and ties with Moscow, forcing the FBI to investigate and leading to the discovery of Welles's membership in the Negro Cultural Committee and the League of American Writers, both considered Communist organizations.

The FBI dossier still exists. James Naremore found dozens of pages of official reports, hate mail, and articles by Hedda Hopper, Hearst's favorite hack, claiming that Welles's work in the theater and journalism was in the service of the Soviet cause. "The cumulative evidence," one report says, "adds to the conclusion that Orson Welles' interests are entirely bound up with those of the Communist Party."[3]

Hearst could not stop the release of *Citizen Kane*, but he did manage to make sure it was poorly distributed. The young filmmaker's career was on the line. Every subsequent film Welles was to make would run into production difficulties, disputes in the cutting room, disagreements with distributors, and commercial failure. While he was shooting *It's All True*, a government-backed project, in South America, producers reedited his second film, *The Magnificent Ambersons*, beyond all recognition. No one in Hollywood was prepared to back a prestigious or ambitious Welles project. He agreed to work as director and actor in the botched *Journey into Fear*; sought commercial success through noir, albeit an unusual version of it, with *The Stranger*; and continued voicing his political views: "The phoney fear of Communism is smoke-screening the real menace of renascent Fascism."[4] He was on a slippery slope. J. Edgar Hoover had his name added to the Security Index as a possible anti-American menace.

The extraordinary creator of *Citizen Kane* was by 1947 a marginalized artist. He tried to woo back the studios by directing the diva (his wife) Rita Hayworth in *The Lady from Shanghai*. Then, more or less as a bet, he made a Shakespearean film, *Macbeth*, for the small studio Republic; he shot the entire film in twenty-three days in the summer of that fateful year.

Roosevelt was no longer president and Truman was intent on fighting an ideological battle with Stalin: the early rumblings of the Cold War. Reacting to anti-Bolshevik sentiment, Republicans and conservative Democrats put pressure on the cultural milieu, including the film industry, whose left-wing sentiment was well known. It was the start of the witch hunt. Beginning in May 1947, the investigation aimed to rid the film industry and theater of so-called subversives. By September the House Un-American Activities Committee (HUAC) had already indicted forty-one prominent figures in Hollywood—the most illustrious being the British actor and filmmaker Charlie Chaplin, who was criticized for his film *Monsieur Verdoux*, "based on an idea by Orson Welles." Soon the hearings were held in public, and in Washington a series of deep throats started coughing up the names of supposed Communists and Communist sympathizers. Accusations were not based on membership in a left-wing party but merely on the profession of certain views. The real aim of the HUAC was to exercise fierce control over American culture by expelling Communist sympathizers from the film industry.

If the HUAC was on your case, you were unlikely to work again. The Constitutional rights of freedom of thought and speech were under attack, prompting many to refuse to cooperate. John Huston, William Wyler, and Philip Dunne founded a Committee for the First Amendment (CFA) to organize a collective defense, publicly criticizing the methods and aims of the hearings. One such appeal was signed by Rita Hayworth. At the end of October, Welles attended a few CFA meetings and the actor Frank Fay called him "as red as a firecracker" in the *Denver Post*.

About the most serious thing the FBI had dug up on Welles was a one-time liaison with a stripper. However, when Welles joined the CFA, Hoover's men dug deeper. A few days later, as Gary Cooper on the other side of America was saying he had turned down some roles because the screenplays were "tinged with red," some California members of the HUAC decided to pay Welles a visit to ask him, point blank, if he was a Communist.

Welles was never a party member. He answered the question with a question: "How do you define a Communist?" The bureaucrats replied, "Someone who takes all your money and gives it to the government." Welles rejoined, "Then the IRS must be 87% Communist."[5]

Welles ducked the question and took the opportunity to be sarcastic about the tax authorities, with whom he had been wrangling for some time. After the 1946 musical extravaganza *Around the World* (an adaptation of *Around the World in Eighty Days*) flopped, he owed around $320,000—and the taxman was relentless, adding fines to arrears.

Welles was vulnerable politically and was being hounded financially. Yet the HUAC had not formally summoned him and he was not short of ideas for the future. He needed money and work, but was unwilling to kowtow to Republicans, William Randolph Hearst, or the taxman in terms of what films to make.

He thought about leaving. In August he traveled incognito to France, where he was preparing *Cyrano de Bergerac* with Marcel Pagnol, a project apparently backed by Alexander Korda. On his return, the producer Edward Small talked to him about a job in Italy. He listened. The film, *Black Magic*, was to be made in Rome by Gregory Ratoff, and Small wanted him to take the lead role. A beautiful city, plenty of money, an undemanding role—and close to France, where he could continue working on *Cyrano*. How could he say no?

The witch hunt intensified. The public hearings were wound up on October 30, when the Hollywood Ten refused to testify and were indicted. Hollywood's major studios fell in line, isolating or firing supposed Communists and jettisoning screenplays that did not celebrate the American way of life. Many filmmakers went to Europe: John Huston to Ireland; Jules Dassin, John Berry, and Ben Barzman to France; and Edward Dmytryk, Joseph Losey, Cyril Endfield, Carl Foreman, and Sam Wanamaker to England.

Welles accepted the *Black Magic* proposal, hoping to start again on his own terms. His situation was not as critical as those of other directors, who had more evident ties to left-wing organizations or who were more blatantly witch-hunted. But this made his departure all the more a slap in the face to Hollywood and its artistic values.

Accused of Communist sympathies after the release of *Monsieur Verdoux*, Charlie Chaplin was the first to talk about Welles's maverick genius in opposition to the majors. When Welles left for Italy, unhesitatingly, he declared, "Hollywood is dying. It no longer produces cinema as art; it just prints miles and miles of film. I should add that it is impossible to penetrate into the realms of the so-called seventh art if you happen to be an anti-conformist or gain a reputation as an 'adventurer' by not heeding the warnings of the majors. I am not pleading my own case here, but look, if you will, at Orson Welles. I may not agree with all his ideas about the cinema, but his career and his fate were decided when he said no to the Hollywood magnates. He no longer has a career or life in Hollywood."[6]

Welles was fleeing—that much was clear even then. America could not offer him the creative opportunities he sought and Hollywood was no longer willing to give him artistic or financial credit. In step with the mood of the times, with treacherous Reds under the beds, Hearst's men threw as many obstacles as they could in Welles's way. The *Black Magic* deal would not have beckoned him away from a more tolerant and understanding America—but the America of Truman and Hoover, where the best filmmakers were humiliated and ostracized daily, was not about to give carte blanche to an upstart and maverick genius who had made his reputation by attacking the most wealthy and influential media tycoon in the land.

Hearst was not above getting involved personally, and told the *Los Angeles Examiner* on November 3 that the film industry was "riddled with Communists." This was perhaps the very day Welles flew to Europe, before the release of *The Lady from Shanghai* and the editing of *Macbeth*. He stopped over in New York on his way to Ireland, accompanied by Barbara Laage, his latest flame. From Dublin he flew on to London and in London he climbed aboard the twin-engine Consul.

November 9, 1947. At Rome's Ciampino Airport a small welcoming party was getting increasingly worried. It comprised Gregory Ratoff, Ratoff's wife, production chief Charles Moses, actress Linda Christian, an advertising executive, a photographer, and an anonymous reporter from the newspaper *Espresso* (he was probably the only journalist present when Welles finally landed).[7]

He was due to arrive at 3:00 PM. At 5:00 PM the only news was that the plane had run into bad weather. Linda Christian and Mrs. Ratoff returned to Rome, leaving the men to wait it out. Rumors began to circulate in the airport; they said the journey had cost Welles as much as £250.

The plane touched down at 9:00 PM, six hours late, and practically out of fuel. Welles appeared, a frown on his face, his eyes red. Despite the evident strain, he looked rather elegant in a blue suit and scarf, light brown overcoat, and shiny black shoes. He was holding a black hat and displayed a healthy mane of hair. "Clean-shaven, he looks much younger," wrote the journalist for *Espresso*, "but no women were there to welcome him, so it is hard to say if they find him attractive."

Customs officials and airport staff took eight leather suitcases out of the plane. The journalist started firing questions. Despite the recent ordeal and his evident tiredness, Welles managed to be complimentary about postwar Italian film and said Alida Valli was becoming a big star in the States. He thought the storm had blown over as far as the hearings featuring Hollywood filmmakers and actors were concerned, but couldn't say what the consequences might be. Political opinions? No comment. Was he planning to make a film about the life of Mussolini? Welles had never had any intention of making a film about the Italian dictator. Divorce from Rita Hayworth? Future marriage plans? No comment.

Just before getting into the car with Ratoff, Welles apologized and went back toward the runway. He rummaged around the cockpit of the Consul for a while until he found the book he had been reading on the flight over, *In the Steps of St. Paul* by H. V. Morton.

Henry Vollam Morton was a journalist and travel writer from Manchester, England, born at the end of the nineteenth century. He had gained some fame by announcing the discovery of Tutankhamen's tomb and from his travel and history books, some of which are still in print. *In the Steps of St. Paul* was a geographical, historical, and cultural reconstruction of St. Paul's journey through the Holy Lands, Greece, and Italy, based on biblical evidence. Welles, too, had repudiated one life for another and, like St. Paul, could have said, *Civis romanus sum*—I am a citizen of Rome—before going on to his own martyrdom.

In Italy, no one expected Welles to start preaching, mainly because he was practically unheard of. A few months earlier, the theater journal *Dramma* had asked, "Who is this Orson Welles?" The journalist Gigi Cane had called him an "intellectual terrorist," in light of the *War of the Worlds* episode and *Voodoo Macbeth,* which he called a "shot from a small caliber gun."[8] The only film that had established a reputation for Welles in Italy was Robert Stevenson's *Jane Eyre,* in which he played Rochester. *Citizen Kane* had not been released in Italy; very few had managed to catch it in France, and among those who hadn't it had an ambiguous reputation. And only the most attentive critics could have seen *The Magnificent Ambersons* and *The Stranger.*

Twenty copies of *The Magnificent Ambersons* had been distributed in Italy in the second half of August (the worst period for film distribution in Italy) 1946.[9] Two cinemas in Rome had shown the film, the Imperial and the Super, together with an MGM documentary on the second atomic explosion on the Bikini Atoll. The film was shown from Wednesday, August 21, to Sunday, August 25, and had then been passed on to the Attualità Cinema until Wednesday, August 28—one week in all. The Corso Cinema in Milan also showed the film for a week, from Saturday, August 24, to Friday, August 30—again with the atomic bomb documentary. Reviews were generally good, and some very good. An anonymous reviewer in *Corriere della Sera* called it a "heavy" picture, but "well-made, particularly in the reconstruction of the late-nineteenth-century setting, acted with style and elegance."[10] The equally unknown stand-in critic for *il Messaggero* was fascinated by the "pared-down, significant cinematic language, with an atmosphere of melancholy and regret," and found the acting "exceptionally measured and delicate ... perfectly in keeping with the overall balance of this excellent movie." Fabrizio Sarazani in *il Tempo* was dazzled by the art direction ("the framework of the film is extraordinarily beautiful") and considered the aesthetics of the film not in the least gratuitous: "The precious elements of many of the film's shots and the oblique camera angles often enhance the characters and their personalities." Even the Vatican's Centro Cattolico Cinematografico spoke of "the constant search for a visual style," "masterly direction," and "real class." The film also went down well with the general public. Release in two major cities for one week was no mean achievement during the torrid summer period. One filmgoer wrote to the magazine *Hollywood* and praised the film for its "marked difference from the standard Hollywood movie."[11] Famed scriptwriter Suso Cecchi d'Amico began to learn her trade by watching the film over and over again, in order to study its structure.

One dissenting voice came from Umberto Barbaro—co-founder with Luigi Chiarini of the Centro Sperimentale di Cinematografia (the Italian National Film School) near Cinecittà—writing for the left-wing newspaper *l'Unità*; he informed readers of Welles's reputation, his attention-grabbing and of the general conformity of Hollywood, making Welles "not so much a rare talent—as they would have you believe—as an eccentric one." Barbaro reported that there was "nothing miraculous" about *The Magnificent Ambersons*. The Marxist critic compared it to the "overly refined" pictures of Soldati and Castellani for Lux, criticizing the excessive aesthetic concern and hence the lack of "political commitment." "Art direction, costumes, and photography," wrote Barbaro, "are certainly very refined, but are showy and without significance, more expensive than elegant. . . . The story, which might have lent itself to interesting historical and social treatment . . . is reduced to one of individuals with no psychological depth or interest. The purpose, if one can call it that, is a tired and indolent exaltation of the capitalist bourgeoisie."[12]

Today these words raise a smile. The film actually records the decadence of the middle class and the devastating effects of industrialization on the social fabric. Newspapers with different political leanings came out in favor of the film, but Barbaro's influential review set the tone for the next ten years—sowing doubts, curbing enthusiasm, and raising eyebrows.

In 1947 the Venice Film Festival featured *The Stranger,* a film of considerable interest, albeit not one of Welles's best. Compared to the melancholic sobriety of *The Magnificent Ambersons,* this new and discomfiting movie baffled the audience, and critics were quick to slap down Welles's unjustified reputation. "We Italians," wrote Arturo Lanocita in *Corriere della Sera,* "don't know much about this explosive artist, who has been causing such a stir in America for some years. . . . All his artistic works have the violence and noise of an explosion. This work, too, has its detonator."[13] Guido Aristarco, in *Sipario*, said "there are some good things" but complained of the "frenetic storytelling with sudden changes of scene, extravagant shots, full of not always justified close-ups of people and things." Adriano Baracco, editor of *Cinema*, was unrestrained: "It's difficult to say whether the 'wunderkind' is a worse actor or director. . . . He obviously wants to astonish, but the director manages to do so only through his utter failure to use the cinematographic medium of expression."

Until his arrival in Rome, however, Welles interested only a handful of cinemagoers and critics. To most people Welles was Rita Hayworth's husband, a strong-looking yet baby-faced man who had won the heart of the world's most beautiful woman—unworthily and temporarily, of course, given the rumors of divorce.

From Ciampino Airport Welles was taken to the Excelsior Hotel, the most famous and luxurious on the Via Veneto. Checking in, he wrote "Negro" on the guest form opposite the question "Race?"

The following day he had lunch with the journalist Luigi Barzini, Jr., former editor of *Corriere d'America* and future author of *The Italians,* and the actor Tullio Carminati, who had spent the 1930s in America. He told them the story of the twin-engine plane running out of fuel, explaining that he had never been afraid for his life. "It would have been illogical to crash into the Mediterranean with a complete stranger, in a rented plane. . . . [J]ust now that I'm throwing myself into new worlds, new experiences. In spring I want to make a film on Cyrano de Bergerac with Sir Alexander Korda, in Rome. I want to make Italian films with Italian actors, I want to write plays, I have an idea for a book. No. Death comes with attendant trappings, everyone gets the death they deserve, which they have earned in life. That was not going to be my death, I could see that straight away. It was too banal, insignificant, futile."[14]

Welles was too optimistic and full of ideas to read anything into that risky flight and narrow escape. He set up court with the help of three Italians who spoke good English: Barzini became his press agent; Carminati was a kind of spokesman and representative; and Antonio Centa, another actor, became his private secretary.

Apart from *Espresso*, no newspaper had reported his arrival. Italian cinemas were featuring Tyrone Power in two of his best-known movies,

The Razor's Edge and *Blood and Sand,* the latter starring Welles's wife, Rita Hayworth. Power had just left town, kicking up dust.

Some newspapers did not come out on Monday so Welles's late Sunday arrival perhaps contributed to the lack of coverage. The story was picked up two days later by *l'Unità,* probably because of the filmmaker's reputation for having Communist sympathies. His almost total obscurity led to a strange misprint: news of his arrival appeared under the photo of the Most Beautiful Baby of 1947, and the baby competition was graced with the photo of an admittedly boyish-looking Orson Welles. *Il Messaggero,* close to Christian Democrat Prime Minister De Gasperi, kept the information of Welles's arrival to itself and did not send anyone to the press conference at the Excelsior some days later.

Osvaldo Scaccia, of Scalera Film, and Luigi Barzini, Jr., organized the press conference on the afternoon of November 12: American actor and director Orson Welles wished to announce his participation in the film *Black Magic* and to discuss his new projects.

Journalists present included Gian Luigi Rondi, the young film critic for *il Tempo,* Sergio Sollima, the future director of the TV series *Sandokan,* then working for *l'Unità,* and Doriana Danton—one of the few women present—of the weekly *Hollywood.* She was not impressed. The photos show Welles in a three-button gray jacket that was a size too large and rather formal for the afternoon, with a large white carnation in the buttonhole, pinstriped pants, and initialed gold cufflinks in starched cuffs. "Well dressed for an American, perhaps," wrote Danton, "but shabby for an Italian."

Others noted that Welles was getting into his role as Cagliostro, who was brought up by gypsies, hence the Errol Flynn mustache and long, curly hair.

The press conference was quite informal. After the initial announcement about the role and movie, the journalists sat in a semicircle around Welles and interpreter Barzini.

Welles was quick witted and affable, if somewhat temperamental when talking about his hopes and projects for the future or about American politics. He used his hands a great deal to talk: "knotty hands," thought some, "a magician's hands," "rather fearsome," "expressive." Sollima recounts, "In actual fact the journalists there knew almost nothing about Orson Welles. Most of the questions concerned Rita Hayworth, from whom he was separating. Orson was irritated and at one point asked us whether we wanted to talk about cinema. I took him up on it. I had already seen *Citizen Kane,* which I quite liked, without thinking it was a masterpiece. The shots were all so bizarre; you end up forgetting the plot and wondering what the director will do next. I asked him if he considered himself a self-indulgent director. It was a barbed question, asked by a journalist who had only a vague notion of cinema, which he deftly answered with an ambiguous smile."

Welles ducked questions about Mussolini and divorce. One reporter found him "blustery, a bit touchy"—perhaps because Danton kept asking about Hayworth until he flared up in anger. But mostly he was good spirited and amiable, and sounded off his famous laugh more than once.

At the end of the press conference he had won most of the reporters over. "Welles is clearly an intelligent man," wrote Sollima, "and an able communicator; his conversation is unusually cultured and tasteful." Cecchi of *Film* thought it was the first decent press conference with a foreign actor since they had started arriving in town. Rondi wrote, "You certainly get the impression you are dealing with a man of intelligence. A number of questions were designed to test him. . . . Welles replied to everyone courteously and good-humoredly, spontaneously and openly." "As if he had learned the part," a colleague insinuated.

"After the conference," Sollima recalled sixty years later, "Welles called me over. 'Now he's going to punch me,' I thought. Instead, he hugs me. Just as well someone asked an intelligent question, he said. Thinking I was affiliated with *l'Unità,* he asked me to arrange a meeting with Palmiro Togliatti. I had to tell him the truth. A friend of mine, the newspaper's theater critic, Luciano Lucignani, was supposed to come to the press conference and I had asked to go in his place, because Welles interested me. I was a freelance journalist. All I knew about Togliatti was that he was head of the Communist Party, nothing more. I told Welles I would pass his message on. I spoke to Lucignani, who probably spoke to the editor in chief at that time, Pietro Ingrao. I don't know what came of it."[15]

Orson Welles

"Hollywood . . . teaches nothing anymore"

PRESS CONFERENCE, ROME, NOVEMBER 12, 1947

Orson Welles's first press conference in Italy took place in the Excelsior Hotel in Via Veneto, in the presence of Osvaldo Scaccia of Scalera Film and the journalist Luigi Barzini, Jr., who acted as interpreter. Numerous journalists attended and the event was widely reported.

The following is a reconstruction of the questions and answers based on the articles in the leading newspapers.[1]

ORSON WELLES: I have come to Rome to play Count Cagliostro, one of my favorite characters, because I feel a little like Cagliostro. I have always liked him because I was once a magician and was good at hypnotizing people. I have come after making *Macbeth,* in which I put all my best ideas: a film I am very satisfied with and which I tried to make unreal and fantastical. But I am also here as a journalist to observe the politics in your country; I would like to meet your leading politicians, De Gasperi, Togliatti, Saragat, and Giannini. I would also like to meet film producers and see if I can make some films in your country.

You mean a film about Italy, made in Italy?

OW: If it is set in the modern day, no. I don't think I could capture your way of life, your spirit, like an Italian director. After *Black Magic,* I hope to direct *Cyrano de Bergerac* here in Rome. And if I direct a film set in Italy I would like it to be about the Renaissance.

Is it true you are thinking of making a film about Mussolini and will play the dictator yourself?

OW: Absolutely not!

But you look a little like him, don't you think?

OW: I am offended! . . . I like dramatic roles, strong, cruel, true to life, but I am not an overbearing, violent man, and I would like that to be known. I'm a quiet man. And I like the characters I play. One I haven't yet managed but would like to play is the hero of *Moby Dick,* Melville's novel. But I will get my own back in London, in spring, when I will do a monologue in the theater.

Do you prefer the theater or the cinema?

OW: It's like asking a painter if he prefers oils or watercolors. I'm happy in both of these art forms.

Do you still paint?

OW: I've almost given it up: I wasn't very good.

Who are your favorite actors?

OW: I understand your question but it isn't very generous to talk about them. You are right to ask and I am right not to answer.

What do you think of Tyrone Power and Alida Valli? Have you seen her first Hollywood movie, The Paradine Case?

OW: Tyrone? A very nice man. And Valli will be a big star, I'm sure of it. I haven't seen *The Paradine Case* but I have seen some reels of RKO's *The Miracle of the Bells;* without doubt she's a great actress.

And Rita Hayworth? What are the reasons for the divorce?

(a diplomatic laugh)

Is that an answer?

OW: No, it is criticism of the question.

Tell us what you think about her as an actress, then.

OW: Rita is an excellent actress. In the film we made together, *The Lady from Shanghai,* she proves it. But she has a huge handicap: she's too beautiful, so the critics see her beauty more than her artistry. She will be appreciated as a great actress a few years from now when she is not so beautiful. In ten years.

What is your opinion of critics?

OW: Critics are harmful, especially when they give prizes and criticize.

Is it true that during the shooting of The Lady from Shanghai *you and Rita Hayworth had artistic differences? That's what the American and French newspapers say.*

ow: No more. Journalists have to invent something!

What do you think of the Italian film industry?

ow: It's very interesting. I'm here to study it more closely. The film I liked best is *Sciuscià*, an important film. And *Roma città aperta* and *Paisà*. Italian films have a future.

Yet your films are very different. They have a tendency toward formalism . . .

ow: I'm aware of it, but I perfectly understand the realism of the best European cinema.

What non-Italian film have you liked recently?

ow: The first half of Carol Reed's *Odd Man Out*.

How did the investigation of actors, including yourself, of the House Un-American Activities Committee go?

ow: I am not a politician and I have never been a Communist. However, I was involved in the recent investigation of liberal actors in Hollywood because I supported Roosevelt's liberal ideas against the reactionary ideas of some American politicians at the moment. At the recent Washington hearings, which in my opinion are against the spirit and letter of the American Constitution, nobody dared call any of these actors to the witness stand, for fear that they would make their protest heard. The unpopularity of the hearings, even among conservatives, was such that nothing came of them. They realized there was no point in going on because they would only have moved public opinion against them, because you cannot stop people thinking what they want in a truly democratic country.

Is it true that Rita Hayworth is a Communist?

ow: Rita Hayworth is a liberal. I can tell you a funny story about this. In Paris they whistled and booed her, calling her the "courtesan of capitalism": perhaps they didn't know she was active in promoting anti-Fascist propaganda during the war. The opposite happened to Barbara Stanwyck, who is a notorious conservative but was applauded by the left.

Have Americans changed a great deal in politics?

ow: Millions of Americans elected Roosevelt four times and they haven't gone away.

What do you think of Hollywood?

OW: Hollywood learns nothing and teaches nothing anymore. The monstrous amount of money required to make a film, any American film, the different sorts of audiences we have to appeal to, the conservatism of businessmen and financiers in Hollywood—interested in recouping the outlay—make it hard to get off the beaten track.

In your opinion, are the capitalists of Hollywood party men and their films promote reactionary politics?

OW: No, they are people who have always been in the film industry, since its beginnings, and now control all of it. They are like sucking fish who instinctively latch onto new ideas in the world, for commercial reasons. It's not easy to win over all markets with just one mentality. The cinema reaches too many people for its messages to be accepted everywhere. Unless you can find a truly universal message that is just as good in Rome as Moscow.

And this message exists?

OW: Perhaps it does. The cinema has huge possibilities. Everybody has something to teach us—including the Italians, with *Sciuscià* and *Roma città aperta,* films made on a shoestring, in which the few resources, poverty, and a certain inexperience become virtues and qualities compared to rich production sets, where the product is shiny, refined, banal. Italians make films that in Hollywood wouldn't get past the producer's secretary, films that start with the intrigue already begun and don't have conventional endings. They can make them because they aren't crushed by the weight of millions of dollars.

Do you like Rome?

OW: It's a city that makes Paris seem new as an army camp. There are bigger, livelier, more dynamic cities. But they don't have what Rome has, a fourth dimension, the dimension of history. Ancient, swarming with life. Ancient and merry. It is not a melancholy museum because everything it has learned is still alive, its famous arts, its ancient wisdom. Rome is a moving city. If I could, I would like to make a film about Rome.

[At the end of the press conference Doriana Danton of *Hollywood* returned to questions about divorce. From here on the questions and answers are between her and Welles.]

How are things with Rita?

ow: I don't really like to answer personal questions. However, the divorce has been decided; no reconciliation is possible. Our characters have too many angles.

Your characters? You certainly have a reputation for having a terrible character, but Rita seems angelic. Aren't these angles all yours?

ow: I'm sorry to hear about my reputation. I may have a strong character, but not a difficult one, believe me!

Who will bring up your daughter, Rebecca?

ow: Rita. But I'll see her often.

Do women like you?

ow: No, they don't like me that much, but on the other hand I admire them. Such a shame they're so costly! Hearts broken, bad dreams, violent palpitations, every time the *dear object* comes into view.

So you avoid them?

ow: Of course! Especially if they are nosy and disrespectful, like you!

[At this point Welles got up and said goodbye with a loud Italian *arrivederci!*]

"I left," wrote Danton, "with the *vague impression* that Orson Welles didn't care much for me and the same was true of my colleagues. I had irreparably lowered the intellectual tone of the press conference."

2

Pizza with Togliatti

Mr. Charles Foster Kane, in every essence of his social beliefs, and
by the dangerous manner in which he has persistently attacked the
American traditions of private property, initiative, and opportunity
for advancement, is in fact, nothing more or less than a Communist!

—Walter Parks Thatcher (George Coulouris), *Citizen Kane*

Welles called the trip his "return to Rome." He had been once before,
many years earlier, and hadn't forgotten.

He was nine years old at the time. His mother, the pianist Beatrice
Ives, had just died of hepatitis. The boy, also a wunderkind at the piano, quit playing and accompanied his father, amateur inventor Richard Welles, on a round-the-world tour. In 1925, they visited Naples and
Rome,[1] and it was then that the young Orson Welles first held a movie
camera in his hands.

The home movies consisted mostly of a single shot on St. Peter's
Square. The young filmmaker was hypnotized by the central fountain.
"Antonioni at the very summit of his powers never held a single shot so
long," Welles recalled many years later. He'd held the shot until, in fact,
the film ran out, so he'd entirely missed the Holy Father's reappearance
"surrounded by Swiss guards and a hundred cardinals."[2]

He had always loved the city of emperors and popes, and had originally planned to include in *Citizen Kane* a scene shot in one of the exquisite rooms of Kane's Italian residence.[3]

Seven years later, *Black Magic* provided him the opportunity to return to Rome and stay for at least several months. Over the first few

days, Welles explored Via Veneto: his immense appetite took him farther afield than the Coliseum and Sistine Chapel, the sights Hollywood stars and tourists normally limited themselves to. He wanted to get to know the city.

However, one of the very first places he wanted to see was the Vatican Museums. A Catholic, he obtained an audience with the Pope, which lasted three-quarters of an hour. The momentous dialogue? He told his biographer Barbara Leaming that throughout the meeting Pope Pius XII had held his hand in his own, "as dry and hot as lizards," and quizzed him about the latest Hollywood gossip—Tyrone Power's wedding and Irene Dunne's divorce.[4]

Welles began to adapt to Italian life, picking up the language from newspapers, waiters, and shop signs. In *Europeo* Luigi Barzini, Jr., wrote admiringly of Welles's metamorphosis: "He has thrown himself into Roman life: tailors, cobblers, bookshops, dingy drinking holes, out-of-the-way museums—he goes everywhere. He went to the Vatican to meet monsignor Ennio Francia, a literary friend of Bellonci, and asked him to dig out some rare documents on Cagliostro, to help him to understand the role. He wants to see and meet everyone. Before lunch, you can see him at Rosati, drinking a 'Negroni' like an Italian film star. Suggest anything and he readily accepts—"I am a glutton," he says."[5]

Dazzled by the beauty of the Eternal City, he seemed ready to settle down there. "Hollywood is far away. Forgotten," he said joyfully. "Forget its pitiful Pharaohs and soulless geniuses. Rome has adopted me and I have adopted Rome."[6] He went so far as to invent for himself illustrious Italian ancestors—the Orsini family no less, hence his first name—a witty and rather childish idea Welles pushed for some years in all earnestness, to the understandable surprise of some and the feigned amusement of others.

But Welles did not just drink Negroni and make up Renaissance ancestors. He asked Barzini to arrange meetings with the leading politicians of the newly proclaimed republic. Barzini started with the toughest one of all, the leader of the Communist Party.

In 1947, Italy viewed Palmiro Togliatti with suspicion and hope. The country had just voted to become a republic but, until the first general election, it wasn't clear which side of the Cold War the country would be on. On Labor Day, near Palermo, machine guns had fired on the crowd at Portella della Ginestra. The usual suspects were Salvatore Giuliano and his gang members, but it is now generally acknowledged that secret service snipers were involved. In January, Prime Minister De Gasperi had returned from Truman's America with a check for $50 million, the first installment of the European Recovery Program, or Marshall Plan. At the end of May, De Gasperi formed a new government with liberals and independents, appointing Mario Scelba interior minister. Togliatti opposed the Marshall Plan and stayed out of government, promoting a general strike to voice his opposition and giving speech after speech in the run-up to Italy's first election as a republic, to be held the following year. Journalist Indro Montanelli caustically recalled, "Togliatti tried to persuade voters that capitalists were latter-day Neros, surrounded by pimps and whores, interested solely in exercising the right of *jus primae noctis* on the poor rice pickers. . . . The Scalera brothers, the Perrone brothers, the Corrieri brothers, the Federici brothers, the Stacchini brothers and other founding brothers of Italy, as is well-known, exercise that right not alone but—surprise, surprise—with their next of kin."[7] The Scalera brothers were the backers of *Black Magic;* the rice pickers were soon to be immortalized by Lux's *Riso amaro,* written and directed by Giuseppe De Santis and starring Silvana Mangano.

Reinvented by Davide Ferrario in his novel *Dissolvenza al nero,* the meeting between Orson Welles and Palmiro Togliatti is now part of the filmmaker's myth, so vague and legendary that one might wonder whether it actually took place.[8] It did, and was widely reported at the time—not least to the FBI—in order to demonstrate Welles's political leanings.

Barzini was hardly a left-wing journalist; ten years later he was elected to Parliament as a member of the center-right Italian Liberal Party. He managed to organize the meeting with Togliatti through colleague and Communist Party member Emanuele Rocco, the parliamentary reporter for *l'Unità* and a man with more experience and influence than Sollima. The time and place were chosen by Togliatti: a dinner—in the presence of Rocco, Barzini, and other journalists—at one of his favorite haunts, the popular pizzeria Romualdo's in piazza della Torretta, near Montecitorio (Parliament).

Welles had a lively curiosity. But what did Togliatti expect to get out of it? Here was a famous Hollywood actor and exile, the victim of artistic and political persecution: Togliatti knew the importance of the cinema and how to turn cultural events to political advantage. Some time later, for example, he criticized comrade Antonello Trombadori for his negative review of *Riso amaro*.[9]

Togliatti may also have been curious about relations between Orson and Sumner Welles, with whom the Italian politician had been arguing heatedly on both sides of the Atlantic. Under-secretary of state in the Roosevelt administration, Sumner Welles had been instrumental in ousting President Machado from Cuba, which paved the way for Batista. In Truman's administration, he'd been a fierce anti-Soviet and, in May, had warned of the dangers of Communism in Europe, accusing the Italian Communist Party of receiving funding from the Soviet Union. Togliatti replied vigorously in the party newspaper *l'Unità* with a front-page article entitled "Ma come sono cretini!"(What idiots!). He also sent Sumner a telegram challenging him to prove his claims or "be exposed as a liar and fabricator."[10] The answer came back via Reuters: the American had nothing to add. The accusation was true: the Soviets were funding the Italian Communist Party, but Togliatti, an opponent of the Marshall Plan, couldn't admit that Soviet money was secretly arriving in Italy and being used by one side only, for its own purposes.

Legend had it that Sumner and Orson Welles were cousins. Barzini said as much in his first article in *Europeo*. Later books and newspapers passed on the error. In fact, the two men were not related. After thoroughly researching Orson Welles's family tree, biographer Charles Higham attributed the mistake to Welles's own mythmaking; he had started the story himself.

During the dinner at Romualdo's, Welles was probably obliged to set Togliatti right on this point. If he did, he nonetheless managed temporarily to foist another myth on the world. The two spoke in English and Spanish, a language Welles said he had learned, as Togliatti had, fighting in the Spanish Civil War.

The dinner took place on December 8, one month after Welles's arrival in Rome and halfway through the shooting of *Black Magic*.

Togliatti wore a double-breasted blazer, with a small silver hammer and sickle on his lapel. Welles, too, had a blue jacket—probably the same one he wore on his arrival at Ciampino. Barzini and Rocco were present, along with three other reporters who had each had disagreements with Togliatti in the past. They were Corrado Pallenberg, author of an enquiry into the Communist Party that made accusations the Party had strongly denied; Vittorio Gorresio, who had argued in print with Togliatti over a literary matter (Togliatti, a literary stickler, had won); and American reporter Emmett J. Hughes, who had published a report on the Communist threat in Europe in *Time* magazine, claiming that there was "blood on the Communist leader's blue blazer." Togliatti sued Hughes, *Time*, and all the Italian newspapers that repeated the claim.

The meeting was a private affair; no notes were to be taken. "We promised not to report the conversation in any newspaper," Barzini wrote, "not because anything untoward was going to be said but because we wanted to feel free to discuss things." They did record the event with a few official photos, however: Welles is sitting opposite Togliatti at the end of the table, against a wall, speaking animatedly, his curly Cagliostro hair dangling over his forehead; the other side of the table was occupied by five journalists.

Although the off-the-record nature of the meeting may have been one of Togliatti's conditions, the restaurant's proximity to Parliament and its popularity—it was famous for its fillet of dried salt cod, a favorite dish of Togliatti's—guaranteed that the news would get out. Rumors circulated and, a few weeks later, articles by Rocco and Barzini appeared in the magazines *Tempo* and *Europeo*.[11]

The two articles say very little: a friendly meeting, pizza and fish, and conversation punctuated frequently by "That's right," and "Yes, I agree" —all very polite and pleasant, not in the least politically explosive. There was probably some truth in this; there were good enough reasons for everyone to be on their best behavior. Unaided by notebooks, the two journalists may not have been able to remember the conversation verbatim and, in view of the prior agreement and Togliatti's record, didn't dare get it wrong.

The dinner began at nine. Some safe topics had been chosen to start the conversation: the difficulty of the Castilian dialect, Julius Caesar's conflict with Brutus, paganism (not the standard menu of icebreakers today). Togliatti and the three reporters found their own way of getting comfortable, by poking fun at each other. "You have written a great deal about me, without knowing me at all," Togliatti teased Pallenberg. "Next time come and see me first." Gorresio pedantically corrected Togliatti's journalism because his vocabulary betrayed an "excessive French influence." Togliatti pointed out that Hughes was pouring the wine "like Judas," by rolling the wrist out, not in: "In Sicily you would be challenged to a duel, no less."

Welles spoke English, Spanish, and some halting Italian, with Barzini interpreting if the need arose. Togliatti said he had read Dumas's novel on Cagliostro in his youth and asked Welles if certain details would be included in the film. To Togliatti's evident disappointment, Welles confessed that the screenplay was a very free adaptation.

Slowly they got around to politics. The Communist leader related an episode from just a few days earlier. During a parade of partisans in Via Nazionale, a four-year-old girl greeted him with outstretched arm, the Fascist salute. Her mother, "a good comrade," had been so ashamed he'd had to reassure her in person.

Barzini complained that he had been fired by *Corriere della Sera* from one day to the next, without severance pay, simply to please the internal workers commission, which considered him a dangerous monarchist. "The liberal party," Togliatti commented, "has drifted so far right you've ended up on the left. Barzini on the left, that's quite something!" Welles broke into such loud laughter that half the restaurant turned to look.

Now it was Welles's turn to entertain. He told the story of when he and Roosevelt had been driving together and come to a fork in the road. Welles had quipped, "Left can't be wrong," and it had turned out to be a good guess.[12]

The more they talked politics, the more animated the discussion became. A waiter hovered near the table, waiting for orders that failed to materialize. In the end he decided to bring some pizza and fish, which Welles left half untouched.

The conversation got around to the situation in Italy. De Gasperi's Christian Democrat Party had recently chosen to freeze out the left, leaving them in opposition, but Togliatti had no regrets: "Leading the opposition is good for the discipline and solidity of the Communist Party," he said. He asked Welles if there was anywhere in America—a city, inner-city area, anywhere at all—where the Communists were strong. Welles hesitated, said no, and then corrected himself: the San Francisco Dockers Union, he suggested.

According to Togliatti, the United States simply could not understand the European left. Welles concurred, but pointed out that the misunderstanding was mutual: "The Polish rebellion, the Chinese Republic, the struggle of the Irish against the British, were all financed by Americans, not just Polish, Chinese, and Irish Americans, but all Americans, because Americans strongly identify with the oppressed. The people who gave Roosevelt his landslide majority are still there in the United States. They might help to build a bridge. Why jettison them? Why not try to win them over with something they can understand? They shouldn't be ignored. This part of public opinion can't make any real contact with the European left and you do nothing to help." Togliatti agreed. Welles went on to say that the Italian Communist Party boycotted the American press: "Right now there are American reporters who sit in the bars complaining that they have to write something about the country. 'Have you met the Communists?' one says, and the other replies, 'I can't get through to them. What do you suppose they are thinking?' He ends up writing an article based on rumor and what a fellow reporter has told him. Which is worse, reporters who make up stories about you, or the fact that—in good or bad faith—they get something slightly wrong?"

The Marshall Plan? According to Welles, if properly managed, it could be a tool for social progress in Western Europe. Togliatti butted in: "It mustn't be charity, which makes both the donor and the recipient poorer; it mustn't come with strings attached so we aren't allowed to create certain industries, or have to put an end to the traditional, life-giving trade between Eastern and Western Europe."

Half in English, half in Spanish, in the company of five reporters of very different political persuasions, Togliatti and Welles had got around to touching on some very sensitive points of foreign policy.

"Strange," one of the reporters said afterward, "Nowhere else in the world are people who don't see eye to eye talking about peace." When the photographer arrived, they joked that they would end up in the U.S. State Department and Russian Cominform. Welles took the opportunity to order a cognac, and toasted to "the day in which people of different ideas and faiths can be photographed together at dinner without fear or consequences."

He was wrong. A few days later an informant (whose name has been crossed out in Welles's dossier) phoned Hoover and told him "one of Hollywood's biggest Communists" had arrived in Italy at a time of social unrest and demonstrations orchestrated by the Communist Party, culminating in the general strike Togliatti ordered (as chance would have it) the day after the dinner. The FBI dossier was later graced with a photo of the dinner cut out from a newspaper.[13] American investigators had evidently failed to pick up on the event half of Rome was talking about, despite the front-page article in *Europeo* and the cover photograph in *Tempo*.

The meeting was still more evidence of Welles's supposed Communism. On its own it outweighed hundreds of other pieces of circumstantial evidence of un-American activity. The presence of five reporters of different political backgrounds counted for nothing.

There is no evidence that the two men discussed any more controversial matters, such as the imminent general strike or what Sumner Welles was up to. Togliatti kept tight control over everything published about the evening. Rocco, a reporter for *l'Unità*, must have cleared his article for *Tempo* with him. Barzini went one step further, accompanying his piece with a declaration initialed P. T.: "I have nothing against the text of this article." At that stage, perhaps, the reports of the meeting had a different purpose than merely to inform readers; they were meant to prove—in defense of Welles and maybe even Togliatti as well—that the meeting had not been secret.

At a tense moment in Italian and international politics, the dinner had been relaxing and enjoyable, a temporary respite—and a rare encounter of two big personalities. At 1:00 AM, Togliatti left the restaurant and returned to Communist Party headquarters. On the way, he confided to Rocco, "This Welles is the cleverest American I've ever met."

3
Black Magic

Self-assured as always, Josef was ready to try anything once.
What had he to lose?

—*Black Magic*

Commendatore Michele Scalera, as he was known, had been one of the most powerful and revered cinema producers in the Kingdom of Italy. He came to cinema quite late, after making a fortune with his brother Salvatore building roads and other public works in Italy and Africa—perhaps stealing here and there and offering bribes in cahoots with the De Bono *quadrumvir.* His production company, Scalera Film, had studios on the Circonvallazione Appia in Rome and on Giudecca Island in Venice, where Mussolini had attempted to move the entire Italian film industry during the short-lived Salò Republic. Dazzled by Hollywood, Scalera specialized in colossal costume pictures, judiciously alternated with a fair number of propaganda films.

After the fall of Fascism, the power and fortunes of the Scalera family had declined, but the name of the production company was still prestigious. Today, if you are elected Miss Italy you may get to be a showgirl on TV. Back then, if you were Miss Scalera, you had a career in films, with all that that entailed: board and lodging in Rome, a place in the world of celluloid, and submission to the sexual appetites of the Commendatore in person, who—like all the film producers of the day—considered his actresses little more than geisha. "Michele Scalera," actress Cosetta Greco told Tatti Sanguineti, "was one of those men who didn't mince his words; [he was] broad-shouldered, thickset, with a rosy-red face and wide eyes, and a large double chin. . . . Believe me, it wasn't a pleasant meeting."[1]

The memory of days gone by and the studio's past glories didn't keep the company going: when the body of Mussolini was hung upside down from a petrol pump in Piazzale Loreto, Scalera lost his political ally and the company's business began to dwindle. Commendatore Scalera sought to make friends among the new powers that be: at the beginning of 1947 he planned to make the usual costume drama, a biography of Cagliostro from the novels of Dumas, and struck an agreement with Edward Small, an independent U.S. film producer.

Black Magic, or *Cagliostro,* became one of the first American-Italian co-productions. Edward Small Productions was to provide the backing, crew, and cast; Scalera would contribute the sets and some logistics, with all the advantages this had in terms of reviving the company's fortunes and publicizing its name. For Edward Small the deal made sense because production costs in Italy were a fraction of what they were in California. Added to that, Edward Small had 120 million lire tied up in Italy—the receipts from his films that were distributed in Italy by United Artists—a sum not released by the Bank of America and Italy because of a law stipulating that these profits had to be reinvested in the film industry on Italian soil.

The real producers of the film were the Americans, so at the end of summer, Scalera officially withdrew from the film but made sure the studio retained an important role. Small immediately asked the prime minister's office for the release of his funds, adding that another hundred million would be added by American partners, and corresponding amounts would be held in Italy. "The funds will be used to hire Italian sets and labor, and for the traveling expenses of the crew and cast."[2]

The official director of the film was Gregory Ratoff, a Russian from Petersburg who had been a dramatic and comic actor in the United States and was now a director (among other things, of Ingrid Bergman's first American film, *Intermezzo*). He was rumored to be a gambling man who had run up debts with various producers. Welles let it be known that Ratoff had agreed to direct *Black Magic* only to pay off some of these debts. But Ratoff had at least one other reason to be far from home. His

1943 film *Song of Russia* had come under the scrutiny of the HUAC for its Communist propaganda, "because it depicted smiling, happy Russian children." The trumped-up accusation was a patent absurdity, but his Russian origins were undeniable and soon he was blacklisted. A film in Rome for an independent producer was just the ticket.

For the role of Cagliostro, Edward Small had only one actor in mind: Orson Welles. He had been wooing him for a long time, pretending to be interested in producing Welles's *Cyrano de Bergerac* or any of a number of the filmmaker's other ideas. When the HUAC turned its attention to Welles, Small saw the opportunity to give him a script by Charles Bennett; he offered Welles a hundred thousand dollars and said he could direct himself in his own scenes.[3] In view of the generous offer, Welles caved.

The Ufficio Centrale per la Cinematografia didn't waste much time in releasing Small's Italian funds. Relishing the prospect of an American crew setting up shop in Rome it informed then-undersecretary for entertainment and future prime minister Giulio Andreotti that in October the Scalera production unit would be used "for the largest production by Americans since *Ben-Hur*," the silent movie directed in 1925 by Fred Niblo. The budget was 250 million lire, all from funds already frozen in various accounts in Italy.

Over the next few weeks the declared production costs continued to creep up. Edward Small Productions festively announced it would spend a further $600,000 "on director's and actors' fees, copyright, scenery, and so on," watering the mouths of the government and Scalera, as well as clearing the way for quick permits and the cheap use of film sets, scenery, and props.

Representatives of the production company asked to meet Andreotti personally, a request passed on enthusiastically by the Ufficio Centrale per la Cinematografia, "given the importance of the initiative, which could be the beginning of a vast production program by Americans in Italy, with evident economic advantages for our country."[4] The very day the request was dutifully passed on, the company was granted something no other production company in Italy would ever again obtain: permission to shoot (free of charge) inside the Quirinale Palace—formerly the property of the pope, then of the king of Savoy, and soon to become the official residence of the president of the newly established Republic of Italy.

Production on *Black Magic* began on October 8, 1947, with exteriors in the splendid Villa d'Este in Tivoli, then moved on to the Scalera production unit for some tricky scenes and interiors. With the arrival of the American crew, a new studio was inaugurated at Scalera, studio 6, and two thousand invitations were sent out by Scalera press officer Osvaldo Scaccia, including to the famed local actor Aldo Fabrizi—one of the "stars" of *Roma città aperta*—and Tyrone Power, who had recently set his eyes on his future wife, Linda Christian, in Rome.

Welles wasn't there. Nor had he yet come on set. Ratoff spent the first month scaring the crew with promises of apocalyptical events as soon as Welles showed up: "He'll show you how it's done!" he would shout at the cowering technicians. The effect was to make Welles as formidable and dangerous as the character he was portraying. When they were making the costumes, based on Welles's measurements, the crew concluded that he was a giant.

Welles graced the studio about a month after shooting began. Escorted by Scaccia and Barzini, he declared in the press conference that he couldn't wait to get started. In fact, he had deep misgivings about the project and, as always when he merely had to act, he did not relish the idea of taking another director's orders.

His arrival on set didn't go unnoticed. One day, Giberto Severi, an amateur painter and struggling journalist who was working as an extra and helping Barzini draw up press releases, heard a kerfuffle in the corridor outside his dressing room. He went out to see what the fuss was about. "A huge man with a mop of hair, bulging eyes, and a short fleshy nose was approaching with what looked like a following of courtiers. He had on a dark suit (ceremonious, despite the fact that it was only ten in the morning) with a red carnation in the buttonhole, a shirt with crumpled collar, and a tie the color of beetroot."[5]

As soon as he set foot in Scalera Studios, Welles realized that he terrified the entire crew, a fact he characteristically decided to turn to his own advantage, immediately dictating the sort of nose he wanted for Cagliostro—not the feeble, childish thing they had presented him with, but a good strong nose, such as he deserved. For his films and stage performances Welles kept a jar of false noses with his makeup paraphernalia, which he did not have with him and needed to have sent from the United States. A month went by. When the noses finally arrived, the production team sent a stagehand to pick them up from Ciampino Airport. The stagehand's name was Alessandro Tasca di Cutò, an aristocrat from Palermo who had lived for some time in the United States. Tasca checked the noses through customs, to the amusement of the officers, and handed them over to one of the assistant directors, Arrigo Colombo. A little later Tasca was summoned by the top brass, Welles, Ratoff, and Warren Doane—Edward Small's Rome representative—each of whom stared at him with an ashen face. "Doane," Tasca wrote in his memoirs, "asked me straight out where the noses were. I said they were in a small jar in the makeup box. Orson interrupted, saying the makeup was all in order but there were no noses. I felt like laughing, it was all so absurd; but of course it was serious, too." Welles looked him over and asked why he had such a mournful look. "I'd be a born fool to look happy," he replied, "given the circumstances." "Fire him," Welles told Doane, who dismissed Tasca with a nod. He returned to his office. . . . The door opened and in came Colombo, sniggering.

"What's so funny?"

"I found the noses."

"Where?"

"In the men's room."

Welles had taken them out of the jar and flushed them down the toilet, but some were left floating in the bowl. "My honor was saved by a nose and a poorly flushing toilet," Tasca concluded.[6]

Welles's attempt to delay his participation in the film for a further few days failed. Doane ordered shooting to start straight away, nose or no nose. The result was that Welles appeared onscreen with his own face—a rarity in the course of his career.

Black Magic was the story of Josef (Giuseppe) Balsamo, aka Cagliostro, a Palermo gypsy, magician, and con artist, based on a loose interpretation of the novels of Alexandre Dumas, *père*. After witnessing the hanging of his adoptive parents, Cagliostro swears revenge on the deceitful Viscount Montagne (Stephen Bekassy). He flees to Vienna with a gypsy friend (Akim Tamiroff) and the lady Zoraida (Valentina Cortese), who is in love with him. There, he meets Doctor Mesmer and learns to hypnotize and feign miraculous feats, abilities he uses at first only as part of a circus show. In France, he joins the court of the viscount and sabotages a plot by Montagne to make the virtuous Lorenza (Nancy Gould) queen of France instead of the perfidious Marie Antoinette (also played by Nancy Gould). Cagliostro falls in love with Lorenza, who has sworn her heart to a young officer (Frank Latimore), so he hypnotizes and seduces her. His desperate love for Lorenza drives him witless to the point of feeling omnipotent. Tried and convicted of all sorts of nefariousness, he avenges his parents' deaths only to lose his love and be killed by his rival.

As a youngster, Welles had admired the Cagliostro character and his magical powers in the novels of Dumas, and was also a devotee of hypnotism. When he wrote an account of the film for the *New York Times*, he dedicated most of it to the subject of hypnotism. "Even under hypnosis, a subject will do nothing for which a strong repulsion is felt," he wrote. "How then, I wondered, could Cagliostro, for all his ability as a mesmerist, have caused the fair and virtuous Lorenza to yield, though hating him in her waking moments, and to impersonate Marie Antoinette, which she considered a fate worse than dishonor?" He added,

> Dr. Freud has pointed out that the more virtuous one seems the stronger may be the contrary impulses clamoring to burst forth. Is it possible, it has been asked, for a man to love a woman and use her so ill? Of course it is. One way or another as another genius of psychological insight has remarked, "Each man kills the thing he loves." . . . Cagliostro used no whirling lights or glittering watches on swinging chains, nor did he have to croon ten minutes of soothing nonsense to a subject. As one who dabbles a bit in hypnotism himself, I can testify to what all stage hypnotists know and most doctors acknowledge: It is much easier to get "control" over a person's will in front of an audience than it is in private, and the magician with his air of mystery, however phoney it may be, is more successful in less time than the legitimate man of medicine. . . . Do not scoff too easily. . . . There are still experts who say it is impossible to saw a woman in half without damaging her in some way. To such skeptics I offer a demonstration any time they happen to be in my neighborhood.[7]

Cagliostro was an ideal vehicle for Welles. A keen magician and juggler, he spent the whole time shooting the film blurring the edges between himself and the character he was portraying. Cagliostro is first seen in a cloud of smoke, pretending to be a medium; Welles then improvises some magic tricks—a chicken pulled out of his coat, a coin trick. On the basis of this trickery Cagliostro offers his audiences a magic potion from the Fountain of Youth: if he had looked into the camera it would have been like one of the many commercials Welles was later to shoot the world over.

Welles clearly enjoyed the role of Cagliostro and found in it subjects that had always interested him: the coexistence of truth and fiction, the ambiguous privilege of tricking an audience, and the temptation and inability to shape destiny according to one's wishes. Cagliostro was one of the powerful, evil men that fascinated him; others were Macbeth, Charles Foster Kane, Lear, and Quinlan—a dominant figure who loses his soul in the Promethean fight against his own weaknesses (the love of a woman he cannot have).

It was not Shakespeare, for sure. Cagliostro was a classic blackguard, liar, cheat, and swashbuckler—a caricature villain. For Maurice Bessy he was one of the many "barbaric scoundrels" played by Welles in the course of his career—"greedy and presumptuous," with a glance that was "heavy and disquieting, threatening and full of ambitious madness, but sometimes warm, with the tenderness of a beast that feels it is cornered."[8] However, *Black Magic* is also one of the films in which a familiar theme in Welles's career—from *Citizen Kane* to *The Immortal Story*—most forcefully emerges: the identification of the showman with the despot.

Poor, brought up by gypsies, and made an orphan by a high-handed, powerful man, Cagliostro is a victim of history; but he has immense theatrical talent and healing powers, abilities that make him first a popular hero and then a victim of his own popularity. Kane, the lying publisher; Arkadin, the financier with a double life; the scientist of *The Fountain of Youth*, who invents a potion to win back a woman; Quinlan, the wise but crooked cop; Don Quixote, the errant knight of the valiant acts of others; and Mr. Clay, the bored merchant who wants to turn a story into reality are all characters whose power depends on the ability to manipulate people. But no other film shows so markedly the Wellesian link between fiction and politics than *Black Magic*. Here the stage, the public trickery, creates a new tyrant; the marvel felt by Cagliostro's audiences is a prelude to dictatorship. *Black Magic* was the perfect way to show two types of stage, the footlights and the rostrum, the showman and the politician,

and was ideal for analyzing their different types of appeal, the hoodwink-
ing and dangers involved in their acts, seeing in both of them a thirst for
attention and power that ultimately ruins them.

Welles let some of this slip in an interview with *Tempo* journalist
Carlo Laurenzi, to whom he announced his intention to make a film
"full of fire and smoke, in which Cagliostro will be a precursor of revolutionary demagogues such as Danton and Robespierre."[9] Fascinated
and terrified by the power of fiction, Welles intended to make the film
such a transparent metaphor for revolution that the critics would not
even notice the sleight of hand (as it turned out, they were so put off by
the coarse filmmaking that the film has forever been underestimated).

Had Welles directed and not only starred in the film, it might have
become one of his most important works. Ratoff's ideas were diametri-
cally opposed to Welles's version of the film. The official director wanted
to make a Hollywood blockbuster, an Errol Flynn–type story of virile
swordplay and intrigue, if anything, even more spectacular and sumptuous. Welles tried everything to bring Ratoff around to his way of thinking. As soon as he arrived he subjected him to lengthy discussions and
arguments behind the partition, where the senior members of the crew
had their lunch. The newspapers of the day called them "Homeric disputes" about the historical context and character of Cagliostro, which
troubled and entertained the rest of the cast.

"The Quirinale is not Versailles," Welles said, "and your Louis XV is
not Louis XV (as your Louis XVI is not Louis XVI), so why shouldn't I
turn Cagliostro into Rasputin?"

"Some people know of Rasputin," Ratoff replied, "and will be surprised to find him in Versailles."

"And some people know the style of Versailles and will be surprised
to find Louis XV in the Quirinale," Welles retorted.

"Certainly there are some but those people will never go to see my
film," said Ratoff.

"No, they won't. They'll come to see my Rasputin."[10]

Welles wanted to make an auteur film with American professionalism and European depth, and was convinced that Cagliostro, the revolutionary shaper of a new society, was the most contemporary slant on an
otherwise tedious story. "We came to Europe to get away from America,"

Welles said, adding that it was pointless to try to make an American film in Rome.

"I am well aware of what really brought us to Europe," Ratoff said. "In America the film would have cost two billion lire, and here just half."[11] And the two continued arguing.

With Small's agreement in his pocket, Welles was nonetheless determined to direct himself in his own scenes (and, thus, most of the film) and used this to try to hijack the whole film. For a while, the two rivals sought allies among the crew and cast, creating two opposing factions that sought not to disappoint one or the other, or both.

Both the official and unofficial directors had whims and foibles. Despite his recent political troubles, or perhaps because of them, Ratoff said he had an old score to settle with the Bolsheviks and came to the set with a beret and visor announcing he was a refugee from the "Red Hell of '17" (the crew reckoned he'd stolen the hat from a chauffeur in Monte Carlo). He had photos taken of himself looking important, waving his stick in the air and shouting at his assistants. He banned smoking on the set, making a sole exception for himself. Welles, for his part, had sunk into character, with eyes blazing, and would be calmed only by the guitar and mandolin music of two Roman musicians.

Superstitious, Ratoff went to the Vatican to have the script blessed by the pope and then sent for a hunchback to bring him good luck. Welles was more refined in his good-luck charms, taking inspiration from Greek mythology. Georges Annenkov, the costume designer for the film, wrote that "Welles asked the production company for two or three Muses to preside over the film: otherwise he couldn't guarantee his inspiration. Directors were sent scouting the whole of Rome until three local beauties with unrivalled charms were found, and three makeshift contracts were signed. Dutifully, the women came to the set for each scene: one was Roman with a Raffaello-like appearance; another Venetian with vaporous, fiery hair; and the third a young Sicilian whose eyes and mouth I shall never forget. One sat in an armchair, knitting like a middle-class housewife, one buried her head in a detective story, and the third dozed off in the corner, yawning discreetly while slowly munching a bar of chocolate. At the end of the day the Muses came down from Parnassus, collected their pay, and went home."[12]

The shooting went ahead rather chaotically—not only because of the arguments between the director and leading actor, but also due to the lack of organization on the set. For the Romans, these big American crews—with their endless assistants, secretaries, and inspectors—were a source of amusement, astonishment, and, of course, livelihood. Luckily, something was always going wrong, and that was when the locals could make themselves useful, fetching whatever was needed from Rome or the provinces.

As Cinecittà was still being used to shelter the postwar homeless, Scalera was one of the most important studios in the country, attracting people from all over Rome with the prospect of easy money. "Those who had been hungry just a few months before," wrote Carlo Laurenzi, "former journalists, some former junior Fascist officers, people who had survived concentration camps, blackmailers, petty delinquents—everyone joined the gold rush from America." The studios and changing rooms were full of Italians from Brooklyn—who were in high demand as translators—girls who knew a little English and could type, and photographers who courted the secretaries of the cast in hopes of getting important photos. But in all this chaos, the most picturesque characters were neither the Italians nor the Americans: Ratoff had brought with him seventy Russians—a court of fellow countrymen—including two former generals, eight ex-colonels, a princess, baroness, prince, count, and even a Communist pontiff. Some—like the costume designer Annenkov—were part of the crew, but most worked as extras. Actress Franca Faldini had a small part and was on set briefly during that time. In her memoirs she wrote, "Ratoff, whose friends called him Grischa, was surrounded by fellow countrymen who had perhaps been in exile for years but remained faithful to their traditions and language. Corpulent, reddish blond, a human wreck, Ratoff sought their loud approval and cheered up immediately if he found it in the aquamarine eyes of Akim Tamiroff, but as soon as the Italian technicians dared to whisper he confirmed what we all suspected—that he was [Darryl] Zanuck's stooge—by screaming in pidgin Italian, *Silentio, reliciosso silentio!*"[13]

Ratoff tried to use his official role to impose his idea of the film—scorning the fanciful notion of metaphorical and political content—to make an adventure story, pure and simple. He was not troubled by the ludicrous historical inaccuracies. It seems that in an earlier version of the screenplay, there was a horse chase with pistols drawn. "They nearly shot a scene," wrote Emanuele Rocco, "in which Louis XV addresses the future Louis XVI as 'My son' while slapping him on the back."[14]

Every time one of these nonsensical pieces of filming cropped up, Welles stepped in, and a fierce argument with Ratoff ensued. The master of arms Enzo Musumeci Greco, who was hired to teach Welles the rudiments of sword fighting, stood by in amazement as these furious arguments developed. His son Renzo, currently Italy's leading consultant on sword fighting and arms for films and the opera, remembers this: "My father told me he had never seen arguments like it in the whole of his life. It was like Welles and Ratoff were going to kill each other." Ratoff came away from these bouts with a fluttery heart and nervous exhaustion, but Welles, always on form and on the lookout for any way to wind him up further, taunted him: "Grischa, you need a little rest." Focused on the morally ambiguous Cagliostro, he played the part off camera, too, and involved the other actors on the set. Nancy Guild played both Lorenza and Marie Antoinette, two quite different characters: Welles continued to court her when she was in her Lorenza costume and paid her no attention when she was dressed in her regalia as Marie Antoinette. For one scene, in which Lorenza apparently dies and is buried alive, Welles insisted it would be more authentic if Nancy, rather than a dummy, was lowered into the ground and earth heaped upon her. Exhausted and no longer in control of the film, Ratoff stood by, powerless to object, as the actress was covered in earth.[15]

Gradually the enemies came to some kind of understanding. As a man of the theater, Welles hated to work until after two in the afternoon. That left the whole morning for Ratoff to shoot scenes without Cagliostro and to prepare for the afternoon showdown. When Welles arrived he simply took over, and sometimes carried on well into the night. At one point Ratoff himself became an extra, directed by Welles.

When the press had first heard of the film, they had hailed it as a new venture for intercontinental cooperation. The law obliging Americans to spend their profits from Italian distribution in Italy was to have a strong impact on the film industry, cast, and crews, as well as on the Italian economy. The Italian magazine *Cinematografia I.T.A.* sensibly pointed out that "a co-production requires good faith, tact, and understanding, if *all* the members of the crew and cast are to be judged formally and substantially by the same measure." In the organizational, linguistic, and cultural chaos of the film, this proved nigh impossible. Working methods, upbringing, origin, social class—everything conspired to exaggerate the differences.

The Americans did not entirely trust the Italians, first of all politically: the largest union of technicians and extras was a Communist organization, and the Americans hated the Communists. "Doane and his wife," said Tasca di Cutò, "and not only they, were paranoid about the Red threat and saw armed bandits everywhere, ready to kill them."

By the same token, the Italians, particularly the poor ones, didn't entirely trust the liberators, since they had immediately become conquerors. Unused to the kind of money the Americans were promising the film industry, they smelled a rat. One evening, when shooting for the final sequence had been transferred to the Sant'Ivo alla Sapienza Cathedral, a rumor started that there was no money left to pay extras or overtime. The crowd began to murmur. Tasca strode over to a table and pulled out a wad of notes, then wisely had the loudspeakers announce that the police were there to protect the money. "Everyone applauded and the work went on until dawn," Tasca reported with relief.

The Italian extras were also nervous about Ratoff's evident preference for the Russians. The two factions had formed rival camps, ready to come to blows at the slightest spark. They were able to let off steam in the scene of the Viennese fighting the gypsies, shot in the Scalera Studios: Ratoff and Welles were equally unable to control the fight, and extras on both sides ended up in the hospital. Meanwhile the journalists were causing another stir, because the set photographer Osvaldo Civirani had been treated so rudely by Ratoff that he decided to quit for a better-paid job. "Quite right, we should do the same," said cameraman Anchise Brizzi.[16]

The film went over schedule by several weeks and leaked money out of unlikely places. In the final duel scene one of Welles's stand-ins feigned an accidental fall and ended up collapsing in a pool of blood, with a knife blade in his throat: the result was a record insurance payout of four million lire. Ratoff's hunchback wined and dined on Cinzano and chocolate cake at the company's expense.

As if that were not enough, on the evening of December 7, 1947, the director of photography, the great Ubaldo Arata, died of a heart attack.

He had done the cinematography for *La signora di tutti* and *Luciano Serra pilota*. For *Roma città aperta* he had worked wonders with film way past its sell-by date and no lighting to speak of. His death, at the age of just fifty-two, hit everyone hard. It seems the death of a colleague, Massimo Terzano (also in his fifties) three months earlier had troubled the cinematographer greatly, and that he was terrified by the "American method" and its "chaotic planning." Some journalists suggested that "his death was hastened by the inhuman intensity of the work directors forced him to endure."

Arata's place was taken by two cinematographers, Anchise Brizzi and Otello Martelli. The two main Roman newspapers, *il Messaggero* and *il Tempo,* published an obituary signed by Welles, Ratoff, Doane, and all the cast and crew of *Black Magic,* but this delicacy did not improve things. Provincial Rome, which had welcomed the Americans, now turned against them, and admiration and gratitude became fear of rough-and-ready colonization. Indicative of this was Francesco Càllari's article on both Edward Small's *Black Magic* and Carmine Gallone's *Addio Mimì* in *Hollywood.* Gallone was finishing up his film for Columbia at that time. Càllari wrote,

> It seems that foreign filmmakers from the other side of the Alps or across the Atlantic Ocean have noticed that it costs very little to make a film in Italy.... Soon we will witness a new barbaric invasion. The advance guard has already taken up position and is making some trial films.... Foreign directors and actors ... are arriving; they wander about Rome, their mouths open ("every ten yards a new wonder!"); they go to St. Peter's Square and their jaws drop still further; they visit the Coliseum and rap the stones with their knuckles to see if they are real; they film inside the Quirinale and can't believe their eyes ("here we should shoot a whole film"); they occupy our studios and can't help admit that everything is perfect; then they are astonished that the costumes are made with real silk (perhaps from exactly the right historical period), and that the scenery has real furniture, real ornaments, and genuine paintings ("in Hollywood it's all fake"); and then in front of two or three hundred extras they say, "Come on, admit it. You've never seen so many people in a film!"[17]

The Americans had arrived with ideas of their own and did not expect to find any excellent technicians in Rome. In the reproduction of sound Hollywood was undoubtedly superior, but Small's production crew was simply stunned by the Italian costumes and scenery. Boxes of wigs from Hollywood were left unopened. Even Ratoff allowed himself to be impressed by the Italian technicians and occasionally found his good humor. "Ratoff is a difficult man," a *Film* journalist wrote. "He alternates between violent outbursts and periods in which he is gentle as a baby, when he goes about saying, 'A very good composition! *Molto bono maestranzo italiani.'"*[18]

When the crew moved to the most luxurious set of all, the Quirinale, where Versailles had been recreated, another fight broke out. The technicians saw a truck pull up with a load of blocks of Formica, complete with holes and doors. Tonino Delli Colli, the assistant cinematographer, went looking for an interpreter and asked the Americans what this truckload of material was for. They had built makeshift toilets for the Italian extras and technicians, fearing that they might foul the rooms of the palace. "Worse than Zulus," Delli Colli recounted. "I said that if they didn't take those things away in five minutes we would all be leaving and that—the Americans could get this into their heads once and for all—we had bathrooms and toilets when they were still scratching about in the dirt. They removed them, but basically that's what they thought of us."[19]

The news that a cinema crew was filming inside the Quirinale spread like wildfire. The guest room was set up as the bedroom of Louis XV; the other rooms for visiting royalty and the Mirror Room were used for the bedrooms of Madame Du Barry and Marie Antoinette. The rooms of the Savoys, one floor up, were not touched, but some landaus from the stables were renovated and used for a scene at Trinità dei Monti, blanking out the royal coat of arms. One of the horses in the movie was Transatlantico, a splendid gray owned by Mussolini.

Nothing is sacred for filmmakers. Even the former throne of the kings of Italy was used for one scene, it was reported. The beautiful rooms of the Palace rapidly became a set like any other, the paving protected by matting, the damask walls covered with "no smoking" signs. Ratoff continued to smoke a fat cigar, even in the Quirinale.

Visiting the set, the film critic Gian Luigi Rondi saw him upbraiding a distinguished-looking gentleman for smoking:

> "Only I can smoke here. Put out that damned cigarette!"
> "Right," said Orson Welles, "That's democracy for you."

The Russian bear stopped and abruptly turned around. "Now they're going to start fighting," a technician laughed. But Welles's derisive expression was merely ironic. The director shrugged and almost ran away, stifling his anger. Whether it was because of the cables on the floor or the protective matting, somehow Ratoff tripped, falling hard against one of the gold-tinted doors and breaking its hinges.

"No matter," he yelled. "I'll have a new one made!"

Welles quipped, "I've seen it already, in *Punch*."[20]

The story of the broken door did the rounds, changing a little each time. Some said that Welles had kicked the door down in a fit of rage and the shocking idea began to circulate that the Americans were reducing one of Italy's most prestigious historical buildings to a circus.

On December 28, the new Constitution of the Republic of Italy was signed. On New Year's Day, President Enrico De Nicola would leave Palazzo Giustiniani and take up his official residence in the Quirinale. Shooting went on. The death of Louis XV was filmed in the guest room at night. English actor Robert Atkins lay down on the sumptuous bed in which William of Prussia and King George had slept, and died sixteen times before Welles—who had by then taken over—was satisfied. "The King is dead," he said finally. "Two minutes' silence." The following morning special editions of the dailies announced that King Vittorio Emanuele III, until recently the legitimate occupant of the Quirinale, had died in Egypt. Perhaps Welles really did have dealings with the occult.

The death of Louis XV was one of the last scenes shot in the Quirinale. On January 1, 1948, the First Grenadiers entered the Great Court to symbolically take possession of the building in the name of the president of the republic (and one of the Scalera tailors asked a soldier which scene he was appearing in).[21] Ratoff was soon forced to leave, not so much out of respect for diplomatic protocol as to avoid further damage to the building. Welles, of course, had to have his say.

"The endless glass gallery," writes Annenkov in his memoirs, "was immediately turned into a depot for the extravagant and picturesque material; two bars were set up, with signs in huge letters: LEMON SQUASH, and bottles everywhere. Some authorized visitors came to the gallery and were amused to see the courtesans of Louis XV nibbling their ham sandwiches and smoking Lucky Strikes under the original Piranesi engravings.... With a friendly pat on the back Orson Welles told one smiling visitor, 'This is nothing. Come back in half an hour when the girls are here!' Scandalized, the visitor disappeared. Ten minutes later the crew was ordered to leave the building. Welles had been joking with the president's private secretary."[22]

Welles has often been accused of making *Macbeth* in a few days and then forgetting about it. His hurried trip to Rome to star in a costume drama is cited as proof that he had no further interest in the project after rehearsals and shooting.

It is true that *Macbeth* had not been edited. Herbert Yates's small production company, Republic, wanted to get the film out in December and had already postponed its release once. After Yates decided to cut ten minutes from the first edited version, Richard Wilson sent the film to Rome with an editor, Lou Lindsay, confident that Welles would do the job as quickly as he had shot the film. As he told Peter Bogdanovich (and as was reported at the time), during his first months in Italy Welles edited *Macbeth* himself, adding some finishing touches; via letters and telegrams his instructions arrived piecemeal to Wilson.

As Welles went about his work Oberdan Troiani, one of the assistant cinematographers for *Black Magic,* watched him. Both men spoke Spanish, and the two hit it off. At one point Welles asked him to shoot an additional scene for *Macbeth,* using a toy model.

"He asked me to shoot a scene for *Macbeth,*" Troiani remembered, "although I was only a second assistant. It featured a miniature camp at night. To do it he showed me a piece of the film and I noticed a close-up of Macbeth, a wide-angle shot, showing a huge square and a woman, whose feet were off camera. I was used to much more traditional shots and asked him about this woman. He said that if he had included her whole it would have given importance to the character, whereas he wanted to minimize her."[23]

Macbeth was not the only film Welles was thinking about during the shooting of *Black Magic.* In mid-February he made a quick visit to London to see Alexander Korda and negotiate his pet project, *Cyrano de Bergerac.* They agreed to postpone shooting until summer, with Alexander Trauner as art director and Henri Alekan as cinematographer; the film was to be distributed by Fox.

Black Magic was the set on which Welles brooded most lengthily about *Othello*, the project that would occupy his mind throughout his period in Italy and which caused him so much torment, one of the few works he managed to gain complete control over, from shooting to editing. Oddly, the inspiration came from Scalera on a day the producer was on set. He caught sight of Welles in costume, face dark, hair disheveled, gold earring in his lobe. "He came on the set," Welles recalled, and

> he looked at me and said, *Dobbiamo fare Otello*—We've got to make *Othello*. I saw no reason to argue. As an actor, since my very earliest days when I first charted an optimistic course that I hoped would take me to some of the great roles in dramatic literature, *Othello* has always been among the highest of those aspirations. But why did Scalera suggest that I should do *Othello*? Well, he loved opera, he was an opera buff and he made a lot of opera movies and made a lot of money making those movies. When he saw me made-up as I was for the role of Count Cagliostro, with gypsy make-up, curly hair and a big gold earring, he was thinking Verdi, and not Shakespeare, and he naturally said, "*Othello*. Let's make *Othello*."[24]

Michele Scalera had had the idea in mind since at least 1942. He intended Welles to act in the film, nothing more. But Welles's imagination immediately got to work. Instead of Verdi's, he wanted to film Shakespeare's *Othello*. Instead of merely acting, he wanted to act and direct. It took him some time to realize his dream, and only then after enormous setbacks and difficulties—of which the shooting of *Black Magic* was just one relatively minor hiccup.

Welles thought about another film during *Black Magic* and actually began making it: a documentary about the circus. All that we could collect about this project, omitted in most biographies, are some summary details and a few anecdotes. The working title was *The Circus*, plain and simple. According to Alessandro Tasca di Cutò it was another Alexander Korda project to delay *Cyrano*. Welles loved whatever was extraordinary and wonderful, and the circus was one of the forms of entertainment he was most temperamentally suited to. Between shooting scenes for *Black Magic*, pending *Cyrano*, he agreed to make the documentary.

The ideal cast would include the Fratellini clowns, much admired by both Welles and Joseph Cotten. From an interview with two of the famous trio, we know that in the documentary they would have performed a simple, yet sensational, number: "One of our best acts was pure pantomime, involving sweeping up the light and putting it into a trashcan, which was then thrown out. . . . The idea didn't come from the cinema but from the spotlights high up in the big top which threw circles of light onto the ground. Gradually we developed it into an act, sweeping up these muffins of light. Orson Welles promised he would put it into a film on the circus. That way, amid all those horses and lions, an improvised routine would be shown to be the symbol of our work and, at the same time, it would become a cinema gag."[25]

Welles never did shoot the scene. The only footage for the documentary was shot at the Zoppé Circus, a small family show featuring horses that had set up camp in Piazza Tuscolo, not far from Scalera Studios, during the final weeks of filming *Black Magic*. Welles was fascinated by one of the most daring numbers: a triple backflip between two galloping horses. He asked Troiani to help him film the somersaults. They went to the circus several evenings running and filmed the number without sound, because Tasca hadn't been able to find a technician willing to lend a hand.

During the last show in Rome a trapeze artist broke a rope and fell about ten meters to the ground. There was no safety net. Normally, a fall of this kind would have been fatal, but the trapeze artist was so nimble and athletic that she managed to somersault before hitting the ground and get up with only a sprained shoulder.

Troiani filmed the fall. Relieved at the outcome, Welles got Tasca to find a bunch of flowers for the trapeze artist and the evening ended at the Grotte del Piccione, a sleazy nightclub behind the central post office in San Silvestro, to which Welles invited the *Black Magic* crew and the circus artists.[26]

The following day a few more scenes were shot: taking down the tent in Piazza Tuscolo, moving the wagons to Tivoli, and setting up anew. The film was developed and printed; according to Troiani, "When I saw the material on the premises of Tecnostampa, Rossellini was there with his entourage, also looking at some rushes. It was my turn with the projector so he asked whether he and his followers could watch while they waited their turn. He liked what he saw, but afterwards the rushes disappeared and were never heard of again!"[27] It was the end of *The Circus*. The negatives could not be found and the project was dropped: one of the many small mysteries of the film's history.

The newspapers reported the accident at the circus and somehow managed to blame Welles. Perhaps because of the sudden death of Arata, Welles had acquired the reputation of someone it was unlucky to be around, and the circus accident was considered further evidence.

Welles quipped that he had brought the trapeze artist good luck, since she had got up virtually unscathed. Welles recommended the circus to his friend Ringling, and soon after, it was invited to tour America with the Ringling Bros. and Barnum & Bailey Circus and be filmed for Cecil B. DeMille's *The Greatest Show on Earth*. Today the Zoppé Family Circus is practically an institution in the United States.

At the end of January 1948, another accident happened on the *Black Magic* set. During a duel, Hungarian actor Stephen Bekassy, who played the cruel Viscount de Montagne, slipped under a barrage of lunges from Welles and fell, pulling a candelabra onto his head. The actor was taken to the hospital with concussion and the scene was deleted from the film. As edited, Montagne dies off camera, a hypnosis-induced suicide.[28]

On February 11 there was more bad news: the sudden death in Moscow of Sergei Eisenstein, the director of *Strike* and *Battleship Potemkin*. Welles was troubled. The two filmmakers had never met but had corresponded ever since Welles had written an unfavorable review of *Ivan the Terrible* for the *New York Post* in 1945.[29] Throughout his life Welles repeatedly stated that this was the only film by Eisenstein he ever saw—so the film or their correspondence must have affected him deeply, because Eisenstein has always been considered one of Welles's most important influences.[30] When the news was broken to him, Welles told Troiani that he had always admired the Russian filmmaker and went to his dressing room. He did no more work that day.

After four months of shooting, *Black Magic* was a wrap. Luigi Barzini, Jr., said the film had cost $1.5 million, about a billion lire at the time. It was more than the budgeted million, but Ratoff said two million would have been needed in Hollywood.

Interviewed by Barzini, Ratoff would not draw on Welles but praised the Italian craftsmen: "Nowhere else could I have made *Black Magic* as I made it in Rome. I would have had to spend ten times the amount and even then the result wouldn't have been the same. Thanks to the Italians, *Black Magic* is the most splendid film ever produced by America."[31]

A year later, when the film was finally released, the critics begged to differ. Ratoff failed to dominate Welles while shooting, so he had taken his revenge in the editing room. What emerged was an evidently commercial film highlighting above all the costumes and scenery: the Quirinale, the outdoor shots at Villa d'Este (the Strasburg scene), the gigantic Scalera film studios (the Tribunal) and Castel Sant'Angelo (the first prison scenes).

Here and there the unmistakable hand of Welles can be seen, temporarily reviving a contorted plot falling between the two stools of action and sentimentality. Welles's touch can certainly be seen in the winding long take of Cagliostro and the gypsy (Tamiroff) entering Versailles; one of Cagliostro's punches shot from the subjective viewpoint of the victim; several low camera angles (including the burial of Lorenza); the habit of shooting the ceiling (the brief prologue in the home of Dumas), as in *Citizen Kane*; and some expressive closeups of Cagliostro. But these are drops in an ocean of mediocrity and tedium.

Welles made light of the poor artistic result and preferred to remember *Black Magic* as "a riotous experience, the funniest, most amusing time I've ever had in movies."[32]

4
Dolce Vita

Women are the gauge of a man's weakness.
—Cesare Borgia (Orson Welles), *Prince of Foxes*

Along with *Black Magic* came something new. Italian journalists had been used to strolling into Cinecittà and Scalera Studios when they pleased and they did not expect (or like) the rigid protocols of the Americans, who objected to strangers wandering about on set. Ratoff got himself a bad reputation and Welles became "unapproachable."

Even an old hand like Ennio Flaiano—the future co-scriptwriter of *La dolce vita* and *8½*—was surprised by the American rules. A few weeks after completion of the shooting of *Black Magic*, he used a review of William Wyler's *The Best Years of our Lives* as a pretext to criticize Welles's fiery temperament and the uncouthness of Americans, cobbling his remarks together from comments by others: "In a country where they sell mayonnaise in tins, being refined is a sign of alarming cynicism. Mr. Orson Welles, whose achievements for us Europeans are the result of a lively, imaginative temperament, in America is thought of as 'too intelligent.' When he was making a film here in Rome a large notice was placed on the set instructing the other American actors not to speak to Mr. Welles. I think this step was necessary in order not to see Welles's lively temperament in action, whose replies may be a constant surprise for a man of the Union who does not know the secret of mayonnaise."[1]

Was Welles difficult, disagreeable, unapproachable? By no means always, although he was capable of being so. Those who worked with him found his way of doing things at times absurd or exasperating; he would occasionally put on a gruff, ill-tempered disposition. But generally he was anything but surly and aloof, as demonstrated by frequent sightings of him sampling the pleasures of Rome's night life.

A week after the dinner with Togliatti, the newspapers spotted Welles and Ratoff in the Wip Club, at a charity gathering on behalf of the Red Cross where a competition was taking place to find the prettiest female voice. This frivolous and pleasure-loving Welles was slightly at odds with the serious Welles the journalists had met at the Excelsior or in Scalera Studios. In the Wip Club he was closer to the stereotype of the brash Hollywood star than the thoughtful, committed *auteur*. Two months into shooting *Black Magic*, Welles had begun to show his face around town in restaurants and night clubs, livening up Via Veneto, later ambiguously celebrated by Federico Fellini. Welles's social whirl was closely observed and criticized by film reviewers: while his films were still unreleased in Italy, *he* was becoming all too visible, dining and barhopping until dawn. Now this courageous filmmaker, a man who had turned his back on Hollywood to look for fresh inspiration, the author of films of worldwide renown Italy had not yet had the opportunity to view—*Citizen Kane*, *The Lady from Shanghai* (and *Macbeth*)—was spotted dining in Tor Fiorenza, camping out in the Grotte del Piccione, visiting Taberna Ulpia where guitarist Alfredo Del Pelo played him *Chiove*, or coming and going at the ABC and Jicky Clubs, more concerned with his dance steps and one pretty girl or another than with his artistic future.

Dutifully, *L'Écran français* informed its readers of the eccentric mariner's attire Welles wore to gatherings at the American Embassy and the improvised parties he threw on the first floor of the Excelsior (one of which was attended by Rossellini and Anna Magnani, also guests at the luxury hotel). Readers were told about an Alfa Romeo valued at five million lire, which Welles drove up and down Via Veneto. "Mr. Welles . . . is the devil incarnate," the caretaker of the hotel would say, sliding another fine into his pocket.[2]

What interested journalists most was Welles's divorce from Rita Hayworth, and how long it would take him to find another woman to take her place. After *Black Magic*, they turned their attention to his female company. The star wasn't shy about it. Nonchalantly he held out his arm and found numerous takers to saunter with him into the most fashionable clubs in town, where the reporters and photographers were waiting for him.

One evening in January 1948, there were at least two reporters at the ABC when Welles made his entrance at 1:00 A M, with his signature "scruffy clothes, ruffled hair, and moody look." He was accompanied by a real beauty: short hair, black gloves, long dress with a high neck, and pearl necklace over an ample bosom. Sensing a scoop, the *Fotogrammi* reporter and photographer jumped to their feet. "Isn't that Jennifer Jones?" Giberto Severi wondered. "Welles turned toward us. We asked him if he would introduce us to Miss Jones. He feigned astonishment: 'Jennifer Jones? Where?' But when he realized we didn't want to interview her, he cheered up immediately: 'Promise?' We promised, so he introduced us. The couple danced in the crowd. For a while we could see their heads bobbing, then Jennifer stealthily moved toward the exit, followed less gracefully by Welles, whose stature made it more difficult for him to slip through the crowd, and they were gone."[3]

Tongues wagged. The two actors had just finished working together—Jones as lead and Welles as the unaccredited narrator in *Duel in the Sun*. She was taking a break from Hollywood and producer boyfriend David O. Selznick. In Rome she ran into Welles and the press imagined the rest.

After that first evening, they avoided the limelight, dining at Tor Fiorenza, an out-of-the-way restaurant on the Via Salaria. The reporters followed them and wrote of quiet dinners for two: risotto and saffron, fillet of veal, potatoes, and red wine—followed by romantic, moonlit walks through the Roman countryside. Nobody actually saw anything compromising, lips touching, an embrace, but that did not stop the rumors. After Rita Hayworth, why shouldn't Welles fall in love with another famous actress?

The couple made no statements, issued no press releases, cleared nothing up. The intrepid *Hollywood* reporter Doriana Danton visited Jones's hotel to ask her about Welles and actually got into her room. Jones denied the romance. She had met Welles only twice in Hollywood and had been pleasantly surprised to find him in Rome. The only scoop was the presence in the room of Henrietta, Welles's tawny mongrel cat, left with her the previous evening to keep her company.[4]

Most likely there was no truth to the rumors and Jones was soon back in Hollywood with Selznick, her future husband. The press concocted some more news: *Oggi* published rumors of a possible marriage to Lana Turner; *Fotogrammi* said Welles had spent an evening with Gene Tierney (before he had arrived in Italy). He was seen at the Capannelle Racetrack with Barzini, Jr., and "a mysterious brunette, apparently a vaudeville star, hired by Welles in Florence." A little later, *Film* came up with her name: Stella Nicolich, a popular entertainer. It suggested she had disdainfully turned down a proposal of marriage, not caring to be a stand-in for Rita Hayworth.

Welles's favorite nightclub was the Boite, where he danced the samba with a number of girls—too many for the reporters to get all their names. He was seen with one Gabriella Battiti, later the director of *haute couture* for the fashion designer Valentino, and with the future star Gina Lollobrigida, who was just starting out in the film business. The actress Cosetta Greco, Miss Scalera, became part of his entourage.

One of the girls he was seen with most often was the precociously beautiful, lissome, sixteen-year old Franca Faldini, a Rita Hayworth look-alike according to the press, and later the companion of the great Neapolitan comic actor Totò. Welles, twice her age, took her to his favorite clubs, the Taberna Ulpia, the Tor Fiorenza, and the Boite, and to Scalera Studios, where she was given a costume of some sort to put on and became an extra on the Ratoff set. Franca also visited him at the various temporary homes Welles had chosen, the Excelsior, Villa Madama, and Villa Manzoni, "where the shelves were covered with notebooks" and where Welles, for her sole delight, acted out scenes from *Othello,* taking on all the roles, apparently with the idea of making a film.

Life, love, Shakespeare, the cinema—one passion poured into another. "Eroticism," Welles told René Clair about this time, "can no longer be a poor man's literature. That's the lesson I've learned in Italy, the country where I want to live."

But something was happening. As they were recording Welles's nighttime outings and erotic conquests, Italy's journalists were beginning to feel irritated by him. In the few short months since his arrival, Welles had slipped from the culture pages of posh dailies to the gossip columns of glossy magazines. The press now treated him as the picturesque protagonist of a freak show. They were less and less impressed with his stature and more and more horrified by his size, his booming laugh, his badgering, and palavering on and about everything. Orson was young, had a reputation for genius, spent his talent on million-dollar films, and courted the loveliest women in Rome. He inspired envy and resentment. The VIP circle of partygoers and nightclub revelers was still willing to show him a certain admiration, but the journalists now openly made fun of him, as if to punish him for being larger than life. Unable to see him at work, to view *Black Magic* or the much lauded *Citizen Kane*, they had no real insight into Welles the artist and dedicated their articles to Welles the man. Not many spoke English. The cocktail parties and sambas on Via Veneto were the beginning of a fatal misunderstanding. The reporters began to write sarcastic hatchet jobs to demolish the myth accompanying his name.

The first chance film critics got to join in the fun was the release of *The Stranger,* which was shown a few months earlier in Venice. In *Film,* Felice smirked: "Among the many postwar disappointments is Orson Welles, unless the so-far unreleased *Citizen Kane* can singlehandedly rescue him from oblivion. From what I have been able to see of it, the film's a bluff."[5] Reviewing *The Stranger* for *la Stampa,* Mario Gromo called it "a tawdry drama" and conceded, "Welles is certainly an ingenious man and, as such, was unable to put up with the ways of Hollywood studios. He made his feelings known and Hollywood showed him the door." However, for Gromo, Welles was essentially the author of the *War of the Worlds* hoax, a man of stunts and gimmicks, unable to outgrow his reputation as the enfant terrible of American film.[6]

As the film critics set about panning *The Stranger,* reporters followed him everywhere to caricature his private life. In *Oggi* he was portrayed as an oversized, inelegant ballroom dancer, and something of an animal: "Welles is as tall as a Grenadier, corpulent, with ruffled hair. His expression is somehow amazed, candid, and simple at the same time: the eyes of a child hypnotist. He laughs loudly, baring his teeth and gums. He wears a baggy sports jacket that might double up as a pajama top at home. He dances frenetically, unbuttoning his shirt top and loosening his tie."[7]

Hollywood's Doriana Danton had a running personal war with Welles, ridiculing him and his entourage at every occasion: "At a cocktail party in the Excelsior . . . as usual Orson Welles held court with a group of rapt admirers, who understood about a quarter of his strongly accented English, exclaiming at regular intervals: 'What a genius!' perhaps because such an unattractive man had managed to win the hand of beautiful Rita Hayworth!"[8]

Paola Ojetti of *Film* dedicated several columns to Welles's manners, barely concealing personal or national jealousy over his female conquests:

> We would ask one thing of the artist: a little discretion. In the end his rolling eyes and booming laugh lose interest. He feels obliged to welcome, wine and dine, court, and caress all the Hollywood actresses that flit through Rome. . . . At the cocktail parties given in his honor he kisses all the ladies who circle around him. Occasionally an Italian man winds him up and gets him to utter sheer nonsense. The other night one such youngster, assisted by a witty lady accomplice, mixed the dregs of twenty glasses of wine and offered this delicacy to Welles, informing him that the cocktail was considered exquisite. And Orsone (as he calls himself, claiming Italian forebears—the Orsini no less) . . . tossed back the glass in robust appreciation. The ingredients were a secret worthy of Cagliostro, they said.[9]

The vindictive piece by Ojetti may have opened Welles's eyes to what was happening. During the springtime of 1948, the original reverence and admiration of his Roman hosts had given way to gossip and scandalmongering. Much as Ojetti had asked, he toned himself down, became more austere. His new demeanor was diligently reported by the press in a somewhat tongue-in-cheek fashion. *Film* stated, "Orson Welles has become restrained . . . his moderation in the capital is beyond reproach. According to Antonio Centa some of his moodiness was due to the indiscretions, and the harassment of admirers. . . . Now his followers number fewer fanatics (in Italy, he is supposed to have said that even glory is capricious, but he may have had another dictator in mind) and he has become reasonable and respectful. I overheard him the other evening at a private party making wise remarks about the length of dresses, the Five-Year Plan, negro eyes, and the third act of *Macbeth*. . . . He said the spring in Rome is beautiful even when it is unfaithful."[10]

It was a cold Easter that year, but Welles, the romantic, thought it beautiful. And there was a reason for his newfound moderation and romanticism: after numerous escapades he had fallen in love.

The actress Lea Padovani was officially twenty-four, but was more likely twenty-eight, according to some sources. Born in Montalto di Castro, near Viterbo, she was of Veneto and Tuscan blood. Dark, petite, with puffy cheeks, she was not a classic beauty but had a lively, sensual temperament (one newspaper called her "tender, maternal, puerile, jealous, furious, or sophisticated, according to her mood") which made her immediately attractive to a man's eyes. She had an endless string of admirers. Her acting career had begun at the Academy of Dramatic Arts, where she had fierce arguments with lovers, and it was said she had been forced to leave the academy because Silvio d'Amico the director, no less, had fallen for her. She moved into the frivolous world of vaudeville, where she hooked up with the surreal comedian Erminio Macario who struck her when he discovered her preference for Massimo Serato, a former lover of Anna Magnani. She continued to work in the theater, however, and appeared in a memorable adaptation of Cocteau's *Les parents terribles*, directed by Visconti. She was the dressmaker Laura in Aldo Vergano's neorealist film dedicated to the Resistance *Il sole sorge ancora* (which borrowed its title, but nothing more, from Hemingway's novel *The Sun Also Rises*).

Lea Padovani had a good reputation as an actress, but Welles knew nothing about her. They met at the restaurant in Scalera Studios at the end of March 1948. Lea was with a former colleague at the academy, Edda Albertini, and other friends. Later, in an interview, she said the meeting had been prearranged to test Welles's mettle. People were sure he would notice her; the group was introduced and Welles became smitten.

He investigated and found out that the woman he admired appeared onstage every evening at the Teatro delle Arti, where she was starring in Noel Coward's *Present Laughter*. That same day he went to see her act. After the show he presented himself at her dressing room door in order to congratulate her on her performance, then waited for her to leave the theater, just to see her walk away in the rain.

He returned several times. After the curtain calls he would go to her dressing room and one evening even managed to persuade her to accompany him to the Boccaccio restaurant. He spoke little Italian, and she no English. Despite this obstacle, after dinner they discussed theater and film until three o'clock in the morning. "The two were never untoward," the *Oggi* reporter wrote. "They observed each other closely, face to face, trying to understand each word, opinion, thought, every gesture and expression." That first evening Welles was particularly euphoric. On leaving, he shook head waiter Gino's hand. Evening after evening, the couple became habitués of the place. Welles walked into the restaurant saying, "Che fame, che fame" (I'm ravenous), and then sat down to ample dishes of spaghetti, salad, and cheese, drank Chianti with Padovani, and left Gino good tips.

Sergio Sollima recalls,

I was a close friend of Lea Padovani, an extraordinary actress, Italy's answer to Bette Davis, only smaller. But she was a little too crazy. She had something of Anna Magnani about her, too, the same determination. Only more beautiful. In one revue she appeared practically undressed, something unheard of at the time. One evening I went to see her at the Teatro delle Arti and saw Orson sitting in the front row. I had no idea about their affair. During the interval I went to her dressing room and told her about Welles, thinking she would be pleased. What a fool! A few minutes later, in breezed Welles, who recognized me. I had been to his first press conference at the Excelsior; he even remembered my name. When Lea went back onstage we had a long chat. He spoke only a little Italian and I had just a smattering of English, so we spoke French and bits and pieces of other languages—a strange mixture—with the help of some mime and showman's antics. He was a natural, and I a beginner. He asked me what I did for a living, and I told him I wanted to be a film director, I had written a screenplay about Salvatore Giuliano, the famous bandit. He was curious: "A fascinating character, to be sure," he said. "Maybe we should take a trip to Montelepre." He could already see himself playing the part, with the dual, multifaceted character of Giuliano. It would have been impressive, but like so many other things it fell by the wayside: we never met again. Lea, of course, kept on seeing him. Welles was head over heels but she was still stuck on Massimo Serato.[11]

That Welles was in love was clear to friends and journalists alike. It was equally clear that Lea was not in love with him. She did not spurn his courtship, but to friends she confessed a certain irritation: "These Americans, they think they can buy everything with the United Nations Relief and Rehabilitation Program, flour, fabrics, dollars, world fame, what have you." The frivolous magazine *Cine Illustrato* invited Welles, Ratoff, and Barzini onto the jury of a competition sponsored by MGM and Warner Bros. to send a girl to Hollywood. But Welles kept away from such temptations and confided to a woman friend that he had taken an important decision: "I've never met anyone as adorable as Lea. *Io la registro."* Or in Welles's half-English, half Italian of the period: "I'm going to register her"—that is, marry her.

Increasingly perplexed about how to handle the situation, she spoke to Guglielmo Cortese, the head of the theater company. He gave the actress some "affectionate advice from a man of the world"; in other words, he told her to accept Welles's advances. Welles was a wealthy, famous, and influential filmmaker and Lea, who was capricious and ambitious, could certainly turn the situation to her advantage, and perhaps launch an international career.

Welles waited anxiously for a sign of her favors. She gave him none. He insisted. She resisted. In the end she informed him she was flying to Sicily, where Serato was shooting *Il principe ribelle* (The rebel prince), directed by Pino Mercanti. Serato would decide what was to become of her. A reporter quoted her as saying, "I have no right to decide. I'll take the plane, go to Massimo in Sicily, and he can dictate my fate." On the evening before her departure Welles dined at Ratoff's with a large group of mutual friends. Everyone could see that Welles was unusually jumpy. Finally he told them why: he had bought Lea a diamond ring and he was afraid she would throw it back in his face. He had been meaning to give it to her for some time but had been too afraid to risk it. The next day he was at the airport to see her off on that fateful journey. Her eyes were full of tears. He slipped the ring on her finger without a word and returned to town overjoyed. "She took it," he told friends, many of whom had heard nothing about his plans.[12]

One magazine estimated the cost of the ring to be a million and a half lire. It was reported that Lea was showing it off in Sicily. The meeting with Serato was probably less than dramatic. He had been unfaithful to her so many times that, as far as he was concerned, there was no engagement.

But Lea kept quiet about that, leaving Welles to stew in his own juice. She left Sicily on April 12, and on the way back she stopped off in Florence to vote in the first elections of the republic, on April 18. For a week Welles paced up and down, "smoking furiously and losing his temper with poor Barzini."[13]

During that week he was invited to a private showing of Rossellini's *Il miracolo,* in which Anna Magnani played a peasant girl who is made pregnant by a shepherd (played by Federico Fellini), whom she believes to be Joseph. The following evening Welles met the director and actress at Le Pleiadi, a nightclub, and congratulated them on the achievement and the forbearance of the Vatican. Michel Sander, the French journalist who reported the meeting, told his readers that Welles had offered to direct the Rossellini script *Life of Jesus* (which no producer had ever wanted to touch) to star Welles as Christ and Anna Magnani as the Virgin Mary.[14]

No other reporter mentioned the episode, so it is possible that Sander was exaggerating or had misheard. The two directors never worked together. Rossellini was busy with other projects: he had a contract with Eduardo De Filippo and he was planning to make a film starring Jennifer Jones for David O. Selznick and a comedy starring Anna Magnani. He was also planning to make a life of St. Francis of Assisi. His private life was in turmoil; he had met and fallen in love with Ingrid Bergman and was about to leave Anna Magnani for her. Welles had expressed his admiration for *Roma città aperta* and *Paisà,* but, somewhat mysteriously, after this meeting he began to criticize Rossellini with a bitterness that suggests a strong disappointment or a fierce argument.

Following the completion of *Black Magic,* Welles stayed in Rome but no new films presented themselves and the projects discussed with Rossellini and others came to nothing. His footage on the circus had been spirited away, and *Cyrano de Bergerac* kept being postponed. Of course, he was waiting for Lea's answer. When she returned from Sicily and Florence, she hadn't decided and told him she could not make up her mind.

One day Welles started flicking through the Milan-based cinema magazine *Bis.* He came across an article in which he was portrayed as a drunk and buffoon: "He gets up around nine still intoxicated from the whisky drunk into the small hours in the nightclubs of the town where he frenetically dances sambas and jitterbugs, loosening his tie and unbuttoning his blue-striped silk shirt. As soon as he gets up he has a drink, shaves with ordinary soap and without a shaving brush, then tucks into a hearty breakfast. He drinks continuously, maybe to forget about his two ex-wives or maybe about the criticism that is leveled against him and his films."[15]

If he had not been in a particularly irritable state of mind due to Lea's continuous procrastination, he might have let the whole thing go. Instead, he called a lawyer and sued the journalist, Roberto De Paolis, the photographer and the editor of the magazine. Then, to everyone's dismay, he got on a plane and returned to the States.

Franca Faldini

"It was just an adolescent flirtation"

ROME, NOVEMBER 11, 2005

In Italy, Franca Faldini (b. 1931) is well known as the partner of Antonio de Curtis, aka Totò, with whom she also worked. But there are several surprising things about her life before and after Totò. They called her "the beauty of Via Veneto" when, while still an adolescent, she left her home in the nearby Via Lazio and turned into the famous street. Her beauty also struck Welles during the filming of *Black Magic*. Later she became a friend of Errol Flynn's and in 1950 she was in Hollywood, hired as an "exotic type" by Paramount. After a little role in *Sailor Beware* with Dean Martin and Jerry Lewis, she returned to Rome, where she met Totò, a man she loved patiently for fifteen years. After his death, she became a journalist and translator and wrote some of the most important pages on the Italian cinema (including *L'avventurosa storia del cinema italiana* [The adventurous history of Italian cinema]—a massive volume of interviews collected and edited with Goffredo Fofi). She agreed to act in only one more film, Alberto Sordi's last, *Incontri proibiti* (Forbidden encounters).

She revealed her brief friendship with Welles in one of her last books, *Roma Hollywood Roma*. Welles noticed her at the ABC, where she was dancing with a boy of her age—sixteen. "Orson Welles can't stop looking at you," her dance partner said. The filmmaker followed her home in his car and had Antonio Centa write down her address. The next morning, he sent her flowers and initialed the note O. W. This went on every day for a week, until they met accidentally at a gala dinner at the Excelsior. "It is rare to meet someone as intuitive and sensitive as Orson Welles," she wrote. "His was the delicate and courteous courtship of a man who has learned at his own expense how quickly the season of daydreams passes and has the moral good sense not to disabuse others too early. He was only ever romantic with me. For as long as he had the heart and patience for it . . ."[1]

She says no more, aware that she was very young and that her words might be interpreted as pompous or vain.

FRANCA FALDINI: It was all so long ago and lasted just a moment. It was just an adolescent flirtation, put it that way.

I have the impression you were not overly impressed by the fame of Orson Welles.

FF: For me, and for most other Italians at the time, Orson Welles was simply Rita Hayworth's husband. That was the first thing I said about him: Rita Hayworth's husband. As an actor or filmmaker I wasn't able to understand or appreciate him. I was sixteen and was dating a boy I liked.

What did you like about Welles?

FF: I remember he was tall, thin, had eyes like a man possessed and a curl of hair that fell over his brow. He was not handsome but could fascinate, especially when he spoke or acted out scenes from plays, with that extraordinary voice of his. And his laugh: he had a laugh all of his own which I can't describe.

How did you communicate? At that time Welles didn't know any Italian.

FF: We spoke English. I was pretty good at it. I had a diploma from the British Institute. When I went to America I was fluent. Languages helped me. After Antonio's death I translated about forty novels from English. It was my job until I started writing things of my own.

Did you ever talk to him about Rita Hayworth?

FF: He admired her greatly, said she was a marvelous person but that she should never have gone into films. She had none of the cunning and egoism of that world. Welles didn't like the fact that his wife was an actress. He said he was still on the best of terms with her. When he said she shouldn't have gone into films, he said it with respect, not to criticize her acting, but as a matter of character.

How did you end up in Black Magic?

FF: I still have the photo. Me, Ratoff, and someone else, dressed as peasants, all of us extras. The scene was set in a barn; we had to come down a ladder, me with a shawl over my head. Ratoff had on sandals and leg garters. I don't remember why we were used and I don't recall ever seeing the film. It was the first time I'd ever been on a film set. It was during Welles's gentle courtship and he had invited me to Scalera Studios to watch them making the film.

Did he think one day you'd be an actress?

FF: No, Welles sold no illusions about the cinema and I certainly had no ambitions to become an actress. The first time I felt tempted was with De Sica. He and Zavattini stopped me one morning when I was going to the post office in Via Lombardia; they had been struck and wanted me to be the statue in *Miracle in Milan.* At the time De Sica was the most famous filmmaker in the country and I thought . . . "Well, if he wants me, why not?" I did the screen test, in a tunic. De Sica told me to move slowly but I was stiff as a post, so Anna Arnova got the part. That was the first time I really had wanted to be in a film. I don't remember how I ended up in *Black Magic.* I think it was just something that just happened, a masquerade, people dressing up as happened in those days on film sets when there were no Union problems or other difficulties.

I read in your book: "If anyone on set made the slightest noise . . . Ratoff immediately seemed to confirm the rumors that he was a stooge of Zanuck's, screaming at us in poor Italian with a strong accent."² Why do you call him a stooge of Zanuck's?

FF: Zanuck was the Twentieth Century Fox mogul and was very right-wing. We thought Ratoff was there as Zanuck's poodle, protecting his interests, because the Italian crew and workmen were all left-wing. It turned out Ratoff had been blacklisted by McCarthy. I really can't say any more. I remember him as rather unpleasant, physically unattractive, blond, tubby, with his Russian girlfriend always on hand . . . I can't remember her name . . . Russians everywhere he went . . .

Where was Welles staying back then?

FF: As soon as he arrived he went to the Scuderie in Villa Madama, converted tracing stables then owned by Dorothy di Frasso. Then he moved to the Excelsior for quite a long time. Then, when he was with Lea Padovani, he rented Villa Manzoni, at the time a marvelous building, but now sadly abandoned. The roof collapsed, and the windows were broken. I don't know the history of the villa but I think it was owned by the Manzoni family. In the late '40s it was still furnished. I had tea there one afternoon. The restaurant, Tor Fiorenza, where Welles used to eat—occasionally with me—no longer exists. It was a lovely place near Piazza Priscilla: an old farmhouse with just a few tables, a fireplace that was always lit, refined, genuine.

Who else did Welles go there with?

FF: Prince Tasca was always with him. And his secretary and a Russian director, Wascinski or some such name ...

Waszynski.

FF: Right. Welles was often with him. And some Italian actors, like Antonio Centa, who was in Castellani's *Un colpo di pistola* [Pistol shot] in 1942. I think Centa procured girls for Welles. And I saw Barzini with him several times.

Girls like Stella Nicolich, Gabriella Battiti, and Gina Lollobrigida?

FF: I don't know anything about that.

And Lea Padovani?

FF: I was there when they met. At the restaurant in Scalera Studios. Orson was simply bewitched. He came in and was introduced to Lea Padovani, who got up and—instead of shaking hands like anyone else would have done—she put her palm next to his, fingertip to fingertip. There was a silence and it was obvious to everyone something was going to happen between them ...

Lea Padovani's films show her strong temperament but it is said she was very sensual.

FF: Above all she was a very intelligent and rather cultured woman. She had always been in the theater world and knew several writers, too. She wasn't a great beauty, petite with big round eyes, but she had a perfect body and there was something about her that men liked. She was well known, was one of Macario's actresses and had been very successful onstage in his *Febbre azzurra* [Blue fever]. When she appeared she didn't take one's breath away, but she was quite fascinating. She had character; she was shrewd ...

What impression did people have of Welles? Genius in exile, driven out of Hollywood, or international star passing briefly through Italy?

FF: My impression was that he was happy in Italy and had no nostalgia whatsoever for his home country. He didn't play the victim. I was young and perhaps I didn't understand these nuances. But he didn't rail against Hollywood, at least I never heard him do so, or express regrets or rancor.

In just a short time Welles went from international celebrity to Mr. Nobody. Did this happen to other American stars?

FF: To all of them. Any American actor who stayed for any length of time in Italy soon got treated badly. We Italians are like that. Generally they booked into the Excelsior, the hotel of the stars. Initially there would be crowds waiting for them to appear. A month would go by and the star would be seen at Doney's, Rosati's, the 54 Club, the Jicky Club, and no one would bat an eyelid. When Tyrone Power refused to go away, they would say, "Tired old Tirone" with a yawn.

But the press wouldn't leave Welles alone. They even reported he had been bitten by a dog.

FF: I remember well. He had to have something like forty rabies shots. Orson loved animals, like many artists do. Anna Magnani used to walk out of restaurants to feed the cats; she would ask them to put something in a bag for them. It was almost a ritual with her. Welles stroked any dog he saw and that's how he got bitten, I imagine.

It was 1951 and you had just returned from Hollywood. Did you see him often?

FF: No. Our relationship ended before it began. We bumped into each other, of course: social life in Rome was practically entirely in Via Veneto and its nightclubs. You could run across anyone there, go on to somewhere else and meet a different crowd, and so on. They were like salons. It was all very pleasant. You went out with three people and met thirty. Journalists did the same, of course. It was a beautiful era. You might come across an eccentric but never anyone who was rude, or worse, like today.

In 1953 you met Welles again on the set of L'uomo, la bestia e la virtù, when you were Totò's partner. Was that the last time?

FF: Yes. We didn't make a big fuss over seeing each other again. It was as if we had met three days before. No reminiscences. Welles and Totò respected and admired one another but the film was a total disaster: Totò didn't want to do it and Steno was not a director who could do Pirandello . . . It was Carlo Ponti's crazy idea and Totò had to do it to honor his contract. Welles needed the money and Viviane Romance was at the end of her career. She brought her busybody husband with her. Shocking...

Did you see Macbeth *or* Othello *when they were released?*

FF: I saw *Othello,* but only years later. I liked good films, not the usual tatter, but I wasn't able to form an opinion back then.

Which of his films do you like now?

FF: *Citizen Kane* was totally original and ahead of its time in its analysis of the press and media magnates. I also liked *The Magnificent Ambersons* and, of course, *Othello,* a role that was just perfect for him. Physically perfect.

What is your most affectionate memory of Welles?

FF: His delicacy with a young girl. It can't have been easy. He managed not to bore me and was never ridiculous. He didn't try to act younger than he was. He was delicate in his letters, too. Sometimes I got into a tantrum because he hadn't called when he said he would. So he would send me his apologies. I kept all these notes. Once he wrote, "Sometimes I wish you were five minutes older so you could understand what it means to be tired out by work." Not five years, you see, five minutes...

November 1947: Just arrived in Rome, Welles and Luigi Barzini, Jr., visit the Vatican Museums. *Photo by kind permission of Andrea Barzini.*

November 12, 1947: Orson Welles holds his first press conference at the Excelsior Hotel in Via Veneto. The journalists were attracted by his fame and the name of his wife. In the photo, Welles listens as Luigi Barzini interprets. *Photo by kind permission of Andrea Barzini.*

December 8, 1947: Orson Welles and Palmiro Togliatti, in a rare photo taken of the legendary dinner at Romualdo's. The hand on the left is Luigi Barzini's. *Photo by kind permission of Andrea Barzini.*

Welles chooses cufflinks in a Rome jewelry store, watched by Antonio Centa and Luigi Barzini, Jr. *Photo by kind permission of Giovanni Austoni and Gabriella Severi.*

(*facing, top*) From left to right: Carla Del Poggio, Welles, Suso Cecchi d'Amico, Antonio Centa, Carlo Ponti, Mario Soldati, and Antonio Blasetti. *Photo by kind permission of Giovanni Austoni and Gabriella Severi.*

(*facing, bottom*) Actors and technicians on the set of *Black Magic*. Gregory Ratoff is standing at the center; Welles is seated. *From the private collection of Massimiliano Troiani, Rome.*

A scene from *Black Magic. Photo by kind permission of Giovanni Austoni and Gabriella Severi.*

Welles and Lea Padovani with Elsa Maxwell on the Lido. Welles seems far from happy. News of *Hamlet*? *Photo: Fondazione La Biennale di Venezia–ASAC.*

(*right*) Suzanne Cloutier as Desdemona. *From the private collection of Massimiliano Troiani, Rome.*

(*below*) Welles, blackened up for *Othello*, shoots Suzanne Cloutier. *From the private collection of Massimiliano Troiani, Rome.*

Morocco, 1949: Oberdan Troiani with Anchise Brizzi.
From the private collection of Massimiliano Troiani, Rome.

Welles points into the far distance, with Troiani and Michał Waszynski.
From the private collection of Massimiliano Troiani, Rome.

Shooting *Othello* in Morocco. *From the private collection of Massimiliano Troiani, Rome.*

An unmade-up Micheál Mac Liammóir resolutely refuses to smile at the photographer. Hilton Edwards (standing), in the dual role of Brabantio and director's assistant, looks on. Welles is seated, checking the scene against a photograph in his right hand. *From the private collection of Massimiliano Troiani, Rome.*

Mac Liammóir as Iago. *From the private collection of Massimiliano Troiani, Rome.*

5

Citizen Kane

"Where's my notice, Bernstein, I've got to finish my notice."
"Mr. Kane is finishing it for you. . . . Mr. Kane is finishing your review just
the way you started it. He's writing a bad notice like you wanted it to be."

—Leland (Joseph Cotten) and Bernstein (Everett Sloane), *Citizen Kane*

In 1948 most Italians had not seen *Citizen Kane*. They'd heard a lot about its revolutionary techniques but few had actually been able to see if the film matched up to its reputation.

The Italian release of Welles's directorial debut had gone the way of many other foreign pictures, held up first by the Fascist policy of homegrown talent and then by the war and its aftermath. Some copies of *Citizen Kane* had managed to find their way into private showings for high-ranking Fascist officials. After the war, some intrepid film buffs went to France to see the movie. In 1946, Alberto Mondadori, son of the publisher Arnoldo, saw it on Boulevard Saint-Michel in Paris and such was his fascination that he sat through the film three times, "tired and giddy with euphoria."

Italian filmgoers had a lot of catching up to do as far as American films were concerned. They had only just been given the opportunity to see *Gone with the Wind* (1939) and *Shadow of a Doubt* (1943), distributed immediately after the war. Other films had been released after impromptu dubbing by Italian Americans who happened to be around. Four years after distribution in the United States, *The Magnificent Ambersons* was released in Italy in the summer of 1946. But seven years after the U.S. release of *Citizen Kane*, RKO executives in Italy were in no hurry to distribute the film. This may have been a ripple effect from William Randolph Hearst's earlier efforts to prevent the film's release extending to Europe, or it simply may have been due to the innovative nature of *Citizen Kane*, which was considered an unlikely box-office hit.

If Welles had not been in Italy, fueling the curiosity of filmgoers, it might not even have occurred to the Italian branch of RKO to release the film. On February 25, 1948, RKO asked the prime minister's office to authorize the review of the film and its release to the public after dubbing into Italian. The copy presented was 3,126 meters long, and had the original title and a laughably infelicitous translation, *Il cittadino Kane*.[1] Permission for public screening was granted soon after, on March 6, accompanied by flattering remarks from the Review Commission.[2] But RKO continued to sit on the film and postponed the dubbing.

A month later, Roberto De Paolis published his article in the Milan film magazine *Bis*, calling Welles a drunk and reviewing the film in advance of its release: "One thing is clear. Not even *Citizen Kane* (a singular film) is all that it's cracked up to be. Even if it did prompt Chaplin to make *Monsieur Verdoux*, Welles is no writer of *The Gold Rush*. Orson seeks a different plane for his films—the intellectual one, let's say, rather than the poetic. His frenzied narrative style overwhelms without being convincing; his camera shots are extravagantly unconventional. Welles wants to dazzle at all costs."[3] Welles sued the unknown journalist for portraying him as an impenitent drunk, not for the remarks about his film, yet it must have ruffled his feathers to read a negative review of *Citizen Kane* before anyone in Italy had been given the opportunity to see it.

Another month went by before *Citizen Kane* premiered at the Excelsior Cinema in Milan, the gala event inaugurating the International Film Festival organized by Cineteca Italiana, on May 12, 1948. Having left for America, Welles did not attend; surprisingly, neither did the Italian intelligentsia, who had been discussing the film for years. Ugo Casiraghi, critic of the Communist daily *l'Unità*, reported, "*Citizen Kane* has been eagerly awaited in certain intellectual circles but at yesterday's premiere precisely those circles, and its men of culture, were conspicuously absent."

The film was shown in its original language, probably with subtitles, since RKO failed to dub it. One critic, Alfredo Panicucci of *Avanti!* confessed his ignorance of the language and reported that the film contained "some mysterious dialogue," inducing him to attribute Kane's wealth to some unspecified dirty dealing.

But even in English there was no hiding the originality of the film. Casiraghi made some apologies on behalf of the absent men of culture, who, he suggested, may have been disturbed by Welles's provocative manner, and went on to praise the film: "It is a highly original work, technically and in its baroque conception." Then he slipped into reporting rather than reviewing by rehashing the *War of the Worlds* hoax; he failed to mention any of the film's numerous narrative techniques or draw attention to the original use of camera angles. Since he said not a word about it, he may or may not have been impressed by the audacity of a twenty-five-year-old actor playing the life of a man from youth to old age. His review was fairly typical of the cockeyed responses to the film in Italy. With few exceptions, the reviewers neglected its technical aspects and searched for its social impact. "Asked about its potential for changing American society," Casiraghi wrote, "Orson Welles replied, 'No influence on society. The film was influential only for filmmaking. It has a revolutionary form.' No judgment of *Citizen Kane* appears to us as revealing as this, from the director himself.... The debate on the film has largely fizzled out because the director of the film isn't very different from the character he portrays. And although Hearst hated Welles with all his considerable might, the truth is that his media empire was left entirely unscathed. Maybe some Americans watched the film and thought to themselves, 'Poor Hearst. How unhappy he was.'"[4]

Quite possibly Casiraghi's review was written before the screening of the film, which had been scheduled to end too late for the presses to roll. Not all the reviewers were as cavalier. Among the exceptions was Arturo Lanocita, in *Corriere della Sera,* who concentrated on the film's formalism and compared it to the crowing of a rooster attempting to fly. He praised only its technical virtuosity: "Welles has blended and innovated techniques and cinematic styles, welding the baroque with the surreal and expressionist; daringly he has insisted on an originality that is not always fruitful but never fails to give the film color and resonance. ... This is a film that doesn't seek to win everybody over, and will not be universally liked. It wants only to dazzle, and it succeeds. *Kane* will be remembered."[5]

In the Socialist newspaper *Avanti!* Panicucci drew parallels with Faulkner and Dos Passos from literature and Dreyer, Lang, Pabst, and Clair from film. Despite the language barrier, and unlike many of his colleagues, he admired the satire and understood the film's "uncommonly audacious" content, and the attempt to show how capitalism renders everything arid, "leaving nothing but money and an overwhelming desire to dominate." His was a positive review, generally restrained, sometimes enthusiastic, concluding: "Citizen Kane is probably not a masterpiece. It's an event, a work that seeks originality at all costs, a hustling and bustling biography, the success of a style (paradoxically) without one single style, an act of photographic pyrotechnics with cameras using three lenses, an array of ceilings, and people shot from below. Yet it's a great film."[6]

Another left-wing critic, Guido Aristarco writing for the now-enemy *Bis,* dismissed the film, comparing Welles with one of the greats of world cinema: "Welles is not Chaplin. He seeks a different plane for his films, the intellectual one rather than the poetic: his frenzied narrative style, his editing characterized by sudden, arbitrary shifts, his extravagant and unconventional shots, not-always-justified camera movements, and closeups of faces and objects. In other words, Welles wants to dazzle at all costs."[7] These words may sound familiar and, in fact, it turned out that Aristarco and Roberto De Paolis, the journalist who, at that moment, was being sued by Welles for libel, were one and the same.

Aristarco was a Marxist critic, a staunch supporter of neorealism and a sworn enemy of formalism. His reviews were dogmatically loyal to these precepts as well as repetitive: during his entire career as a critic, in the name of supposed coherence and integrity, he would trot out his own old remarks again and again in new articles and books. In this case, he borrowed from an article signed pseudonymously. His earlier article for *Bis,* "Un solo Welles non basta" (One Welles is not enough), was a mixture of criticism and gossip. It commented sardonically on photographs depicting such newsworthy events as Welles putting on his shoes, shaving, and having breakfast. Part of the blame may lie with the photographer, who was also sued by Welles, because it was general practice to submit photos to newspapers and journals with a few descriptive words on the back, to be used in the article. In this instance, the photos had been grotesquely transformed by Aristarco into examples of Welles's vice and corruption. According to Aristarco/De Paolis, Welles was a "plagiarist," "eclectic and exuberant"—and since the days of *War of the Worlds* he had been an actor "onscreen" (*Black Magic*) "and off" (his morning bouts of drinking); he concluded that Welles was a conjurer with a showman's angle. The famous baroque style of *Citizen Kane* could be attributed to exhibitionism unchecked, if not enhanced, by prolonged periods of drunkenness.

It is difficult to understand how a normally scrupulous film critic such as Aristarco could produce such a shoddy piece of journalism. The cloak of pseudonymity suggests a malevolence of which even the author seems to have been ashamed. The journalist never again mentioned the incident. No clues as to his motives can be found in the Bologna Film Library, which acquired his papers some years ago. Under the heading "Welles" there are some notes about a conference held in Fiesole in 1974, and nothing more. Nonetheless, Aristarco repeated De Paolis verbatim.

Under two different names, his reviews of Welles in April and May— before and after the Italian premiere of *Citizen Kane*—were practically identical. Evidently, actually seeing the film had contributed nothing to his understanding. The remarks Aristarco added to De Paolis do little to save the author's integrity. Here and there he makes some grudging concessions: "Welles is unconvincing and fails to dazzle: he isn't the first film director to 'photograph the ceilings'; *Citizen Kane* is full of techniques that have become old hat. However, in other ways, it is a singular and courageous film—with a huge teaser (the secret of the word 'Rosebud') and interesting score; some noteworthy sequences, such as the banquet, have excellent rhythm and plasticity."[8]

The complaints about Welles's technique, specifically the "sudden, arbitrary shifts, and extravagant and unconventional shots," were copied word for word from a previous review of *The Stranger*.[9] Not the only Marxist critic to have a bee in his bonnet about Welles, Aristarco accused him of formalism, the bête noire of the neorealist school of filmmaking; the accusation persisted long after the twilight of neorealism, into the 1960s.

A few weeks after the Italian premiere of *Citizen Kane*, Alberto Mondadori weighed into the public discussion of the film, trying to turn it into an informed debate. Addressing his colleagues directly, he was the first in Italy to find in the film unmistakable signs of genius. For him, the film was a true work of art. "Courage, dear Sirs," he wrote enthusiastically, "Finally we have a masterpiece. Do not be afraid of its harshness, do not be fooled by its originality, do not limit yourselves to its light and shade, its peculiar framing, its exemplary editing; imagine you are reading a pamphlet by Swift, a book by Andersen, Faulkner, or Dos Passos (not to accuse Welles of a literary bent, which, Heaven forbid, was far from his intentions, but simply to give *Citizen Kane* its due place, albeit an unusual place for a film)."[10]

Some took Mondadori's admiration for the film as personally, rather than aesthetically, motivated.[11] However, his article in the weekly magazine *Tempo* contained more actual film criticism than other intellectuals had provided. Mondadori rejected the accusations of hyper-formalism and cited Pabst, Lang, Von Sternberg, Dreyer, and Stroheim, adding, "Welles has a Weltanschauung in which the baroque is not style, the wish to shock, or histrionics, but a form of the spirit and the essence of his vision." Unlike the Marxist critics, who could not get past the film's formalism—and, thus, its presumed indifference to social issues—Mondadori took the film to be a strong criticism of American society.

Mondadori's praise went largely unheeded, no doubt in part because of its vehement attack on established film critics, who—like Casiraghi and Aristarco—favored films for and about the masses and were unlikely to credit the opinions of a famous publisher's son writing in a magazine he himself had founded, discussing a film that recounted the life of an American media mogul. Mondadori continued to fight the ostracism of official critics but the two sides merely hardened their positions and the argument came to represent other conflicts in Italian society.

After Mondadori's appeal, two other critics gave the film their attention and tried to offer a reasoned opinion. Giulio Cesare Castello praised the film's unconventional narrative structure, relating a life "in episodes and fragments without slavish adherence to the demands of a straightforward chronology. Uneven in tone, style and quality, the film is the product of Welles's bizarre but undeniable talent.... He is a powerful storyteller in moving pictures."[12]

Glauco Viazzi was the first Italian critic to give lengthy thought to *Citizen Kane*. Researchers into Welles's work have long been familiar with the essay, which intended to rescue the film from the savaging it had received in the press, yet was itself an example of how the film was largely misunderstood in Italy. Viazzi's review was polite, not always coherent, and essentially negative. Analyzing form and content, he pointed out the limitations of the film and then sought to explain and justify them. The stylistic effects, he wrote, "generally remain at the level of effects, pure and simple," although "they are never an end in themselves. ... Welles's conception is rather simplistic ... the myth of individuality which is unmasked, not merely expressed." Viazzi then pointed the finger at "Welles's bloated, disorderly, technically-minded, contradictory style," but admitted that at certain points the film's characters "blend into a perfect stylistic whole, broad and deep." Remarkably, he came to an almost oxymoronic conclusion: despite the apparently revolutionary nature of the film, it was, he believed, "a museum piece. ... Judged on form alone, *Citizen Kane* is a masterpiece, perhaps *the* masterpiece. Yet you don't have to be a film critic to understand, instinctively, that the film is not so grand, that it is basically a product of its time—1941—whereas *Battleship Potemkin*, Pukovkin's *Mother*, Chaplin's *The Pilgrim*, Stroheim's *Greed*, and Vigo's *L'Atalante* are films with a place of honor *in the twentieth century*."[13]

The word "masterpiece" was often used (unfavorably by Panicucci and Viazzi, favorably by Mondadori) to compare Welles's first film with the century's greatest pictures and the most prestigious accomplishments of mature filmmakers. Italian film criticism saw its function as that of confirming or denying the reputation of *Citizen Kane* elsewhere in the world. During the Fascist period, Italians had admired American films from afar, but at a time when Italian neorealist films were themselves establishing a worldwide reputation, the United States' was not the only film industry that had something to say, and "masterpiece" was a label Italian critics no longer used exclusively for foreign films.

All of this touched film distributors and cinema owners not a whit. As the papers fired opinions back and forth about *Citizen Kane*, the film was not being screened anywhere. RKO allowed itself just one small experiment: a week after the Milan premiere it included the film in a week-long program in one Rome theater, advertising the event discreetly in a few newspapers (*il Tempo* described it as "the most intriguing, controversial, and original of Hollywood films").

The film still had not been dubbed and was probably subtitled. The copy may have been the one shown in Milan. The cinema chosen was the Quirinetta, an original-language cinema specializing in American and European films. There, the film critic Jean George Auriol saw it on May 24, 1948. The film competed with commercial offerings such as the exotic *Atlantis*, starring Maria Montez; thus, it had been allocated almost no time at all for a screening—just two days, in fact. Auriol complained to the cinema's management and obtained a token reprieve. "At the end of the last showing, I protested," he wrote, "and accused them of wanting to get on with stuff like *Atlantis*, which was not so far from pornography. So *Citizen Kane* was given one extra day: one day of grace for a film condemned by angry hordes of fanatics in a cinema for the deaf and blind."[14]

So it was that a Frenchman ensured that the film got three rather than two days for its Rome opening (and closing). On May 26, *il Tempo* made the preposterous claim that the extra day had been granted by popular demand. On the third day, like the first two, the cinema was almost empty. "Most of the people who would have come to see anything by Wyler or Capra stayed away," wrote Auriol, who sat and watched seven screenings. "They must be scared of something," he concluded. Later, Welles himself said the public at the Rome showing of the film had whistled and howled during the opening sequence, *News on the March*, aged deliberately for a feeling of authenticity. The three days the film was screened—a Monday, Tuesday, and Wednesday—were also the least likely to attract an audience. The film was already penalized by the language barrier; in addition, not a single newspaper in Rome reviewed the event.

The Milan premiere's hostile reception and the Rome screening, which went entirely unnoticed, cannot have encouraged the distributors. RKO further postponed the Italian version and waited months before applying for approval from the censors who viewed the film—now called *Quarto potere* (Fourth Estate)—on September 9. It was 3,288 meters in length, or two hours, more or less the same as the original.[15] The film was dubbed and twenty copies were prepared for distribution, at which point RKO had second thoughts and the date for release was postponed indefinitely.

They fiddled with the film, cut some scenes, and may have partially reedited it. On several occasions, Aristarco mentions a "severely mutilated Italian version." Fofi, writing in 1963, goes so far as to say that "the flashbacks had been put into chronological order!"[16] Twenty years after its premiere, Guido Fink talked about a "butchered, cut, and reedited version."[17] It's hard to say whether these descriptions are accurate since the Italian version is not from 1948 but from 1966, and has a completely new soundtrack.[18] The dubbing in 1948 and in the subsequent version were certainly different. Censors' records show various attempts to render "Rosebud" as Rosaspina or simply an approximation of the original, Rosbad, before it became Rosabella in 1966. But the editing was almost certainly very similar. In 1966, Aristarco said the new version, released in the summer, was "substantially similar" to the "quite seriously cut" version of the late 1940s.[19] The same permit was used, in an updated form, with the usual proviso "that the film include the same scenes and add no new ones, and not be altered without the authorization of the Ministry."

If Aristarco is right, Fofi and Fink may have credited rumors of reediting or seen the film in a cinema where the owner had his own ideas about how the film should be shown. Whatever the case, the Italian version is a quarter of an hour shorter than the American original.

Many scenes are a few shots shorter—from the journalist's first meeting with Susan to the picnic extravaganza, Leland in the hospice, and the fabulous summary of Kane's marriage at breakfast. The music sequences had all but disappeared; the vaudeville number at the party for the new staff of the *Inquirer* was cut, gone was Dorothy Comingore's piano recital, and some of the singing lessons with the Italian maestro were left on the cutting room floor.

The reason may have been the original film's length. Two hours' running time was unusual for an American film, and cinema owners were reluctant to shorten the intermission (and the sale of refreshments). No scenes were removed entirely, apart from the closing credits, in which the shots of the leading actors were replaced with a simple list of names. Generally the cuts gave a leaner look and quicker pace to the film, without disrespect for the atmosphere, rhythm and content of the original.

This raises a question (and might assuage the anger of purists outraged by the savagery committed): Did Welles agree to the changes?

Given the poor reaction to the film, its excessive length, and the probable insistence of RKO's Italian subsidiary, he might have caved in. Even more intriguingly, did he do the reediting himself? Technically, it was possible; Welles was in Italy editing *Macbeth*, with a Moviola of his own. There are only two pieces of circumstantial evidence, one for and one against this hypothesis, both based on statements to Peter Bogdanovich by Welles himself.

The evidence in favor is the scene in which the journalist goes to interview Susan for the first time in a nightclub. During the shooting, the casting director had included Gino Corrado, a character actor well known to American filmgoers; however, Welles did not want any familiar faces in the scene. To give himself more freedom, Welles had used the ploy of telling the producers he was only rehearsing, not filming, so removing Corrado would have given the game away. "So there he is—spoiling the whole master plan in one of the first shots that I made!" Welles told Bogdanovich. In the Italian version of the film, Gino Corrado has been cut from the scene.

The evidence against is the scene in which Bernstein talks to the reporter about the importance and persistence of memories. "You take me. One day back in 1896, I was crossing over to Jersey on the ferry. And as we pulled out, there was another ferry pulling in, and on it there was a girl waiting to get off. A white dress she had on; she was carrying a white parasol. I only saw her for one second. She didn't see me at all. But I'll bet a month hasn't gone by since that I haven't thought of that girl." This reminiscence was cut from the Italian edition. Yet Welles told Bogdanovich that if he were in hell and they gave him a day off to see any part of any of his movies, this scene—written by Herman Mankiewicz, his co-writer and joint winner of the only Academy Award the film received—is the one he would have chosen.

In its new, lean version, *Quarto potere* was finally released for the 1948–49 season. In November 1948, *Film* announced its imminent release and quoted Welles:

> I wanted to try the cinema after the theater, which I adore: however, with my cinematic language, I wanted to express a precise feeling of rebellion against the hypocrisy of society. I believe only in the good of a humanity comprising individuals with unlimited freedom of thought and action, each respecting

those of others. Naturally whatever I do, I do with passion, or I don't do it at all; nonetheless I am bound to *Citizen Kane* by certain things. I put my everything into it and I owe a deep debt of gratitude to Joseph Cotten. . . . I was satisfied with the performances of the other actors as well. *Citizen Kane* caused a stir, of course, because home truths are always unpleasant to hear.

The newspaper article ended on a buoyant note: "Everywhere else the film has been acclaimed; it is time for Italy to join in the praise."[20]

Italy did not oblige. To be fair, it was hardly given the chance: RKO put off the release week by week, month after month. Exasperated by the delay, two of Italy's future leading film critics, Callisto Cosulich and Tullio Kezich (later Federico Fellini's biographer) went to Trieste to protest with RKO and received the following disparaging reply: "The less films of this sort are seen the better: they ruin the public's taste."[21]

Despite the astonishing stance of the distributor, *Quarto potere* was released in Trieste in February 1949. Cosulich reviewed the film for the local newspaper, *Giornale di Trieste,* and did not repeat others' mistakes. He echoed Aristarco's opinion that Welles was interested only in pleasing his audience, but in a different spirit altogether: "Welles wishes to plunder the treasures of his own imagination and genius." Cosulich called the film "the debut of a major new filmmaker, similar to that of Luchino Visconti with *Ossessione* or Laurence Olivier with *Henry V.*" Summing up, he rebutted the familiar criticisms of Welles, in reply to Viazzi: "The defects of the film can be seen as merits in the light of the personality that is formed within it; if these defects—the barely concealed narcissism, the excessive pleasure in formalism, the baroque no less, and the lack of a serious social commentary—are errors, then they're Welles's errors, and the mistakes of his insufficient subsequent maturing, but they are not the mistakes of his first film, which may not be a film with a place in our century but it is certainly the flagship of the year it was made: 1941."[22]

The film was shown for only a few days in Trieste—mid-week, making way for something more popular at the weekend. A year after its hasty screening in Rome, *Quarto potere* was shown in Milan—again for three days (July 13, 14, and 15), and at the height of summer, when very few people were willing to coop themselves up indoors. An anonymous reviewer in *Cinema* commented, "Such unsuitable scheduling seems to have been chosen deliberately by cinema owners, pessimistic about the returns from the film."

At least the newly dubbed film allowed the Milanese critics, those who had not been to the original showing a year before, to get a better idea of what was on offer. The reviews were detached, mentioning the film's formalism, its complex narrative structure, and the psychological depth of the Kane character—a kind of aristocratic detachment.

The review in Milan's most important daily, *Corriere della Sera*, not signed or initialed, was insipid and botched. Its sentimentality and introspective style were not that of the regular film critic, Lanocita; perhaps the paper had sent a cub reporter willing to sacrifice a warm summer evening to culture. The inexpert reviewer cited a nonexistent premiere in Venice; rehashed opinions expressed during the film's previous showing in Milan; and wrote of "uncompromising technique and taste," banally identifying an "undercurrent of feeling" running throughout the film.[23]

Cinema provided a condescending, superficial slating, also anonymous (Guido Fink thinks it may have been by the editor, Antonio Baracco). The review praised above all the cinematography of Gregg Toland, but called the film "extraordinarily inhuman" and cited Balzac and Gautier to condemn Welles's formalism. "The overall effect," the review concluded, "is one of monotonous extravagance, deliberate and flaunted ostentation, a surprising muddle and fatuous oddity.... [M]ost bothersome is the director's poor taste in repeating his futile exaggerations. Orson Welles has a baroque mind, one of excess and hyperbole, which he mistakes for greatness."[24]

The review was so negative that even Aristarco, the chief editor, tried to tone it down by adding some captions that described the film as "original, anti-conventional," albeit of "debatable" value. In *Sipario*, he returned to his comments in the pages of *Bis* a year before, calling the film "doubtless highly original" and attributing to it "an acrobatic virtuoso technique, drawn from one director after another, one classic after another." Welles, he says, wants to revolutionize film shooting and editing. "After all is said and done," he concludes in a conciliatory vein, "Welles is a phenomenon, and *Citizen Kane* already has a place in the history of cinema."[25]

A lone voice in the wilderness, Volpone—the pseudonym of Pietro Bianchi—wrote a positive review in the humorous and satirical magazine *Bertoldo:* "*Citizen Kane* was shown for just three days in Milan at the height of summer. Yet it is a film of genius, with a powerful story to tell. Why don't we love true cinema in Italy? Maybe the distributors have made it all too difficult for us, with not one Rita Hayworth but a hundred, not one Robert Taylor but two hundred. *Quarto potere* is the story, the exposé, of a man's life. . . . It's a magnificent film, one of the best of the year."[26]

A year had gone by since the first negative reviews and a lot had been happening. Ennio Flaiano had joined in the debate, calling the film "baroque, truculent, with a high, but pointless, degree of precision."[27] The previously scornful Aristarco had softened his original position somewhat, yet the overwhelming impression is of the absurd distance between the opinions of the critics of the day and the unanimous praise, if not veneration, for the film today. Many reviews were lukewarm and gave the impression of a certain relief that the film was not so great after all. A large number of their authors came to regret their opinions and many years later, some even tried to keep their articles away from prying eyes. And that is not the only cover-up: there is no record of the Rome release of the dubbed film and no trace of the film screened in 1948, so no comparison can be made.

Some of the first Italian reviews of *Citizen Kane* were mealymouthed and less than honest: many were published anonymously, or under pseudonyms, or simply initialed, with captions added by someone else— evidence of critical embarrassment (or undisguised lack of interest), which in many cases was equal to their prejudice (or lack of expertise). Uncertainty, ambiguity, hidden sources—these call to mind the scene in which Kane finds Leland drunk at his typewriter and bashes out a poisonous notice himself.

6
Life after Rita

The Chinese say it is difficult for love to last long. Therefore,
one who loves passionately is cured of love, in the end.

—Elsa Bannister (Rita Hayworth), *The Lady from Shanghai*

In 1947, the generally well informed, gossipy film magazine *Hollywood*
reported a tender moment from the making of *The Lady from Shanghai*.
For one scene, the makeup artist suggested adding a drop of sweat to
Rita Hayworth's face. Welles turned on him with indignation: "Sweat!
Horses sweat, people perspire, Rita glows."[1]

On the set something sparked between husband and wife: as the
marriage foundered, the film enabled the two leading actors to seek a reconciliation, if that was what they wanted. Maybe, at a certain point, it was
working. Welles was certainly very protective of his wife; he wouldn't
allow her to sunbathe on the yacht under the tropical sun unless she was
properly oiled, and he had the cliff in Acapulco—from which she was to
dive in one of the scenes—scoured to remove shells and jagged objects.
But Welles was more intent on making his film than on making the marriage work. One Saturday, when Rita persuaded him to accompany her
to her beloved Mexico, Welles packed a typewriter so he could rewrite
the ending of the film; she came to the conclusion that he was more interested in his work than in a family. When the spotlights were turned
off, the marriage was over.

The world's press was full of coverage of the rift. In October 1947,
the Italian newspapers came to their own conclusions: "Rita is tired of
Orson Welles." He was a rover, he wouldn't settle down, and he treated

her cruelly. Hayworth recalled, "When I was pregnant with Rebecca, in 1944, Orson neglected me to the point of driving me to a nervous breakdown. He isn't interested in making a home; he doesn't even have one. He told me himself he shouldn't have married because he needs his freedom. When Rebecca was born he took some interest, and told me he wanted seventeen children. I said three or four would do, and he got terribly thoughtful."[2]

When the film was released in America in a hastily reedited, butchered form, Rita's many admirers were shocked: her flowing locks were shorn, and what little remained of them was dyed blonde. *Gilda* had made Rita Hayworth an international star; her career would never recover from *The Lady from Shanghai*. The film was a box-office flop. Detractors said it proved Welles had only ever been a flash in the pan.

Rita wanted a divorce; Welles readily agreed. While he was adventurously approaching Rome in an airplane, she was in a Los Angeles courtroom filing papers. It would be another year before the separation became divorce. Quizzed by the press, Rita's replies seemed to express more regret than relief. The lady protested a little too much, as if she were trying to convince herself that she wanted the marriage to end. The daily *il Messaggero* quoted her as saying,

> I should never have married him. He has so many things to do, all of them more important than me. He wants to be an artist, a director, a politician, have social concerns. Too much, too many things, of which marriage, for him, is the least important. How can two people who never see each other be happy? I'm still young, after all, and now and again I like to enjoy myself, have friends with the same tastes, who follow the same trends, people I like and who like me. . . . But you just can't live with a genius, can't keep up with him. . . . It's over. I have no regrets and nothing to recriminate myself for. I'm glad I married him; I have a wonderful girl, my little Rebecca, who is everything to me. . . . I learned a great deal from my husband, but I've had enough of men who never come home.[3]

Whether she was still hoping to patch the marriage up—as some reporters at the time insinuated and some historians have repeated—when word got back to America in spring 1948 that Welles was seeing Lea Padovani, Rita was reported to have spat out venomously, "Whatever has happened to Orson? I thought he only liked tall women with a figure."

As his wife was ruefully musing on his tastes in women, and the woman in question was playing—or being—hard to get, Welles, irritated by the article in *Bis,* got on a plane and, without explanation, flew home. His Italian entourage was thunderstruck. Welles's private secretary, Antonio Centa, was seen (by a reporter) with "a forlorn, lost expression of utter solitude."

The rumors began: Welles had been given a hostile reception in Italy and, tail between his legs, he was going back to America to save his marriage. According to *Cine Illustrato,* Welles and Hayworth stayed for a week together at Cranberry Corners in Idaho. But the reason for Welles's sudden return, as Rita certainly realized, was artistic, rather than personal: despite reels sent back and forth between Rome and Los Angeles, Welles hadn't yet managed to edit *Macbeth* and had been summoned by Republic to finish the job.

In Italy, only *Fotogrammi* informed its readers of Welles's departure. Welles had no interest in informing anyone of his return to America because he still hadn't paid the money the Internal Revenue Service demanded in uncollected taxes, and the HUAC was still active (the Hollywood Ten had just pleaded their First Amendment rights before Congress and the major studios were still drawing up blacklists of supposed subversives). But the producers of *Macbeth* were becoming jittery and wanted Welles back, preferably chained to a desk on their premises, to complete the editing.

In Republic's offices he told journalists he would be going back to Italy in June to make *Cyrano,* opposite not Martha Scott, who had turned the picture down, but—he hoped—Michele Morgan. One well-informed journalist asked him if he intended to marry Padovani. "My dear lady," Welles replied, "I find myself in a delicate situation; she doesn't speak English and I speak no Italian, so I don't know if she said yes or no."

On the other side of the Atlantic, Doriana Danton, *Hollywood*'s perfidious journalist, was similarly quizzing Lea and receiving even vaguer answers: "He's a very nice man. Truly remarkable. Yes, maybe I'll be in a film he directs." Asked point-blank if she was going to marry him, Padovani shook her head and delivered a model answer: "Why speak about such things, which are strictly private? If I marry him, it will be public knowledge. If not, what is there to talk about?" Asked if Welles thought her more, or less, beautiful than Rita Hayworth, she smiled, and said, "I would hope he considers me with quite a different yardstick. After all, *I'm* an actress."[4]

Rita held her tongue. She had no intention of taking part in the speculation and gossip, or of replying to Lea's barbed remark. "Certainly I will marry again," she said. "I haven't the slightest idea of what kind of man he will be."[5] At the end of May she began a long holiday in Europe, resting after her latest film, *The Loves of Carmen,* and getting as far away from reporters as she could. She may have been willing to make one last effort to patch up the marriage with Welles, who would also soon be in Europe.

Had one of his daughters not given him chicken pox, Welles might well have gone with Rita after editing *Macbeth.* He stayed home for a few weeks and then flew back to Rome, stopping off in London to talk once again to Alexander Korda about *Cyrano.* The script (co-authored with Ben Hecht) had been finished, the set was being prepared by Trauner, and everything was ready—except for the most important thing. After months of shilly-shallying, Korda backed down. "My dear Orson," he said, "don't you think that man with the nose is rather a bore? I have a chance of making $150,000—hard currency, my dear Orson—so I'm selling it to Columbia. You won't be angry, I know."[6] Welles was used to Korda changing his mind and actually wasn't angry. Besides, he had another film in mind and tossed out the idea to Korda.

Back in Rome at the beginning of June, Welles told the press he had set aside *Cyrano* in favor of a film based on Pirandello's *Enrico IV.* He got hold of the 1943 film version by Giorgio Pastina and hastened off to Capri to write the screenplay, titled *The Emperor.*[7] "I spent months on that. If I ever wanted a script of mine to be published, that would be the one," he told Bogdanovich. "The idea was, the father of the man who believes he is—or is pretending to believe he is—Henry IV is living on an island off the coast of Italy, and is determined to call his son's bluff and shame him."[8] No trace of the script has ever been found and most biographers ignore it.

Bret Wood thought the project for *Henry IV* was related to "The Way to Santiago" and "Carnaval" from *It's All True,* as well as to *Mr. Arkadin* (aka *Confidential Report*), in that it shows Welles's interest in the interior struggle for identity.[9] Quite possibly, the script was prompted by Michał Waszynski, a Polish director. Jewish and homosexual, Waszynski was a spectacular, larger-than-life character Welles had met on the set of *Black Magic,* and who may have reminded Welles of Pirandello's character. The self-proclaimed prince had been Welles's introduction and guide to the good life in Rome.[10] However, Welles was clearly going to make the hero of the film a man after his own heart (or in his own predicament): an American expatriate, isolated, unable to find his feet in his new surroundings, a man who believes in his own extraordinary destiny but is considered by others a madman and megalomaniac. A tragicomic, even ridiculous, figure. Wasn't that how Welles had been made to feel in Italy?

Meanwhile, Rita was in Paris and wasn't having fun. She went to a couple of parties but her health cracked. A nervous breakdown, as the doctors called it, was followed by two collapses, at which point she was taken to the hospital and given blood transfusions. After three weeks of complete rest, she went to the French Riviera and the prestigious Eden Roc Hotel in Cap d'Antibes, where she phoned Welles in Rome. Back from Capri, he was expected to attend yet another gathering at the Hotel de Russie. It was the evening of July 21. As soon as they finished talking, Welles got on a plane to France.

Tongues wagged. Welles had checked into the same hotel as his wife. Were they back together again? the daily *Espresso* wondered on its front page. "What has disrupted the peace and quiet of Antibes," the anonymous reporter insinuated, "is the fact that this evening neither Rita nor Orson have shown their faces. Could it be they have better things to do?"

On the morning of July 23, the two were seen at a restaurant on the Juan-les-Pins beach and were immediately hounded by journalists. "Push off quick or I'll mess with your face," Welles told a reporter from the Nice-based *Espoir.* Only Jean Malin, the French correspondent of the Italian film magazine *Cine Illustrato* managed to get some measured words out of Welles. "After his arrival, Rita has spent her time with no one else. They dine together and the ladies find his demeanor deplorable and sympathize with her. They are unwilling to forgive the former prodigy's table manners, his rumpled clothes and uncombed hair, his booming laugh, and disrespectful treatment of women. . . . Orson Welles was unwilling to be photographed or interviewed, but he did have one thing to say about his intentions: 'I like "Gilda" too much to offend her by marrying her again.'"[11]

The following day they were seen dining at Chez Francis on La Garoupe beach and then dancing at La Jungle in Cannes. They looked happy, and onlookers assumed a reconciliation was taking place, but that same evening Welles returned to Rome, "shutting everyone up," said *Corriere della Sera,* and "disappointing reporters who were already imagining tender stories to come. Rita stayed behind in Cannes while her personal secretary informed journalists that Rita and Orson were 'just good friends.' The suggestion that they had left for Rome together was indignantly denied."[12]

One newspaper claimed that after Welles's departure, Rita had immediately gone to Nice for a visa to Italy; others had her sulking in her room for two days. If she did stay in her room, she may have been hiding from her suitors: the Venezuelan millionaire Alberto Dondero; Audie Murphy, America's most decorated officer; the Shah of Persia, Reza Pahlavi; and Prince Igor Troubetzkoy. She spurned them all. When the prince had the temerity to ask her whatever had induced her to marry someone like Welles, he received a public slap in the face. Playing a more subtle, waiting game was Aly Khan, son of the world's richest man, the Aga Khan.

A few days later, with a hubbub in the world's press about Rita's flirtation with Aly Khan, she sent Welles a telegram and for the second time he flew to France, this time on a cargo plane, since no passenger planes were available. On August 12, there were rumors in Cap d'Antibes of Welles in a jealous rage with Rita and then in a fierce argument with Aly Khan. The reporters sniffed about and found nothing to confirm the rumor; the two had not come to blows, and the trail went dead. Years later, Welles told biographer Barbara Leaming a different, and sadder, story about that evening: "There were candles and champagne ready—and Rita in a marvelous negligee. And the door closed and 'Here I am,' . . . she said. 'Marry me.'"[13] Leaming concluded that Welles, at that moment, was still in love with the tender and fragile Rita but could not bear to make her unhappy again. It was their last evening alone together.

Rita left for Madrid with Aly Khan and the two were treated like royalty. Welles went gambling in Cannes, where he gave five hundred thousand francs to one Monique Baucard, a beautiful blonde who had wheedled her way into high society by pretending to be a Bourbon princess from Parma.

The omens were bad. Welles had been suckered in Cannes, and Rita was heading for another, even more disastrous marriage. As he did with his first wife, Virginia Nicolson, Welles kept in touch with Rita and even claimed to be on good terms with Aly; Rita continued to talk to friends and colleagues about Welles, often surprising them with the intensity of her memories. "He was tormented, possessive, insecure," she said many years later. "A genius, crazy like a horse, and a marvelous man, completely unaware of reality." And Welles, who spoke rarely (and usually badly) about his women, remembered her with affection and tenderness. In the last interview he ever gave, he said, "That's one of the dearest, sweetest women that ever lived. . . . I think I was lucky enough to be with her longer than any of the other men in her life."

After Cannes, Welles headed back to Rome and the arms of Lea Padovani, whose passion seems to have been awakened by the rivalry with Hayworth. The Rome magazine *Fotogrammi* noted, "Orson Welles has returned to Rome amid general indifference. A few nights ago we spotted him in the gardens of the Hotel Quirinale, knocking back numerous cocktails and whiskies and sweating out the toxins in sambas and slow dances with Lea Padovani. This puts an end to rumors of reconciliation between the hoaxer of the Martian invasion and Rita Hayworth. Orson and Lea are in Montecatini for a few days' peace and quiet, taking the spa waters. The wedding date has already been set. Not surprising. Life goes on after Rita."[14]

From Hollywood, Louella Parsons, one of Hearst's hired hacks, played down the fuss on the French Riviera and put a few more nails in Welles's coffin. "I can assure you," she was quoted in the Italian press as saying, "that none of the stories about Orson Welles flying to Cap d'Antibes to make up with Rita Hayworth are true. Formidable Welles, friend of the Italian Communist Party leader Togliatti, is head over heels in love with Lea Padovani. He is also insanely jealous, which is somewhat surprising given that—from what I have fleetingly seen of her—she is neither beautiful nor charming. Rita admits she is still fascinated by Welles but I don't believe she wants to try again with him."[15]

At the end of August, Welles and Padovani made an important decision. He would give up his bohemian ways and move out of the Excelsior Hotel (and the homes of various generous friends) and Lea would come to live with him. He chose to set up home in Casal Pilozzo, a strong-looking seventeenth-century building on the road to Monteporzio Catone. Not so much a villa as a farmhouse with decorated ceilings and terra-cotta paving, it was located on a hillside in Frascati, surrounded by vineyards and fruit trees, overlooking the valley. The house was owned by the family of Giuseppe Bottai, the former Fascist minister pardoned for his crimes the year before. Welles negotiated the deal with Bottai's son and probably had no difficulty since the house had previously been taken over by the homeless. "The Communists will requisition it," Welles told him and got the property for a rent of a hundred thousand lire a month.[16] Welles and Lea moved in immediately with a butler and cook.

They became society people, as if they were actually on the point of marrying. It was about this time that Irving Penn took the famous photo at the Antico Caffè Greco in Via Condotti, which shows a rather provocatively posed Padovani, the only woman in a group of Italian artists, writers, and musicians that included Aldo Palazzeschi, Goffredo Petrassi, Mirko, Carlo Levi, Pericle Fazzini, Afro, Renzo Vespignani, Sandro Penna, Libero De Libero, Mario Mafai, Ennio Flaiano, Vitaliano Brancati, and Orfeo Tamburi. Apparently, Lea had been added by Penn at the last moment to lend some feminine grace to the photo, hence the showiness.[17] What's surprising about the photo, however, is the shy demeanor of Orson Welles, uncharacteristically abashed in the extraordinary company of Italy's artistic intelligentsia.

The photo is the visual record of Welles's supposed integration into Rome society and intellectual circles, although this integration never actually took place. Welles had wanted an Italian love, had looked for friends in the fertile artistic milieu of the capital, and aimed to make pictures in the city of Rossellini and De Sica. But what he had found was a woman who would leave him, intellectuals who were indifferent, if not hostile, to his reputation, and producers with whom he had at best ambiguous relations and with whom he was to argue, as usual. Penn's photo provides the curious illusion of a European, Italian Welles, at home in the kind of society he had sought outside the United States. It is the photo of what might have been.

The same newspaper that gossiped about Welles and Lea in Montecatini also reported on Welles's current projects, informing its readers for the last time about *Cyrano* and for the first about *Othello*. One project had taken the place of the other: after Korda's withdrawal from *Cyrano* (and the idea of adapting Pirandello's *Enrico IV*), Welles turned his attention to another Shakespeare venture. He wanted to get things moving quickly, he told Gian Gaspare Napolitano years later, because he had heard rumors of a similar project in England, so he thought it wise to shoot a few scenes and finalize the financial details with Scalera later. Lea, of course, would be his Desdemona; she was perfect and needed only to dye her hair blonde. He was due in Venice for the world premiere of *Macbeth*, so he could perhaps study some scenes while he was there. The crew would be largely the one he had worked with on *Black Magic*. He wrote to Roger Hill, his mentor at the Todd School, for a few reels of film from America.

No one in Hollywood would have thought of making a film without a script, actors, set, or costumes, but Welles had left Hollywood to seek his artistic freedom—and what could that be if not this type of improvisation? Hadn't Italian directors had to do the same, at the worst moment of their country's history, when Cinecittà was turned over to the homeless? So it was that in summer 1948 a new Welles prepared to make a new film. Without the safety of a studio set, he would film outdoors, produce his own work, and finally have complete control over the costs, the cast, the crew, and the final editing.

This is perhaps the closest Welles got to becoming part of Italian life, by accepting his new circumstances and adopting Italy's famed art of making do. He would put everything he had done behind him and fly by the seat of his pants, use the Mediterranean as a stage, and take advantage of the creative stimuli offered to him in Italy to make a film in Italian style that he could truly call his own.

7

The Fall of Macbeth

Life's but a walking shadow, a poor player
that struts and frets his hour upon the stage
and then is heard no more. It is a tale
told by an idiot, full of sound and fury,
signifying nothing.

—Macbeth (Orson Welles), *Macbeth*

The ninth Venice Film Festival opened on August 19, 1948. *Macbeth* was scheduled for screening on the second-last day. Welles came early, smiling at the photographers from behind dark glasses and a cigar, and—to the surprise and shock of some—strolled about in front of the festival theater dressed only in swimming trunks.

For the inaugural event, he wisely stuck to etiquette and a suit. Lea Padovani, by his side dressed in George Sand trousers, knew perfectly well that Welles preferred women in skirts or dresses. Immaculately turned out, Welles was apparently less than perfectly behaved. According to *Oggi*, he began the evening "snorting out a complaint about the lack of cigarettes and kept on bursting into laughter" and ended up "manifesting his disapproval" of the inaugural film, Powell and Pressburger's *The Red Shoes*, which he couldn't bring himself to sit through until the end. Alfredo Todisco, writing for Trieste's *Ultimissime*, responded by denying all these accusations, adding, "No American filmmaker has such bad press in Italy as Orson Welles."[1]

In the days that followed, the photographers got their shots of Welles and Padovani, she rather diminutive and with lightly shaded lenses, he increasingly gigantic in a white suit with an unnecessarily large double-breasted jacket. A photo in *Fotogrammi* showed them seated somewhere outdoors, Lea shouting into the wind while he looked at her tenderly, his brow furrowed, his baby face enraptured. He had a look of love in his eyes but the journalists preferred to crack jokes about Lea's poor English and her air, nevertheless, of "conducting a serious, intellectual debate."

Welles and Lea attracted a heterogeneous group of admirers, which immediately included Jean Cocteau, an acquaintance from a decade earlier, when they had met during *Voodoo Macbeth* as it was playing in Harlem. They enjoyed each other's company and didn't hide the fact, forming a small Anglo-French coterie. *Combat* even suggested their reunion was *the* event of the festival.[2] They saw each other's films (Cocteau had two: *L'aigle à deux têtes* [*The Eagle with Two Heads*] and *Les parents terribles*), drank cocktails together at the Excelsior, and tried to outdo each other in hugging Anna Magnani, who was presenting Rossellini's *L'amore,* of which part 1, "Una voce umana" (A human voice), was an adaptation of a one-act play by Cocteau.

The Welles clan comprised Lea, Cocteau, Magnani, his long-serving secretary and interpreter, Barzini; Alberto Mondadori, by now an admirer and passionate defender of his films; Alfredo Todisco, a young Triestine journalist (one of the few who spoke English); and renowned columnist Elsa Maxwell, revered by Welles—and his chosen antidote to Louella Parsons and Hedda Hopper.

As always at such gatherings, rivalries and envies abounded. Welles gave the impression of picking and choosing his friends, letting some approach him and keeping others at a frosty distance. As Cocteau remembered it, "In fact neither Welles nor I enjoy speaking about our work. The spectacle of life itself prevents us. We might remain a long time without moving and watch the hotel stir around us. Our immobility would bother busy businessmen and frantic experts of cinematography.... Very soon we were receiving menacing looks. Our stillness had us taken for spies. Our silence caused fright and was charged with explosives. If we happened to laugh, it was frightful. I would see solemn gentlemen pass at top speed in front of us for fear of being tripped up. We were accused of *lèse-festival,* of keeping to ourselves."[3]

The group did not hide its views, which were invariably in direct opposition to the majority opinion; this brought accusations of elitism. Both Welles and Cocteau, experimentalists inclined to bring together cinema, theater, and painting, found themselves in constant disagreement with the professional opinion leaders, who considered it their round-the-clock duty to decree what should or should not be considered cinema—the "good," the "bad," and the "cinematic." As Cocteau put it, "In Venice, again and again, we heard the absurd leitmotif: 'It's cinematic' or 'It isn't cinematic.' . . . You can imagine how amusing we found this, and when interviewed together on the radio, Welles and I replied that we should love to know what a *cinematic film* was and that we asked only to be taught the recipe in order to put it into practice."[4]

On the Lido the hostility that seemed to accompany Welles everywhere became tangible. He shrugged it off, putting it down to his exuberance and complicity with Cocteau, but that was not all it was. A few months earlier, the Christian Democrats and Communists had fought a bitter election campaign, won by the former, and the struggle was continuing in everyday life, including the film industry. The right wing tried to get its hands on the industry Mussolini had called "the most powerful weapon in the world," while the left sought to win over its soul: the right imposed increasingly suffocating censorship, the left responded with films enshrining its own social values; one side made deals with American film studios, the other turned to the shoestring cinema of neorealism. At a time when the market was flooded with American imports, Italian film crews began to feel they were being treated unfairly. With Cinecittà still given over to the postwar homeless, the unrest in the industry came to a head six months after the Venice Film Festival; in Piazza del Popolo in Rome, De Sica, Visconti and Anna Magnani addressed a crowd of 20,000 film workers.

At the election-year Venice Film Festival a certain anti-American feeling was in the air. And Welles—extravagant, ebullient, a protagonist in what many saw as the American attempt to colonize the Italian film industry (*Black Magic* being the perfect example)—became the ideal scapegoat. *Europeo* summed it up pithily: "In the battle between Rome and Hollywood, Welles has had Hollywood, and precisely the sort of

American cinema he himself has always fought so hard against, foisted onto him."[5]

This opposition between European and American cultures was radicalized in the two Shakespeare offerings at the festival, Welles's dark, prickly, American *Macbeth* and Olivier's more conventional, enjoyable, European *Hamlet.* Judgment seemed already to have been passed: no American could hope to understand Shakespeare or rival a countryman of the Bard. Dutifully, the festival upheld Olivier's predictable, elegant film as the ideal all directors should aspire to and no upstart American could achieve.

Compounding the issue were Welles's theatrical origins and work in radio, in which he both acted and directed, a habit he had maintained in films, with the sole exception of *The Magnificent Ambersons.* Mindful of the vainglorious era of Fascism and its inconsequential stagy films, and galvanized by the international success of neorealism, Italian filmgoers and critics frowned on actors who wanted to direct (in Welles's case if not in Olivier's), and on directors who wanted to act. Neorealism, with its sense of authenticity and immediacy, its use of amateur actors, and the discreet presence of the director, was at the opposite aesthetic and ideological extreme from Welles's baroque manner and his insistence on artifice, studio sets, and professional actors.

In fact, the real comparisons made during the festival were not between *Macbeth* and *Hamlet,* but between *Macbeth* and neorealism, the latter in the now-familiar form of Visconti's *La terra trema* (The Earth shakes), Lattuada's *Senza pietà* (Merciless), and Rossellini's *L'amore.* Welles saw the neorealist offerings and just couldn't keep quiet. His criticisms contributed not a little to the hostility he began to feel around him.

Unthinkingly, or uncaringly, he walked out of Visconti's film halfway through, with a bored look on his face.[6] He told Bazin and Tacchella of *L'Écran français* that the film was tedious and badly put together. "The first rule of cinema," he opined, "is to put and keep butts in seats. . . . The camera doesn't have to see everything, but to seek and construct before it attempts to explain."[7] He spoke about a preconstituted aesthetic and openly criticized the choice of nonprofessional actors, provocatively

comparing the Sicilian grandfather in Visconti's film with the extraordinary Raimu in Pagnol's film *La femme du boulanger* (1938). The interview
caused at least one film critic, Renzo Renzi, to fly into patriotic rage: "His
comments were just ridiculous," he wrote in February 1949. "The use of
nonprofessional actors is one of the great strengths of modern Italian
filmmaking."[8]

Welles was equally critical of Rossellini's film. He said nothing
about the second half of the film, *Il miracolo*, on which he had personally complimented Rossellini in April, confining his vehemence to the
adaptation of Cocteau. "What's the point in making a film of closeups
of the human face? Since the shots change with no reason, the film is
already dead after the first minute."[9]

Criticizing Rossellini and Visconti was unlikely to win him any
friends or endear him to the festival, particularly when he still needed
to beg the indulgence of the audience for his own film. Fearing the anticipated reception to *Macbeth*—or out of an uncontrollable provocative
streak, honest or blunt, impulsive or self-destructive—Welles told Jean
Desternes of *Revue du cinéma* that neorealism was like shooting news-
reels, "the true enemy of art in the cinema. This kind of cinema holds
no interest whatsoever. Nothing is easier than getting a passerby to appear in a film. What's hard is to pluck him out of anonymity. Actors are
needed to make art.... Rossellini and Lattuada are talented filmmakers,
but today's cinema has reached an impasse. The last ten years has produced nothing new except *Sciuscià*.... there, and only there, reality was
used as a basis for art. The other films are as old as the world itself. Superseded Italian postwar films had a rationale, that of filmed journalism, but
that moment is past and gone.... Realism in film is either moralistic or
political. Any talk of neorealism in relation to my films is idle chat. I'm
closer to Carné than to Rossellini."[10]

Welles criticized neorealism for aesthetic, stylistic, and—worse
still—moral reasons. Alfredo Todisco, who knew English well, articu-
lated Welles's point of view: "What's the point of showing how ugly the
world is if you aren't also suggesting that such things need to be opposed,
if you don't put forward a solution? The criticism of some neorealist films
in Italy is due to the lack of a clear statement about the horrors being

filmed, and the suspicion that the scenes are meant principally to tug at the heartstrings."[11]

Welles was more interested in Italy's theater than its cinema, and the performer and playwright he admired most was Eduardo De Filippo. In a recently rediscovered article, Giulio Cesare Castello wrote, "He says that Eduardo is the most important European artist working today—not only as an actor. Welles loved *Napoli milionaria* and considers Eduardo's acting the result not only of instinct and tradition but of research and application."[12]

As for his criticism of neorealism, although the Italian reviewers were divided in their appraisal of both *L'amore* and *La terra trema,* they were not about to take lessons from an American. Welles's imprudent attack on the two films had turned the situation into a powder keg; all that was needed now to light the fuse was *Macbeth.*

Shot entirely in the studio, with lingering camerawork and dripping with atmosphere, *Macbeth* differs from Shakespeare in a few essential places: the initial voodoo ritual reprised from the 1936 stage production; a Holy Father who senses the evil in Macbeth and dies at his hand, and—after the battle between Good and Evil (the torches of the besieging army with their Celtic crosses opposed to the darkness of the castle and the forked sticks of the three hags)—the triumphant return of the shrews, representing the very pagan forces supposedly defeated by Christianity.

The film has often been accused of being altogether too noir and unpalatable. To some extent it suffers the inevitable fate of Shakespeare adaptations that wish to maintain the force of Shakespeare's verse (and, as far as possible, the structure of the play): it focuses on visual and sound effects, without concerning itself much with moving the story forward, since the filmgoer would know the fabula of *Macbeth* or *Hamlet,* well enough. As a transposition of Shakespeare onto film, it is the filmic part that interests Welles, who focuses his attention on the evocative and symbolic force of the images and the sound.

The scenery is one of unrelieved bleakness and hostility: cliffs, skeletal trees, crags, smoke, bogs, and torches. The costumes Welles designed are of the same tone: the Scots are a mixture of cavemen, Vikings, and pirates—entirely untamed. Most of the dialogue was recorded before the shooting and overdubbed actors miming with thick Scottish accents—guttural, consonantal sounds almost spat out. But the images and sound serve Welles's purpose, representing and objectifying Macbeth's distorted perception of the world, his drunken, power-besotted, sleep-deprived, haunted consciousness as visions rather than scenes.

James Naremore has said that Macbeth is "arguably the purest example of expressionism in the American cinema."[13] Lang's dark Teutonic influence is obvious. But the editing of Eisenstein is also clearly mimicked with anti-naturalist intercutting and symbolism, indicating how Macbeth lives, according to Rudolf Kurtz's definition of expressionism: "by identification with the fluctuations of nature and hence [he] feels merely emotionally this intensity that is not manifest in the outside world."[14] The crags, clouds, and withered trees are there because they are both inside Macbeth's anguished mind and in the world—and in the world because they are inside him.

Welles was also interested in a contemporary reading of Shakespeare and intended Macbeth to be a condemnation of Fascism and totalitarianism. He told a French weekly in 1950 that "the most interesting part of Macbeth, I believe, is the description of the fall of the criminal king or, to be more precise, his collapse. The public may want to see this in contemporary terms, and thereby they will solve all the film's enigmas and obscurities."[15]

The film was shown privately to a select audience halfway through the festival. Alfredo Todisco, one of the lucky viewers, describes Lea Padovani smoking nervously while Welles attempted self-control as the projectionist made one mistake after another, forcing the filmmaker to explain numerous scenes. Despite these hiccups, the audience— many in Welles's entourage, or coterie, depending on your point of view—liked the film and praised it lavishly. "I've never felt tragedy so violently," said former actress Diana Manners, wife of the American ambassador Duff Cooper. Cocteau, who had been fidgeting in his seat throughout, ran up to Welles, hugged him and whispered in his ear, "Dear fellow, after this, I've decided not to make any more films myself."[16] To this, Welles is (malignantly) supposed—by one of the journalists present—to have jokingly replied, "Pity. If I'd known I would have shown it to you earlier and it would have spared you *The Eagle with Two Heads.*"

Welles undoubtedly wanted to win an important prize in Venice, Italy's leading event. It would have meant a great deal to his post-Hollywood career and his hopes of making films in Europe. The private showing dispelled his fears and he relaxed. Alberto Mondadori remembers having lunch with him and Lea the following day. He was chipper, confident that *Macbeth* would be given a proper reception and looking forward to making *Othello*. He even treated his fellow lunch guests to some playacting.

Mondadori's article begins with a quotation from *Othello,* presumably one of the speeches Welles recited for them: "She loved me for the dangers I had pass'd / And I loved her that she did pity them." In high-flown language, Mondadori described the wind blowing in gusts, hard and hot, from the south, as if a tireless Welles had summoned it from the wide sweeps of the Scottish countryside, which the evening before he had rendered in film, along with the figure of the witch-haunted voodoo-doll fashioned tyrant, as if cast in marble by Bernini. Welles improvised performances over the risotto with scampi as the hot, pungent wind kicked up sand and buffeted the table, causing the tablecloth and napkins to flap; Welles's hands moved from his own face to that of Lea. "O my soul's joy, if after every tempest come such calms," he said as he laughed his childish laugh, his eyes bulging, irrepressibly happy— Mondadori says—in that company of faces masked with handkerchiefs against the wind, like the Tuareg in Pabst's *Mistress of Atlantis:* "May the winds blow till they have waken'd death! / And let the labouring bark climb hills of seas / Olympus-high and duck again as low / As hell's from heaven!"[17]

If Welles had cared to look at the list of festival jurors, he would not have been so confident. The president was Luigi Chiarini. The jury was packed with Italian critics who had already negatively reviewed Welles's work, including Mario Gromo from *la Stampa,* Arturo Lanocita from *Corriere della Sera,* Welles's bête noire Guido Aristarco (whom he had sued only a few months earlier) and Felix A. Morlion, a powerful Dominican friend of Rossellini's, in the pay of the American Secret Services.[18]

The news of the excellent reception given to the film at the private screening actually made things worse. Negative opinions were now whispered, louder and louder, by people who had not even seen the film; invitations went astray, and some publicly snubbed Welles when he greeted them. He began to feel uneasy and decided to take action, calling a press conference at the Excelsior to illustrate the film that would be shown. Unimpressed, the press reported the event with undisguised hostility.

Casiraghi wrote, "Welles was counting on *Macbeth*. His presence at the festival, in the theater, at the gala events, his press conferences—everything was designed to prepare us for the film. He warned us . . . that he would be disappointed if we gave him negative reviews . . . because it would mean we were implicitly siding with the kind of commercial, conformist American cinema he was determined to oppose."[19]

"I don't know if this is the best or worst of my films," Welles declared, "but I think *Macbeth* addresses the most serious problems I have ever dealt with in film. I admit I'm a formalist, but my technique is not a straitjacket. I'm only interested in expressing ideas: formalism is a sign of decadence."[20]

Castello reported, "Welles considers *Macbeth* his most important work. He is convinced he has been totally original and that his version of Shakespeare is unlike Olivier's. However, he also calls *Macbeth* 'a little film' because he made it in twenty days."[21] Only Panicucci voiced a different opinion, criticizing his colleagues: "The most interesting thing that came to light was that *Macbeth* was made. . . . entirely on set, after six months of preparation, studying every camera movement, at a cost of half the going rate in America. The other questions were banal or were asked to show off the ingenuity of the questioner rather than to seek the opinion of the person questioned."[22]

During the press conference, critics and journalists took the opportunity to maneuver Welles away from Shakespeare, teasing and probing. Welles fell for it and the atmosphere became tense. Castello wrote, "His opinions are so resolute, so trenchant. . . . [S]ome of his controversial ideas do not countenance demurral. He rattles them off accompanying them with a gesture of the hand, or with a chuckle, as if to add emphasis. For example, for Welles, the plays produced at the Piccolo Theater in Milan are pretentious and snobbish—if something isn't liked it's because it's ugly, he says. About American realism he has similarly idiosyncratic opinions. Elia Kazan is the most important director in Hollywood, Dmytryk is less interesting, although he admits that *Crossfire* has some merits, but he grows bilious if you ask him about *Till the End of Time.*"[23]

Todisco noted the malevolence in the questions and the fact that many journalists were more interested in the buffet than in Welles's answers. "He's a charmer," he wrote, "but no one was under the illusion that a press conference could restore his popularity; that depends on the so far unproven quality of his film."[24]

On the morning of September 3, in a small underground room beneath the theater, the jury and press sat down to view *Macbeth*. Things went badly right from the start: because of the timetabling of the other films the room was almost empty, and began to fill up only toward the end of the showing. Constant chatter, often of derision, muffled much of the dialogue.

Toward the end of the festival, word was out that Olivier had won and that the jury wanted to humiliate Welles by giving his film a prize for the score—about the only thing Welles had not done himself. After the viewing, Todisco ran into a "bitter, disappointed Welles, who confessed feelingly that he didn't understand the reason for the rift between himself and Italian society."[25]

Hoping to cut through the hypocrisy and prejudice he had encountered in Venice, Welles now made another mistake, convening a second press conference. Gabbling uncontrollably, interpreted by an embarrassed Barzini, he denied his attachment to formalism and the film's debt to Lang and Eisenstein; he claimed importance for an American film made in open conflict with the Hollywood system, and said he had nothing against an important film such as Olivier's *Hamlet*. The desperate attempt to defend a film he said he was proud of riled the journalists still further, and the conference degenerated into an acrimonious farce. *Europeo* described the scene: "Sweating, incredulous, he tried to explain that the film had been made at half the usual cost of an American production, and had been rehearsed for six months before shooting began. He also said no comparison could be made with *Hamlet*, a film of national prestige, costing $4 million."[26]

Welles's words were taken as an involuntary form of self-defense. "All my films have been experimental, including *Macbeth,* although it is not only that. I knew what I wanted to do and tried to do it."[27] Comini, in *Giornale di Trieste,* remarked, "he explained that the scenery was deliberately abstract in order not to distract the spectator, who could concentrate on the acting."[28] "I wanted to use a new method," Welles said, "entrust the storytelling to the characters and make the rest symbolically abstract."[29] To Panicucci, this meant that "Welles has produced scenery that is strongly reminiscent of Lang's *Die Nibelungen* and Eisenstein's *Nevsky*—coincidentally, it would appear, since the director confessed he did not know either of these films."[30]

In typical style, Welles explained, "Leaving aside politics, I think that German art has always been decadent, and cannot be anything else. I'll never appreciate Goethe. It's impossible. . . . and if someone sees Fritz Lang in my film, all the worse for me. I've only seen two of his films, *M* and *Fury.*"[31] "Eisenstein and I are both the sons of D. W. Griffith, but we have gone our separate ways and are no longer brothers—not even relatives—except that neither of us is a realist."[32]

The hostility was evident. "In rough and ready English," Cavallaro wrote in *L'Avvenire d'Italia,* "softened by Barzini, Welles told us that if the film—produced by a small, independent outfit—failed, that would be the end of the 'People's Theater.' Far be it from us to wish to bring about such a sorry event, but in our opinion the people's cause is best served by those who wish to establish the truth without exhibitionism and platitudes."[33]

Alberto Mondadori looked on and drew his own conclusions: "The critics and jury have already made up their minds about Welles. Proof was provided at the two press conferences he convened and, above all, by the condescending questions of Luigi Chiarini. . . . So it would appear that this unbelievable country can do without the genius of a unique filmmaker like Orson Welles, the man who made *Citizen Kane,* the man who has such respect for the Venice Film Festival that he chose it as the occasion to premiere *Macbeth.* He is the most intelligent, original, and extraordinary filmmaker of recent years."[34]

Embittered and irritated, Welles meditated a grandiose gesture. Elsa Maxwell and the U.S. ambassador quietly advised him to withdraw the film before it was shown to the public and the majority of the press. In the end, Welles withdrew it from the competition alone, allowing the public screening. "Why risk it?" he told *Daily Variety*. "It'll never be shown in Italy. Shakespeare can't be dubbed. Better keep it for an audience that understands it. Besides, they don't like me in Italy: my love for the country is unrequited. I know what they'll say, that I didn't have the guts to go up against Rank's *Hamlet*."[35]

That evening the film was given its public screening. The two press conferences had magnified the polemics and poisoned the atmosphere, the audience waited noisily in expectation of a film that had already been tried and condemned. Welles was furious at the decision to show the film immediately after Soldati's *Fuga in Francia,* which he considered a commercial film. Doubtless a well-paced, compelling, Italian film was not the best way to introduce an experimental, *engagé,* transposition of Shakespeare.

Before the screening, the audience was informed by the producer's representative that Mr. Orson Welles had decided to withdraw the film from the competition. There was no "perfect storm of hisses and boos" as Welles later claimed, but the announcement was certainly embarrassed and embarrassing. However, when the film was finally onscreen it immediately appeared to be going well. Alberto Mondadori reported the scene in *Tempo:* "The film began in an atmosphere of hostility, after some whistling, loud coughing, and other forms of disapproval. Unluckily for those who were already rubbing their hands with glee over the fiasco, *Macbeth* is such a powerful work that, after a few minutes, there was absolute silence, it had the audience by the throat, the sequences and shots made the drama of the character the only thing the spectators had on their minds; and this continued, the audience in the grip of the film until the end, having already broken out into spontaneous and loud applause four times during the screening."[36]

Borselli in *Oggi* confirms this: "The audience applauded four times during the film and gave it a long final ovation. Mario Soldati shook Welles's hand and said, 'Very well!' Alberto Lattuada slapped him on the back and told him it was the second time he had seen him onscreen and had enjoyed his performance once again." The jury left the theater in revulsion at the acclaim. "A film suitable for the caves of Postumia, a

Nativity Scene, or the underground baths of Caracalla," they mumbled, remarking on the primitive and artificial semblance of the film.[37]

The next day, almost to a man, the critics savaged the film. The young reviewer Gian Luigi Rondi, who had admired Welles during his first press conference in Rome, wrote, "Everyone knows the heights and terrible depths of the tragedy of Macbeth, the Christian drama of temptation, guilt, remorse and punishment . . . yet Welles sees nothing in it but the drama of the witches, which he throws himself into head first, giving his character just one psychological moment, a sort of negro terror . . . surrounded by cavemen . . . inspired it would seem by the caves of Postumia. . . . Gestures, action, choral composition—everything is theatrical but of the most macabre, the worst kind of theater. . . . [a]n overblown attempt to astound and confound, with editing involving one closeup after another, removing all solemnity and even the semblance of a tragic atmosphere. . . . [I]n Westminster Abbey Shakespeare's bones are turning in their grave [sic]."[38]

Leonardo Mitri of Espresso wrote, with typical vehemence and lack of analysis, "We've had about all we can take of the 'wunderkind.' In his hands the tragedy of remorse—one of Shakespeare's greatest accomplishments—becomes a comedy of the haunted terror of Bozambo or Bouboule I, the Negro King. Whatever has Welles done in this Macbeth to warrant the recommendations of the foreign press, who tried to bamboozle us into supposing this was the best, the greatest, the superlative work of the festival? Instead, it is the most mistaken film ever shown in Venice. It is Welles, the presumptuous director, showing off the histrionics of Welles, the actor."[39]

In Corriere della Sera, one of the jurors, Lanocita, praised the score and cinematography, "often beautifully and plastically imposing," but came to the same conclusion about Welles's undisguised egocentricity: "Here, too, it is clear that Welles has an idea of cinema that depends on its dazzling and shocking effects. . . . The acting is only Orson Welles . . . and this flaunting of a smug self-satisfaction is the worst aspect of what is otherwise a truly original film."[40]

Superficially, Panicucci, in Avanti! also accused Welles of narcissism: "Welles pays continuous homage to himself throughout the film

... photographing himself in endless closeups and relegating the other characters to the background. . . . A mediocre, ambitious, well-intentioned film."[41]

Another juror, Guido Aristarco, attempted a more detailed analysis in *Sipario* but accused the film of excessive formalism and its heavy debt to other film directors, repeating the familiar criticism of Welles that he sought "to dazzle at all costs," adding, "Welles reveals himself to be a trickster who, with sleight of hand, attempts to hide his derivate cinema, copied from Lang and Eisenstein (the atmosphere from *Die Nibelungen* and the final battle scene from *Alexander Nevsky*). So the intent to give a different interpretation to *Macbeth* never succeeds and the scenography takes refuge from the real in the abstract."[42]

One of the harshest reviews was by Ugo Casiraghi in *l'Unità*. He had previously dismissed *Citizen Kane* after its Milan screening in May, and now seemed to take pleasure in venting his anger: "So here, finally, is *Macbeth*, the film that murders sleep. Anyone, after two weeks of screenings at the festival, who might have been tempted to take advantage of the darkness in the theater for a quiet snooze was rudely awakened by the screeching of the hags and shouts of Orson Welles, frightening the audience into mindfulness, according to the tried and tested formula of *Citizen Kane*. This *Macbeth* has almost nothing to do with Shakespeare, and a great deal to do with Orson Welles—who listed its main defects, which he is therefore well aware of: its magniloquence, egocentricity, and bluff. . . . Welles was able to make *Macbeth* (and, hereafter, perchance, a 'domestic' *Othello*, as he calls his project) because it provides him with the opportunity to repeat himself over and over, he with his history as a maverick *enfant prodige*, who loses control of himself and, in the process, becomes a tyrant."[43]

What is interesting about the review in the Communist daily is the underlying ideology, which Welles, the friend of Togliatti, might even have embraced. Yet Casiraghi tries to outflank him on the left: "You can't fight Hollywood conventionalism with the conventionally baroque. You can't fight Hollywood with rhetoric, however daring or crazed." In Marxist style he made a neorealistic appeal to the "message:" "[Y]ou fight Hollywood with new content, new facts and new dramatic situations".

Casiraghi was not a brain-dead or superficial film critic, but his Communist principles, which induced him to admire Soviet cinema, did not allow him to embrace American antirealism, so that he failed to grasp the form and substance of Welles's cinema.

One of the most intelligent observers of the Italian cinema scene, Ennio Flaiano, misunderstood Welles, adopting a mocking tone. His review of *Black Magic* some months later was the epitome of Italy's reaction to Welles so far and an exhilarating caricature of the filmmaker:

> He has a predilection for big parts; his acting in *Macbeth* turns the play, quite accidentally, into a humorous masterpiece. Now that he has set his sights on Othello, it is to be presumed that he will finally work his way up to Henry VIII, to be followed by Quasimodo and Dr. Mabuse. His characters all eat chicken with their fingers—not out of bad manners but an excess of temperament, imagination, and willpower. Exactly the sort of characters that bore us to death and lead us to suppose that their intemperance is not so much due to an ongoing struggle with destiny as to a (treatable) thyroid imbalance. Dressed as Macbeth, Welles has no interest in what he says or in the drama of the situation he finds himself in; he wants the audience to marvel at his performance—like those musicians who think Mozart and Leoncavallo are pretty much the same, or actually prefer the latter because there is a good chance the high notes will bring the chandeliers crashing down.[44]

Few critics dared voice a different opinion, and those who did were amateurs or makeshift reviewers such as Todisco. As usual, the journalist who leaped to Welles's defense was Alberto Mondadori, who would become a close friend:

> *Hamlet* and *Macbeth* cannot be compared. The former is a noble effort at a Shakespeare transposition dominated by the strong stage personality of Laurence Olivier; the latter is a genial experiment, the application of pure cinema technique to Shakespeare and, as such, offers something new— abstract and miraculous—for Shakespeare lovers. It is coherent from the first to last shot. . . . *Macbeth* is Welles's best film after *Citizen Kane*. . . . I haven't read or heard any criticism of the film that substantiates the claim that his baroque style fails to deliver. . . . I haven't read anyone extol the expressive power of the Duncan murder scene (300 meters of film, without a single cut) or of the duel sequence which is edited as never before, or praise the soundtrack, which continuously counterpoints the images on screen, or the music score composed later by Ibert and Welles—frame by frame—in the cutting room.[45]

Mondadori was closer to an objective appraisal of the film than other critics. To be sure, nobody else bothered to mention the extraordinary technique, which included long takes—often entire reels of film—such as the scene before, during, and after Duncan's murder. This was something Welles had already tried out in *The Magnificent Ambersons* and Hitchcock, also in 1948, adopted to show *Rope* in real time, as one continuous take. Nor did anyone mention the distinct Scottish burr, highlighting the violence and drama of the scenes. No mention was made of the cutting and pasting of the soliloquies and rearrangement of certain key speeches, which American critics had considered liberties taken with Shakespeare's text.

Seemingly, in Casiraghi's brazen admission, the Italian critics had tried to sleep through the film. Republic was a small production company and probably hadn't been able to provide subtitles, which explains why the Italian critics, unfamiliar with the text and dumbfounded by the accents, found the film difficult to follow.

However, the criticism in Italy skipped over these minor worries and focused entirely on the formal visual elements of the film. Lang and Eisenstein were mentioned repeatedly—almost as if the critics had swapped notes at the end of the screening and wanted to dangle these illustrious filmmakers in front of Welles and have him deny their influence once more, if he dared. Few of the critics were willing to compare Welles's treatment with Olivier's more conventional approach to Shakespeare, and this was not to spare Welles embarrassment, but to avoid praising him; a comparison with *Hamlet* might have obliged them to point out some merits in the Welles production.

Welles also wanted to avoid direct comparison, stating that the different budgets involved made the films apples and oranges. Few of his listeners cared. *Macbeth* cost about $800,000, not a large sum but not pin money, either. To make a costume drama, shot entirely on set, in twenty-three days and with a low budget was a remarkable achievement, but Welles's insistence on the cost only compounded the confusion. The figure found its way into the press,[46] and critics (and later biographers) began to lower it still further—Bazin to $65,000, McBride to $200,000. The malevolent jumped on these figures as proof that the film was a botched and hurried experiment.

The critics appeared to engage less with *Macbeth* than with Welles's flamboyant personality. They disliked the former wunderkind wander-

ing around the Lido shirtless and smoking cigars, the millionaire returning from Cap d'Antibes and Rita Hayworth only to throw himself
into the arms of Lea Padovani, coming to his press conferences with
a personal bottle of whisky, and surrounding himself with a group of
sycophantic intellectuals. In their eyes he was an egocentric upstart
artist from a parvenu nation that was picking up bits and pieces of the
depressed Italian film industry for a song. They cared little for Welles's
struggle with Hollywood, less still for his aversion to neorealism, and
next to nothing for his fight for independence. The attack on *Macbeth*
became an attack on Welles and, above all, a stringent defense of neorealism, as a genre, as culture, and as an ideology—as opposed to barbarian
abstraction à la Welles.

The next day the Golden Lion was duly given to Olivier, with further recognition for Jean Simmons (Ophelia) and Desmond Dickinson
(cinematography).

Elsa Maxwell accused the jury of bias and ignorance and said that
Italians, only recently freed from the "mental prison" of Fascism, were
unable to appreciate international films made in a democracy. She went
on to complain that some American films had been held by customs for
months, and hinted that American interests in the festival covered 60
percent of its costs. She then invited American filmmakers to boycott
the festival and start one of their own in Europe. Translated and lengthily excerpted in the Italian newspapers, these words made the already
heated debate red hot. In the pages of *la Stampa*, juror Mario Gromo
hurled the accusations back in Maxwell's face: "Last August, Maxwell
called Orson Welles one of the greatest living film directors and *Macbeth*
a masterpiece. For us, Welles is a patchy, pretentious filmmaker of effects.
Macbeth is probably his poorest film, lacking in inspiration, imagination, and intelligence. Hopefully, free America will not begrudge us our
inclination to freely formulate, and give, our opinion. What fault is it of
ours if Olivier's Shakespeare, directing, and acting filled us more than
once with admiration, whereas Welles's *Macbeth* only brought a smile
to our lips?"[47]

Another juror, Giorgio Prosperi, responded in the pages of *Cinema*.
He described *Macbeth* as a "mediocre and pretentious" film that repeated

the "intellectual experimentation of thirty years ago," and, not very chivalrously, attacked Maxwell for her plain looks. Prosperi defended neorealism, which no one had attacked:

> Elsa Maxwell is a close friend of Orson Welles, she thinks of him as her protégé and heaps praises on him. Because of her poor notions of aesthetics, his illusionist's talents, his maverick ways, and hand-me-down intellectualism are the most refined qualities she is able to imagine for the cinema. . . . It is precisely as a reaction to this tired old intellectualism that Italian neorealism came to the fore and is appreciated the world over, especially in America, and is considered a revolution in art. . . . Is it any surprise that we can't work up any enthusiasm for beloved Welles's abstract scenography? Elsa Maxwell knows none of this, of course, but Orson Welles should know it and temper his declarations, which only bring a smile to our lips and even amuse the homegrown monkeys who, yesterday, were willing to sit at the feet of this poor man's Cagliostro of the cinema.[48]

That is what Welles had become after less than a year in Italy: a poor man's populist and mesmerizer. The 1948 Venice Film Festival marked the end of Italy's love affair with Orson Welles. Far from home, instead of finding refuge from Hollywood, Welles had found in Italy another country that didn't understand him.

Two months after the Venice Film Festival, Gian Francesco Luzi went back over Welles's career in Italy, remembering how well *The Magnificent Ambersons* had been received:

> Then the ragged and rugged Welles came to Italy and cinema lovers, critics, and journalists got the opportunity to look at him up close . . . and in less than a year the official and unofficial verdict changed. . . . What happened to Orson Welles in Italy can be explained rather well by the character of many, all too many, of us Italians: our habit of magnifying things at a distance, of fantasizing and making them beautiful and then, when they get closer, of diminishing them, of dismissing them as soon as they actually touch us.[49]

Luzi accuses the critics and the country as a whole of provincialism, of the habit of falling in love with bright, faraway stars, only to shut them out when they come close and their light begins to dazzle.

Unlike the extreme, almost hysterical Italian reviews of *Macbeth*, the rest of Europe was able to respond with a degree of balance. Cocteau recalls a screening of *Macbeth* at Maison de la Chimie, in 1949, that was not well received and Bazin says the critics were divided when the film was released in France the following year. Some critics praised the film, and most were able to see what Welles had been trying to do in his adaptation of Shakespeare. Three reviews, the first written in 1948 and the last in 1951, were remarkably similar in their appreciation of the film: just after the Venice Film Festival, Jacques Bourgeois wrote, "Orson Welles's *Macbeth,* outside the Shakespearean tradition, with evident changes in the ordering of the scenes, an innovative scenography and costumes invented ad hoc, is in fact closer to the spirit of Shakespeare than Olivier's *Hamlet. Macbeth* is a unique play in Shakespeare's canon; postromantic ante litteram, it is a symbolist work."[50]

Cocteau wrote what was to become a famous profile in the first edition of Bazin's extended essay on Welles: "His *Macbeth* leaves the spectator (feeling) deaf and blind, and I can well believe that the people who like it (of which, proudly, I am one) are few and far between. . . . Orson Welles's *Macbeth* has a kind of crude, irreverent power. Clad in animal skins like motorists at the turn of the century, horns and cardboard crowns on their heads, his actors haunt the corridors of some dreamlike subway, an abandoned coal mine, and cellars oozing with water. Not a single shot is left to chance. The camera is always placed just where destiny itself would observe its victims."[51]

In 1951, Claude Mauriac wrote in *Filmcritica,* "When Orson Welles adapts *Macbeth* for the screen, he follows Shakespeare's text and even, in a sense, his directions for mise-en-scène, scrupulously, only extending them in certain directions. . . . Shakespeare is one of the cards Welles plays, but Shakespeare's genius would not be visible if Welles didn't also have genius. Orson Welles doesn't need Shakespeare to make a great film; without Shakespeare, Laurence Olivier would perhaps not make any films at all."[52]

Italy remained substantially hostile to the film for many years, with some timid rethinking and lukewarm efforts at reappraisal. The fate of *Macbeth* was no better in America, which came up with its own brand of sarcasm and ridicule. Alarmed by the reaction in Italy and at home, Republic withdrew the film from US cinemas, and asked Welles to reloop the film (eliminating the Scottish burr) and make hefty cuts to the scenes thought to be tedious or ridiculous. Welles, perforce, agreed and set about the work in person. After it was relooped and cut, *Macbeth* was reduced from 107 minutes (after a lengthy musical introduction) to 86 minutes. It began with a voiceover, cut the now-famous single take of the Duncan murder scene into tiny pieces, and dropped the return of the witches. In the Italian version, the dialogues were translated by Gian Gaspare Napolitano and Welles was dubbed by Gino Cervi. It was 1951 and the polemics from Venice had died down. In its new version, and with Italian dubbing, enabling the viewer to understand Shakespeare's text, the film was given a moderately good reception.

Not that the damage had been repaired. Years would go by before critiques of Welles became more sympathetic to his aims. He wanted to make a film that was faithful to the spirit and letter of Shakespeare's tragedy. In his film, the barren countryside, bogs, and swirling clouds are part of the film's description of a primitive world of passions and violence, reflecting Macbeth's brutality and his hallucinatory, drunken thuggery. Ultimately, the world of *Macbeth* is governed by malevolent spirits, both external (the witches) and internal (his own megalomaniac impulses), and it accommodates those spirits without resistance or qualm. Neither individuals nor the masses that take part in revolutions are the result of free will but of a cruel, deceitful destiny. Like *Citizen Kane* and *The Stranger,* the portrait of Bannister in *The Lady from Shanghai* and Welles's portrayal of Josef Balsamo (aka Cagliostro), *Macbeth* is about the fascination and curse of power.

It was Welles's sixth *Macbeth,* after numerous theater and radio productions, and was built on discoveries made during those productions. It radicalized the relationship between cinematography and the set, before the open-air shooting of *Othello.* It sought to build up layer after layer of sense and symbol, blending text, camera movement, lighting, and scenography (anything but "photographed theater," as Alberto Moravia put it). The countryside, bogs, and clouds were neither the result of an excess of violence, nor derived from Lang or Eisenstein; *Macbeth* was the result of years of preparation and a burgeoning personal vision. If anything, the film owed a debt to Edward Gordon Craig, the English director and scenographer who, in the first half of the twentieth century, had imagined a theater of visions, significant lighting and heavy symbolism, all of which were embodied in *Macbeth*. This idea was put forward in 2001 by Gherardo Casale, whose work on Welles's relationship with Shakespeare is the most illuminating yet published in Italy and is a long overdue rectification by an Italian film critic of the summary lynching of *Macbeth* in Italy in September 1948.[53]

Alfredo Todisco
A Necktie with Dedication
MILAN, MARCH 8, 2004

Born in Melfi, Basilicata, but raised in Trieste, Alfredo Todisco (1920–2010) wrote for the magazines *il Mondo* and *Europeo* and the newspapers *la Stampa, Corriere della Sera,* and *il Resto del Carlino.* He also wrote novels and travel journals.

His career as a journalist began in 1948 as special correspondent at the Venice Film Festival for the Trieste-based daily newspaper *Ultimissime.* He spoke excellent English. On the Lido he mixed with actors and filmmakers, among them Orson Welles. "A big, sixteenth century face," he wrote of Welles in one of his articles. "Two warm, direct eyes, sometimes veiled with a hint of irony, other times boyishly fresh and enthusiastic. His very first words and actions immediately appeared to be those of a powerful yet simple man, dealing with the problems that presented themselves, a refined European intellectual combined with the virgin, concrete, practicality of an American."[1]

Todisco was one of the first to see *Macbeth,* a film he defended. "Rarely," he wrote, "has tragedy been so powerfully evoked on film in images forged from bronze by the force of thunderbolts."[2]

ALFREDO TODISCO: I was at the Venice Film Festival as a reporter for a Trieste daily. The chief editor rather liked me and sent me almost on a whim. I wasn't a journalist. I wrote a few things for the newspapers of Trieste as a freelancer. The festival screened *Macbeth,* which I reviewed positively. I said it was a great film, as it was and still is. I showed the article to Welles, who had it translated—he only knew a couple of words in Italian—and from that moment on he considered me the only Italian journalist who understood him.

What struck you most about Macbeth?

AT: Welles's extraordinary acting. He acted even when he took a gondola ride with us, great chunks of Shakespeare he knew by heart, such as the famous "Tomorrow and tomorrow and tomorrow" soliloquy, which he recited with feeling.

Did you know anything about Welles before you met him?

AT: I'd seen *The Lady from Shanghai,* with the famous scene in the aquarium with the two of them talking and, behind them, the shark: a beautiful scene.

Why did you think Macbeth *was given such a poor reception?*

AT: I couldn't understand it. In my (and his) opinion, it wasn't appreciated as it deserved to be. Let's say it was received with lukewarm appreciation, if not worse. Welles believed there was hostility in the reaction to the film.

The opinion of film critics certainly changed very quickly in relation to Welles. When he arrived in Italy, he was a genius. A year later he was a "bluff." Why did they change their minds?

AT: You'll certainly remember Flaiano's *Un marziano a Roma* [A Martian in Rome] . . . That's Italy for you. At that time, Welles felt a certain animosity towards Italian journalists, because they refused to recognize his artistic value. It was true, not just his impression.

What is your recollection of Welles today?

AT: I remember his state of virtual ecstasy in Venice and with Lea Padovani—he was head over heels. He took a number of gondola rides and looked at every building with rapture; he spoke of Venice as of a miracle . . . It was obvious he was very sensitive to beauty in all its forms. Venice impresses everyone, but it overwhelmed him. I recall that a few times we looked at St. Mark's Cathedral from the square. It isn't exactly the most beautiful building in Venice. He said, "It looks like a balloon about to rise into the air." Or we'd walk past the Salute Church which is another building I don't much like, but he loved the baroque, the great sweep of the architecture. Probably he was more right than I was. In Venice there are many things that are more beautiful than these churches, in my opinion, but he was totally won over by them . . . After I showed him my review, we became friends, and every evening he invited me to dinner with his entourage. We ate here and there in Venice or his friends came to the bar of the Excelsior.

Who did you meet?

AT: I suppose everyone who was with him, like Elsa Maxwell. He introduced me as someone of great intelligence . . . even Elsa Maxwell followed his lead and treated me with the greatest respect. She said, "I'll make you famous," and she was able to do so in her columns. One time I was with Welles in the Excelsior bar when in came Jean Cocteau and they embraced, as artists do . . . We had a drink together. As a boy I used to write down memorable sentences I read in books, so on that occasion I recited to Cocteau a few lines in French from his *Opium: "On ne pais pas fumè l'opium e partager aux avantages de ceux qui ne fume pas"*—You can't smoke opium and expect to share the advantages of those who don't smoke it. In other words, everything has a price. He had smoked opium in the past . . . Then he said that some people have the feeling of what they have and others the sense of what they lack. He was of the latter type; he didn't have money, or love . . . So I recited a few more lines and he looked at me as if I were speaking Urdu. Maybe my French pronunciation was not very good. So Welles stepped in and said I was quoting him, at which point he seemed to remember. I think he had forgotten the lines were his.

Any other memorable meetings?

AT: I remember Luigi Barzini, Jr., a friend of Welles's. They'd met in America and he spoke perfect English with an American accent. He'd studied there.

And Welles the man?

AT: A true gentleman. A Renaissance man. He said he liked Venice above all in winter, when the colors are more tenuous, and the streets are not full of heat or crowds. He had refined tastes. And acting in his bones, as all great actors have, a form of narcissism . . . everything had to revolve around him.

He was vain?

AT: No . . . He was a man who lived in part on this earth and in part in his imagination, his own mind. A purely aesthetic-cinematographic imagination. Seeing St. Mark's Cathedral as a giant balloon about to take off isn't a businessman's point of view. He had a fervid imagination and a keen poetic sensibility. We walked around Venice during and after the screening of *Macbeth*, when he had no appointments. Once in the lagoon in front of St. Mark's there was a Roman warship, a trireme—I don't know for what film—and behind it there was an American Cruiser. The two empires, we noted, of course. I was with him for about a week that time and for about ten days during the shooting of *Othello*, when he invited me to come over and see what he was doing.

Shooting in Venice began a year later.

AT: Maybe my memory fails me but I thought it was later in 1948, just a few weeks after the Venice Film Festival.

Do you remember any specific scene?

AT: I recall Roderigo, played by Carlini, who goes to see Brabantio. Under the Ca' d'Oro a young man is talking to Brabantio. They argue and Brabantio says to Roderigo, "Thou art a villain." To which he replies, "You are a senator!" I watched them shoot that scene.[3]

What was Welles's working method on set?

AT: Not someone who barked out orders, for sure. He used moral persuasion, as the expression is nowadays.

What do you remember about Lea Padovani?

AT: She was very lovely, not at all with the airs of a star. As Desdemona she could have been haughty and superior, but not a bit of it.

Did you ever speak to Welles about Rita Hayworth?

AT: Never, either to avoid displeasing him or upsetting Lea Padovani, I'm not sure which . . . He was in love with Lea but she wasn't with him. She had another man, Papi . . . with whom she had a secret agreement. She would make the film and Papi would be the production director, without Welles knowing anything about them. She pretended to be with Welles. And maybe she was with him, too, because when I went into their room—at the Gritti Hotel, I think—once I saw Welles had written on the mirror in lipstick, "Your eyes are too big." Too big in the sense of praise for her eyes, of course. I knew both Lea and Papi, a rather elusive man, handsome, Roman. I heard all about their affair from friends of Papi's. Lea admired Welles but she wasn't in love with him. "He's too big for me," she said, meaning his physical stature. She was in love with Papi, who cynically accepted the situation, partly—I suspect—because he wasn't in love with her. I love her and she loves him and he loves another and so on . . .

And Welles knew nothing about it?

AT: I don't think so. No one told him. I don't think he would have accepted it, although he was an artist used to strange ways . . . I think they stopped shooting not only because Welles ran out of money but also because he fought with Lea; she was distant and this upset Welles a great deal. It led to arguments . . .

They were fighting already in Venice?

AT: I don't know if it had come to that. I stayed only a short while before returning to Trieste, where I lived at the time.

For an artist like Welles, Venice must have been an inspiration. When did he get the idea of making Othello?

AT: Before he ever went to Venice, I think. But certainly during the film festival the idea became concrete, real. Besides, somewhere in his mind he was perhaps jealous of Papi, without knowing it, as it were . . . I'm not saying he made *Othello* because he was jealous of Lea, but the workings of the unconscious are such that maybe, yes, this was a reason for making the film.

Did you write about Othello?

AT: No, I went as a spectator and friend. I remember those days with great affection, even though they were just a few moments. I took some gondola rides with Welles and Lea Padovani; he would look up and comment on the beauty of the architecture. I went as a friend, not a journalist. No doubt he also wanted a journalist on his side; I don't deny it. It was a pleasure to think of him as a friend. He gave me a tie, which sadly I've lost, on the back of which he had written, "With much much affection from Orson W." So, I think we were genuine friends . . .

Did you see the finished film?

AT: Yes. I liked it. I think Welles had understood something about Shakespeare's play, something modern, let's say. At that time racism wasn't a question, but Shakesepare had understood the sense of inferiority of a black man in relation to a beautiful white woman. Othello kills her out of furious rage and inferiority. Othello, the winner, the commander of the fleet, who feels inadequate . . . this is how Welles understood and portrayed him.

Did you continue to write about films?

AT: No, I changed town at the beginning of the fifties and became a journalist, not a film critic. I'd met Barzini through Welles, and when I moved to Rome to try my luck as a journalist I went to see him. He told me a new weekly magazine, *il Mondo,* had just been set up under Mario Pannunzio. He took me to see him and told him he could use me; I was a good journalist. That was in 1951, I think. Pannunzio asked me to write something about Trieste and they put it on the front page. I was shocked and pleased, of course. The magazine was very authoritative; Croce and Einaudi were contributors.[4] I then went on to other magazines and newspapers and became the Moscow correspondent for *la Stampa.* I worked at *Corriere della Sera* for nearly twenty years.

Did you ever meet Welles again?

AT: No, never. Life is like that. Generally the people who stay are those you can't get rid of, but those you'd like to hang on to vanish into thin air.

8

Othello **Begins Shooting**

O, beware, my lord, of jealousy;
It is the green-ey'd monster, which doth mock
The meat it feeds on. That cuckold lives in bliss,
Who, certain of his fate, loves not his wronger:
But O, what damnèd minutes tells he o'er
Who dotes, yet doubts, suspects, yet strongly loves!
—Iago (Micheál Mac Liammóir), *Othello*

Shakespeare was the flavor of the month in September 1948. In addition to *Macbeth* and *Hamlet,* the Venice Film Festival presented George Cukor's now almost forgotten *A Double Life,* a meta-theatrical adaptation of *Othello.* Not one of Cukor's best, but not without interest, the film features an actor past his prime who is obsessed with the role of the Moor and his jealousy of Desdemona. One of Ronald Colman's lines was "To act jealousy you have to be jealous," and Welles was soon to discover that Lea Padovani could give him plenty of opportunity to act jealous. After the final breakup with Rita, Welles resumed his courtship of Lea, who—unknown to him—was doing some courting of her own.

Used to getting what he wanted, at least with women (including the Italian women he had met in the first months of his stay), Welles was bewildered by Lea's evasiveness. He grew insistent—and more insistent each time Lea failed to answer his marriage proposals. Lea hedged and fudged and denied him the pleasures that, so the rumors went, she granted another.

Welles's rival was Giorgio Papi, not an actor or director but a production manager who would later become a well-known producer of such films as *A Fistful of Dollars*. Welles knew him well; they'd met on the *Black Magic* set, where Papi was head of production. Welles asked him to do the same job on *Othello*. Micheál Mac Liammóir described him as a handsome man "who has the air of a rosy-cheeked and very startled *stag* and is friendly."[1] Lea Padovani had fallen hopelessly in love with him, a married man with children.

The situation was difficult. Welles's courtship was an excellent smokescreen for the clandestine couple, but Lea was forced to keep stringing Welles along with half-promises and Papi was obliged to read about Welles's public adoration of her in the newspapers. Everyone in the Rome film industry knew about the triangle—everyone except Welles, of course, who was blinded, as they say, by love. He chose Papi, of all people, to confide in.

Welles's intention to make *Othello* seems to have hardened during the Venice Film Festival. Romantic walks with Lea through the narrow alleyways of the city and gondola rides with her and Todisco also allowed him to reconnoiter locations for the film. Rather astonishingly, the reception of *Macbeth* in Venice had not put him off a new Shakespeare venture.

He was less familiar with *Othello*, never having produced it for the stage or radio, and he had no backer. The reels sent by Roger Hill would last for a few screen tests and maybe a couple of scenes, no more. Although they had not yet struck a deal, Welles hoped Michele Scalera would come up with the money. After all, had he not suggested the film in the first place? Scalera, however, wanted the film to be made in Italian with a cast of Italian actors, Welles playing the lead and directing the dialogue for the English-language version. The reason he wanted to limit Welles's involvement was not artistic but bureaucratic: the Italian government, through Direzione Generale per la Cinematografia, provided funding, refunds, and tax relief for "Italian films," which required a mostly Italian crew and cast. Scalera intended to update the Italo-American co-production of *Black Magic,* exploiting Welles's reputation and the Italian government's domestic assistance. Welles was never going to agree not to direct the film or to hire a cast of actors unable to speak the language of Shakespeare. The impasse was obvious even at the scripting stage. "The collaboration of Orson Welles on the script," noted an internal memo at Scalera, "soon made it clear that it was more than ever imperative to stick to the classical model of the English stage, at that moment so successfully represented by Olivier's *Hamlet* and *Henry V.* Faced with two English-language productions and the risk of a botched production and flawed interpretation of Shakespeare, Welles said it would be unwise to go ahead with *Othello* in Italy, in the absence of experienced Shakespearean actors. Scalera Film had committed to the project and could not, therefore, back down or refuse Welles's artistic requests, nor did it wish to forgo the opportunity to make a great film in Italy—albeit one that required a considerable financial outlay—or to put to use and promote our studios, guaranteeing work to an Italian crew."[2]

Despite its conciliatory tone, this memo points to an evident tug-of-war between producer and director, each of whom wanted to make the film to suit his own ends, and each convinced he could persuade the other to see reason. Scalera wanted to make an Italian film starring Welles; Welles wanted to make his own *Othello.* Neither budged and negotiations broke down. Scalera kept his purse closed and Welles pressed on regardless. Maybe an American producer could still be persuaded to advance him some money for a future acting role.

During the summer of 1948, Welles had bumped into Darryl Zanuck, head of Twentieth Century Fox, at Cap d'Antibes (this meeting was not so accidental); later in August at a cocktail party in Zanuck's honor at Casina Valadier in Rome;[3] and in Venice, where Welles and Lea met him and his daughter at the inauguration of the festival. Welles agreed to act in *Prince of Foxes* and intended to invest his $100,000 paycheck in *Othello.*

Directed by Henry King, *Prince of Foxes* was Twentieth Century Fox's first Italian production. The script was officially an adaptation of Samuel Shellabarger's novel, but Duilio Coletti claimed it was a remake of his 1941 *La maschera di Cesare Borgia:* "After the War, the Americans bought the film to do another version with Orson Welles."[4] *Prince of Foxes* told the story of the intrigues of Andrea Orsini (Tyrone Power), an unprincipaled agent of the Borgia family, who unscrupulously renounces his mother (Katina Paxinou) and the love of Angela Borgia (Marina Berti) in order to seduce Camilla (Wanda Hendrix) and kill her husband, the aging Duke of Città del Monte (Felix Aylmer), who stands in the way of Cesare Borgia's plans to annex the territory. But the beauty and dignity of Camilla inspire a change of heart; Orsini falls in love with her and extracts himself from the clutches of the Borgia family. He heads the resistance to Borgia rule (of the besieged town, Città del Monte) and is present as the heroic duke draws his last breath. Imprisoned and tortured, he is saved by Mario Belli (Everett Sloane), frees Camilla, and the siege of the tyrannical invader is repulsed by the town.

Welles was the last to join the cast and could have no other role than that of the villainous Borgia, an evildoer able to intimidate, if not terrorize, his opponents with his sheer physical presence. A "Renaissance man," as Welles believed himself to be, in bearing and exuberance, Borgia represented the dark side of his times. Welles intended to portray him with mischievous glee.

An almost forgotten film, *Prince of Foxes* was nonetheless a cut above other costume dramas of the era. In the interests of fidelity to the story's settings, the film was shot on location in San Marino, Florence, Venice, Siena, Ferrara, Viterbo, Ravenna, and Rome. King wanted to film the lavish interiors and exteriors in color, but Zanuck confined him to cheaper black and white. After filming *Black Magic* in the sumptuous locations of Villa d'Este and the Quirinale Palace, Welles would be traveling farther afield—first to San Marino at the end of August, as the Venice Film Festival was in progress. Filming locations were taped off and signs reading, "Los Angeles City Limits" were erected; this provoked some disquiet among San Marino locals, who believed the Americans were taking over their small republic. King began with the most spectacular part of the film, the siege of Città del Monte—complete with cannons, catapults, and a battle involving a thousand hired extras.[5]

Welles's attitude toward the film was very different from the one he had shown toward *Black Magic*. Some biographers claim that he helped in the direction, and he may well have made suggestions regarding the scenes in which he appeared, but by and large he left King to do his job. He appeared in only a few scenes, albeit long and complicated ones. The film was a vehicle for the virile, expressionless Tyrone Power (angry with Zanuck for not hiring his girlfriend Linda Christian), so Welles was able to study *Othello*, try out a few scenes, and attempt to solve the difficult problem of teaching Lea/Desdemona English.

Welles notified the press of his decision to cast Lea via *Fotogrammi*, which assigned Amy Ravagnan to write a piece about the famous couple. Ravagnan, reported, "There are a thousand things to do: direct, write, act in other films—four of which are to be made in Italy—attend conferences abroad, finish annotating the Bible, follow political developments, and write newspaper articles. A strange man, Welles, with his lively, changing expressions, ruffled black hair; he is moody, simple, and generous with his money, which comes and goes with surprising ease. Can beautiful Rita have understood his flamboyant character? Certainly Lea does. This fragile, sensitive woman, down-to-earth and intelligent, has changed Welles a great deal. No more idiosyncratic lifestyle. . . . As he gets ready to play Cesare Borgia in *Prince of Foxes*, Lea is studying Shakespeare's English and has dyed her hair blonde, tinged with gold."[6]

Welles wanted her as his Desdemona and Scalera wanted to cast his quota of Italians, so the decision to use her was a foregone conclusion. However, after six months with Welles, her English was still heavily accented. Why not dub her? As Welles explained later, "In Italy the audience is used to their favorite actors being dubbed, with very few exceptions. In the English-speaking market, it is unimaginable."[7] Lea needed to take lessons. Welles was not worried about grammar or her understanding of Shakespeare's lines so much as the cadence of her voice. He needed a teacher who was a native speaker and used to working with actors.

As chance would have it, on the set of *Prince of Foxes* Welles met Harriet White, an English actress who had appeared in one scene of Rossellini's neorealist masterpiece *Paisà*. She was working as a diction coach. Charlie Moses, a director of production who was also working for Welles, discreetly approached the actress and arranged a meeting in Casal Pilozzo. Harriet White went to the villa, surrounded by vineyards and with the ghostly presences of stiffly respectful household staff, where Welles appeared to her as a king. He explained that he wanted Desdemona to sound like her. She accepted thirty-five thousand lire a week to teach diction to Lea, to whom she immediately became a friend and confidante.

Astonishingly, by Welles's later admission, Lea had not yet slept with him. The more he laid siege the more she held out. As if that were not enough, Lea had moved her parents, sister, brother-in-law, and sundry others into the villa in Casal Pilozzo. Welles paid for everything and was barely bid good day. Out of love for Lea, he accepted her entourage. "I knew one day something of the kind would happen to me," he told Alessandro Tasca, "but I never imagined it happening while I was still young."[8] Maybe it was this absurd situation that led him to drink too much on occasion. Drunk one evening, he fell down in the villa's luxurious bathroom and got stuck between the toilet bowl and bidet; Harriet and the butler had to call the fire brigade to get him out.

Padovani continued to pine for Papi. Her relationship with Welles was by now a way to spite the married man who could not, or would not, abandon his wife and children. They argued continuously. Lea also argued endlessly with Welles. "You're just a Machiavelli," she once hurled at him. "Not even that . . . at least Machiavelli left something behind in this world."[9]

"When I didn't know what she was shouting at me," he told Leaming, "it was just marvelous Italian theater. . . . Through the months she learned English and I learned Italian, and we discovered that we detested each other."

Welles began to smell a rat; Lea was away too often. Harriet White was witness and accomplice to several of her transgressions but remembered one in particular, when Lea took off with one Maurizio, a former racecar driver (one of her many admirers, according to Harriet White). They went first to a race in Pesaro and then to Cortina d'Ampezzo. From the hotel Harriet wired her husband, art director Gastone Medin, that she would be away for a few days. She unpacked and had just got into the bathtub when the door was flung open and a familiar voice boomed, "WHERE IS SHE?"

"I could see Orson's face," she wrote, "moving in and out of the steam, his neck bristling like a woodcock's, with his Chinese eyes way up, crazed with anger! He had been able to trace us to the hotel because of the telegram I had sent to Gastone. "She's over there, next door!" I told him, sinking down beneath my suds. So he stomped out through the mists, went next door, and dragged Lea out of her room. I heard him out in the hall yelling, 'Come on, pack your bag, we're going!' Then he stuck his head back into my bathroom and said, 'Get dressed, we're going!' So I got out, dried myself with miles and miles of Turkish towels, got dressed and went with them down the grand staircase, each of us on an arm of Orson."[10]

Out of the blue, Alexander Korda phoned with some extraordinary news. Maybe *Cyrano* or *The Circus* or *The Emperor* would finally get made? Nothing of the kind. The producer had simply thought of him for a film by Carol Reed, *The Third Man*.

At first Welles didn't want to take on the small but pivotal role. Korda sent some people from the production unit to Rome to persuade him. He went to a hotel and refused to speak to anyone. Korda smoked him out through his love of magic he sent a well-known magician to the hotel and told Welles the man would teach him a few tricks if he would only come out of his room. Welles fell for it, got caught up in discussions about the film, and agreed to take the part.[11] Besides, he needed money for his production of *Othello*, in case Scalera failed to come through and no other backer could be found.

The Third Man is the only story Graham Greene wrote directly for the screen; he turned the screenplay into a novel only afterward. The teaser, a man who buries his friend only to see him plain as day not long afterward, had immediately attracted Korda, who was anxious to repeat the success of *Fallen Idol*, another Greene/Reed collaboration.

Holly Martins (Joseph Cotten), a writer of pulp Westerns, is looking for his old friend Harry Lime (Welles), who was reported dead in an accident. Holly attends Lime's funeral and sees the coffin lowered into the ground, but something does not seem right. Two shady men were there with him when he died, he discovers—maybe also a third man. Then, one evening, he sees his friend. At first incredulous, Holly begins to believe Lime is guilty of illegally—and lethally—peddling diluted penicillin: why else feign his own death? When the two meet up again on a Ferris wheel, it is evident that Lime has become a cynical racketeer (the film is set in war-torn Vienna, where the black market is rampant). Lime's Czech girlfriend, Anna Schmidt (Alida Valli), continues to believe in him but Holly, who is by now in love with her, turns Lime over to the police. After a chase through the sewers of Vienna, Martins shoots Lime dead.

Written in Vienna, Ravello, London, and Santa Monica, the original script had a happy ending, which was changed by Greene at Reed's insistence into one of the most famous finales in cinema history: Anna Schmidt walks away from the cemetery where Lime has been buried for the second time—past an adoring but, in her eyes, culpable Holly Martins. She doesn't so much as look at him.

Welles agreed to play the part of the cynical profiteer but had no contract. When the production company contacted him to formalize the commitment, Welles took his revenge on Korda, a man who had always promised so much and delivered so little. He gave Korda's emissaries the runaround, setting up appointments and then failing to show. Korda sent his brother Vincent and nephew Michael first to Paris, then Rome, Florence, Venice, and Naples. The chase went on for days; Welles proved to be as elusive as Harry Lime. Korda began listening to David O. Selznick, who had never wanted to cast Welles and suggested Noel Coward for the role. Meanwhile Korda's men saw Welles smiling at them from a boat off Capri. They finally caught up with him in Cagnes-sur-Mer on the French Riviera, where he was devouring a roast chicken with artichokes provençal. They loaded him into a plane and took him to London, where he signed onto the film. Never a businessman, Welles took the agreed-upon $100,000, which he needed for *Othello,* and turned down 10 percent of the gross (excluding US receipts)—a deal that would have made him a very wealthy man.

In mid-October his presence on set was required. Working on *Othello* and still not finished with *Prince of Foxes,* he wired several times that he was unable to make the date. From London, Korda bombarded him with phone calls and telegrams and finally threatened to replace him with Coward. Once more, Welles fell into line and reported for duty in Vienna a week late. Twiddling his thumbs, Reed thought about the scene in which Lime would finally appear: a pair of shoes, a cat that rubs up against them, then an upstairs light suddenly illuminating Welles's face—the greatest entrance ever filmed.

Of all the films Welles acted in without directing, *The Third Man* is by far the most Wellesian. The wide-angle shots, the presence of Joseph Cotten, the satanic magnificence of the title character, whom Welles somehow manages to make both noble and ignoble, have as much to do with Welles as with Greene and Reed. Welles was modest about his contribution; he admitted to authoring his own dialogue and suggesting the final shot of the fingers appearing through the sewer grate, but the rest, he said, was pure Reed. If this is the case, we have to admire Reed for learning so much of the art of expressionism, rhythmic editing, and the layering of dialogue from Welles's films. Certainly, Welles suggested shooting part of the final escape scene on set rather than on location, but only a few such shots were added. Yet it is unlikely that Welles would have been able to influence the entire film. He had other things (*Othello* and Lea) on his mind.

From Vienna, Welles sent Lea lengthy telegrams that ended with soothing, intimate, unabbreviated words such as *allora arrivederci cara* and *dormi bene e profondamente.* So besotted was he with Padovani that he barely noticed "the sexiest thing you ever saw in your life," Alida Valli, who filled him with lust years later whenever he watched the film on television. Despite "losing his mind in some way" over Padovani, a little flu, the stench of Vienna's sewers in his non-false nose, and the lack of falsifying makeup generally, he delivered a near perfect performance and the film, ironically, became one of the most successful productions he was ever involved with.

Shooting for *Othello* began in autumn 1948; *Prince of Foxes* and *The Third Man* were still unfinished. Micheál Mac Liammóir believed that some scenes from the film were shot in September, but documents held in the State Archives in Italy indicate a start date of October 18.[12]

Roderigo was to be played by stage actor Paolo Carlini, and the role of Emilia, at Lea's suggestion, had gone to Harriet White. Giuseppe Varni, a character actor who had been on the *Black Magic* set, was to be Brabantio. Antonio Centa was initially drafted onto the cast (probably as Montano), but on October 18 Welles wired him from Florence that he could not pay the minimum wages required by Italian law. Welles's buddy Everett Sloane (Bernstein in *Citizen Kane* and Bannister in *The Lady from Shanghai*) was to move on from *Prince of Foxes,* in which he played a similar double-crosser, to be Welles's Iago. Michał Waszynski, author of the classic of Yiddish cinema *Dybuk,* was appointed to head up the second unit, after co-directing (with Vittorio Cottafavi) the instantly forgettable *La grande strada* (The long road), as well as *Lo sconosciuto di San Marino* (The stranger from San Marino) and *Fiamme sul mare* (Flames over the sea). Cinematography was entrusted to Alberto Fusi, and the adaptable Giorgio Papi had the roles of head of production and Welles's lover's secret lover.

The cast, crew, and technicians numbered forty; Welles did a few sums and rapidly concluded that with extras, the cost of film, costumes, and hotel bills, the $200,000 from *Prince of Foxes* and *The Third Man* were not sufficient. Yet he persisted, perhaps afraid that someone would beat him to it, and was still hopeful that Scalera would come through—after all, the crew and majority of the cast were Italian.

Without a word to anyone, Welles booked himself and Lea into separate rooms in the Europa Hotel in Venice, where the cast of *Prince of Foxes* was expected the next day. Everett Sloane was shooting a scene with Tyrone Power, so it is possible that *Othello* began with Sloane as Iago, and not the unnamed Italian actor recalled by Mac Liammóir.[13]

There was not a whisper from the press until October 30, when *il Gazzettino*—tailing Ernest Hemingway, on holiday in Venice—bumped into Welles at the Gritti. Cotten was also there before he returned to Vienna for *The Third Man*. A few days later the newspaper published a photo of Welles shooting a scene on the marble staircase of the Giganti.

People finally noticed when the crew took up their positions in St. Mark's Square. Under the powerful lights stood a blonde, elegantly dressed Lea with Harriet White, around them a semicircle of curious onlookers. *Il Gazzettino-Sera* humorously reported that Desdemona, accompanied by her loyal servant Emilia, had taken a gondola to the Doge's Palace to seek an audience from the Council of Ten. Two valets attended her on the gondola, from which descended the beautiful bride of Othello, the Moor of Venice, the Serenissima's faithful general. Hearing of the event, a large group of extras asked for autographs. Waszynski held the crowd back during the four takes, while Alberto Fusi aimed his camera at Padovani and White as Desdemona and Emilia. "Per-fect," he said, finally, to everyone's satisfaction. And they broke out the sandwiches.[14]

Another scene was shot on the eastern side of St. Mark's Cathedral, featuring Desdemona and Othello. Under the watchful guidance of Waszynski, the couple was simply to walk between two Byzantine columns. After the shot, the protagonist said, "Xe finio tuto?" ("Are we done?" in Venetian), setting off a chorus of exclamations as the crowd marveled at Welles's mastery of the local dialect, but the autograph sought by the admiring locals was that of Alfredo Lombardini, a local actor hired as stand-in for Othello when seen from a distance.[15]

That day Welles was either in Vienna shooting *The Third Man* or in Florence for *Prince of Foxes,* in which case he would have been up to his usual tricks with Henry King. As he told Bogdanovich, "I used to hide and wait until he'd start to scream, 'Where *is* he? I know that son-of-a-bitch is away in Venice shooting that goddamn Shakespeare!' And then I'd step out of the bushes fully dressed and say, 'Do you want me, Henry?'"[16]

October and November were busy months, full of traveling, new projects, and old hopes. After the panning of *Macbeth,* Welles was working on three films at the same time and in his kaleidoscopic mind ideas for one film ended up in another. The dark Venice in which Orsini is almost stabbed is the same Venice in the first scenes of *Othello.* The punishment inflicted on Orsini—being kept in a cage without food or water, carrion for the birds—became the non-Shakespearean punishment of Iago. The cat that wraps itself around Harry Lime's feet the first time he appears in *The Third Man* crossed over into the prologue of Welles's Venetian production; and, of course, Borgia provided Welles with the most famous lines in *The Third Man:* "Don't be so gloomy. After all, it's not that awful. Like the fella says, in Italy for thirty years under the Borgias they had warfare, terror, murder, and bloodshed, but they produced Michelangelo, Leonardo da Vinci, and the Renaissance. In Switzerland they had brotherly love—they had five hundred years of democracy and peace, and what did that produce? The cuckoo clock."

As King and Reed were finishing their films, Welles got cracking with *Othello.* During Welles's absence, Waszynski shot Emilia walking through alleyways and the like, plus some more complicated scenes— the meeting of Roderigo and Brabantio and the scenes at Ca' d'oro and the Doge's Palace involving hundreds of extras dressed as commoners, squires, and noblemen (at a reputed cost of three hundred thousand lire a day)—were shot only on Welles's return. The myth of the homeless, maverick film director starting films he never finished is a journalistic concoction. With or without him, the filming went ahead apace. A local reporter for *il Gazzettino-Sera* said Welles would be staying in Venice, weather permitting, until the end of November and then would be in

Rome to shoot some interiors (presumably at the Scalera studios), to be followed by Castel Sant'Angelo and finally Sicily, somewhere near Palermo, for the Cyprus scenes. If everything had gone according to plan the film would have been wrapped up by the end of the year, edited, and released in early spring. Too optimistic? Maybe, but the reason things did not go according to plan were neither financial nor organizational; they were romantic.

Lea Padovani continued to string Welles along as she conducted her affair with Papi. The crew was so used to the goings-on that even an outsider like Todisco got to hear about them. Lea kept away from Welles's bed. Occasionally, he would phone Waszynski in the dead of night and ask, "But why, Mike, why?" Like everyone else, Waszynski kept quiet.

By late November, Welles's courtship of Lea had become desperate. "One evening at Harry's Bar," Todisco wrote in *Europeo*, "after a gondola ride on the Grand Canal, Welles ordered two whiskies and looked at Lea Padovani without a word. Then he lowered his eyes and said, 'It's the first time I have really loved. Until now I'd only ever thought of women as pleasure, like a glass of wine when you're thirsty or a dish when you're hungry.'"[17] In the mornings the actress would find Welles's words of devotion written in lipstick on the dressing table mirror. Sometimes, he left her photos of future gifts, including a luxury Buick under which he had penciled, "This car will reach Italy in a few days. It belongs to Lea Padovani."

Lea refused the car but accepted the continuing siege. "We went on for a little while," the actress recalled. "He said he wanted to marry me, whatever it took. He said he had only ever thought of women as objects, as pastimes. Even the 'bombshell' Rita, and all the others. He said he had taken those women like you eat a dish or drink some wine, but with me it was different. I, on the other hand, was immensely embarrassed by his fierce courtship."[18] "A genius like that," she added many years later, "does nothing by halves and for him love was a delirium. He followed me everywhere, sat in his car under my window for hours just to see me for a few moments. . . . He was capable of unforgettable things. One day at the Caffè Cipriani in Venice he got down on his knees, kissed the edge of my skirt, and pronounced my name quietly. I was breathless with emotion."[19] Finally she caved and spent her first and—according to Welles—last night with him. Overjoyed, Welles ran to tell—who else?—Papi, who could only—what else?—heartily congratulate him.

What happened next is not clear. Charles Higham, the only Welles biographer to include an interview with Lea Padovani, wrote that Papi immediately asked her to dump Welles and she did so. Welles's furious reaction and Padovani's character did the rest. The argument ended when the tiny Lea managed to hit him over the head with a hefty doorstop. As Welles lay unconscious on the floor, a terrified Lea packed and left for Rome. But the conviction in Rome, even today, is that things went differently: Welles caught Lea and Papi together and flew into a rage. "In the nine months I was with her," he told Maurice Bessy, "I paid for everything I'd ever done to women, but in two days I made her pay for everything she'd done to me in nine months."[20] Payment included firing her from the film. He would have fired Papi, too, but his rival now had the reins of *Othello* firmly in his hands. Welles contented himself with confining Papi to Rome, spoke to him as little as possible, and promoted Walter Bedogni to joint production chief.

Padovani tried to stop the tongues wagging by taking responsibility (and credit) for the breakup with Welles. She chose her friend Dorothy di Frasso to give her side of the story. "She would prefer to sell violets in Piazza di Spagna rather than marry without love," Dorothy told everyone. The film ground to a halt. The adaptation of *the* play about jealousy was held up (first time round) by Welles's jealousy. A series of accidents and misadventures further delayed the film. In mid-December, in a luxury clothes store on Via Veneto, Papi was relieved of a bag containing all the contracts for *Othello* and about four million lire in cash and checks. That same evening Welles was informed that his divorce from Rita was final and that he would soon be paying alimony for Rebecca. Finally, Everett Sloane came to the conclusion that he had gotten himself nowhere fast with *Othello* and gave up the role of Iago.

When Welles was called to Shepperton Studios, near London, to finish *The Third Man* it must have been a relief. He had time for one more scene for Henry King, a terrifying cavalry battle shot on the Rome coastline, in which twenty extras were injured. Reporters wrote that Padovani wanted to continue her English studies, and that was why she was accompanying Welles to England. Evidently he hadn't yet cut her loose, emotionally or artistically. She was a perfect Desdemona and Welles may even have thought that his performance as Othello would be all the more convincing because of his genuine jealousy. The newspapers caught the scent of trouble on January 27, 1949, at the wedding in Rome of Tyrone Power and Linda Christian. Lea was still Desdemona blonde, but where was Welles?

Officially the relationship ended in mid-February. The four-year (some said seven-year) contract between Welles and Padovani was torn up by mutual agreement, without damages to either party. A few months later, using the English Welles and White had taught her, she made the best film of her career, *Give Us This Day* (aka *Christ in Concrete*) directed by Edward Dmytryk, one of the Hollywood Ten forced into exile by the HUAC. During the shooting of the film, in London, she agreed to talk to a *Film* reporter about Welles: "We were going to be married. But it isn't the first time a wedding has had to be canceled. Orson is a true genius, but I couldn't stay with him only for professional reasons. We agreed to separate and are now good friends. I'll never forget how much I learned about films from him, how much English, but . . ."[21]

But she was in love with someone else, who did not love her as much as she wanted. "You're the only woman who ever sent Orson Welles packing," Humphrey Bogart told her. To her credit, Lea was not proud of this. She even came to believe that she had made one of her worst mistakes in life by leaving Welles.

For his part and for many years to come, Welles breathed hellfire about her and the time he had wasted chasing after her. With Barbara Leaming he even withheld her name, referring to her only as an actress with "a face like a spoon."[22] He said everyone had come to hate her and that she had made scenes in every region of Italy. It had not been worth it; not even that one night had been so marvelous. But he believed it had been more his fault than hers and he had been egged on by her continuous refusals: a woman who did not want him!

One thing is certain: he threw away most of the film he had shot in Venice (thought to be, according to the Venetian press, 3,000 meters, or an hour and fifty minutes) and lost his leading actress. He had run out of time, money, and patience with Lea.

She had the good taste to turn down large sums offered by American newspapers to publish Welles's letters and telegrams to her. He reciprocated when she ran into legal problems by providing her, at his expense, with his team of attorneys. Welles—the impulsive, generous Renaissance man.

9
Scalera Gets Cold Feet

You'll find the game's ready.
I always make the first move.

—Bayan (Orson Welles), *The Black Rose*

The false start on *Othello* cost Welles about a month. In mid-November the crew weighed anchor in Venice and returned home without the slightest idea of when shooting would resume. Welles did not lose hope and set about getting the film moving again.

He tried Paris. The Italian press claimed that Charles Philber, a former Paris industrialist who had made his fortune in leather goods, had offered Welles sixty-three million lire to finish *Othello*. Meanwhile, here were nineteen million to do something else: rewrite the script of *Portrait of an Assassin* and adapt the dialogue for the English-language version of the film, as well as act alongside Maria Montez and Erich von Stroheim.[1]

The contract was signed on December 2. While Papi and Rocco Facchini, based in the Excelsior Hotel in Rome, held the strands of *Othello* together, Welles and his friend Charles Lederer worked on the script for the French film at the Lancaster, in Paris.

In late 1948 and early 1949, Welles was spotted working on both films while courting young French and Italian actresses, who were pleased to allow some of the light of his fame and fortune to fall on them, however temporarily. In Paris, Welles was spotted most often with Suzanne Bernard, a stage actress who immediately informed *France dimanche* of her new status as Welles's girlfriend, and volunteered, "Not for anything would I marry him. I understand why Rita left him. Living with a genius is too complicated."

In Rome, he met a budding actress and former beauty queen (originally first runner-up at the Miss Italy pageant of 1946, but proclaimed a co-winner after popular uproar), the curvaceous Silvana Pampanini, a girl with magnetic green eyes and some experience in films. "How Orson Welles looked at me," she wrote in her memoirs. "My friends made a point of introducing me to him after his flirtation with Lea Padovani. Guido Celani told me Welles could get me into serious films. They invited me to dinner in Tor Fiorenza and contrived to leave us alone together. In the car—we had a chauffeur—he was all over me. . . . 'You must be mine, tonight!' he screamed. I gave him a good slap in the face. What else could I do? He drove me home and didn't even get out of the car to say good night."[2]

Back in Paris Welles met Ernest Borneman, a Canadian scriptwriter working for the Cinema Department at UNESCO, who wanted him to work on a film on Ulysses. Welles invited him to write the script in his villa in Frascati for a thousand dollars a month. Borneman could hardly believe his luck. Over Christmas, in the villa in Casal Pilozzo, reeling from the beauty and chaos of the place, he found notebooks with Lea's English lessons strewn over the house and numerous messages and pierced hearts lipsticked onto mirrors.

Welles went back to Shakespeare, visiting Castel Sant'Angelo, which he thought of turning into a Cyprus fortress, sometime in January or February. He was battle-hardened and optimistic, and had adapted to Italian ways to the extent that he was making the most of the little he had, in contrast to the luxurious and spendthrift ways of Hollywood. Around this time, he told his friend Barzini, "Films are like parties. There are some where you have a whale of a time with bread and salami, Frascati, and a gramophone. At others you stay up to the early morning talking. And there are parties where the serving people in livery, the ladies' fine jewelry, the frescoes on the walls, and the lobster, caviar, and champagne don't stop you getting bored to tears. . . . Hollywood is often a big boring party, which every now and then redoubles the number of lackeys, the rooms, the orchestras and lobsters, but everyone wants to leave all the same. With a few dollars in Italy you can make something different, enjoyable, experimental, that no one in America would allow you to do."[3]

Borneman wrote page after page of the Ulysses script, quit UNESCO, and had his family come over from Ottawa. He intended to start a new life at the court of King Orson. According to Welles's biographer, Peter Noble, Borneman stayed at the villa in Casal Pilozzo for a couple of months and did not receive a dime from Welles. He finished his script as the creditors were beating at his door. Welles didn't pay the rent, either, and the electricity, water, and phone were cut off.

Just before he left the villa, Borneman managed to track Welles down with a telegram, in which he asked him how he and his wife were supposed to make ends meet. "Dear Ernest, live simply," Welles replied.

Welles sent two hundred and fifty dollars, which Borneman used to leave the country, probably reflecting on the latter-day, multifaceted Ulysses he had got himself mixed up with. Later, when Borneman was writing for the radio in London, he received a surprise visit from one of Welles's secretaries—who bore him greetings, apologies, and a briefcase containing all the money he was owed.

Bad news came from America about *Macbeth*. The film had been given a hostile reception at its premiere in autumn; Republic was going to rerecord the dialogue and have the film reedited with substantial cuts. Alberto Mondadori had asked him for a copy of the film. Welles's reply from Paris in February, in Italian, said:[4]

Dear Alberto,

It was a great pleasure to get your letter, but sadly there is no copy of *Macbeth* in Europe. The copy sent to Venice was sent back to England, where the dragons of Republic Pictures want to save it from who knows what in the most remote hiding place in the British Isles.

Worse still, in Hollywood they're now thinking of reediting the film according to their own exquisite tastes—in the hope, I assume, of changing the verdict of the doges of Venice by remixing the celluloid. I can't bear to think of what the result will be.

... What they will do with *Macbeth* after they've finished ruining it I can't say. In the meantime I'm working hard on *Othello*, which I will finish partly in Italy, partly in France.

I want to spend most of March and maybe April in Rome. If you're in the area, it would be a great pleasure to meet with you again. You are a real friend and I want you to know I appreciate it and am a friend to you too.

My most cordial and affectionate regards,

Your Orson[5]

Welles told Mondadori that he expected to complete *Othello* "partly in Italy, partly in France." Presumably, he was thinking of Charles Philber; consequently, art director Alexander Trauner chose Victorine Studios in Nice, where he had worked on *Cyrano*, rather than Castel Sant'Angelo and Sicily, for the Cyprus scenes.

After Everett Sloane's departure, Welles needed a new Iago. His first thought was James Mason, who had made *Odd Man Out* with Carol Reed in 1947. Reed considered Mason unsuitable for the part and recommended Irish stage actor Micheál Mac Liammóir, the man who had given Welles his first acting job in Dublin. They hadn't met since the 1934 Todd Summer Festival in Woodstock. The two actors respected each other's talents and had been friendly—and sometimes unfriendly—rivals. Wispy but with a round face and introspective demeanor, Mac Liammóir actually resembled Mason: the Mason of *Lolita*—suggesting something tainted, treacherous, and corrupt. Welles took Reed's advice and, at the end of January, wired the actor in Dublin to invite him for a screen test in Paris.

Mac Liammóir had just been through something of a nervous breakdown and had no wish to get on a plane to Paris. He said he was tired, had aged, put on weight, and was not suitable for the role of Iago or any bad guy. Perhaps these protests were dictated in part by a smoldering resentment of Welles. But repeated phone calls and the advice of Mac Liammóir's doctor and his companion, Hilton Edwards (who also joined the cast) finally persuaded him at least to try.

In Paris, the actor had no screen test to do. Welles had already made up his mind; he asked him only to go through a few scenes and discussed costumes with him (Welles had in mind the type of puffs, laces, and frills in Carpaccio's portraits).[6] He revealed to the actor his take on Iago—a man motivated by secret impotence—and tempted Mac Liammóir with dazzling locations: Rome, Venice, Nice, a holiday in Europe's most beautiful locations. And still the actor hesitated, reluctant to give up his beloved theater. To reassure him, Welles said the film would be finished "by August at the latest."

The best record of the subsequent shambles and vicissitudes of *Othello* is Mac Liammóir's *Put Money in Thy Purse*—partly a tasty and elegant record in diary form of the shooting of the film, partly an entertaining autobiography—published in 1952 with a preface by Welles. For Welles's biographers it is an invaluable source on what are otherwise the relatively unknown Italian years. But the book is not without malice and unresolved, even unaddressed, questions. No explanation is given of Lea Padovani's disappearance from the project. Mac Liammóir met her, a "beautiful creature" in February at the Lancaster in Paris and spent some evenings with her and Welles, including a "tumultuous dinner." She had dyed her hair blonde.

Could she learn enough English to play the role in time for film? Mac Liammóir asked Welles, skeptical. "If not, she could be dubbed," Welles replied.[7] On February 15, Mac Liammóir made a diary entry: "Long day of working and eating with Orson and Padovani. She is fascinating and doesn't seem to like Desdemona at all."[8] The next day she was fired and Mac Liammóir returned to Dublin wondering if the film would ever be made.

Meanwhile, Alexander Trauner, who was already in a studio on the French Riviera for the Cyprus scenes, now suggested also rebuilding parts of Venice in a studio. This was in order not to give a patchy overall visual effect to the film, with "those famous and familiar old Venetian stones" looking too dissimilar to the Cyprus scenery, which had been made of paste and then painted over. Welles agreed and began to think of *Othello* in an abstract, unreal world. It was one of the many compromises the production conditions of *Othello* obliged him to make and was a partial recantation, a return to the *Macbeth* model of shooting on a set.

Ten days after his return to Dublin, Mac Liammóir received the contract. He was to fly back to Paris on March 7, where he found Welles in the virtually hopeless enterprise of finding a Desdemona with delicate lineaments, good English and, if possible, a Shakespeare pedigree.

In the hotel, Welles interviewed an array of unlikely candidates; irritated by their ineptitude, he decided some might serve another purpose. The first actress with a real chance was Cécile Aubry, currently all the rage in Paris for her performance in Henry-Georges Clouzot's *Manon*. Welles met her on March 4 during the Miss Cinémonde pageant, for which he was one of the judges. A week later, Maurice Bessy, chief editor of *Cinémonde*, visited him with the actress. Her broad smile, child-like looks and graceful and delicate sixteen-year-old figure made her an ideal victim of a husband's rage and jealousy. Two days later, the actress informed the enthusiastic pair that she had signed for another film, and left them high and dry.

The following week, the director Anatole Litvak met Welles at the Ritz and invited him to view a few reels of *The Snake Pit*, which featured actress Betsy Blair—Gene Kelly's wife—in a small part. Perhaps she would do the trick. "Longish, lovely face crowned with light hair, and a performance full of gentleness and understanding. O. likes her," wrote Mac Liammóir,[9] oblivious to the fact that Welles had already met her, in 1942, when she had been promoting the interests of the working classes. Welles called the Kelly home in Beverly Hills. Betsy flew to Rome, dyed her hair blonde and met Welles and Trauner. It was one fewer problem to solve.

English actor Robert Coote was brought on board as Roderigo in late March, which left Bianca, Cassio, Lodovico, a new Emilia, and a new Brabantio still to find. Of course, money was running low, since Welles continued to stay at the Lancaster and to treat himself and his actors to the best restaurants in town. It was part of the lure of the film; he played to the vanity of the cast, although, as producer, he made no attempt to hide the lack of funding from them. Besides, he was a generous man; Papi could worry about the money.

It wasn't the best moment for generosity. His French co-producer had just vanished into thin air and Trauner had had to leave the studios in Nice after making just a series of sketches that served no purpose (although they were admired, it seems, by Picasso, no less). Welles was back to square one, with no money and needing to make further changes to the artistic setup of the film.

No one was surprised when, on the verge of bankruptcy, Welles left for London on March 29 to take a small role in *The Black Rose*, the film Cécile Aubry had preferred to his *Othello*. It was another costume drama with Tyrone Power. And Mac Liammóir? No matter. He could wait for

Welles in the villa in Frascati, try on some costumes and wigs, and get into the role.

The Black Rose was set in the thirteenth century, mostly in the Far East, and featured two Saxon noblemen—Walter of Gurnie (Tyrone Power) and Tristram Griffin (Jack Hawkins)—exiled after an unsuccessful rebellion against the Norman throne and the hated King Edward. In Antiochia, they join forces with Bayan (Welles), a Mongol warlord who is due to hand over the beautiful Maryam, aka the Black Rose (Aubry), to Kublai Khan as his bride. After some hokum, Walter returns to England, is pardoned, and is reunited with his beloved Black Rose, with the blessing of Bayan.

Directed by an irascible and unapproachable Henry Hathaway and shot in dazzling Technicolor for Twentieth Century Fox, the film was a convenient way of spending five million dollars that were frozen in England. Hathaway frittered away the budget on extras and a series of locations, while skimping on the battle scenes. He ignored Welles and did not even sit down to eat with him. This time Welles would not be allowed to write or direct his own scenes.

The film suffers for it: the direction is perfunctory and flat, without a trace of Welles's gifts as a director. In the scenes in which he appears, he manages to show off only his acting skills, imparting an extraordinarily natural air to the rhythm of the dialogue. Bayan of the Hundred Eyes is not the type of tyrant that interested Welles. Helmeted and draped in sheepskin, he is something of a parody of a bloodthirsty megalomaniac, interested only in what he can lay his hands on—especially gunpowder from China, with which he intends to destroy Rome. The script never explains what he sees in two erudite Saxon runaways.

Most of the film was shot in French Morocco, where Welles spent two months perhaps, among other things, trying to convince Aubry to change her mind. In fact, she met a Moroccan prince on the set, married him, and never made another film.

At the end of May, news reached the crew of Rita Hayworth's ostentatious wedding to Aly Khan. The cast was in Meknès, at the palace of Califf Moulay Ben Zidan. Welles disappeared from the set and was not on the veranda where the actors rested after shooting. His seat was left vacant for days, said *Cine Illustrato*: "A certain embarrassment ran through the company. Where on earth was he? Tyrone Power wondered. One evening, Jack Hawkins stumbled upon him furiously looking for something in the garden. When he enquired what it was, Welles replied, 'Why, the harem, of course, there's got to be one in the palace of a Caliph!' Hawkins didn't dare imagine what might have happened if Welles had found his harem."[10]

Actually, a Berber woman, a "great, tall, dark, tattooed creature," as Welles later described her to Leaming, was acting as his secretary, interpreter, and consolation, and he was out in the torrid sun looking for locations for *Othello*. This was his new idea. Morocco was uncontaminated, cheaper, and historically closer to Cyprus than Italy or the French Riviera. In Mogador (now Essaouira), he found a fifteenth-century Portuguese fortress—complete with towers, battlements, bells, secret passageways, ramparts, and even a bronze cannon pointing out over the Atlantic (which would become the Mediterranean around Cyprus). Some scenes could be shot in Safi and Mazagan (now El-Jadida).

Welles called Mac Liammóir over in mid-May and prepared to tell him that the beautiful, expensive, and relaxing locations in Europe—with which he had convinced the Irish actor to join the crew—had become scorching Morocco. Not even Venice would be used. In addition, when Mac Liammóir stepped off the plane in Casablanca he was greeted not by Welles but by the news that Welles was still shooting *The Black Rose*, so he flew on to Rome and sat again in the villa in Frascati with Robert Coote (Roderigo) and a new member of the cast, Michael Laurence (Cassio)—all of them twiddling their thumbs.

The cast was now Welles, Betsy Blair, Mac Liammóir, Coote, and Laurence—not an Italian among them. Scalera had not given in, however; nor had Welles forgotten his Italian producer. Scalera had simply come up with an idea: if Welles wanted to direct himself in an English-language film and the producer needed an Italian director and cast, what was the problem? All they had to do was hire two crews and two directors, and shoot the film in two languages. Only Othello, Desdemona, and Iago would be the same.

The idea wasn't new; under Fascism, they had done something similar for a few Italo-German productions. One cast shot a scene in its own language under one director, and the second cast then shot the same scene in a different language with a different director; only the leading actors remained the same. Rossellini and Ingrid Bergman were about to make *Stromboli* in both English and Italian, but without changing the cast. Scalera probably intended to use Welles's footage from Morocco, and interiors shot in his own studios, using Italian actors. The Italian director may have been no more than a front, merely supervising the doubling, so the Italian version of the film could be given the name of an Italian director. All this was necessary for certification of Italian nationality and government funding.

On May 22, Scalera applied to Direzione Generale per la Cinematografia for a permit to begin shooting *Othello* in English and Italian. The schedule included four weeks in Mogador (exteriors of the palace in Cyprus), one week in Safi (exteriors of the governor's palace), another in Mazagan (exteriors of Desdemona's residence), five weeks in Scalera Studios (interiors of Desdemona's, Brabantio's, and Roderigo's residence, and exteriors of the tower in Cyprus) and a final week in Venice (Doge's Palace)—with a budget of 271,678,000 lire.[11]

The application lists the three main English-language actors plus Antonio Centa as Montano, Luca Cortese as the Doge, neorealist filmmaker and actor Vittorio De Sica as Ludovico, and Gina Lollobrigida as Bianca. Two days later Commendatore Scalera confirmed that shooting would begin on June 15, under the direction of Oreste Biancoli, writer of *Bicycle Thieves* and one of De Sica's right-hand men.

Today, Gina Lollobrigida denies all knowledge of the film and the role. She may have been included in the parallel cast because Welles had met and serenaded her in 1948; Centa had been Welles's private secretary for a number of months just after Welles's arrival in Italy; and De Sica was Italy's most revered filmmaker and, for Welles, perhaps the only Italian filmmaker worthy of such acclaim. The cast list was intended to suggest heavy Italian involvement, which, in fact, was merely marginal: Montano, the Doge, Bianca, and Ludovico had very few, brief scenes. The Italian cast seems to have been chosen by Welles himself.

The application for funding included a copy of the script, not obligatory but certainly a good idea, to avoid problems later with the censor and the bureaucrats who approved the funding. The script was reviewed by the censorship office on June 3, the summary beginning exactly as the film was actually to start: a prologue in Cyprus, the bodies of Othello and Desdemona held aloft, and "the imprisonment of Iago in an iron cage." The censor approved the script with some reservations, given its evidently provisional nature. Annibale Scicluna, the senior executive, wrote, "There are few directions, the camera position and movements are not specified. . . . However, it would appear to be essentially a filmed stage production. . . . The focus is on the machinations and choreographic aspects of the plot, to the detriment of Shakespeare's depth and universal human interest. The impression is that the adaptation will be revised again before shooting."[12]

The censor was busiest clipping and trimming Shakespeare's lines of sexual innuendo, including these: "Even now, now, very now, an old black ram / Is tupping your white ewe"; "if you canst cuckold him, thou dost thyself a pleasure / Me a sport"; "You rise to play and go to bed to work"; and "[Lie] With her, on her, what you will." Scicluna, who ran the department with an iron hand, concluded, "These lines should therefore be recommended for removal since they damage the overall tone of the work." A handwritten note next to this recommendation indicates that it was delivered to Scalera, or Papi, only verbally, no doubt to avoid exposing the censor to ridicule.

It is unclear whether Welles ever found out that a zealous bureaucrat had seen fit to amend Shakespeare's work. Probably he would not have been unduly surprised. In any case, it was the last of his worries. Despite the agreement with Scalera, there was very little money to make the film. As Betsy Blair was shooting a scene in Mogador—Desdemona impatiently awaiting the arrival of Othello—the crew was waiting for the other shoe to drop.

Even Welles had premonitions. He told Leaming, "I was convinced I was going to die. The wind blew all the time, which seemed to me to be associated with my death. And things were so terrible, there didn't seem to be any way out of it. And I was absolutely, serenely prepared never to leave Mogador. I was sure they were going to carry me out dead."[13]

With Hilton Edwards (Brabantio) and Doris Dowling (Bianca), the crew for the film was complete. However, the arrival at Mogador on June 9 of Mac Liammóir, Laurence, and Coote brought bad news from Rome: Scalera was in financial straits. Mac Liammóir found Welles pacing up and down under the full moon; he soon confided the endless financial difficulties, problems with costumes, and high labor costs. The costumes were urgently needed because they were about to shoot a scene with many extras as Venetian senators, all splendidly dressed in Renaissance pomp.

The following afternoon, Welles and Trauner phoned Rome and were told the men's costumes were still in Scalera Studios. Betsy Blair recalled, "Orson pleaded on the phone to Rome; he shouted and threatened and appealed in the name of Art, civilized values, and future work. It was to no avail. If there was no cash on the table, no costumes would be on the plane. And there was no cash. Orson roared into the dining room and ordered two meals for himself. He inveighed against Fate, the Italians, and his production manager. The rest of us sat in silence."[14]

Welles could hardly send sixty people home when he had everything he needed to carry on shooting for at least a couple of days—everything but the men's costumes, that is. The next morning, he gathered everyone around him and explained they would shoot the Roderigo murder scene, not in the street, but in a Turkish bath, with actors in robes or towels.

This is the episode of the precarious shooting of *Othello* that everyone knows and is most often cited to illustrate Welles's indomitable ingenuity. Welles told it over and over, never hinting that the idea had not been his. Betsy Blair, however, said it was the brainchild of Trauner. As Welles was cursing fate and everything else under the sun, Trauner sat quietly sketching and finally showed Welles what he had drawn. Betsy Blair described how Trauner explained in his Hungarian-inflected English, "'It could be the senators are in old Turkish bath near to the ramparts. They wear towels or maybe not. We make steam,'" and "Orson roared with joy. He threw his arms around Trau, picked him up and danced from table to table. Everyone relaxed, laughing with relief. And so the scene was shot in a Turkish bath and looked great. That crisis was over."[15] Blair—still unaware that she had taken over the role from Lea Padovani and was about to be replaced herself—may have had her own reasons for demythologizing Welles, but the entire episode is narrated in such detail and with such affection that it has a ring of truth.

Over the next few days the crew rehearsed while a local tailor stitched up a costume for Mac Liammóir (it was used for every shot of

Iago). Trauner and Waszynski got some local residents to improvise a Turkish bath in one of the towers of the fortress. On the morning of June 19, Welles was able, once again, to say, "Action."

Welles always maintained that the costumes failed to arrive because Scalera had gone bust. He was exaggerating. The company was in trouble, but not yet bankrupt. Welles himself later shot some scenes in their studios in Rome (on the Appia orbital road) and Venice (on Giudecca Island). It is more likely that Scalera himself had used the costumes in his fight with Welles in an attempt to impose his own director or at least regain control of the picture. When Welles pulled off the steam trick, Scalera played his last card.

On June 21, two days after the resumption of shooting in Morocco, Commendatore Scalera personally took up pen and paper and informed Direzione Generale per la Cinematografia of what appears to have been a unilateral decision:[16]

> Scalera Film   Rome, June 21, 1949
> To:
> Direzione Generale per la Cinematografia R O M E
> Please be informed that our agreement with Mr. Orson Welles for the production of "O T H E L L O" has been temporarily suspended.
> In the light of the fact that Mr. Welles is currently shooting on location in Morocco, we have decided to postpone the renegotiation of the agreement until he, the cast, and crew return to Italy.
> Therefore, we have agreed that the film will be distributed by us but will be produced by Mr. Welles at his expense, at least until he returns to Italy and renegotiates the agreement with us.
> Yours faithfully,
> (Michele Scalera)

Scalera was trading punch for punch. If Welles wanted to go it alone, let him.

Welles accepted the challenge but, wisely, did not slam the door in Scalera's face. The country that had snubbed him over *Citizen Kane*, massacred *Macbeth*, and cut off his funding for *Othello* was still where he wanted to live and work, despite his feeling a certain embarrassment there, as he confessed to Mac Liammóir: "[N]octural walk with Orson . . . discussed Italy and her people, decided that former was a large and sumptuous Aviary and the latter its feathered inmates, pecking, fluttering, scratching, hopping, cackling, making love, and rhapsodically singing. Our only point of disagreement is that I am partial to Birds and Orson not at all, and he cited humorous drawing in the New Yorker which depicted the Birds with flapping wings and yapping beaks lecturing hell out of a cowering St. Francis, and said that was how he always felt in Italy."[17]

Welles and the crew continued shooting for another month in Mogador and the chateau in Safi, with an additional cameraman and assistant, Anchise Brizzi (cinematographer of Welles's beloved *Sciuscià*) and Oberdan Troiani, both of whom he had met while working on *Black Magic*. After the Turkish bath scene, they shot one of the longest takes of the film, the dialogue between Othello and Iago in which Othello shows jealousy for the first time. The scene was shot from a moving jeep as the actors walked among the ramparts of the chateau. Cassio's drunken scene was also shot while wine and Coca-Cola was handed out to the extras (who were Jews and Arabs), adding a little more confusion to the proceedings. Fay Compton (Emilia) and Nicholas Bruce (Lodovico) arrived, followed by technicians from various countries, a French bookkeeper, a Swiss script girl, and a Jewish costume designer. A couple of Swedish journalists came on set, having got to Morocco too late for *The Black Rose*, and were enrolled as extras into Othello's army.[18]

Other problems included an eye infection Mac Liammóir picked up from the spotlights, forcing Welles to use the sound technician, who had a similar build, for long shots. The local extras cooperated enthusiastically on a market scene, but one had to be persuaded that sewing machines were not a regular feature of the sixteenth century. When some seagulls got into one shot, Welles was forced to try to include them later as well; he tried to bellow them down from the skies, then sprinkled ten kilos of sardines over the ground. Hilton Edwards had a car accident in France and arrived with a bandaged arm and head, then caught pneumonia.

Finally, Welles decided Betsy Blair just wasn't right for the part of Desdemona and asked her to pack her bags. In the hotel in Casablanca he explained that it was not fair to keep her away from her family for so long, in Africa or Rome, in such a precarious situation in which he did not know whether any more funding would be forthcoming. He would let her know when things looked up. And while they were on the subject, he didn't have the money for her return ticket to Los Angeles. When Betsy left she was convinced Welles was doing her a favor by sending her home for a few weeks and her role as Desdemona was secure. She bought her ticket home (for which she was never reimbursed), and left. She met Welles a few years later in Via Veneto after only recently reading in the newspapers who had taken her place in the film. "Welles had such a magnetic presence that I was happy to see him," Blair recalls. "I introduced [my friend] Jeannie. Orson said, 'Are you suing me?' I laughed and said, no, I hadn't thought of that. 'Good,' he said, 'Then I'm taking you both to dinner.'"[19]

Without a Desdemona and low on cash, Welles got ready to postpone shooting once again. In Italy, Walter Bedogni organized the return of cast and crew to Rome and applied for an import license for 30,000 meters of still-virgin negatives. At the last moment Welles was given an unexpected hand by Jean David, a French distributor, who managed to sell the film "in strange places such as Turkey and the Dutch Antilles," which bought him one or two more weeks of shooting. In gratitude he was given the small role of Montano, despite his "utter inability to act."

Shooting broke down on July 25. "Two axes have fallen," Mac Liammóir wrote in his diary. Hilton Edwards was diagnosed with bronchitis and hallucinated "hooded Figures who sit in the corner watching him," and "Orson, pale as his shirt (only it was a black one) announced yesterday that money crisis had again arisen and we would have to knock off work until things were settled. Complete scattering of our forces." He ended his ruminations with this: "I fall to pondering on this Othello film of ours and on what will happen next."[20]

Before disappearing to Casablanca, Welles made one last effort to keep the film going. That same day, in Hollywood, his friend Richard Wilson announced that Welles was working on a story of the *Iliad* and the *Odyssey*.[21] At the same time Dragosei broke the same news in *Hollywood*, adding that the film—*The Adventures of Ulysses*—would be Welles's first in Technicolor and that he would take the leading role.[22] Of course, Welles planned to use Borneman's script. The idea was to attract producers, sell some options, and use the money for *Othello*. But no producer showed interest and the cast and crew broke up a few days later.

Mac Liammóir wrote, "*Othello*, ushered by Orson and the rest, seems to have faded out of life."[23]

There was just one other chance. Fox owed Welles fifty million lire for *The Black Rose*, a sum that had to be spent on Italian soil. Although he'd requested it of Banca d'America e d'Italia in Rome, the money had not yet been released.

10

The Last Desdemona

"Sometimes I feel we are walking across the world on a tightrope."
"Don't worry. I won't fall off. I know how to keep my balance."
—Zoraida (Valentina Cortese) and Count Cagliostro (Welles), *Black Magic*

While he was filming in Morocco, Welles's press in Italy didn't improve; journalists took thoughtless, carefree aim at him in unsigned articles and under the cover of pseudonyms. When a reader asked *Hollywood* what the magazine thought of Welles, Zorro replied on its behalf, "He's a self-propelled bluff, far less crazy and great than he would have us believe."[1] *Oggi* wrote, "His star has been on the wane in Italy ever since his extravagance got out of hand and he turned out to be not a genius but a puffed-up charlatan."[2]

One of Hearst's people, Hedda Hopper, wrote a full-length hatchet job about people who "fall victim to the myths" they create about themselves; a translation was printed in *Hollywood.* Hopper called him a megalomaniac and a "Martian in the clouds" in her narration, and distortion, of the failure of *It's All True.* She went on to hint at Welles's all-consuming envy of Olivier. This was gossip, of course, but it contributed to public opinion in Italy. "In a continuous effort to impress people," Hopper concluded, "Welles has lost sight of the true mission, which is to make art."[3]

In autumn 1948, *The Lady from Shanghai* arrived in Italy, in the form Harry Cohn had hacked out of Welles's film, and with the additional blemish of hurried, botched dubbing. Distributed just a month after the *Macbeth* debacle in Venice, the film was ambiguously received, closing the gap between Welles's admirers and detractors. Among the admirers, Alberto Mondadori noted its failings and played to its strengths in his review in *Tempo:* "The finale of *The Lady from Shanghai*—a mediocre film compared to Welles's other work—is a truly remarkable piece of cinema, summing up all the previous feelings of estrangement, fear, and hallucination captured in the film's other great scene: the aquarium (one day we will have to come to terms with Welles's so-called debt to German expressionism, something the critics have got into their heads). The film suffers from a cold storyline, shaky psychology, and, sadly, a poor performance by Rita Hayworth. . . . Yet it shows Welles once more as an innovator of cinematic language, the first to break with certain hallowed traditions and to explore new depths of expression."[4]

Among the detractors, Guido Aristarco returned to his favorite characterization of Welles as a director who sought to "dazzle at all costs." He praised his originality in eschewing a happy ending (many such endings had been foisted on noir), but his review was once again negative, if better thought out this time, under the scrutiny of Mondadori, his leading film critic rival in Milan. Aristarco noted the attempt "to denounce a bourgeoisie deluding itself that the pursuit of money is a noble and joyful occupation" but he found that trite, and described the two scenes praised by Mondadori as "Salvador Dalí applied to the scenography of *The Cabinet of Dr. Caligari,*" the play of mirrors a mere "hedonistic game," and Hayworth as one of Welles's few accomplishments (here Mondadori had paid Welles a backhanded compliment for "managing to get his ex-wife to stop moving about and putting on a face"). According to Aristarco, Welles had "managed to transform a cover girl into a sometimes expressive actress."[5]

Dino Risi, then a journalist in Milan, joined in the discussion a month later. Unlike Mondadori and Aristarco, who appeared once again to be debating ideology and canons of style, he wrote about the film itself and begged to differ with them: "Welles, so poorly received and shabbily treated in Italy, described as a man who senses cinema as a dog sniffs a tree, contributes hugely to the cinema by renewing its means of expression: Welles's sequences are like trout in a hatchery. *The Lady from Shanghai* is all bits and pieces, but is full of invention and glimpses of the future: this is the film of an energetic director."[6]

Other reviews were favorable; there was a feeling among some in the film industry that Welles had been given a raw deal at the Venice Film Festival and in the press. From Trieste, Callisto Cosulich wrote that Welles had "shown humility making a straight mystery story. *The Lady from Shanghai* is his best film and reconciles him with his audience after the disappointment of Venice."[7]

In *Bertoldo*, Pietro Bianchi launched himself into a passionate defense of Welles, almost outdoing Alberto Mondadori, who was usually Welles's sole defender. "Ours is truly a strange country," he wrote. "Take Orson Welles for example. He is a world-class filmmaker, an innovator of the cinematic means of expression. We have the great fortune to have him in Italy and what do we do? We fight him. Doubtless he is everything they say he is: egocentric, histrionic, proud as Mephistopheles. But he also happens to be the man who made *Citizen Kane* (a masterpiece), *The Magnificent Ambersons, Macbeth,* and *The Lady from Shanghai*. Italians are supposed to love ingenuity and artistry. So why this ostracism? *The Lady from Shanghai* is reckoned to be an arid film, dark, damned. I dare say. But how much invention, what extraordinary creativity! And what a lesson for conventional Hollywood producers. Orson is a rebel angel, for sure, a great artist who deserves to be treated better, to be left to get on with his work. And made to feel at home."[8]

Something appeared to have changed in the circles that mattered and critics were at least willing to concede some merit to the extraterrestrial filmmaker. In January 1949, Giulio Cesare Castello published the first serious Italian study of the American director, entitled *The Magnificent Orson Welles*. The title was praise indeed, after the lynching Welles had received only four months earlier in Venice. Welles is barbaric, Castello admitted, and prone to mystification and amateurism; then Castello changes tone: among other insights, he suggests that Welles was "uncontrollably dominated by the impetuous need to give to others, to expand his chaotic, rich inner life."

Castello did not mince words. "I think Welles has not yet been given the balanced, thought-out critique he deserves." He saw in Italian criticism "the tendency to take him or leave him—meaning leave him—and a refusal to discuss his films beyond the heat of the moment." Castello attributed this attitude to a reaction against the excessively positive criticism of the French and their somewhat facile enthusiasm, and to the "strange" way Welles had been brought to the attention of Italian film-goers by critics obsessed with formalism and cinema technique at the expense of a film's overall architecture and narrative. So what if Welles filmed some ceilings? Castello documented his article more fully than other critics, revealing, for example, that Welles had invented "the subjective viewpoint film" with the unmade *Heart of Darkness* in 1939. The critic had not seen *Journey into Fear* but knew Welles had repudiated it, and expressed regret that *It's All True* was unfinished.

One by one, from the first to the most recent, Castello discussed Welles's films. The "fractured syntax and chronology" of *Citizen Kane*, Castello wrote, was not gimmicky or quirky, but an essential part of the storytelling, counterpointing conflicting elements of Kane's character and life. Welles was an enemy of "sentimentality" who told stories "objectively," and ran the risk—in certain lengthy scenes and dialogues in *The Magnificent Ambersons*—of reducing the camera to virtual stasis. Castello criticized *The Stranger* for falling into a baroque finale at the end of an admirably paced story. Castello treated only Welles's more recent films harshly, declaring *The Lady from Shanghai* to be "gratuitous" and *Macbeth* "sterile and a step backward." However, he concluded that even if Welles never made another film "his reputation has been established; far from being presumptuous, an arrogant exhibitionist, he speaks through images in a new language that is foreign to nine American films out of ten."[9]

The revaluation of Welles's career suffered a setback in May and June 1949 when *Black Magic* finally got its release. Ratoff's anxiously awaited film fell flat on its face and the recent momentum in favor of Welles was stopped in its tracks.

In *Corriere della Sera,* Lanocita peremptorily asked Ratoff what he thought he'd been doing in this "gross film from beginning to end." He described the story of the necklace as "narrated laboriously within an asthmatic scenario edited with childish simplicity. . . . [S]ome episodes don't come close to being ridiculous, they achieve it." He excused Welles for being unable to act his way out of such a mess, while accusing him of failing to do so: "even Welles is caught up in the absurdity of the melo-drama and often falls into pompous, insincere, declamation."[10]

Less kind still was Dino Falconi, who wrote an open letter to Welles in *Film:* "This time it isn't a private showing in Venice, as for your *Macbeth*. It's a film before a paying public with no cultural prejudices. I realize you didn't direct the film, Mr. Welles. It was made by Gregory Ratoff, but so strong is your personality that any film, even one you only act in, becomes *yours*. Well, I have to say we're tired of you, Mr. Welles. I dare say you're too good for us, too much of a genius, and we're just mediocre. Which only means we don't deserve each other."[11]

Flaiano added his own characteristic vitriol, joining the ranks of the detractors of *Citizen Kane*—which he described, along with *Black Magic* as "highly questionable." The former he called "baroque, gratuitously violent, and with a futile precision," and the latter "tedious and humdrum," practically a joke.[12] Who knows whether he'd actually been one of the few to see *Citizen Kane* during the three days it had been shown in Rome the previous year, or whether he was basing his review on what he'd heard. The overlapping, jumbled release of Welles's films in Italy was not helping; the bad reception of *Macbeth* had adversely colored *The Lady from Shanghai,* and now *Black Magic* was tainting the Milan audience's reaction to *Citizen Kane.* Just when Welles had finally taken one step forward in his adopted country, he was knocked two steps back.

"We're tired of you," Falconi had said, and set the tone for Welles's return to Italy from Morocco. Some producers were up in arms: Scalera had wanted a different film and was contemplating pulling the plug on the project; Sandro Ghenzi had been obliged to set aside his own *Othello,* to be directed by Castellani; and Dino De Laurentiis, who had been working on an *Odyssey* for six months, didn't take kindly to news of a *Ulysses* by Welles.

This climate may have contributed to the freezing of Fox's payment for *The Black Rose* in the bank. On April 28, the director general of Twentieth Century Fox in Italy, Mario Luporini, asked the Ministry of Foreign Trade to release Welles's fee of fifty-three million lire from Banca d'America e d'Italia, specifying that Welles would spend the money "on board and lodging, travel expenses, studies in Italy, and secretarial costs."[13] To get the money cleared immediately, it would have been sufficient to say that the money would be spent on making a film in Italy—a film like *Othello,* as chance would have it. But because *Othello* was not a Twentieth Century Fox film, the producer couldn't care less about it; Luporini, therefore, did not mention it. Was it a trick to keep the money on hold? To obstruct Welles's film? Maybe. When Fox asked Direzione Generale della Cinematografia for approval, the bureaucrats replied that nothing had been sent to them and asked for more details about how the money would be used. In the meantime, the money stayed put.

Correspondence between Fox's Italian subsidiary, the prime minister's office (which controlled Direzione Generale Spettacolo, the visual entertainment department), and Welles's production unit (now at the cheaper Boston Hotel in Via Lombardia) resumed in mid-July, when Welles was about to return to Italy due to lack of funds. Papi put the wheels in motion. On July 16, he obtained the approval of Direzione Generale Spettacolo; two weeks later he informed them and the Ministry of Foreign Trade "in [his] capacity as head of production and legal representative of Orson Welles in Italy" that the money would be used "solely to shoot *Othello* in Italy," and production would begin as soon as the funds were released by the relevant government authorities "to Mr. Orson Welles."[14] With his letter he enclosed an estimate of costs for another four weeks' shooting in Venice, listing the fees for the production head (Papi), the director's assistant (Waszynski), cinematographer (Anchise Brizzi), cameraman (Alberto Fusi), and sound technician (Umberto Picistrelli)—"all hired at the end of March by Orson Welles, both as a first option on their work and because shooting was scheduled for earlier." The estimate was for 47,244,500 lire (costumes topped the list at 4 million) and did not include anything for the director or actors' salaries.

Confident that the money would come through, Welles spoke to the cast, now scattered across half of Europe, and convened them for the resumption of shooting in Venice. On August 1, the Foreign Trade Ministry gave the go-ahead for the payment of about a quarter of the sum, 11,222,500 lire. Ten days later, "following information received and the submission by the production company of an estimate of costs," the release of a further 38,777,500 lire was authorized, to be spent on the production of *Othello*. The payment likely also needed to be rubber-stamped by the Foreign Exchange Department, and a few more weeks went by before the money materialized. Mac Liammóir and the rest of the crew waited patiently in Venice as Welles did a passing impression of the Scarlet Pimpernel, disappearing no sooner than he had arrived from Torcello.

Anxious to get back to work, and suffering from the intense summer heat, Welles saw Lea Padovani again in Venice.[15] A few weeks later, she would be presenting *Christ in Concrete* at the Venice Film Festival. Suzanne Cloutier, a twenty-two-year-old Canadian actress with a delicate, Renaissance face, did a screen test for the part of Desdemona. Welles went to an exhibition on the European Recovery Program (aka Marshall Plan) signing the register, "With the gratitude of an American who loves Italy."[16] On August 8, he ran into Mac Liammóir and Edwards behind the Frezzaria, near St. Mark's Square. "How terrible to be broke," he said, hauling them off to the notoriously expensive Harry's Bar, only to disappear for another two weeks.

Mac Liammóir doesn't say what happened next, but the events can be reconstructed. Welles was working on some interiors in Scalera Studios on Giudecca Island. The economically strapped production company had received some funding from a mysterious Milan company called Mercury—in fact it was Welles's own company, and Scalera was confident he could weather the storm and perhaps even get back on track with the distribution of *Othello*. Meanwhile, the shots with Betsy Blair needed to be redone: Welles and the Scalera people worked day and night on the lighting and scenery (some of which Welles painted himself).

Mac Liammóir didn't just twiddle his thumbs, however. One evening he accosted a gondolier, who ended up in the Grand Canal, and the incident threatened to mar the reputation of the entire crew and cast. Welles hushed it all up with a fistful of dollars. "The gondoliers cost you lawyers' fees just to row across the canal anyway," he told Leaming—much more "if you knock them into the canal making forbidden love to them!"[17]

Othello's running costs from October 18, 1948, to August 20, 1949, alone amounted to over forty million lire.

In August 1949, Hoover received an anonymous letter from Paris, asking him to proceed against Welles for un-American activities. The letter was accompanied by a newspaper photo from December 8, 1947, that showed Welles dining with the Italian Communist leader Palmiro Togliatti. The FBI reopened the Welles file and began to poke around.

Some informants in Italy were contacted, and Hoover discovered that Welles had been trying to make a film in North Africa and that the crew had been sent away from Nassour Studios for lack of funds. In England, George Orwell wrote a list of 130 Communist sympathizers for the Foreign Office, which included Charlie Chaplin and Orson Welles—with a question mark beside their names.[18]

The FBI had no proof Welles was up to anything untoward. In fact, he seemed to be involved in a complicated costume production in out-of-the-way places, rather than plotting the downfall of the U.S. government. One of their informants, a joker—probably Italian—said he thought all Welles had ever been trying to do since he arrived in Italy was get together enough money to return to America. Ultimately, the agency couldn't do much to hurt Welles. After all, he lived abroad and could hardly be openly accused on the flimsiest of grounds. The head of the enquiry recommended that the filmmaker's name be removed from the Security Card Index. Hoover agreed, but told his agents to review the situation if Welles returned to America and got mixed up with the Communists.[19]

Shooting for *Othello* resumed on August 24 on the Grand Canal; a few kilometers away, that year's Venice Film Festival was about to get underway. There were tourists everywhere and it was baking hot, not the cold Venice Welles wanted. The first scene to be shot was Brabantio (Edwards) on the balcony as Iago (Mac Liammóir) and Roderigo (Coote) shout up to him from a gondola. As the actors and crew went about their business, the new Desdemona appeared, enchanting them with her long silk dress and flowing blonde hair.

If Cécile Aubry is included, Suzanne Cloutier, a twenty-two-year-old model, was the fourth actress hired by Welles to play Desdemona, although the press book of the restored film of 1992 (which appears to have been prepared after consultation with the actress) claims she was the eleventh. Cloutier had appeared in some films and plays with the Comédie-Française. Her fragility, light complexion, and elegance were the perfect foil for Othello's dark skin, brooding manner, rough looks, and burly physique. Suzanne was a woman of character, however, with a strong will, as Mac Liammóir noted in his diary on August 3, 1949: "bi-lingual, a lingering echo of Canada in her English here and there, but voice warm, flexible and soft; her face a Bellini with large grey eyes that bestow lingering and slightly *reproachful* glances, perfect nose and mouth . . . somewhere in her There is Steel. . . . [I] prophesy that Orson will have trouble with her (as she no doubt with him)."[20]

Welles wasted no time in trying to seduce her. Cloutier took advice from Lea Padovani and stoically prepared herself for the siege. Soon, however, Welles desisted, although he continuously teased and humiliated her on set, declaring himself, take after take, unsatisfied with her acting. Enigmatic, indestructible, she took it all, bursting into tears over and over again in private but showing not a chink of weakness to the gruff Welles, and thereby earning the admiration of the rest of the cast, who conferred upon her the nickname of "Iron Butterfly."

By now, the crew and technicians were close to exasperation. During summer and fall 1949, many came and went, according to the location and their other commitments. Tonino Delli Colli, for example, worked on the film for some time before quitting for "family reasons." "I made half of *Othello*," he said later. "But the film dragged on and I was getting married."[21] Cinematographers Alberto Fusi and Anchise Brizzi and their assistant, Oberdan Troiani, hung on. However, only Troiani managed to be philosophical about it all. "Welles didn't want a straight shot," he said:

> Always tilted, off axis, and I was the only one who could do it right. He'd shown me how. You get one element of the shot on axis and forget about the rest. Sure, it was hard work. . . . Welles used a Debrie camera, where you can see the shot only through the film; and with the red filter all you could see of Othello was his eyes. With the Mitchell camera it was even worse; Mitchells have viewfinders that are fine for long and medium shots but hopeless for closeups. All you could see was an ear or an eye. It took a quarter of an hour to get the thing right, because Welles, maybe, wanted a tower in the distance to be seen between two strands of hair. Move a bit to the left, a bit to the right—and the actor had to be absolutely motionless, barely breathe. Welles always came on set in the morning completely made up and with curly hair, but he never stood in front of the camera. I ended up blacker than him because his makeup came off on the lens. For Brizzi, *Othello* was a continual annoyance; he never agreed with this way of shooting. For him, when it was over, it was a relief. Welles wanted straight answers. Fusi and he argued all the time.
> "So?" Welles would say. "Was that OK?"
> "Fine," Fusi would reply. "Except . . ."
> "Except what? Do we print it or not?"
> "Yes, for me it was fine, except . . ."

And Welles would start shouting, "I'll shoot the whole goddamn film over again if I have to. Just tell me, was it good or not?"

"Yes, it was good, except . . ."

Sick of Welles's working methods, Fusi and Brizzi signed a contract to join the German set of *Amore e sangue* (Schatten über Neapel). "The first Saturday we were in Venice for the shooting," Troiani explained,

> Brizzi and Fusi bid Welles goodbye, partly because their contracts had expired. I get on the motor boat with the head of production and Welles, who starts to shout, "There they go! Cowards! They don't understand anything about the importance of this film. Only Troiani here has been honest!" I was contracted with Brizzi, however, so I had to leave, too. When I could get Papi alone I told him so, and he said I'd end up in the canal if I quit. So I stayed. I knew Welles would offer me the cinematography but I didn't want it. Welles was too changeable, never the same from one moment to the next, let alone from one day to the next.[22]

Troiani convinced Welles to hire Aldo Graziati, aka G. R. Aldo, the Franco-Italian cinematographer of Visconti's *La terra trema*. So frightened of Welles was Aldo that he would agree to join the crew only if Alvaro Mancori was also hired. Mancori had known Welles at the time of the affair with Lea Padovani, and Aldo's trusted assistant Nino Cristiani was part of the deal. While they worked in the studios on Giudecca Island, Troiani was sent to photograph Venice—for a documentary, Welles told him, but actually for locations to be cut into *Othello*.

Stimulated by the setting, Welles began to create under the curious gaze of journalists and passersby. Ennio Flaiano, covering the Venice Film Festival for *il Mondo*, met him behind St. Mark's Square. "The actor," Flaiano wrote, with less hostility than before, "was standing on one of those small bridges over the canals with a group of people, but he seemed absorbed, his eyes staring at the decorations on a façade, just like in Poe's beautiful story of Venice ["The Assignation"] and just as capable of throwing himself into the water to rescue a child or an idea. With his new whiskers, Orson Welles looks quite venerable."[23]

Bazin also bumped into him. In the first version of his famous monograph on Welles, the French critic portrays him affectionately as a chivalrous and kind man:

> It was August, in Venice, Campo dei Miracoli. I had gone to watch the shooting of *Othello*. I'd had some trouble locating them and their Elizabethan-style

equipment, hidden away in a back alley. I was there with some curious onlookers who hadn't a clue what was happening in front of them. Welles was sitting on an iron chair he'd borrowed from a nearby restaurant and was thinking deeply about something while waiting, who knows what for, as often happens in film-making. I can assure you that the scene that then unfolded was not put on for anyone's benefit. A woman was watching the shooting, her shopping basket tucked under one arm and a youngster in tow. Welles got up from his chair, as if he were on a bus or train, and gave her his seat.[24]

Journalists from the Festival came to see what was going on and were pleased to discover that Welles could now speak pretty passable Italian. Carlo Martini, from *Film,* met him outside the Danieli Hotel at two in the morning, a cat in his arms—Harry Lime in person.

"Do you like cats?" the journalist asked.

"'Very much. See? This one will soon be an actor' (and Welles laughed that wonderful, warm laugh of his). 'I want to do a prologue to my film. . . . Yes, a prologue to prepare the atmosphere: dawn in Venice, a wintery dawn. Venice slowly waking as if—a new Atlantis—it were rising out of the eternal depths of the sea. The canals: lazy, gray, quiet. The silence of a dawn in Venice. What better than to show silence than the stealth of a cat. Cats waking up and then, suddenly, the silence is broken by a woman screaming. Then silence once more. Then music from far off. Men and women going home after a night of revels. Weak torch lights that finally go out . . . and then the cats again: meowing, the sound of winter in Venice slowly coming out of slumber at daybreak.'"[25]

After the Grand Canal, the crew moved on to a location in front of the Doge's Palace, to shoot the dialogue between Iago and Roderigo, envious of Othello and his recent wedding. On August 28, Joseph Cotten and Joan Fontaine arrived from the festival on their way to shooting *September Affair.* Welles wanted his friend Cotten to be in at least one shot in the film, dressed as a senator. It would bring the film good luck, he thought. Fontaine, Welles's co-star in *Jane Eyre,* good-naturedly agreed to dress as a page boy. Sadly, there is no trace of either Cotton or Fontaine in the finished film.

Later that day Welles had Mac Liammóir endure a grueling sunset session filming the "I am not what I am" soliloquy, which he wanted to color with the oncoming darkness. Mac Liammóir forgot or flubbed his lines until the sun had set, angering Welles. The scene was completed the next afternoon after a full day's frenetic shooting. The crew then moved on to Torcello to shoot Desdemona comforted by Emilia and Iago egging Othello on to murder, and worked until the dead of night.

The crowds of onlookers were thinner than the year before, when Lea Padovani was the leading lady, and the local population was now used to seeing people in costume roaming the city. This was maliciously interpreted by *Film* as indifference: there were no more people at the shooting than generally stood behind a street artist drawing the Rialto Bridge, the newspaper informed its readers.

On September 4, after ten days' shooting in Venice, the cast and crew moved to Rome for the interior scenes, without completing the exteriors. Mac Liammóir did not say why. Maybe the Scalera Studio in Venice was ill equipped, or Welles just could not get Venice to look wintry. He may have been worried—if he kept everyone on in one of the world's most expensive tourist resorts throughout the high season—that he would run out of money before he could return at a more suitable time.

When Welles returned to Rome, *Cine Illustrato* felt the need to say that he had not been missed and to report that he was staying at the Grand Hotel and wore "a crumpled white jacket morning, afternoon, and evening, which evidently makes him look very artistic"; with his "thick beard" he "strides about Rome, frightening youngsters."[26]

He was hardly the charismatic figure of a year before. Càllari in *Cinema* rubbed salt into the wound: "The Italians in general and the Romans, in particular, knock false celebrities off their pedestals pretty fast" (meaning not only Welles but also, by now, Tyrone Power). Magniloquently, he added, "Here, only true celebrities survive."[27]

Welles had not returned to Rome to be a celebrity, but to finish a film, and that's what he set about doing immediately, using Scalera Studios after two o'clock, as he had for *Black Magic.* All Emilia's scenes were shot, including her death at Iago's hand, as well as the arrival of Lodovico and Othello slapping Desdemona. For the latter, Welles told Suzanne Cloutier to relax, since they would shoot the very last part of the scene the following afternoon; when she finally relaxed, Welles slapped her.

Actually the entire cast and crew had relaxed. Welles was in excellent form, the work was going ahead, and the money had not dried up. In the evenings, Welles entertained the actors and technicians with magic tricks. He asked Troiani for a 100-franc note; he then tore off a corner and burned it, only to retrieve the note—torn corner and all—from an orange on the table.

Slowly the crew was beginning to realize they were not dealing with a madman or an amateur, but a technically skilled director with a strong personal and aesthetic vision. Welles insisted on the utmost accuracy in shooting and often did a dozen, or two dozen, takes. They had been perplexed by the changes in set, location, and Desdemonas, and the chaos and confusion, but now they discovered Welles could be finicky to the nth degree or improvise solutions to problems as they arose. The camera wasn't perfectly steady? Put a bucket of water on it. For Othello's epileptic fit, Welles adopted an idea of Troiani's: the camera was tied to a big roller skate; Welles made it circle around himself by pushing it with a stick. As Troiani recalled in an interview, "We made the trolley and followed him as he approached Iago; he wanted the camera to follow him at exactly his speed and to stop precisely when he stopped. But it was impossible to coordinate; there was always a split-second delay, the trolley, and therefore the camera, made a tiny movement toward him. Welles first tried towing the trolley with some weird contraption, but that didn't work. So we did the scene again and this time, when he stopped, he moved the upper part of his body fractionally to compensate for the slight movement of the camera."[28]

The manic insistence on detail didn't always bring rewards and there were arguments with the crew. "For the theater Welles created the strangest things. One day," Troiani recounted,

> he wanted a six-meter-long track; the camera was to pull away over five minutes as Desdemona was singing a lullaby to Emilia. The audience wasn't supposed to notice that the field of vision was slowly widening. We needed to rig up a winch over a wheel, which we silenced with talcum powder. We did the take but Welles didn't use it in the final cut. Another time, Aldo refused to do what Welles wanted, he said it just wouldn't work. Welles was furious; "If you don't do this shot I'll get Troiani to do it," he said. Aldo just knew it would never get into the film. "Shoot the picture," Welles said. "I'll worry about what works and what doesn't. Nothing's impossible. I'll cut it if it doesn't work out." I went over to Aldo and said, "If you don't do the shot, I will. I've been with him for three years. If I refuse he'll sack you and me together." Aldo did the shot but things were never the same between them and, after a while, Welles got rid of him.[29]

On September 18 everything ground to a halt once again for lack of money. Welles tried to detain the Irish actors (who had yet to be paid) by promising them a *Julius Caesar* in spring, to be directed by Edwards and with Mac Liammóir as Brutus. After hesitating a few days the two actors returned to Dublin, hoping to be just in time for the new theater season. They promised to return to Italy, that "large and sumptuous Aviary" to finish the film. Mac Liammóir noted in his diary, "What has been really good about this latest stage of things has been that so much of the picture is now achieved that the idea of not going through to the end is surely out of the question."[30]

The hiatus was less than a month. On October 16, Papi wired the Irish actors, forcing them yet again to drop everything and come running. Welles was shooting in Tuscania, in the crypt of a decrepit eleventh-century church. The scene of Othello undressing in front of the mirror, assisted by Iago, was also shot in the underworld, when Mac Liammóir and the others returned.

All that was missing now was the scene of Desdemona's murder and Othello's death. Things between Welles and Cloutier were tense. Coincidentally or not, she was soft and he was rough. "You great, big cosmic mass of uncompromising egocentricity," he called her in public, to which Cloutier replied bashfully that all Welles was lacking was "l'amour d'une brave femme."

The scene of Desdemona's murder was shot in Viterbo, inside Santa Maria della Salute, a deconsecrated thirteenth-century church that Alexander Trauner transformed into a solemn and ominous-looking nuptial chamber where Othello, before falling onto the bed with his dead bride, asks Cassio and the other onlookers to tell his story: "Set you down this."

As he was shooting Othello's death, Welles had the idea of saying his last words looking up at the ceiling where the audience was supposed to imagine a peephole. Welles wanted to give his spectators the idea of drawing aside the cover of the peephole—a kind of gigantic, divine eye—to look down on the tragic scene. When Othello dies, the peephole cover falls back into place. Welles almost certainly got the idea from Mantegna's fifteenth-century painting of the nuptial chamber in the Castello di San Giorgio in Mantova, commissioned by Ludovico Gonzaga for his bride, Barbara of Brandenburg. The extraordinary trompe l'oeil of the painting creates a fake peephole in the ceiling, through which cherubs appear to be looking down from the bluest heavens. Welles asked Troiani to make a tiny peephole-like shutter close to the camera lens, which a technician could open and close with a simple control mechanism. Perched on a platform, the actors would have made the movement of opening and closing a life-size peephole that didn't actually exist.[31]

Welles asked Troiani to make him quite a few models. For example, all the Venetian ships were miniature models created by Troiani, and a sailor seen clearly on board one of the ships was, in fact, a technician on the roof of the Scalera Studio restaurant filmed with the model in closeup. The lances held aloft by an array of soldiers were small splinters in thimbles on each finger of a hand; a sheet flapping next to a basin of water was a sail on the Mediterranean Sea, and so on. Most of these ingenious, money-saving devices are unnoticeable in the film. About this time Welles wrote a preface to a book on cinematic illusion, in which he says, "There is no place for trickery in films . . . and it isn't a question of enlisting the complicity of the spectator . . . [f]or the simple reason that a camera is a recording device. . . . If a magician on stage makes an egg disappear, the audience wonders *how he makes it vanish*. In films, if an egg disappears, the audience wonders *how it was made to vanish*. Past tense. That's the difference between theater and cinema, trickery and magic. . . . Tricks in the cinema are devices to show reality and are entirely without fascination; they're meant to go unobserved."[32]

The shooting of Desdemona's death scene continued for a few days. At the climax of the scene, after several hours' work, Cloutier was not able to cry. The crew tried onions and smelling salts, but in the end the tension and frustration made her tearful. Mac Liammóir noted ironically in his diary that, in the end, "she did it unaided."[33]

The cast and crew were working all hours, every day. As they were working to kill Desdemona, Welles shot a scene with Iago on the steps of the Papal Palace in Viterbo (a reverse shot of one photographed in Morocco in July) and probably some other scenes in Orvieto, a few kilometers to the north of Viterbo. Welles was a demanding director but set a good example, as Mac Liammóir noted in his journal on October 21: "O has no time for sleep and never seems to need any."[34]

As a result, Welles almost collapsed a week later. The doctors told him to rest for a few weeks, and not to smoke or drink coffee. Welles pretended to comply, simply moving the set away from Viterbo. On October 31, they were all back in Venice, where, according to Mac Liammóir, Welles told them "there was no money for anyone, anywhere, and ordering *fine champagne* and delicacies all round."[35]

The following day they were shooting in St. Mark's Square and outside the Doge's Palace. To complete the scenes with Cassio and Lodovico, Michael Laurence and Nicholas Bruce were recalled. On November 2, a crowd of tourists and onlookers was kept from using Ponte della Paglia to leave the balustrade overlooking Riva degli Schiavoni free. Welles applied black eyeliner to the eyes and nose of Hilton Edwards as groups of extras, dressed as senators, waited for everything to be ready. It was an overcast day but when, unexpectedly, the sun peeped out from behind the clouds, Welles immediately invented a new shot, one of the most beautiful in the whole film, using the pigeons he otherwise hated. A reporter for *il Gazzettino-Sera* described the scene thus: "Welles suddenly brightened up with the sky and scurried off into a small flock of pigeons, feeding them with grains of corn, attracting the attention of the passersby. In the place of the previous five or six, now hundreds of pigeons arrived and, as they did, Welles shouted, 'Action!' The cameras rolled and the spotlights threw beams of light onto the figure struggling with the birds. Wardens stopped people from crossing over. On the brightly lit bridge, as Brabantio and Othello's followers passed by, the frightened pigeons took off in all directions. "Magnificent!" Welles cried. "Absolutely magnificent!"[36]

Two days later, the crew moved on to Ca' d'Oro. It was a cold, damp day. The extras hopped up and down to keep warm and the actors hid in the porter's lodges of the museums, as a numbed Suzanne Cloutier tried for the sixth or seventh time to walk up the steps from the courtyard to the raised gallery of the palace. In the grip of the freezing cold, she pressed one hand against her stomach, while the other was held by a stand-in for Othello. After a few moments Welles stopped the camera because the stand-in was walking clumsily. The *Gazzettino* reporter saw what happened next: "Welles was berating the stand-in but Suzanne Cloutier thought he was yelling at her. She replied in fiery French that she was sick and tired of his outbursts and temper tantrums, that he treated her worse than a novice, to which Welles replied in somewhat less refined English. The crew held its breath as the scene unfolded, Desdemona giving as good as she got. Cloutier stormed off the set. Then the little rebel was seen on the second floor, under a pearl-shaped vault, her elbows on the balcony, her head in her hands, sobbing her eyes out."[37]

The incident shows not only how tense were the relations between the director and leading lady but also Welles's determination to shoot the film, and complete it, exactly as he wanted. He had returned to Venice in late autumn for its melancholic, fading light. He had told Todisco that was the light he loved most, not only for itself but because it enhanced the spirit of the film.

Work continued until November 11. The unit occasionally bumped into two other film crews then in Venice, with some of Welles's former assistants. Anchise Brizzi and Alberto Fusi were working on *Il ladro di Venezia* (Thief of Venice), an Italo-American production, and Tonino Delli Colli was the cinematographer for Scalera's co-production of *La rivale dell'imperatrice* (The empress's rival).

Welles and Trauner headed for Perugia to look for locations for the Senate, leaving Waszynski and a cameraman, American George Fanto, in Venice to film some segue material and reverse angles.

Mac Liammóir did not say so, but in all likelihood money had run out again. Accounts used to justify Fox's payment show that between August 20 and November 10, 50,463,305 lire, more or less Welles's fee for *The Black Rose,* had been spent. Production ground to a halt for the fourth time.

Welles left for France. At the end of November 1949 he and the cast were on the French Riviera. He continued to book them into the most luxurious hotels and to keep them hanging on with prospects of a *Julius Caesar* (and a *Salomé* and a *Carmilla*), or a European theater tour performing Shakespeare and Wilde.

When no money could be found, the cast drifted away and Welles flew to Paris to present *The Third Man* for European release. In Italy, Reed's film received some favorable reviews but the reception was generally condescending. Like a broken record, Mario Gromo spoke of "excessive effects, the wish to surprise,"[38] and the usual deputy at *Cinema* criticized, "Orson Welles is unable to control his mimicry and seems to infect with his own lack of expression and meaning everything he touches. He is an actor who seems to be perpetually admiring himself in the mirror. His only good scene is when he first appears."[39]

Cinemagoers in Italy and the rest of Europe were at odds; the film was a box-office smash and its reputation was indissolubly associated with Welles's presence. His famous remark about the Renaissance and Switzerland sparked an amusing incident in Geneva, where Reed was given a cuckoo clock at the premiere, accompanied by a note that read, "No hard feelings." In Paris the zither became fashionable. Whenever Welles went to a nightclub or restaurant, the orchestra interrupted what they were playing to perform Karas's theme music. Barzini wrote, "Orson is never allowed to be himself. No sooner had he stopped being Rita Hayworth's ex-husband than he became Harry Lime."[40]

Feted and pampered, Welles enjoyed his sudden popularity, but the French newspapers continued to ask him when he would finish *Othello*. Hopefully before Christmas, he replied, taking advantage of the news coverage to explain that it was hard to find a backer: "I'm the worst businessman in America," he said, "and I'm forced to spend 95 percent of my time discussing business!"[41]

Alvaro Mancori

"Every now and then he would shout, 'Traitors!'"

ROME, JUNE 14, 2005

There were at least five cinematographers (including their assistants) on *Othello,* as shown in the credits. Some were fired by Welles, and some abandoned the film when it got into trouble. Others preferred not to be credited for tax reasons.

Today it is hard to know who shot what. Many sequences comprise shots from different cinematographers, and Mac Liammóir's account isn't complete. No mention is made of camera operators working with Waszynski while Welles was on another set. Certainly, in October 1948, the man behind the camera was Alberto Fusi, sometimes assisted by Tonino Delli Colli. In spring 1949, Fusi was helped by Anchise Brizzi, Oberdan Troiani, and George Fanto. When Fusi and Brizzi quit, their place was taken by G. R. Aldo and Alvaro Mancori, with Nino Cristiani acting as assistant. The three men also worked in Scalera Studios in Rome and possibly in Tuscania and Viterbo (where Brizzi briefly reappeared—he is mentioned by Mac Liammóir in his diary entry of October 17, 1949) and again in Venice. After the departure of Mancori and Aldo, the cinematography was the work of Fanto and Troiani, the latter being one of the few to have worked on practically the entire film. Alvaro Mancori (1923–2011), later a highly reputed cinematographer in his own right, is not included in the film credits. Until recently his work on *Othello* was unknown.

ALVARO MANCORI: I'd say ten or twelve cameramen worked on *Othello,* one of the reasons I withheld my name from the credits. I worked mainly in Scalera Studios in Rome, but I started a little earlier, on location. I was a sort of technical assistant for Welles; we sketched locations we hadn't yet found.

How did you meet Welles?

AM: I was the assistant cinematographer on *Black Magic.* I worked on the scenes in the Quirinale. Only someone like Scalera could have persuaded the authorities to let us shoot there. The crew treated the palace with respect. There were guards everywhere. You had to come to work with your shoes polished, you weren't allowed to rest your jacket over the back of an armchair, and if you sat down you were in trouble!

What was Welles like?

AM: Shrewd, intelligent, extraordinary. Full of little manias. He always blamed someone else—the actors, the stagehands, the cameraman. He treated actors terribly, and that includes Lea Padovani, with whom he was quite fierce.

So you were there when she was still in the cast.

AM: Yes, the film started up with her and me. Welles and Padovani can't have hit it off sexually because they were both always a bundle of nerves. She wasn't a kid, of course, and about a third of the way through the shooting she thought she had him in her grip and began to make him suffer. One day when she wasn't there he said, "Get this scene ready. I'll be back straight away." He went to the hotel where he found her in bed with someone on the production staff.

Giorgio Papi.

AM: Exactly. I didn't want to say who.

It seems everyone knew about him except Welles.

AM: Well, he had his suspicions because the time he said he'd come straight back he went directly to their hotel room, so he must have known what was going on. "Whooooooooore!" he shouted. And everyone tried to calm him down. What could we say to him? She likes him, she likes others, that's what life is like . . . "I've had the most beautiful women in the world and no one has betrayed me like this!" Padovani offended his pride and vanity. The strong and successful man made to suffer by a nonentity, a silly little girl. Well, Papi was a handsome man. Welles fired them both and the film resumed, as so often happened with that film. Another actress arrived, from England, a beauty, Suzanne Cloutier . . .

Not immediately. After several months.

AM: Yes, we wrote down the scenes and then reconstructed them . . . It was a lot of work, all this starting and stopping . . .

How did you start work again on the film?

AM: At the time I was working with G. R. Aldo on *Domani è un altro giorno* (Tomorrow is another day) by Léonide Moguy, starring Annamaria Pierangeli, among others. Aldo asked me if I wanted to come and work on *Othello,* because he thought he would not be able to work easily with Welles. "You be the Director of Photography together with me," he said. "I'll do one thing, you another." Why not? Aldo was fabulous. Visconti had taken him to Rome for *La terra trema* and he won a Silver Ribbon straight away. Genina then asked him to work on *Cielo sulla palude* (Sky over marshland) and he won another Silver Ribbon. He was an exceptionally gifted cinematographer.

Why did he think it would be difficult to work with Welles?

AM: Welles had fired so many already. In Morocco he got rid of three. He stopped the film and waited for the replacements. Aldo thought he would get the same treatment, particularly because so much for him was new . . . Photography is the business of two people, the camera operator and the person who does the lighting. The director is closer to the cinematographer; he looks through the lens and sees what the cinematographer sees. He can check what is going on. With the lighting man he generally speaks only a little, because he doesn't understand the job. Aldo didn't really know how to look through the camera, so he was happy if I came along with him. Welles was also happy to have me behind the camera because he'd been told I did a good job. But Welles was always on the alert. You couldn't tell him he'd made a mistake, that the shot needed redoing . . .

Was there a script or did you tend to improvise?

AM: No, Welles had everything down in detail. He loved Shakespeare, the text, and he wouldn't allow the slightest change. The film was entirely scripted. The Anglo-Saxons considered him an expert in English literature and he was proud of that reputation. However, he wrote three or four scripts. He wrote, rewrote, threw away, started again. He spent five or six months in Morocco and when he came back he shot everything over again, because he preferred Aldo's cinematography. He wanted to rebuild Morocco in the Venetian studios. He threw away the negatives and we started again. But it was very difficult to reproduce the Moroccan light in the studio. Scaccianoce, Scalera's architect, was worried about the spotlights. We needed to get some more in from Rome. So the film was endless! And there was always an argument, because Welles was exasperatingly precise; he framed and reframed. The stagehands and electricians stood by because for every camera placement something needed to be changed, there was something in the frame that shouldn't be there—the lens screen, mini-projector, track . . . something. We had to stay on our toes. In one scene there were about thirty camera positions. Welles stopped, spoke to someone, turned to someone else, they spoke, the tracking shot needed to start backward, then go forward, then backward again: there were no zooms back then, you had to do it all on the track. It needed to be very accurate. Welles looked at everything. He had 360-degree vision. The stagehands wrote 1, 2, 3 on the floor, but he didn't want any chalk marks on the ground . . . A real stickler. The rehearsals went fine but then when we came to actual filming, you heard the motor, silence . . . everyone was tense . . . He made two or three movements, as in closeup, but I could see through the camera that he got it wrong; instead of moving with one leg he moved with the other and he was off camera. He realized and shouted, "Stop! Alvaro, the camera wobbled," he said. I reply, "Orson, the camera was perfectly still. But if you say it wobbled, then it must have wobbled . . ."

How was the relationship between Welles and Cloutier?

AM: The first few days . . . Welles had the habit of nibbling pumpkin and he would spit the seeds at her as she was doing her part. He knew what the camera would and wouldn't pick up. He wanted her to speak perfect Shakespearean English while he spat at her, the poor woman. And then he would say, "That's no good. Do it again." And he would do it for her. Perfectly. She used to come to me in the evenings to cry, and I said, "Either you walk out or you carry on, but if you continue this is what it'll be like. Nobody can fire *him*." One day she was told that her mother in London was unwell. "Alvaro, I'm leaving," she told me. I said, "Better tell Welles first, otherwise he'll look for you." She went to Welles and said she had to go to see her sick mother, her dying mother, just for a day or two. Welles replied, "You're not moving from here, you're going nowhere." I looked at the script. I knew there were no scenes with her for the next few days. "You're OK for three or four days," I told her. She leaves. Welles says nothing, doesn't look for her, but goes to London, too, where he has some business. He walks into a restaurant and there she is! She bursts into tears, poor thing. So he walks over to her and starts beating his fists on the table. "I told you not to leave Rome, who told you to come?" "I told Alvaro, and Alvaro . . . ," she begins. Welles continues to pummel the table, to push it towards her and she goes on crying. From another table, Peter Ustinov stands up and comes over. He told me how it went later. He goes over to Welles and says, "Enough. You're making her cry. A gentleman doesn't do such a thing . . ." They argue and the next day Cloutier is back in Rome. Something serious must have happened. "Alvaro, I had to tell him you let me go." "Holy Mother of God. Now he'll fire me," I tell her. When I see Welles he looks me up and down. "I've got a bone to pick with you," he says. "Go ahead," I reply. "Get it off your chest." "You did something that went against my wishes. I had said no, because . . . I know why I didn't want her to go!" I was ready to pack my things and go. He looked me straight in the eye, expecting me to avert my gaze but and I looked back at him. And that was that. He didn't fire me. I had a reputation in the film world and didn't accept criticism lightly. Papi, of all people, told me to stand my ground.

Why didn't Welles fire Papi?

AM: He got him away from Venice and kept him on only in the Rome office. He couldn't have been sacked; he knew everything about the film. But from then on, it was as if he and Welles didn't know each other. They became total strangers. Then Ustinov came to Venice to visit Cloutier and I realized there was now something between them. In London, Ustinov was everyone's darling; the queen loved him; he was in Buckingham Palace as often as he was in his changing room. So Welles tried to win him over. He wanted to make peace. Maybe he didn't know who he was when they argued in the restaurant. But Ustinov held up his hand and said, "It's better if you keep your distance. Better for you, not for me." That evening we ate in a restaurant and Ustinov was there, in the same restaurant; when one arrived, the other left. When one got up the other rose from his table. They were like two Neapolitan comedians on the stage.

So it was because of you that Ustinov and Cloutier met and married.

AM: Yes, I suppose so. They had children but later separated. Years later I went to Sicily to make a film for Fregonese with Ustinov. One day he asked me to take him to the airport. When Suzanne Cloutier got off the plane she hugged me, not him. "Alvaroooo!" "You know each other?" Ustinov said. "I made that film in Venice . . ." He didn't remember. Then he came to Rome and he and his wife rented a villa with swimming pool on the Appia Antica, near Mastroianni's place. He came round to see me here at home. And he took me to dinner in London with Her Majesty, no less.

Cloutier may have cried quite often but she was far from a helpless little girl.

AM: Yes, far from it. She looked at Welles with utter hatred and he didn't forgive her. I think he would have liked to hit her but he stopped himself. They were always at each other's throats and I often had to step in to keep them apart. Of course I took her side, not his. When Cloutier told Ustinov that Welles used to spit at her while she was acting, he followed him around the set and tried to hit him with a chair. Welles had a terrible character. Frightening if riled. A bully. If he bellowed at you he did no more than that. But if he was quiet . . . watch out. A strange animal indeed.

I have the idea that he put people to the test.

AM: I dare say.

And when you passed the test . . .

AM: He let you be, otherwise you were in big trouble.

Do you remember any particularly difficult scenes for the film?

AM: The last one, constructed in the Scalera studios in Rome. With huge scaffolding, right up to the ceiling.

And a hole at the top.

AM: Exactly. The dolly was to move down slowly over twenty meters —there was no zoom—and stop at the level of Othello dead on the bed.

Didn't you have a crane?

AM: No, no crane. We had a pulley and rail system rigged to the scaffolding. We had to keep the rails in place, because there were joints and the camera wobbled. At that height it was very noticeable, so we used talcum powder to smooth the dolly over the rail . . .

A strange idea.

AM: Yes, but it worked. With the cameraman on the dolly and an electrician holding a lamp, the wheels moved to the edge of the rail and began to squeak. It was one hell of a job. Welles was extremely tense, but he made us spill blood *throughout* the entire shooting of the film. I made one film with him and would never have done another. But I managed to let off steam somehow, whereas Aldo kept it all in. He said, "Keep calm," and I would say, "You keep calm." We Romans have seen it all. However, Orson was a genius. His framing drove you crazy but was truly beautiful . . . And when everything went well he was adorable and you could do no wrong. He would tell us to be on set at nine o'clock the next morning and then arrive at six in the evening. Stagehands, electricians, the entire crew, just waiting for Welles. He knew we'd be angry so he came surrounded by women and someone playing the accordion! What can you say to someone like that?

He tried to win you over?

AM: Of course, because he knew it was his fault. The women danced, kissed your cheeks . . . and when one of us smiled he would get us to start work.

Do you remember Waszynski? At the beginning he was credited as co-director.

AM: Nooo, he was an assistant director, though, a close friend of Welles's.

Do you know anything about the idea of including Lollobrigida or De Sica in the cast?

AM: Nothing about Lollobrigida, but there were words about De Sica from time to time. They needed an Italian cast for financial reasons. Some extras had been hired from the Centro Sperimentale. They were told to sit and wait, paid, and sent home. The only Italian actor was Lea Padovani, fired by Welles.

Did you know Mac Liammóir?

AM: I saw him in his makeup but never spoke to him. I don't speak English. A good actor.

Where did you shoot in Venice?

AM: On the Giudecca and in the church in Torcello.

Did Welles ever do any magic tricks?

AM: Yes, but as soon as he started I walked away. After work, I had things to do, whereas he wanted to entertain. "Wait," he would say, and I would answer, "I'll be right back," and leave. He enjoyed magic.

He liked to be admired, perhaps.

AM: That is what he most enjoyed and what he tried to achieve all the time. He wanted people to think he was good. Of course, he was good. I would pull his leg, but there was no doubting his ability.

What did you learn from working with Welles?

AM: Framing. Camera movements, which with him were subtle and gentle . . . He got us to repeat them maybe twenty times but he knew what he wanted. I learned to be precise with him. Because if you didn't get it right, he would look at the rushes and then remind you of how he'd wanted you to do it. You'd moved the lens screen, say. There were always arguments over the rushes.

How many people looked at them?

AM: Welles, the director of photography, the assistant directors and assistant cameramen, and sometimes the editor, Lucidi, but only toward the end. Never the actors.

How did Welles manage to keep the crew together after months of interruption?

AM: He didn't. There were always new people. I started in Venice, with Aldo, when the others refused to go.

You never went to Morocco?

AM: No. There, the camera operators were English and French. I don't even know their names.

Anchise Brizzi?

AM: He did, yes. But he was in Rome when they did the screen tests. At the beginning. Then they went to Morocco and Brizzi didn't want to go. He was a superb cameraman and had understood what kind of man Welles was.

George Fanto?

AM: I don't know.

Alberto Fusi?

AM: I think he did go to Morocco, if I'm not mistaken.

Oberdan Troiani?

AM: He took my place at the end of the film in Scalera Studios in Rome. Maybe he was in Morocco, too. The crew went to Morocco three or four times in all.

Tonino Delli Colli?

AM: One of the best in Italy. He was with Brizzi at the beginning, I think.

How did Welles manage to put together so many shots from so many cameramen? How did he keep the light uniform?

AM: Orson told us what lighting he wanted . . . He preferred three-quarter light. In Morocco he wanted violent beams of light. He put Vaseline on his face so it shone and you could see the pores. His eyes bulged. He wanted Aldo because he did three-quarter lighting well. I was a little calmer but also did that kind of lighting.

Had Welles seen Visconti's La terra trema?

AM: He'd seen it, and the film by Genina, and the one we did with Moguy.

Did you speak Italian with him?

AM: A little Italian and a little French. The others all spoke English. He had learned some Italian, especially how to swear.

What did he think of the Italians?

AM: He didn't say, but it was clear he wasn't very enthusiastic or trusting. Every now and then he would shout, "Traitors!" And we would tell him to fuck off in Italian. "You don't tell me to fuck off," he'd say, and we'd reply, "Then don't call us traitors."

Did you see the completed Othello?

AM: I saw it because as director of photography I had to go to the development and print plant. Welles asked me to go and "put in the lights" because I hail from that type of plant.

Did you like the result?

AM: Yes. An extraordinary film. Moving, excellent, tough, wonderful scenes. The painters were all from Scalera. Welles loved them dearly because they were good at their jobs. He painted the shooting plates day and night, too. It was a very difficult film, partly because of Welles's character, partly because of lack of money and other situations. But it was a complicated film anyway. He didn't always manage to pay us on time. *Othello* made Scalera bankrupt. Scalera, who built the roads during Fascism, millionaires, it wasn't easy to bankrupt that family . . .

But they were already in serious difficulties.

AM: They were always in difficulties, millionaires in difficulties . . .

Why didn't you finish the film with Welles?

AM: I had other commitments. I'd promised Gentilomo I'd make *Atto di accusa* with him. The producers, Carpentieri and Donati, begged me. They started with an English cinematographer. Gentilomo fired him and then I arrived. The film starred Marcello Mastroianni, a friend, and Lea Padovani, who behaved as if nothing had happened . . . Aldo finished the scene at the Scalera studios and quit. We left at about the same time. Aldo was angry with me for not following him, but you have to start somewhere, and *Atto di accusa* was my big break . . .

Why did Aldo quit?

AM: It was hard working with Welles. Aldo was fascinated by him. He was also good at his job, but directors feared Aldo and his poor expertise . . . you know, if you don't know what you're doing with a camera, the framing, the camera positions . . .

But Welles understood the camera.

AM: He certainly did. He was extremely precise, a technician, a brain. In the Debrie there's a mirror in front that opens and closes when you change the lens and in the darkness the person lit up is reflected in the mirror. Out of the corner of his eye, Welles looked at this image as he was delivering his lines to make sure the framing was correct.

Why are you not credited?

AM: Taxes. I had too many films out. I made a pretty penny with Welles and I didn't care if my name wasn't in the credits. We made three hundred films a year in Italy at that time, so I always had work. Not being credited damaged me professionally because Welles's film was important and I would have got the same recognition as Aldo, but I didn't want to pay the taxes. Make just one famous film and the taxman is after you for the rest of your life.

Maybe you also thought the film would never be finished?

AM: We were all convinced of that, everyone in the crew. Even the makeup people.

Welles didn't scare anyone in Italy, it seems, with his reputation.

AM: Robert Taylor made some great films, but he was a laughing stock in Italy. Rome is like that. Even Jesus Christ, after a few days in Piazza Navona or Campo de' fiori, is a nobody. Welles was soon out of fashion and the photographers began to ignore him. They'd moved on to Richard Burton and Elizabeth Taylor.

11

Blessed and Damned

"Why do the Creation?"
"It's in the Bible, Mr. Behoovian."
"In the Bible perhaps, but not in the budget."

—*The Unthinking Lobster*

Edmond Tenoudji, a French Algerian producer, came to the rescue, investing twelve million francs in exchange for the French distribution rights to *Othello*. Production resumed on January 31 in Mogador. "Strange sense of eternity in relation to film of *Othello* overcame me as we alighted yet again in Casablanca," Mac Liammóir noted in his diary entry of January 20/21, 1950.[1]

The chief cinematographer was first Alvaro Mancori, then G. R. Aldo, and Fanto soon after, although many of the shots were the work of Oberdan Troiani: "Aldo gave up after a while because he just wasn't up for it. He paid no attention to what had been shot by the two camera operators before and didn't want to shoot as Welles told him. They argued. At that point I had to do things my way.... Fanto had been with Welles for a long time; he was a kind of secretary and cameraman."[2]

Alexander Trauner and Michał Waszynski had also jumped ship, replaced by a new art director, James Allan, and a young assistant director, Patrice Dally. Of course, the cast needed to be recalled. If someone was busy, Welles improvised. "Every time you see someone with his back turned or with a hood over his head, you can be sure that it's a stand-in," Welles explained.[3]

In Mogador, Welles finally managed to finish some dialogue between Othello and Iago, and shoot Othello's epileptic seizure. Some
connecting shots were done in the chateau in Safi. The biggest job was
shooting inside a huge fifteenth-century stone cistern built in the Portuguese heart of the city of Mazagan. It had a hole at the top, like the ceiling above Othello's nuptial chamber. For days on end the crew breathed
in the fetid air of the tank, their feet in a few inches of Venice-seeming
water, filming fight scenes with stand-ins for Iago, Cassio and Roderigo.
Welles had the water blacked with aniline and enthusiastically threw
buckets of the stuff over the walls until Troiani had the better idea of
spattering the stagnant waters with sand.

Every now and then, Welles disappeared. One day he told the crew
he was going to Portugal and left Troiani a detailed list of scenes to
shoot in Mogador, three and a half typed pages in imperfect Italian,
accompanied by photos and screen tests on which Welles had drawn
the positions of the actors and the effects he wanted to achieve. The
instructions were extremely clear in terms of camera movements and
additional observations:

> Cannons firing from the walls, as already established. . . . This scene should look
> like sunrise/sunset. Dawn that looks like sunset or vice versa. Suggest shooting
> morning and late afternoon. Second scene: shot down the tower. Use a 40 if that
> was the lens used for the two photos I've marked and enclosed here. . . . The grass
> along the walls must be pulled out and nine or ten soldiers placed there, one or
> two marching slowly up and down but not ostentatiously. . . . If there is a wind-
> less day, remove the flags from the standards because they would look ridiculous
> without wind. The camera doesn't move from Othello to the castle but from the
> castle, through the wall, to Othello: the opposite of what would seem logical. . . .
> Hand-held camera following the flight of seagulls for idea of delirium. . . . Shot of
> cannons firing and Othello rising to his feet after epileptic fit: use English film.

Welles concluded, in threateningly large capital letters, "DON'T FORGET
THE CANNONS. DON'T FORGET THE CANNONS."[4]

Iago's torment was still left to shoot. Shakespeare leaves his fate uncertain, having Lodovico say, "To you, lord governor / Remains the cen-
sure of this hellish villain; / The time, the place, the torture: O, enforce
it!" Welles had Iago put in a cage, hoisted on high for the birds to peck at.

Where did the idea come from? He told Bogdanovich it was taken
from the death of Abd el-Krim, head of the Arab insurrection, who was

caged and exhibited to the rebel forces on the back of a donkey. But the very first inspiration may have come from a scene in *Prince of Foxes*, in which Orsini is told: "Tomorrow you shall be exposed in a cage on the castle tower, there to remain as a spectacle and a warning, until your bones drop apart."

In all, three cages were built: one miniature, one medium sized, and one life-size. The smaller versions were used to prefigure Iago's punishment and death. Poor Mac Liammóir was chained around the neck and pulled this way and that by various extras across a Mogador square for a day and a half. The final punishment was shot in the port of Mazagan, where Mac Liammóir was hoisted and lowered repeatedly in the largest cage, provoking continual applause and laughter in a group of onlookers nearby.

On March 7, Welles and Mac Liammóir shot the scene of Iago provoking Othello to paroxysms of jealousy with a false report of Cassio's bragging about sleeping with Desdemona ("With her, on her, what you will"). In the scene—a long tracking shot, as Mac Liammóir described it—the characters walk and pause, then walk on again under a roof of slats and branches, their faces cut by beams of sunlight and strips of shade, while the actors needed to step gingerly over an intricate network of tracks. Seven takes were required before Welles was satisfied, after which he hugged Mac Liammóir and told him, after a year of shooting, that he was now an out-of-work actor.

Mac Liammóir's journal ends with a note on an additional week's work in Perugia to shoot the Senate scene and the hope that he would be able to team up with Welles again, whether in Ireland or on the European theater tour or even at a festival to be organized in Vatican City. He and Hilton Edwards breathed a sigh of relief and flew back to Dublin.

Mac Liammóir may have finished his job, but that was not the only reason his journal entries run dry at this point. He evidently didn't want to record the excruciating months that followed, in which he was forced to contact Welles over and over again for his pay. He and Edwards had been treated to the best hotels in Morocco, France, and Italy, but otherwise had not received a penny. They had also given up two theater seasons for Welles's Shakespearean adventure and the film was far from finished. It would be another year and a half before *Othello* saw the light of day. Welles was unable to go to Perugia even for the one week required because he had run out of money again. Everything came to a halt for a fifth time, with just a few shots remaining.

In less than two years, Welles had spent everything he had earned from *Prince of Foxes, The Third Man,* and *The Black Rose;* he had sold distribution rights for *Othello* in Italy (to Scalera) and France (to Tenoudji) and now wanted to sell them in America and England to the highest bidder, so it was time to go back to the only person who had given him a hand, Darryl Zanuck.

Legend has it that Welles boarded a taxi in Rome and told the driver to go to Cap d'Antibes on the French Riviera, where he arrived at four in the morning and paid an astronomical fare. In the hotel, without further ado, he asked to speak to Zanuck, waited for him, hugged him, and— they say—got down on his knees. "Only you can help me," he is supposed to have said, "I've nearly finished *Othello* but haven't paid the cast."

Zanuck caved in and ordered his people to prepare a sack full of money—but not out of the goodness of his heart, of course. In return Twentieth Century Fox would receive 50 percent of the distribution rights in the United States and British Commonwealth. The contract was signed by Fox, represented by Francis L. Hartley, and Orson Welles Productions on March 28 at the Hotel Eden in Rome. The 195 million lire was to be paid from Fox's Italian account at the Banca d'America e d'Italia, which involved the usual bureaucratic entanglements.

A few days later Papi submitted the application to Direzione Generale della Cinematografia. It specified that a further ten weeks' shooting was needed: four in Perugia, "in the Town Hall, Notaries Room, and in some squares and streets," two at Scalera Studios, "where the construction of a Castle will be constructed [sic]," two in Pavia for "interiors and the Certosa exteriors," and two more in Venice.[5] Mac Liammóir said one more week, the application said ten. Welles had probably played down the problems to the Irish actor and played them up to the bureaucrats— unless, in the light of the agreement with Zanuck, he changed his mind and extended the shooting from one to ten weeks.

Meanwhile Orson Welles Productions slid one more step down the ladder of prestige: from the Excelsior in Via Veneto to the Hotel Boston to the Eden and now to an anonymous address—Via dell'Oca 27, in care of a phantom company, Arcadia Film; later still he used Scalera Studios as his address. Papi dutifully produced an estimate of additional costs, totaling 216,295,000 lire. The Ministry of Foreign Trade was not to be railroaded so easily and objected to the director's fees (first 20, then emended to 30 million lire). Papi was obliged to produce receipts and documents for costs of over seventeen million lire between August and October 1949 (salaries, severance pay, transportation, costumes, and sundries), in addition to the 50 million he had already accounted for. Then he remembered a further 10 million for the use of Scalera Studios, making debts of 27 million. He said 60 percent of the film still needed to be shot and no fewer than ten weeks were required, as the functionaries could see from the revised script Papi enclosed. He explained that Welles's fee also included board and lodging in Italy for the shooting and the start of the editing. Since Welles was producer, director, and actor the sum was certainly not excessive. Other sums had been included "logically on the generous side" in the event of delays or price increases. The 195 million the production company was asking for would be used to pay off old debts (costs from October 1948 to August 1949, theoretically already paid out of the fees from *Prince of Foxes* and *The Third Man*).

The correspondence between the parties (including the Italian Ministry of Foreign Trade), shows that the release of funds was in doubt until the very last minute, attracting the attention of the director general of cinematography himself, Nicola De Pirro. He wrote to Luigi Attilio Jaschi—the man who could open or close the purse strings—at the Foreign Exchange Department of the Ministry of Foreign Trade.

The end of his letter—probably decisive for the release of funds—is revealing, since it indicates esteem for the director but also the prevailing sense that he was a spendthrift, somehow responsible even for *Black Magic*'s going over budget: "Given the amount of work already done, whether you look at the costs already sustained or the estimate of future expenses, in light of Welles's costly direction—which, it should be said, in the case of *Black Magic*, involved the use of 120,000 meters of negatives—and the time still required to complete shooting, the sums indicated seem to correspond to actual needs. The largest items are 32 million for Welles, whose multiple functions and caliber through two years of work certainly justify the expense . . . [and t]he hire of studios, construction of sets, art direction and so on, amount to 80 million, a sum that is required to meet the tastes of foreign, especially American, filmgoers. In the light of the above I would be grateful if you could see to it that any reservations about the application are set aside and deal with the matter with benevolence, releasing the sum requested."[6]

Four days later De Pirro informed Jaschi that Anica and the Producers Union no longer objected to the release of funds. Originally they had considered it funding to another country, but Scalera's financial straits persuaded them to turn a blind eye.[7] On June 22, after more than two months of back and forth, the Ministry of Foreign Trade authorized the Banca d'America e d'Italia to release 195 million lire to Orson Welles Productions for the completion of *Othello,* not in one lump sum, of course, but "gradually, as production necessities dictate."[8]

Welles stayed aloof from such matters; in the spring of 1950 he was busy with myriad other problems, none of them in Rome. On March 31, the press leaped on a lawsuit filed against him in France for the rewrite of *Portrait of an Assassin.* The producers were suing him for the money they had paid him and for considerable damages; Welles said the final installment was still owed and the whole suit was a way of wheedling out of paying it.

While Papi was traipsing about in ministerial departments and knocking on doors to obtain the Fox money, Welles returned to the Ulysses project as a source of funding. Dino De Laurentiis still wanted to make an *Odyssey* and still did not brook rivals. When the press started talking about Welles's project, De Laurentiis got ready for a fight. The papers reported some legal squabbling, then retracted. A few weeks later De Laurentiis announced that he had hired George Wilhelm Pabst—the author of *The Joyless Street* and *Pandora's Box*—to direct *Ulysses.*

Welles didn't bat an eye, and informed French journalists at the beginning of April that his film would go ahead. Pabst arrived in Italy; went looking for locations in the south of Italy; and called a press conference to inform reporters that the film would be shot in Calabria and Sicily, in color, and that Greta Garbo—star of *The Joyless Street*—would be coming out of retirement to play Penelope.

This announcement trumped Welles's offering. According to his biographer Peter Noble, he sent De Laurentiis Borneman's script and asked him to finance *his* version. The producer read the script, found it utterly unviable commercially, and returned it. Welles continued to declare that he would be directing and starring in *Ulysses*. It was now up to De Laurentiis to make a counteroffer. At the end of April, a journalist found Welles at the Diodoro hotel in Taormina, where he had taken a quiet room with an excellent view. He told the concierge not to disturb him for any reason. The journalist managed to speak to him in the hotel restaurant (the only place he was willing to show himself), where he ate with his secretary Mary Alcaide and a large Alsatian dog, which ate from a plate on the table. Welles greeted the journalist and invited him to join them. He was sporting a beard and said he had just been offered the part of Ulysses.

"The trip to Taormina is a promise I made myself some time ago," Welles said.

> I come to Sicily every year and in the peace and quiet of these villages and the countryside, I can concentrate on the roles I have played and want to play in the future. This time I came with a lengthy script sent to me by Pabst: before accepting I want to see whether my temperament will manage to properly represent Ulysses in the way the film wants to portray him. Currently I'm finishing another important film: *Othello,* which I began in Morocco and will finish in Perugia, in the quiet of Umbria. The film requires not only an artistic but a spiritual preparation and I hope I have succeeded. Every time I come here I think about a film to set in Sicily, and I've received some offers—particularly after *Vulcano* and *Stromboli*. But I haven't made up my mind yet. I'd like to write the script myself, about the humanity of Sicily, its peace and love of beauty.... [M]aybe I'll come back here for inspiration to write it, if I have the time.[9]

Welles stayed several days, no doubt tempted by the offer to make some more money for *Othello* with another acting role, but it is unlikely that he ever seriously thought of accepting the role. He had a better idea.

Both Welles and De Laurentiis continued to claim they were about to make the film they knew only one of them could make. In the end, Welles got what he had been looking for all along: De Laurentiis paid him a considerable sum not to make his film.[10]

Welles announced he had given up the idea in June and De Laurentiis made his *Ulysses*, the most expensive Italian film in the postwar period, without Pabst, who withdrew in October for reasons that have never been clarified. His place was taken by Mario Camerini, who had his hands full with an undisciplined Kirk Douglas in the title role. Penelope was played not by Greta Garbo but by De Laurentiis's wife, Silvana Mangano.

One of the things that Welles, the latter-day Pico della Mirandola, was working on in Taormina in spring 1950 was the preface to Kenneth Tynan's *He That Plays the King:* "Since Stanislavsky there is an established assumption that the best acting company is a permanent one, that the nomadic life of the actor in commercial theatres leads nowhere but down. Unhappily, however, the hard economic facts have been such that we have had precious few Moscow Art Theatres. If it is hard to find a producer with the gifts of Stanislavsky it is just as difficult to find one with his money."[11] For some time, Welles had been thinking of returning to the tough nomadic life of the stage actor. He'd discussed a European tour with Mac Liammóir and Edwards, which he intended partly as a form of recompense for the work they had put into *Othello.* In Taormina, Welles was working on *The Blessed and the Damned,* the project he intended to stage.

The event was divided into two theatrical sketches and was a parodic/serious analysis of the sacred in contemporary society. The "blessed" in the first sketch is a Hollywood typist who performs miracles on a film set; the "damned" of the second sketch is a black Faust (music composed by Duke Ellington).

In his rereading of the Faust legend, *Time Runs,* Welles mixed Goethe, Dante, Milton, and Marlowe: on the stage he was Faust; Edwards, Mephistopheles; and the beautiful Eartha Kitt (with whom, it is thought, Welles had another of his tempestuous affairs), Helen of Troy. But what got people's attention was the first part of the show: *The Unthinking Lobster,* based on an original story by Welles. The curtain opens to the projection of the rushes of a costly film based on Genesis, in the presence of a Hollywood magnate, Mr. Jake Behoovian (Welles), who is less interested in the biblical story than in cutting the budget. In his satire, Welles ferociously attacks Hollywood's commercialism and hypocrisy, willing to tell the stories of the miracle worker Bernadette and Joan of Arc for a buck. The butt of the jokes was not only Hollywood, however; Welles also took aim at Cinecittà. The invisible star of the play is the Italian director, Alessandro Sporcacione (a misspelling of the Italian word for "lecher"), a sort of neorealist director who is never onstage but whose florid language is heard from the wings. He insists on hiring extras who are genuine cripples and invalids, fires the star of the show for not looking spiritual enough, and replaces her with his typist. When she miraculously cures the extras, Hollywood becomes a kind of holy city; the sick make pilgrimages and Tinseltown begins to rival Rome (in its Jubilee year in 1950). After the typist's miracle, there are no more divorces, strips of film are sold as religious relics, and Hollywood is unable to make any films. Behoovian and his ilk are ruined. An archangel descends (in an elevator) to suggest a compromise: there will be no more miracles in Hollywood if Hollywood stops making religious films.

Rehearsals began in Paris, where the show was to debut. As usual, Welles worked the stagehands and actors hard. "It's two in the morning," they told him. "These people have wives at home who are expecting them." "We'll find them new wives," Welles replied.

The show was scheduled to open at the Edward VII Theatre on June 15, but the date was put back four times (to June 19). Duke Ellington arrived, the actress Deanna Durbin was there, and so—to everyone's amazement—was Rita Hayworth. "What's so strange?" Welles said, "Aly, me, and Rita, we're friends."[12]

The Blessed and the Damned was a moderate success. *Le Monde* called it a "masterpiece of scenic art" and the Italian weekly *La Settimana Incom* reported condescendingly that for an English-language show in Paris, the theater was rather full.[13] An anonymous wit, writing for *Film*, damned it with praise, calling the piece "highly respectable" and complimenting "the drunk" on his performance. In Italy, the hue and cry was all about neorealism and who had inspired the character of the filmmaker. In *Film d'oggi* Marco Ramperti jokingly asked Alessandro Blasetti if Sporcacione's first name did not make him wonder, and if he intended to ask Welles for an explanation.[14] But it was no mystery that the model for director Sporcacione was Roberto Rossellini, a man Hollywood had tried to woo as they were seeking to win back his new love, Ingrid Bergman (who had made a mediocre Technicolor *Joan of Arc*), whose defection to Rome still smarted. The actress replacement in *Lobster* recalled the ousting of Anna Magnani in favor of Bergman for *Stromboli*. The miracles performed in Welles's piece were a clear reference to Rossellini's *Il miracolo,* which Welles had seen in April 1948.

The scene of the crime was obscure but the murder weapon—satire—was in plain sight. *Lobster* seemed to be a vendetta against neorealism fashion, perhaps related to Rossellini's failure to deliver on the *Life of Christ* or some other real or imagined lapse by the notoriously unreliable neorealist filmmaker.

Rossellini said nothing and kept well away from journalists who wanted to provoke some kind of fight with Welles. He was trying to obtain a divorce and marry Bergman, who had just had their love child, Robertino. Three years later, in *Cinema Nuovo,* Giuseppe Grieco took up his cause against Welles.

The film journal founded by Aristarco dedicated two pages to *The Blessed and the Damned,* in which Grieco called Welles "an amateur" and the show "of little artistic value." In point of fact, he didn't bother to mention the second sketch at all and spared Welles nothing for his parody of neorealism:

> It now remains to discuss the caricature of Italian neorealism Welles stages in the first part of the farce. It is without bite, almost always gratuitous, practically without an original line. The best is this one: "Italy is a country of actors, the worst of whom are professionals." The director Sporcacione—and the name should alert us to Welles's intentions—is a generic figure portrayed only very approximately. He is never onstage, but is heard swearing and cursing. Perhaps, Orson Welles thinks this is very neorealistic. We beg to differ. And believe that if in Hollywood miracles become a farce and the Bible is a pretext to make a "sexy" movie, Italian realism, should it ever get there, would end up like Welles's squalid caricature.[15]

The success of *The Blessed and the Damned* was short lived. From Italy came news of the 195 million from Zanuck, but Welles preferred to delay the completion of *Othello.* He needed to wait for the autumn light and cold.

Welles stayed in France and thought of what to do next. Provoked by the Rossellini caricature, in Italy the newspapers started to joke about Welles's career. In July 1950, a pseudonymous reporter, Gulliver, in the Rome weekly *L'elefante,* quipped, "He has moved to France after a long period in Italy. Here, he made an unforgettably atrocious film, *Black Magic,* and lived a life of animation, hustle, bustle, and oddity. In the end he tired of us and we of him. His life in France promises nothing new. There, too, his words, actions, deeds seem to be dictated by one imperative: to maintain the curiosity about, and interest in, Orson Welles. It is sufficient to read the interviews he gave to Parisian journalists in June to come to this conclusion. In these interviews he says (1) he will make a film based on Henry IV; (2) he will become a war correspondent in Korea; (3) he will buy a ranch in America and grow roses and birch trees for the rest of his days; (4) he will perform four Shakespeare plays on a European tour with a theater company he has yet to create; (5) he will take part in the next French Grand Prix; (6) he will write a series of articles on linguistic problems in answer to Stalin; (7) he will start upon a career as a radio entertainer; and (8) he will move to the Alps and take up winter sports, particularly bobsleigh on ice."[16]

The hilarity and sarcasm conceal a fair degree of ignorance about Welles's career to date—Gulliver seems not to have known that Welles had been a very famous radio entertainer in the 1930s—and make even the plans that were actually true appear ridiculous: he was thinking once again about Pirandello's *Enrico IV* and of touring Europe with a Shakespeare production, and he was about to become a correspondent for several newspapers.

What he came up with next was *An Evening with Orson Welles*, a show with a variable repertoire including *Time Runs*, excerpts from *The Importance of Being Earnest*, songs by Eartha Kitt, a magic show or scenes from *Henry VI, Julius Caesar*, and *Othello*. The show was to run first in Germany. In return for more funding, Welles had promised some newspaper articles about Hitler's homeland, one of which—"Thoughts on Germany"—was published in 1951 in the London journal *The Fortnightly*; the others appeared in France and Italy (in *Corriere dell'Informazione*, the afternoon edition of *Corriere della Sera*).[17]

The articles were thoughtful and entertaining, lucid and heartfelt descriptions of postwar Germany before the Wall: the nostalgia for Nazism in Munich; the suffering of Berlin, where Hitler had committed suicide; and Frankfurt, unchanged since the time of Kaiser Wilhelm. Here and there he remembers Italy with affection: "The commonplace of the hardheaded German is like that of the indolent Italian, a racist and mistaken notion of a country's traits. How is it that Italians, who are exuberant, have managed to convince us—and themselves—that they are idlers, good for the siesta and serenades?"[18] "A few months ago, I walked out of a restaurant in Venice because the owner had accused Toscanini of all manner of evil, including treachery";[19] "Watching these children . . . playing inside a shop on Friedrichstrasse, I was reminded of some Italians talking in a restaurant at the Caracalla baths or a loving couple kissing outside the Coliseum: the innocent joy of those who have not seen past glories";[20] and "Is Hitler still alive? The subject is good only to revive a flagging dinner conversation. Yes, he's alive, but only in the sense that Mussolini is still alive here and there in Italy. But solely in that sense."[21]

An Evening with Orson Welles made its debut in Frankfurt on August 7 at the Altjakobstheater am Zoo. On stage were Welles, Eartha Kitt, Mac Liammóir and Hilton Edwards (honored as director). The show moved on to Hamburg, Munich, Düsseldorf and Bad Oeynhausen, reaching Berlin in September, where all hell let loose.

In one of his articles Welles recounted an episode in Berlin. In one of the city's nightclubs the orchestra began to play "Horst Wessel," a tune that had become famous under Nazism. There was applause, and a man gave the Nazi salute. A woman invited him to lower his arm and threw a vase at him when he refused. The man then slapped the woman, and was applauded by onlookers. Welles threw himself into the brawl and managed to get a second vase broken over his head. In the passivity of the others, Welles saw a sort of reverence towards the American invader and made his chivalry appear slightly culpable. But he also said that despite self-pity and denigration "German instincts have been damaged far less than their cities," adding that the country had not been entirely invented by Josef Goebbels. The article was published in France and translated (poorly) into German. Readers saw themselves portrayed as members of the SS and the reaction was prompt: no orchestra played *The Third Man* theme, and cinemas in the Rhine and Palatinate boycotted *Prince of Foxes*.

More surprised than pained ("Every day I am accused of being a liar and charlatan"), Welles wrote another article in defense of his intellectual honesty and respect for the Germans. Twentieth Century Fox called a press conference to dissociate themselves from Welles's opinion: "Our company is astonished at how Welles has frivolously and superficially passed judgment on an entire people—we repeat, Welles has no permanent contract with us."[22] Faced with letters of protest from far and wide, Zanuck was forced to withhold distribution of *The Black Rose* in Germany.

It is often wrongly assumed that Welles's theater engagements distracted him from *Othello*. In fact, during the mornings and afternoons before the Paris performance of *The Blessed and the Damned*, he had been editing the film with Jean Sacha and had had it dubbed (for which presumably he paid out of the box-office returns for the show). In Germany, Welles included some scenes from *Othello* to reacquaint himself with, and perhaps deepen, the role.

Back in Italy, Welles's men were trying to keep the distributors (Scalera, Tenoudji, and Zanuck) at bay. In August, the head of administration, Walter Bedogni, asked for permission to export 15,000 meters of developed film from Rome to France, in order to reassure distributors about the footage and progress of the film, "its quantity and quality."

The German tour ended on September 9 and moved to Brussels for ten or so shows, after which Welles and the cast took up residence in a luxury hotel on Lake Como. But the money ran out again, the Italian leg of the tour was canceled, and the company split up.

At the beginning of October, Welles stopped over in Rome to talk to Papi. They buried the hatchet and joked about current trends in Italian cinema, the so-called neorealistic formula and Papi's view that, after amateur actors, they would soon start using amateur directors. Amused, Welles cited *Cristo proibito* (*Strange Deception*), the directorial debut of writer Curzio Malaparte. He told Papi *Othello* would be finished within the month and then he would be filming *The Damned*, based on *Time Runs.*[23]

And still Welles kept away from *Othello*, waiting for late autumn. During October he had other things on his mind. *Film* reported he was working on a movie based on the life of the Sicilian bandit Giuliano, perhaps because of something Sergio Sollima remembered;[24] he was actually preparing a script called *Lovelife*, the film he likely wanted to set in Sicily.

He had mentioned it in Paris in May while preparing *The Blessed and the Damned*. Arturo Lanocita reported Welles's idea from France

in *Corriere dell'Informazione:* "'I'm going to make a film on lazy people, the kind you meet at the French Riviera and do nothing but spend
money.' Welles believes men and women with means and no desire to
work can have dramatic lives, and intends to investigate that drama,
since the cinema largely ignores it."[25] Englishman Francis Koval jotted
down details about the project in his interview notes: "[Welles] entrusts
me with the secret (an open one) that in his free moments (where on
earth does he find them?) he is scripting a picture about sexual obsession called *Lovelife.* 'Despite the subject, it will not be endangered by
any censorship,' he proclaims. 'It will be so respectable that families
will take their children to see it without the slightest hesitation. But if
I succeed—the picture will shock every adult with human feelings and
social conscience."[26]

Lanocita returned to the subject in November in *Corriere della Sera,*
reporting that the film—to be entitled *Luna di miele* (Honeymoon)—
would comprise eight episodes, each dedicated to the decline of the rul-
ing classes. As Welles explained, "Without a political or class message, of
course; politics doesn't interest me. How about you? Today it is no longer
a clash of ideas, just a conflict between opposing interests between two
worlds that see survival only in the elimination of the other."[27]

The following January, Gian Gaspare Napolitano revealed, "Welles
describes it as film dedicated to a world destined to disappear: a world
of snobs. The story takes place in Paris, Rome, Capri, and the French
Riviera. Italian neorealism has given us the world of the poor. Welles
wants to give us the world of the rich in the postwar period. He includes
himself among the snobs."[28]

Welles contacted Pierre Frasnais and Yvonne Printemps about the
film, and the name Michèle Morgan was mentioned. The filmmaker
looked for funding in France, Italy, and—despite the recent debacle—
Germany. The project may have been another of Welles's ideas to dangle
in front of producers to see who would take the bait, but he worked hard
on the script, found time to return to Taormina in October, and even offered Truman Capote (a frequent visitor to Sicily) a part. After spending
an entire evening with Welles, during which the novelist recited chunks
of *The Lady from Shanghai* without requiring a single prompt, Capote
turned Welles down.[29]

The project took Welles to the most spectacular locations in the Mediterranean—ending in Capri, where Welles gave Roman Prince Dado Ruspoli some lessons in hypnotism. This is what Ruspoli told Ludovica Ripa di Meana about the meeting over thirty years later:

> He came to Capri to shoot some scenes for *Othello*, but the work went ahead slowly. He joined our group and must have felt at ease because he gave us an exhibition of his extraordinary powers. One evening, entering Villa Vuotto in the famous Piazzetta, he asked me what I wanted to see next. As it happened, a lady was crossing the square, immaculately dressed and with a drink in her hand, ready for dinner. I told Welles I wanted to see her spill her Bloody Mary all over her new dress. And that is exactly what happened. Welles gave out an inhuman roar, as if from the mouth of a wounded elephant, a peremptory gesture like Mandrake pointing his magical ring at a victim, and she spilled her tomato juice all down her front. You may think Welles had frightened her. Maybe so, but what does it matter? There's room for doubt, otherwise things would just be too terrifying. He did a few more tricks, too. After that he taught me hypnotism . . . this shifting of roles from subject to object and vice versa is very oriental. If you look at a beautiful girl she captures my attention, Welles said. She is the subject and I am the object, because she captures my attention, mesmerizes. . . . Try to mesmerize something that does not capture your attention, a crust of bread, for example. Take it to your room and concentrate on it for fifteen minutes. If you can do that, four out of five people you try to hypnotize will fall under your spell, because you will have become the mesmerizer, irradiating magnetism.[30]

Lovelife soon ran out of steam, and Welles ran into trouble. Back in Italy, a series of remarks about alcohol, cocaine, and morphine consumption in Italy found their way into a French newspaper and then into *La Settimana Incom*. Welles said, "The level of alcoholism in Italy is scandalous. The consumption of cocaine and morphine is so routine in certain classes that young people inject themselves through their trousers between one samba and the next. In one cabaret in Rome, they set out on the table boxes of papers to sniff cocaine." Revenge? Simply the truth? Whatever the case, these declarations further fueled Welles's reputation for being a disquieting and irritating guest.

The autumn light became suitable for *Othello* and Welles wasted no time. According to the work schedule drawn up by Papi in April 1950, more shooting was needed in Perugia, Rome, Pavia, and Venice. The only location that Welles didn't shoot in seems to have been Perugia, which Welles may have visited in April, as suggested in the interview from Taormina.

At the beginning of November, Welles was certainly in Rome with Mac Liammóir, Lanocita, Rispoli of *Film,* and another reporter for *Araldo dello Spettacolo,* who met him in Scalera's Studio 2. The three journalists watched Welles record the final scene in almost total darkness, surrounded by actors perched on a trestle. Welles broke off for a half-hour interview in "fluent and picturesque" Italian, revealing his ambitions for *Othello:* "Another Shakespeare, this time closer to the time and spirit of the play. Perhaps *Othello* will be less Shakespearean than *Macbeth* but it will be more Elizabethan, describing the conflict of a brutal, instinctive foreigner and Venetian culture and power.... But I don't know if I have got it right this time, either. Or even if there is a right way. I don't make films, I carry out experiments. Everything I do is experimental."[31]

Rispoli tried to rile him with a question about his well-paid experimental holidays making films of dubious value such as *Black Magic* and *The Black Rose.* "He laughed and smiled as if to say, you have to make a living, and the films had nothing to do with him. 'Maybe they're masterpieces,' he said, feigning propriety, 'but I haven't seen them.'"[32]

Then it was the turn of the anonymous reporter for *Araldo dello Spettacolo* to try to shake Welles's equanimity: "Is it true you don't like neorealism? What do you think of De Sica?" Welles replied, "I think people are beginning to tire of realism, but I admire De Sica a great deal. His films are truly lyrical."[33]

The three journalists left the studios won over, yet puzzled. Welles was utterly unlike the way he was usually described, an ogre who chewed up and spat out stagehands and technicians. The reporter for *Film* ended his piece by musing, "What is all this nonsense in the papers?"

When the money from Fox arrived and the light was right, Welles finished shooting *Othello* in a few weeks, helped by his most loyal assistants Troiani and Fanto. The work included some closeups of Othello, some crowd scenes at Castel Sant'Angelo, and other scenes in Pavia and Venice.[34]

A few weeks later he was in Venice, bearded, with black scarf and raincoat. It was the fourth time he had been there to shoot and the second that he found it shrouded in melancholic mist, without tourists. No one paid any attention to Welles in Venice. The famous director had not completed a single film in Italy and was considered little more than a curiosity. The reporter for *il Gazzettino-Sera* asked him about everything but the cinema: Martians (the question was met with a loud guffaw), his favorite sport (bullfighting), soccer fans (a little mad, perhaps). He repeated what he had said about Venice a year earlier: "an underwater city, a mysterious Atlantis, a world that germinates from water."[35]

In Pavia Welles did just one complicated take. Troiani described it this way: "Iago had to walk behind a passageway in front of St. Peter's Cathedral. God knows how Welles had found it. The passageway was blocked and the reverse shot, with Iago looking down through the columns, was shot with a tiny model because we couldn't get a camera up there. Behind the model you can see a bit of paving in Rome, in the EUR district."[36]

1950 was drawing to a close and with it, at last, the shooting of Welles's first Italian film.

Welles and Troiani (seated) prepare to shoot *Othello* using some of Troiani's models.
From the private collection of Massimiliano Troiani, Rome.

The fortress in Cyprus and the rigging of the Moor's ship.
From the private collection of Massimiliano Troiani, Rome.

Welles about to shoot with another model. *From the*
private collection of Massimiliano Troiani, Rome.

Battlements of plywood; rods and flags become spears and standards.
From the private collection of Massimiliano Troiani, Rome.

The reverse shot, the arrival of Othello, shot by Troiani in Ostia,
using a model of the building and a boat about 1 meter long.
From the private collection of Massimiliano Troiani, Rome.

(*facing, bottom*) The scene of Desdemona in the fortress
of Cyprus was shot in Viterbo, Palazzo dei Papi.
From the private collection of Massimiliano Troiani, Rome.

George Fanto (next to the camera), Welles (seated), and Troiani (with hands on hips) in Morocco. *From the private collection of Massimiliano Troiani, Rome.*

Ca' d'Oro, Venice, probably in November 1949. Troiani is standing on the left.
A fleeting image of Iago. *From the private collection of Massimiliano Troiani, Rome.*

Othello in the crypt in Tuscania (Viterbo). *From the
private collection of Massimiliano Troiani, Rome.*

A self-mocking Christmas card from December 1950, the last phase of shooting *Othello*. *From the private collection of Massimiliano Troiani, Rome.*

June 19, 1952: Welles looks over the EUR district of Rome for *Caesar!*
From the private collection of Massimiliano Troiani, Rome.

(*facing, top*) Welles with Luigi Troiani, Oberdan's brother. Both Troianis
were asked to take photos of possible locations. *From the private collection
of Massimiliano Troiani, Rome.*

(*facing, bottom*) January 1953: Welles, Viviane Romance and Totò making
L'uomo, la bestia e la virtù in the studios of Ponti and De Laurentiis. The
child in Welles's arms (the beast's son), Giancarlo Nicotra, would go on to
become a film director. *Photo by kind permission of Giancarlo Nicotra.*

Another scene from *L'uomo, la bestia e la virtù*.
Photo by kind permission of Giancarlo Nicotra.

12
Waiting for *Othello*

There was once, in Venice, a Moor: Othello.

—Othello (Orson Welles), *Othello* (1955 version)

When a dog bites a man it is not news. Unless the man in question is Orson Welles. On January 16, 1951, it was reported that Welles had been bitten on the finger of his right hand by a small dog with reddish fur, in Piazza Barberini in Rome. At four in the morning Welles had tried to shoo away a dog that had been yapping at his heels, and, bending down to stroke it, had been bitten on the hand. The dog had been shot on the spot by a night warden, Achille De Angelis, taken to the municipal pound, and found to have been rabid. The article concluded, "Stroking a stray will cost the filmmaker forty days of unpleasant treatment."[1]

A Rome newspaper, *Momento Sera,* picked up the story and printed three columns with a photo; from there it crossed the Atlantic. In America, animal protectionists criticized the warden for slaying the dog before it had been tested for disease. It was rumored that Welles had kicked the dog. Bob Hope quipped, "Officials should stay out of family squabbles."

The treatment forced Welles to give up his plans and travels. He stayed in Rome, taking advantage of the enforced rest to edit *Othello* with Renzo Lucidi. Work at the Moviola was extremely complicated due to the conditions in which the shooting had been carried out. Reverse shots had often been made long after the original takes; some of the dialogue began in Morocco and was finished in Rome's Scalera Studios; a scene begun in Morocco ended, perhaps, in Orvieto; and the deep focus in

Viterbo had reverse shots in Ostia. Different emulsions had been used (Dupont, French Kodak, American Kodak, and Ferrania), the cinematographers behind the camera were not the same, and the shots had been made using different lenses in a variety of lighting conditions. During most of the shooting there was no script girl and some of the work had no continuity supervision. At the time there were no monitors to check the work just completed, and in Morocco there were no rushes at the end of the day.

According to the records of the Scalera studio, Welles had shot 24,000 meters of film, about fifteen hours' worth, including many tiny fragments. Some scenes had been shot a dozen times, rethought, then shot again months later in an entirely different location. Desdemona was played mostly by Suzanne Cloutier, sometimes by Betsy Blair, and occasionally even by Lea Padovani; several sequences were broken up into rapid shots, or even just a few frames.

To pick their way through this mess, the crew had printed the screen tests for the reverse shots on numerous pieces of paper but many of these had got lost in the lengthy downtime during shooting or because they'd been used to sell the film to distributors and had not been put back. So the crew began to put a series of complicated, coded notches in the negatives to indicate the intended effect when passing from one shot to the next. Troiani remembered being praised by Welles for his ability to understand what other camera operators had done. "When the material was projected," he told Alberto Farina, "he wanted to kiss my feet . . . I just told him he'd done all the photography for the film himself."[2]

Certainly the film could be put together only using Welles's memory, as he was to say later in *Filming Othello*. On the set his ideas had been clear: Venice wintry and in a watery slumber, Cyprus resplendent with light or suddenly in shade. While editing he sometimes needed to invert the negative so a character looked left instead of right. Despite this considerable mess, he was able to turn some defects to the good and the chaos almost into style, incorporating the visual disintegration into the look of the film and taking advantage of the "tottering instability" and hesitation caused by the shooting method. These were made to represent Iago's disturbed logic and "shattered syntax" and not technical and organizational deficiencies.[3]

Meanwhile, Angelo Francesco Lavagnino was composing the oft-praised score (solemn funereal music for Othello, graceful dance music for the scenes in Venice, mandolins for the murder of Roderigo). Writer Gian Gaspare Napolitano, fresh from completing the Italian dialogues of *Macbeth,* agreed to oversee the dubbing of *Othello.*

As the film was edited, Welles jotted down one or two shots in which things could be improved, and reshot some frames. Napolitano says Welles did some work in the studio in January. "The film is over and being mixed," he wrote, "but he hasn't yet shaved off the close beard of the Moor of Venice, in case he still needs him.... He speaks Italian fluently, a little flirtatiously. He likes Italy but knows very well Italians don't like him. His is a case of unrequited love. He doesn't even have fun here. Italy is not a place where you can have fun. It has become important, by now he can't do without it, but he feels that his life here is an utter mistake."[4]

During the period of quarantine, unable to travel or shoot, working on the editing of *Othello* with microphones and a Moviola, Welles turned his hand to dubbing films into English, an uncredited but well-paying job. After teaching Lea Padovani English, Harriet White had become proficient at dubbing. One day she was summoned to work on Giacomo Gentilomo's *Enrico Caruso, leggenda di una voce* (Caruso, the legendary voice) and found Welles in charge: "I was hired by somebody else, so you can imagine my surprise when I entered the studio to find Orson directing the looping! In order to raise money for *Othello,* Orson agreed to direct the English dubbing of some Italian pictures. He was probably paid something like $20,000 per film, and naturally, he took no credit for the work. He directed the sessions with a great deal of warmth and humor. He would tell the actors, 'Take your time; it's just tape, it's not film. We can do it over as many times as you need.'"[5]

Welles may have got the job through his old friend Gina Lollobrigida, the star of the Caruso film. Or he may have picked it up by hanging around the studio where they were dubbing *Othello.* He also dubbed Julien Duvivier's *Don Camillo* (like *Caruso,* produced by Peppino Amato), which has Welles as the offscreen narrator (Emilio Cigoli in the Italian version) and the voice of the Crucifix (played by Ruggero Ruggeri). He didn't work only on Italian films. *L'Écran français* reported that for the English version of *Le trésor de Cantenac,* Welles would dub the protagonist, played by director Sacha Guitry.[6]

Welles didn't confine himself to editing *Othello* or dubbing other people's films. He took an active part in the social life of Rome and, whenever he spotted a new talent, hatched new ideas. On January 26, photographers besieged the Fiammetta Theater, which was conducting rehearsals of *Se il Tevere parlasse . . .* (If the Tiber could speak . . .) a two-act show by Fiorentini and Gigliozzi performed by members of high society in Rome. It cost the princely sum of ten thousand lire to get in, and the receipts were to be given to charity. The audience comprised those of the Rome aristocracy not already onstage as well as famous actors such as Anna Magnani, Wanda Osiris, Totò, and a pensive and whiskered Orson Welles, the only foreigner, who continued to draw on a large cigar despite the no-smoking signs.[7]

Most of the audience was struck by a seventeen-year old blonde girl, Countess Gisella Sofio, who did some imitations. At the end of the show Antonio de Curtis (Totò) and Welles headed for her dressing room to sign her—Totò to his theater company, and Welles to his adaptation of Pirandello's *Enrico IV,* "to play Henry's daughter, who, in his version, was just another girl."[8] This is how Sofio remembered Welles:

> That evening was my theater debut. I started doing imitations of the ladies who came to my home for afternoon tea. One day Princess Belmonte, a close friend of my mother's, said, "Do send us your daughter, we're doing a charity show. She doesn't have to do anything, just stand in a basket with some roses on her head. We're doing some tableaux vivants." They put me in a vase with some flowers. After a few days I was in despair. I kept looking around, imitating the dressmaker, a girl who wanted to be a singer, anyone. On the evening of the dress rehearsal I made an agreement with the director Enrico Glori, Pupetto as he liked to be called: he would let me do my imitations. Anna Magnani and Orson Welles were in the front row, with Totò and Wanda Osiris, and they applauded everything I did. I just went through my routine, a lamb to the slaughter, but it didn't matter to me. Afterwards Welles offered me the part of Henry IV's daughter. Of course, I jumped at the chance. I went to somewhere on the Appia, where Welles had an office, to do a small screen test. I wore a red trouser suit, because red's my lucky color and I believe in that sort of thing. There he was, surrounded by people, at a huge table, it was like a dream. Welles spoke Italian quite well; he was a bit overpowering, huge, tall, with that beard, but very nice, very courteous. The script was in English, and I knew English. It was a good part, very long. I'd read some of the script and learned it by heart, so I acted it out.

Without the camera. It went very well. Afterward, Welles got in touch with my parents, because I was still a minor, and they had to give their permission. My grandmother refused because I hadn't finished school yet. A newspaper actually reported it—"Grandma says no"—imagine that. She turned everyone down, Welles, Totò, Wanda Osiris, who wanted me in her show with Gianni Agus. So that was the end of *Enrico IV.* I know Welles had changed Pirandello's play; I used to have the script but I haven't got it any more. A pity . . . everything lost. I met Welles again, some years later, when he married Paola Mori, who was a friend of my family. They'd gone to live in Fregene and I used to see him there, occasionally, on the beach, very much in love with his wife. He was a passionate fellow, hot-blooded, full of character. I liked his persona, put it like that, but I didn't know him well. I was shy, and angry that my family wouldn't let me do the part . . . furious with all of them. Strange thing is I forgot all about it. Welles offered me my first role in the cinema and I forgot! Until you reminded me. But I forget things that don't work out so my life always seems perfect. I "repress" them, as the saying goes nowadays.[9]

A few weeks later, the revised version of *Macbeth* was released with the changes Republic had insisted on. Welles had done the work while finishing *Othello*—cutting scenes, whittling down the closeups, relooping his part and sending detailed instructions to America about how the other parts should be overdubbed. In *Epoca,* Alberto Mondadori wrote, "The Italian edition has been cut a little here and there but it is still a film with a place in the history of the cinema, alongside Welles's other masterpiece, *Citizen Kane.*"[10]

Supervised by Gian Gaspare Napolitano, the Italian version was released in March, and this time was received quite well. A few critics even changed their minds about the film.

Ennio Flaiano, for example, seemed to regret some of his sarcasm of three years earlier and praised both *Macbeth* and *Citizen Kane.* However, he still accused Welles of "self-indulgent sorcery" and "the suspicion of pyrotechnics," "the nouveau riche intelligent taste for whom money is no object and who seek to strike the imagination of an audience by lighting a cigar with a large bill." The review ends in light and shade, associating the artistic merits and defects of *Macbeth* with the personality of its creator: "Welles . . . has emphasized in the work its similarities with his own personality, a struggle between faith and sorcery, guilt and remorse, power and decline. In the gallery of faces the cinema has given to Macbeth, that of Orson Welles is certainly the most faithful, the most responsible."[11]

There was even a partial recantation by Guido Aristarco, who had the same reservations as Flaiano, seemingly without much reference to the Shakespeare adaptation. Once again he focused on Welles's formalism: "Welles has an instinctive primitivism, unleashing crude and barbaric forces which are captured in stylish, studied shots. . . . This is very much the territory of the conjurer Welles, the narcissist, portraying the dictator Macbeth and showing us screaming witches . . . for which Welles doesn't only use the positioning of the camera but also deep focus. . . . *Macbeth* is a controversial but fascinating film; this might be the right occasion to reexamine Welles's personality."[12]

Mario Gromo, another member of the Venice jury in 1948, was less conciliatory, criticizing the film for its expressionism and lèse majesté in relation to Shakespeare. He did not tell his readers that the new edition had been severely trimmed by the producers: "Having established— Welles, that is—that the spectator's attention and the film's tension cannot be maintained for more than an hour and a half, the fearless director cuts great chunks out of Shakespeare. The text was supposed to be preeminent in the film, so the scenery is reduced to a minimum . . . and the acting is dense, sustained . . . with such an intense focus on the protagonist . . . that it slips into exhibitionism." After this, he magnanimously grants that the film is worth seeing.[13]

Callisto Cosulich dusted off the old comparison with *Hamlet*: "Compared to Olivier's measured direction, Welles's exhibitionism cannot but irritate: however, it must be said that the critics were not always objective about the film. . . . Welles . . . could have respected the text where he wanted to: he was *the* self-made man par excellence with a thousand different experiences, an *enfant prodige* . . . Two years later, far from the polemics of the first showing, things are a little clearer. . . . Welles may have done the cinema harm, but of all the various disservices rendered to this unhappy medium, Welles's is perhaps the best kind of damage."[14]

Gian Luigi Rondi did not budge from his original opinion. His review was practically word for word what he had originally written, with a new introduction in the same tone of voice, unfavorably comparing Welles with Olivier: "Whereas the English director was intent on approaching his fellow countryman with devout and intelligent respect, and included the priceless treasures of European civilization in his work, the American director uses Shakespeare for his hand-me-down cinematographic culture, coupled with such vainglory that he seems to think any kind of exaggeration is likely to impress a naïve audience."[15]

Fernaldo Di Giammatteo reminded his readers about the goings-on at the Venice Film Festival and the rivalry with Olivier's *Hamlet*, then commented, "There is no better way to appreciate Welles's film than to go back to Shakespeare, . . . Welles sees in the tragedy violence and horror . . . which he certainly did not invent." He criticized Welles not for the horror but for a "certain sadistic delight in the horrid" and the excessive citation of the masters of cinema, "Lang, Eisenstein's *Alexander Nevsky*." He was disturbed by Welles's contradictions in *Macbeth*, a "tangle that cannot be undone," which he saw in all his films but which in *Citizen Kane*, in places in *Macbeth*, and in his "minor" works, "aren't always negative."[16]

Alberto Moravia also returned to the Shakespeare play but came to the opposite conclusion, calling the film "photographed theater. We don't know whether this was a deliberate choice or was dictated by the rapid schedule and lack of resources . . . but Welles, an undoubtedly talented actor and director, is often a little too sure of himself, and keeps the film within the confines of the play, focusing on the acting and the virtuosity of the shooting." Moravia's superficial review rehashed all the old prejudices about Welles: "Almost German in its expressionism," "a shallow attempt to surprise," "would have been better with more sobriety, humanity and simplicity," "the characters seem to be on the verge of epilepsy," and "we knew the Kings of Scotland were poor, but didn't think they were cavemen."[17]

Allergic to opening nights and galas, Welles stayed away from the premiere of the new version, reducing the publicity but also avoiding a new round of polemics. He spent the spring of 1951 working on *Othello* and finding the money to finish the film. Despite the 195 million lire from Fox and various odd jobs, Welles had run out of money again. The debts were piling up; Welles intended to honor them all. Wanting to overcome problems with synchronization and editing, he asked Michel Olian for a loan. He was a guest of the colorful Latvian wheeler-dealer in Villa Madama (he described him to Bogdanovich as a "crazy Russian," and the idea for Arkadin began to take shape in his mind).

Olian, who possessed patience and an understanding of bureaucracy, was known in Rome as someone to go to if you needed the government to release funds for a film. He could make false declarations,
move money around, act as a front, and get the film funds released (from
which he took a handsome cut). When Welles, his nightclub drinking
companion, asked him for money to complete *Othello,* Olian probably
thought it was just another deal. He gave Welles thirty-five thousand
dollars to begin with; the sum gradually rose to two hundred thousand.
In return, Welles was forced to give him a larger and larger share in the
film. Olian was under the impression that the film was just a few weeks
from completion; the perfectionist Welles then kept postponing it until
Olian remonstrated with him in the lobby of the Excelsior Hotel. "Tu
as reason, Michel," an embarrassed Welles said in an attempt to mollify
him.[18]

Money was disappearing fast, and not because of Welles's scrupulous
finishing work. In the accounts Orson Welles Productions presented to
Direzione Generale dello Spettacolo, expenses between March and July
1951 included post-production costs (musical score, printing, development, editing, synchronization); salaries for the actors, extras, workmen,
and camera crew; and traveling expenses. Some of these may have been
old debts, but it is also possible that Welles had shot some additional
scenes or made other improvements.

According to *Hollywood,* in March Welles was once again in Casablanca, writing *Masquerade* (a script that would become *Mr. Arkadin,*
aka *Confidential Report*), a love story between an American of a certain
age and a young Italian woman, to be shot in Casablanca and "a small
Adriatic port."[19] But the real reason for visiting North Africa was to shoot
some additional material for *Othello:* the press release prepared by Scalera for the Italian premiere of the film has Welles shooting some outdoor
scenery in Mogador in April. And so the costs kept mounting.

How much did *Othello* cost in the end? According to Frank Brady,
the total cost was around five hundred thousand dollars,[20] whereas the
Scalera press release (which includes only the costs of the Italian version,
without the subsequent changes) puts the figure at one million.

In May, inspectors viewed the Orson Welles Productions balance
sheet. "After examining the accounts and salary slips," the inspectors

wrote, "all the expenses have been fully documented, although a large number of receipts appear to be simply pieces of paper with illegible signatures (especially during the first period of shooting) and some of these receipts are for large sums."[21]

Was three million lire too much for photographs and screen tests? Or a hundred thousand a week for Papi's salary, even when the crew wasn't filming? For a normal production unit, perhaps. However, as the inspectors also noted, no salaries had been included for the foreign actors (the entire main cast) and a number of items still appeared to be due, making the cost higher than the sums paid out by Fox. The expenses in Morocco were paid by Tenoudji and hence were not included in the Italian accounts.

How could *Othello* have cost so much? Direzione Generale put it down to Welles's now infamous spendthrift ways: "Given the subject matter and type of film and the expensive direction of Orson Welles— who evidently wishes to challenge Olivier's *Hamlet*—and given the fact that the film took nearly three years to make, with a large number of scenes shot several times, the list of expenses appears, overall, to be acceptable."[22]

The following pages examine these expenses, as detailed to Direzione Generale dello Spettacolo for the purposes of having the Fox money released in installments to cover the costs in Italy. The accounts are unlikely to be perfectly accurate and do not include the expenses incurred during downtime, equipment rental, salaries, board and lodging, travel expenses, and so on. However, they cannot have been too far off, because there were receipts of one kind or another for just about everything.

Expenses for the period from October 18, 1948, to August 20, 1949 (shooting in Venice with Lea Padovani and the search for a new Desdemona), totaled 40,037,468 lire. From August 20, 1949 to November 10, 1949 (shooting in Venice, the Scalera studios on the Giudecca and in Rome, and in Viterbo and Tuscania), the total was 50,463,305 lire. A third accounting period ran from October 23, 1949, to October 18, 1950 (almost no shooting in Italy), during which expenses totaled 41,001,157 lire. The fourth period, from October 18, 1950 to March 3, 1951 (final shooting in Rome, Perugia, Venice and Pavia and the start of post-production), expenses came to 60,686,796 lire. Expenses for the final period—from

March 3, 1951 to July 11, 1951 (final shooting and the rest of post-production)—were 52,831,987 lire.

Expenses for the first period together with the last three add up to 194,557,408 lire, and were to be set against the 195,000,000 given by Fox in exchange for 50 percent of the distribution rights in the Anglo-American market. The second period corresponded to the 50,000,000 lire paid by Fox for *The Black Rose*. The overall total is 245,020,713 lire, which covered only the official costs in Italy. To this must be added the 12,000,000 francs (about 20,000,000 lire) that were paid by Tenoudji for shooting in French Morocco and were not included in the Italian accounting. An undated summary of costs written later by the director of Orson Welles Production, Rocco Facchini, gives a total of 264,848,228 lire, about 20,000,000 more than the money released by Fox.

SUMMARY OF COSTS FOR THE FILM "OTHELLO"

Preparation, organization, and music	5,843,668
Executives and administrative and secretarial staff	32,415,933
Technicians	33,325,778
Leading and secondary actors	45,160,677
Workmen	11,861,142
Film, development, and printing	26,626,719
Studios, lighting, and machinery	12,824,848
Scenography	12,700,843
Costumes, makeup, and sundries	13,037,042
Transport, customs duties, etc.	19,331,113
Expenses for actors and crew	17,687,915
Insurance	9,330,968
Taxation	1,824,916
Editing, synchronization, and mixing	11,474,034
Postal, etc.	4,145,743
Overheads and sundries	7,256,889
TOTAL COST	264,848,228
Libero Balduini	Rocco Facchini
Accountant	Director of Production

These are the declared and certified sums. The equivalent cost in dollars was $424,000, to which Welles's acting fees for *The Third Man* and *Prince of Foxes* ($100,000 for each picture, according to Barbara Leaming) should be added, as well as the $200,000 paid by Olian, making a total of $824,000. Tenoudji almost certainly spent more than the amount declared; a letter from Patrice Dally to George Fanto mentioned the sum of 18,100,000 francs, together with a promise of further funds to make the "promised advance of 28,000,000."[23]

The figures above do not include Welles's other sources of income, including dubbing Italian and French films, his theater work, contributions to newspapers, prefaces, and radio work in England—not all of which, of course, would have been spent on *Othello*. The Scalera accounts refer only to the first edition of the film, and not to the subsequent improvements that led to the official version of the film.

Scalera's estimate of a million dollars is probably a little high, but not far off the mark.

According to Scalera's financial records, Welles worked on the Italian edition of *Othello* until July 11, 1951. However, by then, Welles had resumed his travels in Europe, visiting the Cannes Film Festival and London, where he made the radio series *The Adventures of Harry Lime*. Several of the thirty-nine episodes were written by Welles himself, but most were the work of Ernest Borneman, the unlucky writer of *The Adventures of Ulysses*. A few episodes were recorded in Paris; nine were translated into Italian, directed by Anton Giulio Majano, and broadcast by Italian state radio (Rai Radio 2).

After radio, Welles worked in the theater. He met Laurence Olivier in a restaurant and told him he wanted to stage an *Othello*. Olivier gave him use of St. James's Theatre, of which he was then director. Welles had the *Othello* reels sent from Italy and began rehearsing. He worked on the editing with John Shepridge, the third editor after Jean Sacha in France and Renzo Lucidi in Italy.[24]

By summer, the editing work was almost finished, and Welles was happy enough with the result to want to present the film personally. He may also have seen it as an opportunity to win over the Italian critics. After the long takes of *Macbeth*, *Othello* featured rapid editing and quick changes of scene. Welles also wanted to keep a promise to the now almost defunct Scalera Studios: "Of all the English-language films made until now, and there are tens of thousands of them, *Othello* is the first to be given its world premiere in Italy," wrote Gian Gaspare Napolitano, as the finishing touches were being put on the editing. The film was entered into competition at the Venice Film Festival, the ideal location for its world premiere, but also a festival with which Welles had a score to settle.

The Italian press announced the coming event without recalling the disastrous screening of *Macbeth* three years before or mentioning the troubled production of the film. *Cento Stelle* turned its attention to Welles for its seventy-sixth issue, addressing its readers directly and calling Welles "the actor whom—in spite of yourselves—you have probably admired in numerous films."[25]

A special edition of *L'Eco del Cinema e dello Spettacolo* published the biographies of all the directors competing at the festival. Welles was described as being "considered among the best of contemporary filmmakers, one of the most original, most technically skillful and certainly the most gifted in various media."[26] The two pages about the film that follow mention only the Scalera Studios in Rome and Venice. Morocco was omitted because of Scalera's continuing effort to garner official recognition of Italian nationality for the film, despite the fact that the cast and some of the crew were foreign. The English-language version was to be screened but Scalera hoped Italian nationality would help improve the film's reception among critics, domestic cinemagoers, and above all, the jury—which could use state funds to reimburse expenses only for Italian films.

The problem was that *Othello* still was not finished. The synchronization of the original dialogues was proving difficult, and the schedule for delivery of the finished film had to be pushed back.

On August 24, after the inauguration of the Festival, Orson Welles Production stipulated a contract with Loew's International Corporation (the parent company of MGM until 1959) for the remaining 50 percent of distribution rights in Great Britain and the Commonwealth. The Italian State Archives have a record of the agreement, which explicitly refers to an unfinished film. "In order to complete the English version," the note reads, "which requires some shooting, synchronization, and dubbing, as well as the payment of debts and unpaid salaries, about 100 million lire is needed."

On the day Welles was scheduled to arrive on the Lido, he was in England trying to get the film finished. When he finally arrived, his face was as dark as the rather large blue suit he was wearing, and his mood was grim.

The news that he had come without the film started up a new round of barbed comments. Casiraghi immediately launched into an attack on Welles and the Christian Democrat appointed director of the festival, Antonio Petrucci. "The atmosphere of nervous anticipation, with the director growing thinner and thinner each day, has ended. Heaven be praised! Orson Welles has arrived. His film, *Othello*, scheduled for screening in the competition section, hasn't."[27]

It was then rumored that the film had arrived but Welles had found it unacceptable, or that it was held up in customs. In the end Petrucci was forced to issue a declaration to the press: "If it has not been possible to screen the original version of *Othello* it is simply because the film has not yet been finished. No customs holdups could prevent a scheduled film from being screened at the Venice Film Festival."[28]

Perhaps on Scalera's insistence, Welles suggested that the festival screen the Italian version of the film, which had now been dubbed. Petrucci agreed, and Scalera hurriedly printed a copy and sent it to Venice by train.

Welles waited anxiously for the film to arrive. Spectators saw him pacing up and down outside the main theater and Alberto Mondadori, who had seen a working copy, had this to say in his August 31 article for *Epoca*: "No film so far screened at the 12th Festival is comparable to Orson Welles's *Othello*." By that point, the films that had been shown included Renoir's first color film, *The River*, Bresson's *Journal d'un curé de campagne*, and Billy Wilder's *Ace in the Hole*.

When the reels arrived, Welles and a projectionist went through each one, while journalists waited outside the main theater for news. A spokesman for Petrucci then announced that the film had been withdrawn by the director and that there would be a press conference that afternoon to explain this decision.

It is not hard to imagine the journalists' reaction. After three years, another of Welles's films had been withdrawn, this time not only from the competition but from the festival. It was all a bad joke. Luigi Fossati of *Avanti!* was indignant. He also wondered how Gian Gaspare Napolitano—who had been in charge of dubbing *Othello* into Italian—could be a member of the jury, since the film had been entered into the competition until moments before. He suspected favoritism—perhaps forgetting that the president of the jury, Mario Gromo and another juror, Gian Luigi Rondi, were not known for their sympathies for Welles.[29]

A new battle was about to commence. Even Callisto Cosulich, until then an admirer of Welles, lost his temper and boycotted the press conference. "Could Orson Welles come to the festival without creating some sort of ruckus? Of course not. This time the fuss is not over a statement he has made, nor has he presented an *Othello* that calls into question fifty years of cinema history. . . . It is simply that he, and not the film, has come to the festival. . . . As the director, he has the right not to show a copy he doesn't believe is up to standard, but as the producer he should have anticipated this eventuality and made sure it didn't happen. He has a commitment to the festival."[30]

Welles went back to the Excelsior to change and get ready for the press conference. He was overheard mumbling the hope that the press would listen to him. He then returned to the main theater to face the music. This is how the journalists present recorded the event:

> "He came to the press conference symbolically dressed in white. A declaration of peace. His suit was baggy and, although a large man, he continually had to roll up the sleeves of his jacket. The journalists were irritated, in view of their past experience with him and were inclined to go back to 1948 to criticize him for withdrawing *Macbeth* from the competition. Why enter and then withdraw? Is the festival some kind of game? The room was full of disgruntlement and embarrassing questions."[31]

> "He started by saying in Italian that he no longer remembered Italian and in English that he had even forgotten his English. . . . He thanked the organizers of the festival for their kindness at a time, he said, when directors counted for less and less. He was sincere, pained . . ."[32]

> "Seraphic, dressed in white, a large smile on his creased face, he spoke devotedly and with humility, addressing Festival Director Petrucci and the press in rather faltering, subdued Italian, from which we understood that he was making a sincere and pained apology. He explained why *Othello* had been withdrawn."[33]

"Welles said: 'The other directors all move on, but I am stuck. This film is my last chance and I can't afford to make the wrong move.' He spoke Italian with a childish lilt, every now and then lifting his eyes heavenward. 'The film is finished but the print and mixing are of poor quality. We were too anxious to take part in this festival. I just can't allow this version to be screened. It would ruin three years of hard work.' Welles recited contrition perfectly and perhaps he was genuinely sorry. 'My next film will be called *The Intimate Diary of Othello,* and will tell the story of the film you haven't been able to see today.'"[34]

"Shot with a variety of materials in a number of different locations and climates, the film needed end treatment, accurate fixing and printing. But in the haste the print had come out only here and there as a dry canvas. The soundtrack was also defective. Last but not least, the copy Welles had was dubbed by Gino Cervi, an excellent dubber, as Welles said, but it was the Italian version all the same, and not the version he had hoped to screen. Welles should have the right, as the director and leading actor, to present the film with his own voice, and not the voice of another actor, however good."[35]

"He was kind, funny, a little awkward. He said that he did not want to ruin three years of hard work; he said the film had been dubbed excellently but too quickly, hence the technical imperfections. He said Shakespeare was magnificent; he said everything. in other words. except why the film, entered three months earlier, was not ready and why the English-language version was still in London while its author meditated in or around Versailles. But geniuses have the right to forget things every now and then and Welles is doubtless a genius."[36]

"The gifted American filmmaker torments his right ear as he speaks in public; it helps him think. However, we didn't get the impression that it helped him clarify the reasons one of the films scheduled for the festival wasn't screened. 'Will you take part in the Festival in the future, with other films?' they asked him. 'It all depends if they still want me after today,' he replied."[37]

"He concluded by saying that after three years of unstinting work, he was in a sorrier position than those who had come to see the film, and was as disappointed as they were. Except for a few exceptions, the journalists accepted his apology. And Welles won his battle, once more. A strange fate, his: triumphant in life, defeated in his art."[38]

"He was applauded, a homage to the solitary and stubborn fighter, to one of the few filmmakers and actors today able to throw himself headlong into a generous—nay, a noble—enterprise."[39]

Welles understood he had sailed very close to the wind. He managed to placate the journalists and organizers who had been furious. Wryly, he commented, "The Venice Film Festival treated my badly when I was the great Welles. Now that I'm only a little Welles, they are good to me."

The news of the withdrawal of the film was given out too late to prevent the public from crowding in front of the gates of the main theater.
The gates remained closed; the screen stayed blank. When the cancel-
ation of the screening was finally announced, several filmgoers tried to
attack Petrucci.

Some thought the press conference was nothing more than an example of Welles's acting skills. Vittorio Bonicelli wrote, "What's dramatic is
that he acted contrition although he genuinely felt it, acted an apology
although he felt really sorry and was worried by the consequences of
what he had done." Later, Welles and Bonicelli went to dinner together.
They ordered meat, and when Welles was brought a skinny half chicken,
he burst out, "This is what producers give me when I want to shoot a
scene in a certain way."

Perhaps, as some suspected, Welles regretted promising the film to
Venice and by now preferred Cannes. His reputation had not suffered
in France as it had in Italy. But it was also true that *Othello* needed more
work and more money before it could be screened satisfactorily.

The presence in Venice of Olian and a business partner gave Welles
hope. He arranged to have breakfast with them at the Excelsior. Welles
assumed his most persuasive demeanor; recruited a guest of the festival,
Joseph Cotten, as assistant; and made sure they had a table near Winston
Churchill, who was resting in Venice before the new general election
in Britain. "Winston, how nice to see you again," he said to his august
breakfast companion. When Churchill failed to rise to the occasion,
Welles explained that Churchill was not feeling well. Welles's two guests
(described by Cotten as "tough and exceedingly wealthy businessmen")
suggested meeting again in the evening and disappeared to make some
mysterious intercontinental phone calls.

Later that day, as Cotten recounted, they "spotted Churchill swimming in the Lido. In a flash, Orson had his swimming trunks on and
was in the water beside him." Welles apologized for his earlier ruse and
explained that he had wanted to impress the two gentlemen he was with.
Churchill again said nothing but that evening, when a gloomy-looking
Welles, Cotten, and the potential backers passed in front of Churchill's
table, the statesman "stood up," Cotten remembered, "looked directly at

Orson, and bowed slowly and deeply." Olian was so impressed by Welles's friendship with Churchill that the deal was struck that evening.[40]

Exactly what the deal was is a mystery. It seems to have been some kind of addition to the agreement with Loew's, granting them 50 percent of the distribution rights for Great Britain and the Commonwealth for 100 million lire. The mechanism was the same as before—the American funds would be released from an account held by the Banca d'America e d'Italia. However, the record of the agreement in the State Archives is not accompanied by the usual documents for the release of funds, so it may have been a phony contract arranged by Olian to obtain the funds on behalf of one of his clients.

The following day Welles met Churchill on the beach and thanked him for his help. From then on, Welles told Bogdanovich, every evening, as he entered the dining room, Churchill *rose* to acknowledge him, "probably thinking, 'Well, every time I stand up, he gets some more dough—so why not?'"[41]

On September 3, 1951, Venice was the focus of worldwide media attention. Mexican millionaire Carlos de Beistegui hosted a masked costume ball with fifteen hundred illustrious guests, including Gene Tierney, Salvador Dalí, and Christian Dior. Cecil Beaton photographed the event. High society from Rome and Milan danced the night away in Palazzo Labia on the Grand Canal, to sambas and the music of Mozart, Boccherini, and Gluck. The neighboring square, Campo di San Geremia, became crowded with curious onlookers. "I happened to be invited," Welles related, "and of course Churchill was, too, but he was hoping to get back into office and everybody was attacking the ball as conspicuous luxury and all that, so he couldn't go. And here we are all going off in our speedboats to the ball, and there was Churchill down at the end of the dock watching us leave, ready—and miserable."

Welles had two excellent reasons for attending the lavish event. He wanted to see Louise de Vilmorin, the fascinating writer with whom he had fallen in love,[42] and to write an account of the evening for his friend Alberto Mondadori's weekly, *Epoca*. The playful article is a mixture of good humor, irony, self-deprecation, and razor-sharp wit, as the following excerpt shows:

Venice is the most beautiful home in the world. I know its ins and outs, its finest and its most tawdry spots, the secret alleyways off the Grand Canal . . . as far as the Doge's Palace . . . The newspapers have spoken insistently of a scandalous event. I'm a playboy and many have said, some even written, that I like scandals. Meaning that I cause them. They say so even when it isn't entirely true. Or when it's totally false. But on this occasion, I was downright curious to know how the Venetians would cope with Don Carlos. A city that in its long history has never rebelled or had a revolution—except Fornaretto, poor fellow—but now everyone seemed to be revolting against the Mexican. What I wanted to know was whether the Venice I had got to know shooting *Othello* was the same Venice that had always managed to find a perfect point of balance between luxury and good taste, the good life and a life of discipline. Rehearsing at St. James's Theatre in London I thought about the costume I would wear to the ball. Impossible to move Othello into the eighteenth century. Too far. Cagliostro was just right. I got there without the costume, of course, which hadn't arrived from Rome. I get distracted, as everyone knows. Some think I do it deliberately. But that evening, at eight o'clock, I suddenly realized I had no costume. I had to improvise. At the Danieli they found me a turban, something between a lady's art nouveau hat and the headdress of a Sioux Indian chief . . . The port workers, in floating attendance on the Grand Canal, opposite Palazzo Labia, would occasionally burst into applause, or whistle their disapproval, with genuine feeling and participation, as the guests arrived by boat. . . . It couldn't happen in any other country or any other city in Italy . . . This city under the siege of water is a world unto itself. The Italian art of balance finds its greatest expression here. Over the centuries the ordinary folk of the city have rubbed shoulders too often with its aristocrats, merchants, warlords, and artists not to become like them, actors and protagonists in the same great comedy of life. The comedy of Veronese and Tintoretto, Othello, Tiepolo's Pulcinellas, and Titian's magnificent women . . . the same ordinary folk now crowding the adjacent Campo San Geremia. When they recognized us, they called us by name, me Othello actually. From the windows came eighteenth-century music, slowly becoming modern. The guests danced until dawn . . . Don Carlos smiled throughout, even to the tired guests who had taken off their shoes and the women who had cut their feet on some broken glass. At seven o'clock in the morning Don Carlos said that the following year he would give another ball, dedicated to a different century. At eight o'clock I sat down to type this article: you see, I had to prove that I can keep a promise.[43]

Tullio Kezich
"A maverick filmmaker"
ROME, APRIL 23, 2005

An essayist, playwright, and screenwriter, Tullio Kezich (1928–2009) was one of Italy's best-known film critics. He was a close friend of Federico Fellini, about whom he wrote extensively. He started his career writing about the Venice Film Festival for Radio Trieste and was present at the first screening of *Macbeth*. He was also in Venice three years later when *Othello* was withdrawn from the event. Perhaps more than any other critic he was aware of the atmosphere of hostility and distrust between Welles and the leading Italian film critics of the day.

TULLIO KEZICH: Today Welles is a legendary filmmaker, but that was not at all the case back then. His immense reputation perhaps didn't help. The idea that this wunderkind had created what some people considered the world's greatest film made the critics suspicious. Just Hollywood marketing, we thought. They're trying to foist on us the next generation of filmmakers, who may or may not have talent. There wasn't a great deal of anxious expectation about *Citizen Kane;* it was more grudging than anything else. In Italy, RKO practically threw the movie away, along with *The Magnificent Ambersons.* Back then, I was the film critic for a radio station in Trieste and Callisto Cosulich wrote for *il Piccolo.* We knew all the film distributors in town. When we went to the RKO distributor, he asked us why on earth we were interested in *Citizen Kane.* It was scheduled to be screened from Tuesday to Friday, not the weekend, which was reserved for popular, successful films. I'm not even sure it made it to Friday.

The same thing happened in other cities, at least in Milan and Rome.

TK: *Citizen Kane* was released only here and there. It was a minor event. People seemed disappointed by it and *The Magnificent Ambersons* also got nowhere. Trieste was in a strange situation. All the theaters had been requisitioned by the Allies, so Callisto and I put on some oversized sweaters and pretended to be American soldiers. You paid and said up or down, circle or stalls, and went in. They were the only English words we knew. We got to see a lot of films that way, but not *Citizen Kane* or *The Magnificent Ambersons,* because they were not shown by the army. The soldiers had seen them years earlier. In Italy, they were screened in the less important theaters; *The Magnificent Ambersons,* I recall, was shown in Novo Cine, a theater that normally showed B or even C movies, horror films, or Westerns made on a shoestring. But *The Stranger* was presented at the 1947 Venice Film Festival, where it was poorly received—perhaps rightly so. It certainly wasn't Welles's best work.

What happened at the festival a year later?

TK: Welles came to the festival with *Macbeth* and things began to get interesting. It wasn't like now, when the big names show their faces for a few seconds then go to their hotel rooms. Then it was all a huge melting pot. You could speak to anyone. Welles had a clan of his own: Luigi Barzini, Jr.; Lea Padovani; and Alberto Mondadori, a rather exuberant fellow—always with a glass of whisky in his hand, addressing the crowd in a loud voice. This group was viewed with a certain ironic detachment.

Alfredo Todisco was another member, I think.

TK: In Trieste, young Todisco was a sort of Sunday journalist. During the week he worked in the offices of the Allied military government, in public works, I think. He came from the Guf Theater groups and had the ambition to write. But he spoke good English, hence his job with the Allies. In Venice he introduced himself to Welles. Nobody spoke English back then, so Welles surrounded himself with people who could talk to him. He didn't speak Italian and he felt like an Italian might in Finland. Orson liked Todisco immediately and changed his life, inspiring him to go to Rome and become a very successful and well-known journalist. One day, he showed us a white tie autographed by Welles that he was very proud of. "He told me to call him Orson," he said. We were a little envious, but we didn't speak English, so what could we say?

What happened at the screening of Macbeth?

TK: It was shown the same evening as Mario Soldati's *Fuga in Francia* (Flight to France). We were in the main theater of the cinema building. It was the first year the festival had returned to the Lido and the theater was packed. Back then, journalists watched the films together with the public, and although there weren't nearly as many journalists as there are today, the theater could barely cope with the numbers. I had to sit on a step—next to Soldati, whose film was onscreen. Welles didn't want his film to be shown with what he considered to be a commercial picture; it was bad scheduling, he thought. When *Macbeth* came on, I must say the public appeared to like it, but the critics didn't. There was a press conference that immediately became rather tragic. Orson had an interpreter, but he was facing a group of people who refused to believe that he was all that he was cracked up to be. It was an extremely hostile press conference, as I recall, after which Welles withdrew *Macbeth* from the competition because he had been told Olivier's *Hamlet* was favorite for the Golden Lion. Barzini was the interpreter, and I remember him rather exaggerating Welles's remarks, which he made somewhat casually, but the translation came out different. For example Barzini said, a little pompously, "Mr. Welles accepts the definition of baroque for his work." Or another time, and this is amusing: "Mr. Welles and Eisenstein exchanged letters in which they both acknowledged themselves to be sons of D. W. Griffith, although not related to each other." I think the whole press conference was riddled with misunderstandings and incomprehension. I remember Welles saying, and I heard this with my own ears, "What can you expect . . . mine is a small, low-budget film and I'm up against the British Empire." Which was totally untrue. *Hamlet* was certainly not a product of British artistic and economic power. It was the film of an Italian adventurer, Filippo Del Giudice, who appreciated Olivier's genius and had the great merit of putting him onscreen with *Henry V* and *Hamlet*. He was an independent producer who had struggled to get financial backing for his films, as everyone did those days.

Do you think the critics favored Hamlet *because it was produced by Del Giudice? Did they have a bias towards an Italian producer?*

TK: No, Del Giudice had left Italy for England . . . There was an obvious misunderstanding. I remember Mondadori writing, "This *Macbeth*, sculpted in bronze and steel," and some objected that it actually seemed to have been sculpted out of cardboard because the caves were made like Neapolitan nativity scenes, and the actors were good theater actors, although somewhat perfunctory. It was clearly a film made on a low budget . . . Welles had agreed to do it and had made a great job of it. Few understood that Welles was not only a great director and actor but also a resourceful producer. He would turn anything to some use, in true Italian style. Anyway, he said he just couldn't compete with *Hamlet* and withdrew the film from competition. For this he was criticized. When they challenged his decision, he replied, "But this film will never be distributed in Italy because you can't dub Shakespeare." In fact, it was dubbed, excellently, by Gino Cervi, who also dubbed Olivier's *Hamlet.* And the dubbing was expensive. Let's say it's as if you wanted Giancarlo Giannini to dub a film today. Anyhow, that changed nothing; it was all a gigantic misunderstanding. The hostility was palpable. Welles was given the assistance—before, during, and after—of Elsa Maxwell, the famous columnist, a shrew who must have been seventy if she was a day and who was also rather plump and plain. Oddly, Welles, who had fought his battles with the Hollywood gossip columnists Hopper and Parsons, brought Elsa into his group. She was part of his coterie. I remember him obligingly helping her into her fur coat; it was obvious who was boss. He needed her. And she launched into an attack on Italy in her newspaper, saying we had treated Welles badly, he was right to withdraw the film because it had been made perfectly clear that no one liked it and the disgraceful jury was going to deny him any award. Her article was quoted widely in the Italian press and was deeply resented because she had turned the defense of Welles into an attack on Italy and the festival, which she claimed was rigged. Well, there were one or two strange things at the festival, admittedly; for example, the jurors were allowed to review the films in their newspapers, which is unimaginable today.

Were the films subtitled? From the reviews, it seems that none of the Italian critics understood Macbeth *very well.*

TK: Most of them were, yes. But in this case, I don't think so . . . I don't remember. The film was made on a shoestring, so I doubt it. It was produced by Republic, which made Westerns with Gene Autry and Roy Rogers, the cowboy singers, all the films under the *Three Mesquiteers* umbrella, and B movies with John Wayne before he moved up. It's not as if they were going to splash out money to compete in Venice.

What do you remember of Welles's failure to take part in the Festival in 1951?

TK: That was completely different. *Othello* was scheduled for screening on the evening of August 31 but that morning it was rumored the viewing had been canceled. There was a press conference. Welles stood on the stage, alone, in front of a large number of journalists from all over the world. This time he surprised everyone by speaking Italian. He was quite fluent, although he sounded like someone who had learned his Italian from Dante and Machiavelli. He said, "Other directors move forward. Only I stay put, and this doesn't seem right to me." Then he mentioned the difficulties he had encountered in making *Othello* and said, "As it stands, my film is currently a little midday and a little midnight," meaning that in the print you could see the different work of the various cinematographers and the fact that some scenes began in one continent and finished in another. "I'd hoped I would be able to finish the film for this occasion, but I have not succeeded." That year in Venice the films in competition included *Rashōmon*, Bresson's *Le journal d'un curé de campagne,* and Billy Wilder's *Ace in the Hole.* So maybe he had understood it would be a difficult competition, or else someone from Cannes had promised him something, so he delayed completion . . . Anyway, he was right to withdraw the film because he won Cannes, albeit with Castellani, which will not have pleased him at all. Looking back over the following years, I think directors and producers in Venice and Cannes started covering their asses about that time. Still, the film had a number of problems. But at the press conference, the fact that he spoke Italian, in confidence, almost in despair, and not like a big star but more like a man with serious problems on his mind, who complained that Hollywood directors had enormous resources while he had to make do with what he could find . . . this made us think of him quite differently, with far more sympathy than before. Only a few were resentful. I remember an English journalist, Francis Koval, who introduced himself and challenged Welles: "You mean we can't see the film because the print isn't perfect . . . but we are specialists, and since we have come all this way, you can and should show us the film. We'll understand the improvements a new print will make." Welles apologized: "I must beg your pardon, you'll see the film when it is finished, because until it is finished . . ." and he drew a circle around himself in the air. "I have this fortress." A neat way of saying that he had the right to decide.

How did the public react?

TK: I was a meter away from something quite sensational that happened on the steps leading up to the theater. People were coming from far and wide to see Welles's film. Antonio Petrucci, the Christian Democrat director of the festival, was passing by. He was a tough man, put there by Andreotti to take the festival away from the Venetians—an arrogant man, surrounded by flunkies. To speak to him you had to get past row upon row of filters. Someone saw him, started insulting him, and came close to hitting him. "You don't know how to run the festival! We came here to see a film and now they tell us this film isn't here!" Petrucci was standing next to the chief of police and simply told him to remove this ugly disturbance. The man was arrested and others who were protesting were also taken away. It wasn't Petrucci's fault that *Othello* hadn't arrived. So in addition to the new light in which we were disposed to see Orson, after his humble apology, there was also a minority, outside the theater, who were angered by his failure to bring the film. That evening the festival screened no film at all, which was odd. Many people didn't forgive Welles for that.

One of the little mysteries of Welles in Italy is the photo in the Caffè Greco.

TK: I don't know who organized it, who got everyone to come, but it's certainly artfully posed and composed. Welles is surrounded by the most formidable intellectuals of the day, but is clearly an odd man out. Lea Padovani was everyone's friend; they treated her well due to her beauty, so I'd say he was included because she was there and he was with her. Welles was a routine presence in Rome, although, in my opinion, he never fit in, was never part of the community. He didn't help himself with declarations such as the one about Italy being a country of born actors, except for the professional actors. The photo shows the pseudo-integration of Welles into Rome society. I think Welles was Flaiano's famous *Martian in Rome.* The story was published in *il Mondo* and it more or less recounts Welles's reception in Rome, first in Via Veneto—a curiosity—then somewhere else in the city—nothing surprising—then later, somewhere else—not him again! And, finally, why doesn't he go home? That is just how it was with Welles in Italy.

However, this conflict also had an artistic dimension: he represented one view of the cinema and Italy then espoused an opposing view. He was accused of formalism and rebutted by continuing to criticize neorealism. Our critics went too far but Welles was hardly diplomatic . . .

TK: No, he certainly wasn't. Our film industry at the time was somewhere else entirely. It was the worst possible moment to do Shakespeare. Castellani's *Romeo and Juliet,* in 1954, was made in an entirely different climate. An Italian director wouldn't have dreamed of making *Macbeth* in 1948. It ran against everything our cinema stood for. But Welles rather liked running against what something or someone stood for. He was a maverick filmmaker. His was literary cinema, based on a close relationship with the actors. When he made *Citizen Kane* he transferred the entire Mercury Theater to the screen and made some actors world famous: Joseph Cotten, Paul Stewart, Everett Sloane, Agnes Moorehead, and others who stayed in Hollywood. At that moment *Macbeth* was just wrong for Italy. And Olivier was able to do his *Hamlet* because of a certain aura he had . . . Later, the various versions of *Macbeth* in Italy, including the famous one by Tino Buazzelli in 1968, restored a lot of what Welles had had in mind. But you're right. It was the wrong moment; our taste was elsewhere. Our critics didn't understand Welles and Welles didn't understand them.

The first Italian film critic to give Welles a proper hearing was Giulio Cesare Castello. A close friend of yours, I believe.

TK: I adored him. He was one of the first critics to write both about theater and film. Historically, film critics couldn't care less about the theater and vice versa, with the added complication of the inferiority complex of the theater critics, too. Neorealist cinema hated actors. Once a friend of mine, a Triestine actor, Mario Valdemarin, who had worked in theater with Visconti and Strehler, went for an audition with Pietro Germi. Germi went up to him, had a lot of pictures taken, and said, "Very interesting. What do you do in ordinary life?" "I'm an actor," Valdemarin replied. "Ah, OK. We'll let you know," and that was that. Germi wasn't interested. That was the neorealist attitude toward professional actors, and

eventually it included Anna Magnani, Fabrizi, and the actors that came
from vaudeville. Welles was a professional theater actor and was the opposite of a neorealist. Castello, however, was an expert of both cinema
and theater, so he understood actors. One fine day, he had a sort of crisis;
something terrifying happened. He taught at the Centro Sperimentale
but wanted to be a university professor: when he wasn't accepted, he
took it very badly. He felt that he was the victim of an injustice and gave
everything up overnight. "I've ruined my life for something stupid like
the cinema when there is music," he said. "One page of Mozart is worth
everything the cinema ever made. I'd like to write about music, but now
it's too late." For the last twenty or thirty years of his life he was very
withdrawn; I don't even know how he made ends meet. Maybe he had a
little money set aside from the family. I never saw him again at a festival,
but he was an excellent critic.

Did you ever see Welles again?

T K : I didn't, but my wife did. When she was a girl, Alessandra lived
in Largo Bradano 4, where Paola Mori's family also lived. So she would
see Welles sometimes, down in the street below. The Martian was now
just a regular visitor to a place, like any other, in Rome.

Do you know anything about the article by Roberto De Paolis?

T K : Roberto De Paolis . . . I don't know him.

*It's a pseudonym for Guido Aristarco. The real name came up because
Welles sued him for some remarks about his drinking habits.*

T K : Show me. *"He gets up at nine, already drunk . . ."* Nonsense. I
never saw Welles drink too much. In 1951 Joseph Cotten gave a press
conference on the terrace of the Excelsior Hotel in Rome and he, for
sure, was tipsy, swaying this way and that as if tossed by the wind. Dana
Andrews and Van Heflin were drinkers. When American actors drink,
they drink. I'm not saying Welles never had a drop of alcohol but if he
was excessive, it was in his food. Which also suggests he didn't drink:
alcoholics aren't usually great eaters.

*I have an article by Aristarco which contains some lines practically iden-
tical to the ones signed by De Paolis. They're both about* Citizen Kane.

T K : Well, Guido wasn't like Castello, who had skills he didn't possess. If he wrote about the same thing for two newspapers, Aristarco just
rehashed the same thing. Once Castello wanted to review *I capricci di*

Marianna (Marianna's whims), which was being staged in Capri, with De Lullo. To pay for the trip, board, and lodging, he had persuaded four newspapers to buy his piece. So he wrote four different articles. Aristarco was in awe of him. He used to ask me how he did it. I said he could do the same and he said no, he couldn't because it wouldn't be right to change his mind. So I said it wasn't a matter of changing your mind, but of changing the focus, the wording, and writing about another aspect. Aristarco was an anti-journalist. "*Welles wants to dazzle at all costs . . .*" Yes, that's Aristarco all right. I think the battle with Welles was because although Aristarco wrote about films all his life, he wasn't a film person at all, and in fact, wisely, he didn't write much about the cinema—he just reviewed films . . .

13

Reviewing *Othello*
The World Premiere

Ah, *Othello* . . . I saw it this year at the St. James's Theatre.
I didn't like the leading actor very much but I got a big kick out of the play.

—Sigsbee Manderson (Orson Welles), *Trent's Last Case*

When *Othello* was withdrawn from the Venice Film Festival, the possibility that Welles and Italy might be reconciled faded away to nothing. Although many of the journalists present at the press conference allowed themselves to be persuaded by Welles's fine oratory, nearly every article they wrote had a touch of rancor. Four years' worth of gossip and criticism had dug a deep hole for Welles that no press conference could fill.

The battle resumed, if less openly than the one over *Macbeth*. The unwitting catalyst this time was Alberto Mondadori, Italy's most vociferous—and perhaps only real—champion of Welles. On September 8, 1951, he published the first review ever written of *Othello*. He had seen the Italian version of the film just before Welles had rejected it for the festival. The review was an enthusiastic defense of the film's baroque manner. More than that, it sought to rescue the baroque as an art form from the cultural margins to which it had been consigned by one of Italy's most influential philosophers and intellectuals of the interwar period, Benedetto Croce. Mondadori tried to persuade his readers that the baroque was more eclectic than Croce had admitted, and a system "rich with intimate tension, movement, vitality, imagination, filling every possible void," in opposition (down through the ages) to classical taste. Welles was a product of the baroque, Mondadori wrote, "a follower of Tintoretto and El Greco, bringing together the rationalism of Pascal and the labyrinth of Theseus." Such a description went against the grain of the aesthetic tastes of Italian critics, and was bound to be challenged, as Mondadori knew perfectly well: "God only knows how Welles's latest work will be judged."[1]

Mondadori's long article was full of praise for the Shakespeare adaptation, the technique, and the style of the film. It anticipated the objections of other critics, defending Welles's formalism from the usual accusation of gratuitous violence and exhibitionism by showing how the form of the film enhanced its content. "The most evidently original part of the film," wrote Mondadori, "albeit aesthetically mediated, is the use of lingering closeups to reveal the thoughts and feelings of the characters." Welles gives new life to the ancient drama through a "modern interpretation of a range of feelings and states of mind, and the workings of fate—which, as in Wagner, override even the will of the gods." The film's "overwhelming" visual effect is achieved through a series of "enchantments," as "the story is presented at times sparsely, at other times as if unleashed from the precarious senses of the characters." These images "are not themselves precarious; their rhythm is dictated by the needs of expression." He concluded, "Cinema can take its rightful place among the arts only when its technique becomes a language."

With proud citations and erudite references, Mondadori was attempting to ward off negative criticism by placing the entire argument on a new plane. However, he also gave vent to strong feelings and an evident resentment prompted by past criticism: "Welles the actor takes second place to Welles the director, so it will not be easy to repeat the accusations of three years ago, when critics found his performance exhibitionist and mannered." Mondadori returned to the thorny issue of the Venice Film Festival of 1948 to point the finger: "At that time the welcome given to *Macbeth* was, to say the least, brusque and offensive, despite the fact that—whatever Luigi Chiarini or Gian Luigi Rondi might say—the film is one of the few recent cinema offerings of note."

Mondadori intended to wage war on Welles's critics, and the skirmishes began immediately. When Paolo Valmarana wrote of the troubling Orson Welles affair, he questioned Mondadori's status as commentator, confirmed his previous panning of *Macbeth,* and upbraided Welles for his foray into high-society journalism (neglecting to cite the publication in question, Mondadori's *Epoca*). However, Valmarana also compared Othello's relationship with Desdemona to Welles's ongoing fight with European culture:

> When we are told—by well-informed albeit not authoritative sources—that *Othello* is Welles's most important film, his best, his most sincere, we have no difficulty in believing it. Othello's love for Desdemona, overwhelming, immense, primitive and irrational, tempestuous and unruly, to the point of suffocating its object, is exactly like Welles's love for European culture.... [A]nd who is the utmost expression of this culture if not Shakespeare? ... In *Macbeth,* a homage to the Bard, doubtless full of love but altogether lacking in respect and all too untroubled, the drama of Macbeth and Lady Macbeth collapses into nothingness. What is left ... is an empty shell: a horrid and bloody episode ... the characters bawling at each other, persecuted by a fate decided on paper by the insensitive and superficial scriptwriter. This time, we were expecting to see *Othello,* but instead we get another puzzling affair: ... this non-event, this non-appearance of the film.... At least, that is what we have been led to believe, but opening one of the leading Italian weeklies the other day we couldn't help noticing the latest sad episode in the life of the American filmmaker ... there, on glossy paper, was an article signed by a man who had once terrified America with a Martian invasion, a man whose first film had shocked the world, albeit without entirely winning it over, and who now—we hope only temporarily—has become a crepuscular and decadent society reporter, informing us of the grooming of Emanuela Castelbarco and Simonetta Visconti.[2]

The next shots were fired by Luigi Chiarini, who, like Rondi, was accused of rudeness at the Venice Film Festival. In an article in *Cinema,* he feigned continuance of an ongoing discussion of the specifics of film language in a long preamble on cinematography in general, and on film adaptations of theatrical and literary works in particular. He then got to the point:

> I don't want to bore my readers with Mondadori's entirely unjustified, insolent tone, which he seems to use regularly when referring to me, solely because I have expressed reservations about Welles's *Macbeth.*.... I have never denied Orson Welles's talent and his mastery of cinema technique, nor can I comment on *Othello*—which I haven't seen and which may indeed, as Mondadori claims, be a wonderful film, because the ebullient American director is certainly a man of character; but excessive technical virtuosity should not be taken for a new cinematic language, and the only one which should be spoken.[3]

Despite the conciliatory tone, Chiarini was accusing the film of "excessive technical virtuosity" at the same time as admitting he hadn't seen it.

Mondadori reacted with ironic composure. Later he wrote to Chiarini privately, thanking him for quoting his review of *Othello* and saying he had no time for a full reply to be published in *Cinema*. He concluded with one last jibe: "I am pleased by the fact that you have changed your mind and are now prepared to recognize that the talent and character of Orson Welles deserve respect. I, too, am willing to concede that technical virtuosity can sometimes be mistaken for an authorized cinematic language, but about this the discussion could go on at length."[4]

Rondi and Welles's other opponents stood ready to join in the fight, but an immediate pretext could not be found: *Othello* had not been released and Orson Welles was in London, working on a theater production of the same work.

The show opened on October 1, 1951, and was given an uneven reception. As usual, Welles took it philosophically; presenting a magic act to Princess Elizabeth and the Duke of Edinburgh, he said, "I have just come from the St. James's Theatre, where I have been murdering Desdemona—or Shakespeare—according to which newspaper you read."

A few weeks later, the Milan court summoned Welles to plead his suit against *Bis* and the journalist De Paolis (Aristarco), who had called him a drunk. The legal battle had been going on for over three years, and the hearing was scheduled for November 5. The last edition of *Corriere della Sera* reported on the case:

> The eleventh section of the court, presided over by Dr. Biotti (and State Prosecutor Balsamo, Clerk of Court Galante), this morning heard the libel suit brought by the American actor Orson Welles against the cinema weekly *Bis*. None of the protagonists was present—Welles; Salvato Cappelli, editor of *Bis*; photographer Stefano Vanzini; or the author of the article, Guido Aristarco. The piece, accompanied by a series of photographs, included insinuations Welles considered injurious to his dignity as an artist and a man. He had appointed the attorney Serrao to assist him in the suit. *Bis* was represented by attorney-at-law A. Pestalozza. The hearing had been set for this morning after numerous delays caused by the absence of the plaintiff. This caused the public prosecutor to invoke section 144 of the code of criminal procedure and demand a fine for Welles and a court order to force him to appear, accompanied by officers of the law if need be. After brief deliberation, the court imposed a fine of five thousand lire on Welles but did not issue a subpoena or order court officers to produce Welles by force. A new hearing was scheduled.[5]

Nothing came of the suit, which had lost interest for everyone. *Bis* had been closed down and the suit would hardly have reflected well on Aristarco, who had criticized *Citizen Kane* and invented stories of Welles's drunkenness under the cover of a pseudonym. Even if Welles had wanted to come to court on previous occasions, it is unlikely he would have managed to get there, busy as he was with the reediting of *Macbeth* and the shooting of *Othello.*

The day of the hearing, Welles was in Cannes—"on private business," the newspapers said—probably negotiating for *Othello* to be included in the upcoming film festival. It was a strategic decision for Welles. He had tried for some years now to restart his career in Italy and had failed to win over the Venice Film Festival; Cannes might be more benevolent. Perhaps he was not so disappointed that *Othello* was not shown in Venice.

Welles stayed on the French Riviera for a couple of days, during which he called a new press conference. He spoke mostly about his theatrical production of *Othello,* which after London he wanted to take to Paris, Brussels, Milan, Rome, Venice, and Madrid. Of course, he was also quizzed about the film and the dual Shakespeare adaptation. "Some criticize me for giving two different interpretations of the same play," he said. "But why not? Shakespeare is immense. He contains everything. He is forever present. All interpretations are valid and possible. I have also been criticized for making cuts. It's true. You can't put on *Othello* without cutting. A French critic, who otherwise praises me, says that my Roderigo is a clownish figure. Only a French critic could say such a thing. The French will never understand Shakespeare just as the English will never understand Racine." He also spoke about Italy, with affection and increasing diffidence and perplexity. "He says he loves the Mediterranean and Italy," wrote journalist Angelo Maccario, "but he finds the Italian public cold, detached from what is onstage . . . perhaps this is because the Italians have the theater in the streets, which are so animated, picturesque, and full of life."[6]

Yet he had promised to premiere his new film in Italy. Film festival rules were not as strict as they are today; the film would be allowed to compete in Cannes even if it had previously been released in Italy. The English-language version presented at the Cannes Film Festival has always been considered the "original"—although a dubbed version approved by Welles was already in general release in Italy.

It was first shown on November 29, 1951. According to the "explicit wishes of Orson Welles," the world premiere of *Othello* was at the Barberini Cinema in Rome, where a gala evening was organized, the proceeds going to the Don Carlo Gnocchi Institute for children mutilated by war. Scalera was on the verge of bankruptcy and publicized the premiere poorly. The press release consisted of four typed pages informing the public that, after Venice, Welles and Waszynski had taken a month to obtain a properly printed and dubbed version of the film and that the original language version would be ready in a few days, at the beginning of December.

Rome's *il Messaggero* and *il Tempo* publicized the premiere right up to opening day, informing their readers that tickets could still be obtained from the box office of the theaters themselves. But they sent no reporters and the critics stayed away; they would see it later. The two leading newspapers did not cover the event or review the film; this appears to have been a deliberate snub. Only *L'Eco del Cinema e dello Spettacolo* told its readers that the beneficiaries of the charity event, the war injured, had decided to turn the proceeds of the gala over to the victims of flooding in northeastern Italy.

The evening of November 30, another gala event was held—this time at the Missori cinema in Milan, where the film was beginning its general release. The proceeds would once again go to the flood victims of Polesine. In Rome the film was scheduled for release on December 5 at the Fiamma and Ariston, after a typically Wellesian publicity gimmick using an airplane vapor trail: *il Tempo* advised its readers to look into the sky at 1:00 PM to see the title of a great film, *Othello*, flying above their heads.

In *Corriere della Sera,* Lanocita wrote,

> *Othello* is much to be preferred to *Macbeth.* It is a dense film, expressive, evocative, and poetic—qualities we no longer expected from a director whose character leads him into an opulent display of techniques, many of which have only incidental importance.... Alongside the genuine poetic effects, his pompous, corrupted decorative style strives for poetry and fails, lacking in penetration and interpenetration.... Nor is the relationship between Welles the actor and Welles the director ever settled. Which prevails? Who is at the service of whom?

... The film presents an Othello in line with the most perceptive commentators
of Shakespeare, a man with the meekness and violence of a generous lion, unri-
valed in a straight fight yet easily tricked and overthrown by deception.... For
all its scintillating hyperbole, its resonant and luxurious texture, it is the most
deeply thought out of Welles's films, after the revolutionary Citizen Kane.[7]

Vittorio Bonicelli noted that when Iago admits his guilt ("What
you know, you know"), he looks directly into Othello's eyes, as if to accuse him of complicity in his wickedness. The critic had expected to see
Welles's horrified and pained expression as he learns of Iago's treachery,
but instead, Othello appears lost in thought, murkily conscious of his
own guilt. Struck by this scene, Bonicelli dared express the unimaginable—a preference for Welles over Olivier: "The film, now on release
in Italy's two biggest cities ([I]s this world premiere the homage of an
itinerant Welles to the country he says he loves the most?), will be given
a rough ride. I can already hear the accusations of excess and megalo-
mania. It saddens me. Overall, the film is an important work. Maybe I
suffer from fascination with generous, imperfect natures. Here the film
is rather more than a wager: it displays the energy of life that always go
hand and hand with error and is closer to greatness than the righteous
could ever be, with their subtle calculations. True, Welles is unpopular.
So what? The cinema has too many popular actors and directors: a disaster at a time of conformity. There is more Shakespeare in the "arrogance"
and "ribaldry" of Orson Welles than in the refined academic work of
Laurence Olivier. (Here endeth my reputation.)"[8]

In Oggi, Angelo Solmi was measured. The film has "some inexplica-
ble highs and lows," he wrote. "The copy on release is far from perfect....
The formal virtues, when the director overdoes them, become vices." For
Verdi lovers "the arrival of Othello in Cyprus will be a disappointment,"
he said. After these introductory remarks, the review was largely positive,
suggesting that perhaps the time was right for a reappraisal of Welles:

> Othello is far from being photographed theater. On the contrary, it is pure
> cinema, with a dynamism we are no longer used to. Even if the film had no other
> merits, it would be enough to say that, unlike so many postwar films, it isn't the
> trite and straightforward telling of a story (in the current fashion of misunder-
> stood realism). This is a film narrated with all the means the cinema has at its
> disposal, many of which have unjustly fallen into neglect. After Citizen Kane,
> which stunned, The Magnificent Ambersons, which perplexed, and the others

(*The Stranger, The Lady from Shanghai,* and *Macbeth*), which some considered bluffs, *Othello* is a step in the right direction. Welles is no bluff. When he learns to control his verve and limit his magniloquence, aestheticism, and penchant for symbolism, the cinema will acquire a first-rate artist. *Othello* is already halfway there. Even if Welles doesn't live up to all his promise, he will be spoken of for years to come.[9]

Other reviews in the Italian press pointed out the qualities of the film, but in general, it was received poorly. In *il Messaggero,* Ermanno Contini criticized the cuts in the first three acts, reducing Iago's scheming to a "rather mechanical, naïve and unsubtle game." He saw the film as insufficiently narrated cinematographically, with a visual density that, in conjunction with the play's original dialogue, left the viewer perplexed rather than convinced. He struck a positive note only toward the end of the review:

Despite these defects, which are due in part to Welles's cinematic style and in part to a mistaken calculation of proportions, rendering the film inexpressive, *Othello* contains numerous dramatic scenes; with the Ruskinian beauty of some Venetian alleyways and especially the shots of the fifteenth-century bastions of Mogador; it has a visual plasticity and strength that is reflected in Othello's jealousy and rage, his passionate fury, and alternating love and hate, pity and violence, scorn and adoration, ferocity and remorse, creating moments of raw emotion. Perhaps they're not as moving as Welles thinks, but they are undeniably highly charged.[10]

Alberto Moravia trashed the film. Apart from an interesting observation about the dreamlike quality of the film's depiction of Othello's delirium, he repeated his previous attack on the baroque: "Welles is a talented filmmaker interested more in force than intelligence, in the grandiose rather than the natural, in trickery rather than truth. You could say that, like some fish, he is unable to plumb the depths but must stay close to the surface in order to breathe. Hence the need to make a big splash. The more baroque the artist, the bigger the effect and the less the substance. It seems that Welles believes the job of the artist is to dumbfound rather than to win over and move. This is due to his inability to penetrate to the depths of art and life."[11]

After waiting for the right opportunity, Rondi now responded to Mondadori. Nothing after Venice 1948 had made him change his mind about Orson Welles. This *Othello* was no exception, he wrote, although he might have been writing about *Macbeth* rather than *Othello,* dusting off the old idea of a Welles seeking to rival (or emulate) Olivier:

> *Othello* would appear to lend itself more naturally to the obsessive, ferocious and exasperated style of Welles the actor and director . . . but this time he has not remained faithful to his usual inspiration, which would have produced a questionable although sincere film. With all these staircases, castles, terraces and funerals, he appears to have had Olivier in mind. . . . The style, for all the more settled outdoor locations, appears to be striving for the strongest possible effect . . . no doubt this will please the general public and the moviegoer's taste for ready-made emotions. Criticism, however, sees in it all the risks run by Olivier together with all the risks run by Welles, which make it impossible to be anything more than respectful about this film. It has nobility, commitment, and poetic intent, which are not always to be found in the cinema.[12]

In the Catholic journal *La Rivista del Cinematografo,* Giorgio Santarelli criticized Welles for cutting great lumps out of Shakespeare while praising his "measured" performance and damning the other actors. He was the sole critic to question Mac Liammóir's Iago. Santarelli joined the chorus of criticism about Welles's direction, specifically the "barbaric, exaggerated imagination of the American . . . intent on striving for effect; without losing sight of what is good in each invention, the overall inventiveness produces an effect that is not one of art, but of bedazzlement, which just isn't moving. . . . This doesn't mean the film is not fascinating, but we shouldn't confuse fascination with genuine expressive value."[13]

The harshest criticism came from the left. Still angry the film hadn't been shown in Venice, Luigi Fossati weighed in: the film was overblown, it was a betrayal of the original play, it employed folklore elements in the Cyprus scenes shot in Morocco; Welles was a funambulist (unlike the exquisitely poised Olivier) with an "excessive" mastery of the camera. "*Macbeth* was baroque, in its worst sense. *Othello* isn't so different . . . not 'filmed theater' or such like, no. To make cinema, Welles moves the camera around willy-nilly, so we get to see colonnades and shafts of light: all very pointless."[14]

In the Milanese edition of *l'Unità,* Casiraghi surpassed all others in ferocity:

> If Orson Welles's *Othello* hadn't been withdrawn at the last minute by its author, we would have seen it at the Venice Film Festival, flying the Moroccan flag. Now that we have been able to see it, we understand the flag. The film is a Moroccan

marocchinata.[15] Shakespeare's tragedy was duly raped . . . Welles dedicated several years to it. And he sought, with his wandering eye, in various lands, to feed into his greedy camera buildings, ramparts, stones, pillars, windy harbors, flying birds, banners, colorful items—the more Levantine, Cypriot the better—making such a mosaic, so confused a patchwork of sensations, that the actual story of Othello's jealousy comes in a distant second. The story deflates, to be inflated by what Welles calls his "plastic vision," i.e., his confused formalism.[16]

In *Cinema,* Aristarco was particularly stubborn, repeating—word for word—the adjectival characterization of *The Stranger,* this time echoing Rondi's unfavorable comparison with Olivier: "If we don't go into a detailed analysis of *Othello,* it's because it adds nothing new to what we already know about Welles the director; over the top, exuberant, ambitious, talented, wizard-like . . . here he is, once again, anxious to dazzle at all costs with his technical virtuosity, complicated architecture, a revolutionary-seeming appearance without a revolutionary content. . . . Welles is a hedonist, narcissistically indulging his extravagant camera positions, both as director and actor . . . he repeats himself ad infinitum."[17] And so Aristarco continued, ad infinitum.

Happy to have found the occasion to rebut Mondadori, Chiarini took over the baton in an issue of *Cinema.* He accused Welles of betraying the original inspiration of Shakespeare's tragedy: "In my opinion, the film . . . falls into the trap of believing that to make something cinematographic you need complicated technique. However deliberate and refined, it is nonetheless technique for its own sake."[18]

Much of the criticism seems to have been written without reference to the actual film, focusing instead on Welles's intentions and the experience of watching the images on the screen. Rondi appears to have seen *Macbeth,* Moravia goes on about excessive virtuosity, and Aristarco is proud of his own unflinching opinions. Chiarini went so far as to accuse Welles of seeking an "illusory cinematography," of exemplifying American cinema technique, described as the leftovers of "criticism derived from the empirics of film theory," misguided since the days of silent movies, "dubious baggage," he concludes, for a film director to be carrying around with him. He concludes by accusing Welles of "suffering from the nightmare of the specificity of film," and here it is hard not to see Chiarini's own baggage and film theory coming to the fore.

Massacring Welles became the favorite pastime of Italian intellectuals, an increasingly vicious circle. Franco Berutti praised the acting in *Othello* but could find only three memorable scenes in the film: the Moor's epileptic fit under the flight of the seagulls, the murder of Roderigo in the Turkish bath, and Othello's funeral. Among his criticisms, he accused Welles of "using the camera to film plays to be shown in the absence of theaters," of being "the peddler of Shakespearean wares," of suffering from "visual restlessness," with the camera "panning in wide angles," added the familiar accusation of the debt to Eisenstein, and—perhaps most insultingly—complained that Welles had learned "nothing in ten years, the time between the countless futile cinematic effects in that festival of the baroque that goes by the name of *Citizen Kane,* effects other directors had given up long before. Ten years to learn something, but no, in terms of the specificity of film, this *Othello* cannot bring itself to speak the grammar of a new cinematic language."[19]

It was not until February 1952 that a well thought out, positive, and courageous review of the film appeared in print. Written by Fernaldo Di Giammatteo for *Rassegna del film,* it sought to clarify Welles's debt to Schlegel's vision of Shakespeare, acknowledged by Welles in a 1950 interview for *Film,* promptly picked up and repeated by the critics. Di Giammatteo shifted the focus away from romanticism and towards a sort of Übermensch culture. He began by summarizing Italy's hasty and superficial reactions to Welles:

> First, from *Citizen Kane* to *The Lady from Shanghai,* he was called baroque. Now, after the two films dedicated to Shakespeare, he is seen as a romantic, given the interest of the romantics in the Bard. . . . In other words, a barbarian because a tardy romantic . . . which would be all well and good if it weren't for the fact that, as a filmmaker, Welles is entirely extraneous to this strain of romanticism . . . From *Citizen Kane* to *Othello,* often in a confused and uncontrollable way, all of Welles's characters have demonstrated blind ambition and the will to power, emerging from a culture that includes popular versions of Nietzsche; this is the world Welles, sometimes knowingly, sometimes less consciously, explores.[20]

Without the aesthetic and ideological blinkers of other critics, Di Giammatteo discussed the core of the film, the heart of the Moor: "symbol of an uncontrollable force, good or bad, no matter," and hence—he says—beyond good and evil, not susceptible to moral judgment. It was

the first attempt in Italy to understand Welles's fascination with powerful, charismatic figures and the positive and negative reactions of supporters (Mondadori) and "dogged detractors" (defenders of neorealism
and "the message") of the film. "With pomp and magniloquence, the
refined barbarian Welles brings out in his film—with a technique that is
both disconcerting and puerile—the frenetic will to dominate the world
and the people within it, the product of a culture that can still be sniffed
in the air today, unsure of its aims yet certain of its ambition to conquer
and subdue. No other filmmaker deals with this subject matter; it isn't
hard to see why it is so controversial and why Welles is either loved or
hated for forcing us to look at these issues."[21]

In 1951 and 1952, this criticism, driven by an awareness of the politi-
cal issues of the day but without ideological bias, went largely unheeded.
Subsequently, this line of thinking has become one of the most credited.
Up to and beyond *The Immortal Story*, whose dictatorial Mr. Clay is
determined to turn a fable into reality, all Welles's films are complex
investigations of power. Yet it was not until the end of the decade, when
Italo Calvino saw Quinlan in *Touch of Evil* as a deformed Stalin, that
Italian critics began to revise their opinions of Welles.

Their failure to understand him was partly because of their need to
focus on content rather than form. Formalism was considered a symptom of bourgeois decadence. Nor did the influence of Eisenstein help
Welles with left-wing critics, since the influence of the Soviet filmmaker
extended far and wide (for example, Visconti's neorealist *La terra trema*
owed something to Eisenstein). Welles was certainly a formalist, but he
could not be accused of slavish imitation. Unnoticed by the reviewers of
the time, *Othello* begins and ends with the protagonist's funeral, just as
Olivier's *Hamlet* had begun and ended with Hamlet's, but this is far from
imitative; the effect is very different in the two films.[22]

Despite the evident differences between the studio film *Macbeth*
and the location film *Othello*—one shot in gray, the other in contrasting light and darkness; long takes versus rapid shots; the former using
symbolic scenography, the latter exalting real architecture; monologues
and soliloquies versus dialogue and interplay (*Macbeth* is a tragedy of
individual ambition and remorse, and *Othello* one of psychic and physical overpowering, a drama)—Italian film critics tended to lump them

together and, in particular, failed to see how *Othello* might be considered a response to the criticism leveled at *Macbeth*. The critics saw no virtue in Welles's ability to improvise on location, exploiting the moment, and making the best use of the resources available. In other words, they didn't appreciate Welles's shooting a film in Italian style.

This may have been because—although the individual shots, locations, and editing were very different—the narrative style and use of metaphor and symbolism in the two films was quite similar. *Othello* is the story of a man at the height of his power and happiness, *Macbeth* details the rise and fall of a tyrant, from victory over the Norwegians to defeat at the hands of Macduff. Both are victims: Macbeth of fate and the forces of darkness, Othello of envy and prejudice. Their fates are made clear in the very first shot and their destinies are unavoidable, hence the claustrophobia of both films (shown in the grottoes in *Macbeth* and the iron bars in *Othello*). In both, Welles shows the psychological and physical decline of a man poisoned by his own obsessions. The expressionism of the films derives less from Lang or Eisenstein than from the objectivization of the inner worlds of the protagonists, from their hallucinations—the dagger, Banquo's ghost, and Othello's jealousy-induced seizures—giving *Macbeth* the appearance of steamy darkness and *Othello* the inescapable sense of a prison (the cage, gates, and masts and rigging of the ships).

The films show the world seen through the eyes of . . . well, whom? *Macbeth* had been filmed as if seen through the darkened mind of the maddened despot. It is more difficult to establish the subjectivity of *Othello*. At first sight, it would appear to reflect the vision of the general; after all, the film begins with the face of the Moor and ends with a false subjective shot, as if—already dead—he were observing the huge trapdoor closing over him. In the European version of the film—replaced by a brief prologue in the American edition—this interpretation is reinforced by the voiceover, which associates Othello with the narrator (Welles) throughout the film. Yet *Othello* could be seen from quite another viewpoint: Iago's. Thrown into a cage and raised aloft to public scorn, he looks down at the soldiers of Cyprus and the coffins of Othello and Desdemona, and appears to be remembering. His unmoved expression, shown in every stony detail, might suggest that the film is a flashback seen through his eyes.

As the events unfold, the viewer is shown both points of view (inside the cage or inside Othello's seizing mind). The film is a reliving of events from this dual perspective. As Jack Jorgens has said, the film is the perverse marriage of Othello and Iago.[23] They are the true couple; it is the differences between them, not between Othello and Desdemona, that lead to the tragedy.

The story is told by two voices, alternating—with different tone and accent, different emphasis and elocution, and generating different modes of vision—until they begin to mingle, mesh, and cross over. Both fall into the abyss of deranged narration, provoked in Othello by his delirium of insecurity and jealousy, and in Iago by the Byzantine, duplicitous mentality of an evil man. If *Macbeth* was the nightmare of a usurper, *Othello* is a double nightmare—that of the betrayed commander and that of his confidant, the betrayer.

Bazin pointed out the fragmented editing and the non-naturalistic use of natural locations, "a dramatic and imaginary architecture," a drama that takes place "in the open air but not at all in nature."[24] Michael Anderegg suggested that the strongly contrasting light and darkness underline the racial element of the play.[25] Joseph McBride called Othello, after O'Hara in *The Lady from Shanghai,* the only "innocent" character in the Welles canon and believed that Welles—somewhat adrift in European postwar cinema and suffering from a sense of victimization over his career—wanted to explore the adventurous side of his character.[26] *Othello,* made in Italy, France, and Morocco, seems to be a battle with the hostile environment in Italy, where the mellifluous Iago represents the suave reviewers who had butchered *Macbeth.*

But it is once again to Jorgens we should turn, not least because Welles endorsed his words, citing them here and there—making them his own—in *Filming Othello.* Jorgens called Cyprus "the frontier of the civilized world," which is identified in the "rich harmonious architecture" of Venice; according to Jorgens and Welles, the film is about "Venetian Christianity overpowered by paganism." James Naremore also noted the opposition between Venice and Cyprus, rendered in the kaleidoscopic vision of Welles in some densely symbolic scenes that appear to operate almost at a subliminal level, so quickly do the fragments pass in front of our eyes.[27]

Venice is the world of harmony, ambiguity, politics and political intrigue, penumbra and sunsets; it is gray and its element is water. Cyprus is a world of strong contrasts, of warriors who understand only war and peace; its colors are those of blinding light and utter darkness, its elements air and stone. Venice is an exhausted beauty, decadent, adorned with double lancet windows and low relief, inhabited by domesticated pigeons. Cyprus is essential, virile, phallic (with cannons firing into the Mediterranean); its seagulls are wild, the fortresses rough and unadorned.

The contrast reflects the two protagonists: Iago is Venice—elegant, refined, subtle, and malicious, with an ambiguous sexuality, impotent, labyrinthine, insinuating; Othello is Cyprus—force, loyalty, military discipline, and an inability to understand the subtle and indirect. All the more interesting is the fact that each acts in the other's world: in the first part of the film, Othello is in Iago's realm, Venice: he is spied upon, envied by Roderigo, hated by Brabantio, almost brought to trial, insulted, and cursed. But his heart and mind are honest, straightforward, and uncomplicated. After Iago's plotting (shown by the rapid sequence of shots in the penumbra), Othello arrives, serene, his face fully lit. He pleads his case with the Senate, demonstrates his honesty and rectitude, and the sincerity of his love for Desdemona. Their secret wedding takes place at dawn; the sun is just rising as the hasty hearing takes place before the Senate, and the light comes to dispel the nebulous world of Iago. Round 1 to Othello.

In the rest of the film Iago is in Cyprus, in Othello's world, where he maintains the same self-confident swagger. Used to shadowy Venice and the swaying motion of gondolas, for the first time he is forced to go about his subterfuge in the cold light of day. Astutely and patiently, he approaches Othello, takes him by the arm, and pretends to be guided by him. He walks with Othello over the ramparts and falls into step with him, mimics his movements, and feigns allegiance to Othello's directness. The syntax of the film is still quite simple and linear. But in Iago's company, Othello begins to lose his balance: his brightness is dimmed, his mind clouds over, his strength oozes out of him. It is as if Iago took over the direction of the film, which begins to fragment and disintegrate; love is turned to hatred, beauty to corruption. Afterward, consistently, the scenes between Iago and Othello take place in the shade, in back alleys, or outside in the open air where cages and gates appear to be closing in and are superimposed on the faces of the protagonists, imprisoning them metaphorically and physically.

There is another antagonism in the film, representing the continuous duel between Iago and the Moor and involving two primordial elements, water and stone. Iago, with his rocking motion and cloudy stare, is fluid water; and Othello, massive, rigidly armored, with his proud profile, is hard stone slowly worn down and eroded. The contrast is reproduced in the worlds they inhabit: fluid, spectral, fugitive Venice; and hard, substantial, stony Cyprus, with its parched streets, tall buildings, and sheer drops that seem to turn everything into massive burial chambers. Welles uses water to show Iago's complexity and duplicity. The first shot of him is as reflected in the water, his facial features flickering and unstable. Water is the element of evil for Iago, used to "drown cats and blind puppies," adaptable to any container yet impossible to grasp. Roderigo and Cassio fight in the water of a stagnant tank; Roderigo is murdered in a Turkish bath. Cassio loses his office through drink.

Othello is stone-faced from his first appearance, in that upturned face that already seemed to be a funeral mask. When Iago instills jealousy in him, his rigidity becomes even harsher. Of his jealousy, he complains, "My heart is turned to stone, I strike it and it hurts my hand." In an epileptic fit, he has the appearance of a monstrous statue; Welles uses the same frame to freeze him into motionlessness. The final, enlarged shot of Desdemona gives her a stony appearance, as if Othello had transferred part of his nature to her. Welles's measured performance is aimed at bringing out Othello's erosion and ruination, like an Egyptian Colossus cracked by time. Mac Liammóir noted this effect in his diary, referencing the early rehearsals: "He is speaking many of the lines . . . with a queer, breathless rapidity: this treatment, with his great bulk and power, gives an extraordinary feeling of loss, of withering, diminishing, crumbling, toppling over, of a vanishing equilibrium."[28]

Water and stone. The heart of the film seems to lie in this geological relationship between the two antagonists. Their first fight can be seen in the Mediterranean waves beating against Othello's fortress and the island of Cyprus. As Othello asks for ocular proof—the certainty of the senses—slowly the water of malice and deception seeps into the stone, undermines its solidity, and finally causes it to crack. The loyal, disciplined Moor, a soldier who relates the world according to a military code of honor, succumbs because he is unable to think that people can be other than righteous and honest. Similarly, Iago is punished by the opposite of his own perversion, by the straightforward self-sacrificing Emilia and the conscience of Othello, coherent in suicide. Hung up in a cage outside the fortress, he will be shriveled by the sun and wind, dehydrate, and turn into a parched skeleton.

As the duel rages, Desdemona is a shadowy figure—first unsee- ing witness, then resigned victim. As he had reduced the role of Lady Macbeth in his previous film, so now Welles eclipses Desdemona and the love story, focusing on the struggle between the two men. Where she does appear, she indicates the distance between the two lovers: his rough-and-readiness, her sophistication; his bestiality, her beauty; and his inferiority complex not only toward her but toward the impenetrable Venetian world she represents.

There is a distance between the two lovers, who are rarely shown engaging in physical contact; even when they are hand in hand, or later, when Othello's hand is raised to strike, Welles shows us the shot and reverse shot, Othello or Desdemona—never the two together. Similarly, sexual relations between them are distant, almost chaste: we see them embrace but only in the distance, their kisses are hidden by their ample clothing, and they appear to be shadows fleetingly commingling even on their wedding night: "I have but an hour of love to spend with thee. We must obey the time." Welles shot the scene of Othello and Desdemona kissing in front of Iago several times (as the so-called *Othello Doubles* in the National Film Library show). In one shot, the lips are pressed close but are tightly shut. When editing the film, Welles chose an even more chaste shot, in which the kiss is partially obscured by Othello's cloak. This gives the sense of an impossible relationship, not only a psychologi- cal and spiritual distance but, more concretely, a racial and class divide or—even more appropriately—an abyss. The relationship between a Moor and Venetian lady is inconceivable.

The only real sexual passion we see in the film is in the last few hours of Desdemona's life, ending with the deadly and deathly kiss. In these scenes Desdemona is transformed in Othello's mind from an angel into a common whore—first barely flesh and blood, then all-too-solid flesh. As he kisses her belly, he is disembodied by the shot. Just afterward, the final kiss of death is the only moment of true sensuality between them.

Desdemona has prepared the bed with the nuptial sheets. The violent opening of the silk canopy alludes to the loss of virginity. Her fear contrasts with her earlier serenity, when the weight of Othello's body on the bed made it gently rock. Now her sobs are that of a victim, the prefiguring of her death by sexual violence, the caricature of the initial moment of love between them that cannot be repeated and can only be mourned; the sexual energy pent up throughout the film finally explodes and Othello seems to overcome his sense of inferiority only now, in this final, fatal embrace.

Welles makes a substantial change from Shakespeare in the murder scene. Instead of strangling her, Othello suffocates her with his wedding sheets, through which he kisses her, turning them into a shroud (it is also a reminder of Desdemona's handkerchief). The sheet is a further separation between the spiritual Desdemona and solid Othello, a foreign body put between them at the moment of the unhappy consummation of their love. Othello kisses her lips through the shroud; even now she is unreachable, untouchable. Soon, the peephole above them will close, the light that bathed Othello's figure in the Senate will be put out, blackness will prevail, and the nuptial chamber will become a tomb.

The final scene resumes the opening shot as the body of the Moor is carried over the battlements, followed by the body of Desdemona. Othello is a solitary, monumental, petrified silhouette. The sun and stone, the sky and harsh walls of the fortress of Cyprus swallow him up, to be replaced, as the credits roll, by the shining reflections of the water in Venice—Iago's multiform and ambiguous world, which has the last word in the film.

Othello was shown at the Missori Cinema in Milan for a week, and on December 8 was replaced by *Mago per forza* (Perforce, a magician), a comedy made by Vittorio Metz starring Tino Scotti and Isa Barzizza. At the Fiamma and Ariston Cinemas in Rome, the film also lasted a week, from December 5–12, and was replaced by *Daughters Courageous* by Michael Curtiz (of *Casablanca* fame), a 1939 comedy starring Claude Rains.

On December 15 Welles finished the last performance of *Othello* at St. James's Theatre in London. He had no money left to carry out the planned tour of Europe, and what little he had he needed to prepare the film for Cannes. As usual, he set to work immediately, playing Moriarty in a radio version of *Sherlock Holmes*. He then visited his friends Edwards and Mac Liammóir in Dublin. At the Gate Theatre he was greeted by a hundred or so members of the Catholic Cinema and Theatre Patrons Association, who threw bottles at him and called him "Stalin's star," telling him to go back to Moscow. The police were unable to disperse the crowd, which continued to heckle outside the theater throughout the performance; finally Welles was forced to make an announcement from the stage. The Dublin visit included work on the short film *Return to Glennascaul*, an Academy Award–nominated ghost story directed by Hilton Edwards, who co-produced the film with Mac Liammóir. Perhaps in partial payment of what he owed the actors, Welles provided the voiceover. The film opens and closes with Welles as himself; he is first seen directing *Othello,* probably at Scalera Studios either in Rome or Venice the year before.

Welles then went on to act in *Trent's Last Case,* a British whodunit directed by Herbert Wilcox, whom Welles had met during the *Citizen Kane* period and bumped into again during the London performances of *Othello.* Welles plays the American millionaire Sigsbee Manderson, found dead in his luxurious villa. It is thought to be a suicide but journalist Philip Trent (Michael Wilding) has his suspicions—in the shape of Manderson's wife (Margaret Lockwood), in cahoots with his private secretary (John McCallum). Welles enters the film after about an hour, in a flashback that explains the mechanics of the death, a suicide made to look like murder, for which his rival is supposed to be incriminated. Wise to the trick, the secretary procures for himself a new alibi, fiddles around with the clues to the case, and ensures a verdict of suicide at the coroner's court. The film is allowed to end on a happy note, after a partial send-up of the American hardboiled detective story, with a kiss between the widow and the intrepid journalist who has solved the case.

Rather humdrum and with a bizarre plot, the film moved Welles to give the perfunctory performance it deserved; he was no doubt pleased to find some funding for the post-production of the English version of

Othello. On the set he was alternately good-humored and cantankerous. "He could be moody," Margaret Lockwood said. "Some days he would just sit on his chair on the set and not say a word to anybody. No doubt he was worrying about his long-drawn-out production of *Othello,* which still awaited completion. Or maybe he was in love? At any rate, he was certainly very poor company at times."[29]

Welles's bushy eyebrows and enormous rubber nose—the largest in his collection—made him something of a caricature of himself, a role he might have actually enjoyed, embellishing the words of the jealous millionaire with a few quotations from *Othello.* Manderson also complains about the performance of the lead actor in the production he had seen at St. James's Theatre. The film stumbles forward until Welles appears, when the screen suddenly bursts into life. Welles also contributed not a little to the film's structure. Like *The Third Man* (and *Othello*), the film begins with the death of the protagonist and then proceeds to shed light on the mystery via flashback and investigation (as in *Citizen Kane*). The similarity with *The Third Man*—and Welles's entrance halfway through the film—even gave Italian distributors the absurd idea of calling the film *Ritorna il terzo uomo* (The return of the third man).

Meanwhile, *Othello* was officially selected for the Cannes Film Festival. On the ferry ride across the English Channel Welles met Peter Brook, who was working on a *Salomé* for Covent Garden, with scenery and costumes designed by Salvador Dalí. Would Welles like to play Herod? Welles replied by suggesting they turn it into a film. He described a Paris café, a young man and woman, an elderly gentleman who starts to tell them about Wilde's play, and doodles on the tablecloth.

In February and March 1952, Welles was in a club on the Champs Elysées, looking for a sixteen-year-old or thereabouts to play Salomé. Newspapers said that unsatisfied, he went to Belgium, Holland, and even Denmark to look for the actress. He then returned to Italy, where part of the film would be shot. "Only Italian girls have the freshness of their years," he said. As preparations got underway for Cannes, Welles was on the French Riviera holding auditions.

Italy sent a number of exceptional films to Cannes that year: De Sica's neorealist masterpiece *Umberto D.,* Lattuada's *Il cappotto* (*The Overcoat*), *Due soldi di speranza* (Two cents' worth of hope) by Castellani, and *Guardie e ladri* (*Cops and Robbers*) by Monicelli and Steno. These had been given preference, but not without argument, over Visconti's *Bellissima* and De Santis's *Roma ore 11*. Off the coast some U.S. aircraft carriers yielded Senator McCarthy, who was there to talk to the French minister Louvel about renewing an agreement for the export of films to and from France.

Immediately, *Othello* ran into trouble. The first problem was to establish its nationality. According to the rules of the competition, each film had to have a certificate of origin and the Americans, French, and Italians did not want to provide it. They had their own films, as Welles told Bogdanovich.[30] The film therefore became Moroccan. After all, over half of it had been shot in Morocco. In addition, Welles had not yet decided on the definitive version of the film. He was allowed to present the film on the penultimate evening of the festival. On May 10, Welles had two versions of the film, the English version of the film distributed in Italy, and another he preferred but had not had the time to reedit as he wanted. He was not altogether happy with the English version, but in the end chose it despite the fact that it was printed poorly from a working copy and had no subtitles.

The next day, Welles was in his hotel room when he received a phone call from the festival director, Robert Favre Le Bret, who asked him, "What's the Moroccan national anthem?" He had won first prize. Welles told Bogdanovich, "There *is* no Moroccan national anthem, or wasn't then, so they played something out of *Chu Chin Chow* or something, and everybody stood up. There was no Moroccan delegation or anything. I think I'm the sole winner in the Arab world of a great international prize."[31]

In fact, he shared the prize with *Due soldi di speranza*. It was the second year in a row that two films had shared first prize (previously it had gone to De Sica's *Miracolo a Milano* and Sjöberg's adaption of Strindberg's *Miss Julie*). The Italian critics were dumbstruck. They'd already had occasion to express their opinion of *Othello*, and considered Castellani's film an "exceptional artistic achievement" compared to what Lanocita described as Welles's "ornamental and solemn" offering. Casiraghi called *Othello* "a photo album without substance," and Di Lauro, an essentially "formalist and pretentious" film. After a press conference in which Welles appears once again to have been undiplomatic about Italian actors and filmmakers, Rondi replied on behalf of the offended Italian film industry:

> Although . . . *Due soldi di speranza* by Castellani," he wrote, "received the admiration and approval of the jury . . . Welles's *Othello* was almost certainly given the award due to the inexplicable inferiority complex the French still suffer from in relation to Welles: an inferiority complex that seems unconsciously to reappear every time judges from refined, cultured civilizations are put in front of the visual expressions of a copious and almost barbaric art. Welles did not deserve any prize, and his attempt to intimidate in the last press conference of the festival increased in his admirers the displeasure of seeing him earn recognition for talents he does not possess. Asked by the journalists, he found a way to be discourteous about Italian actors and did not hesitate to opine that no Italian film is a complete success. His insults and boorishness were answered by the French jury, which made the mistake of giving two prizes but made up for it to some extent by awarding the prize for best participation to Italy.[32]

Others suspected the competition had been rigged. No one said so openly although Casiraghi mentions "considerations it would be too long to go into here."[33]

French critics were similarly hostile. Jacques Gautier of *Le Figaro* called *Othello* a film "dripping with literature and intellectualism . . . a hodgepodge of magniloquent effects obtained by the most artificial means."[34] Henry Magnan in *Le Monde* called the decision "extravagant" and the film "monstrous," wondered if the jury had fallen asleep, and stated that the poor style of *Othello* would appear outdated in less than ten years, more old hat than *l'arroseur arrosé*, the prehistoric sprinkler gag filmed by the Lumière brothers in 1895.[35] Perhaps the oft-repeated maxim that Welles enjoyed excellent press in France needs to be reviewed.

Renato Castellani refused to take part in the award ceremony, officially because the organizers had not found time to show his film again. Welles stepped up to take his prize and was booed and jeered off the stage.

14
Byzantine Timekeeping

"If anyone here should be on edge, it's me."
—Captain Perella (Welles), *L'uomo, la bestia e la virtù*

At the end of August 1952, Welles was once again at the Venice Film Festival, which opened with Blasetti's *Altri tempi* (*Times Gone By*), a film in various episodes based on the sex appeal of Gina Lollobrigida. Welles probably was there only to see her, perhaps to ask her advice about a lady friend of his. Despite his assurances that he would stay to the end, after one evening at the festival he returned to Fregene, a small seaside resort not far from Rome.

Fregene was also the hometown of actress Paola Mori. A newspaper article said the two had become acquainted through a film director named Vishinsky, doubtless a typo for Waszynski, the assistant director of *Othello*. Waszynski had been hired as art director of a costume film starring Errol Flynn and Gina Lollobrigida, *Il maestro di Don Giovanni* (*Crossed Swords*). In March 1952, he had invited friends to a cocktail party in Rome, where Welles noticed a beautiful, elegant, and lively brunette, who had a small role in the costume drama. Welles introduced himself and discovered that Paola Mori spoke good English. She was born in Somalia, where her father worked as a colonial official. During the war, she, her sister Patrizia, and her mother, Countess of Girfalco, had been interned in English prison camps. Liberated in 1942, they were reunited a year later and settled in Fregene, where Paola replaced the gazelles and leopards she was used to with cats, dogs, and hens. Welles fell head over heels for the beautiful, animal-loving aristocrat.

"Waszynski had nothing to do with it," Patrizia Mori recalled, overcoming her customary reluctance to talk about her sister:

> Maybe there was a cocktail party, but they had already met. I think it was in 1951 in Fregene where the family had a villa. June, not the high season. Orson was staying with Luchino Visconti. They were on the beach when Paola walked by and Orson commented on her beauty. I wasn't there but that's what Orson and others told me later. He wanted to meet her at all costs and convinced Visconti to act as go-between. Luchino sent someone over to our house to say he (Visconti) wanted to offer Paola a part in a film. She had already been offered a few parts, but my father had always said no. He refused this time, too. I was only small but I remember this occasion. Paola insisted. It's Visconti, she said, at least let me go and see. My father agreed, Paola went, and that is how she met Welles. Visconti didn't care about Paola.[1]

Welles began visiting the family villa in Fregene and Paola's mother's home in Largo Bradano in Rome. When he was away from Rome, he telephoned or sent telegrams and flowers. Fourteen years his junior, Paola was fascinated by his intelligence and creativity, and flattered and intimidated by his attentions. She convinced her father to let her act in a few films and, after all, she couldn't prevent Welles turning up on the set, where she greeted him merely politely, leaving everyone else agog.

Welles redoubled his efforts, sent more flowers, and had a word with the competition. "While working on a television documentary about Walter Chiari," said film critic Tatti Sanguineti, "I asked him how his friendship with Orson Welles began. Walter told me of a summer in the early fifties in Fregene, when the beach was full of fishermen rather than tourists, and, 'as if born out of the sea in a song by Modugno,' two beautiful aristocratic Sicilian girls had appeared. The comedian considered it his duty to court the prettier of the two, Paola, improvising silly beach gymnastics and telling her jokes. One day he found himself confronted by a large man who said, more in a melancholy way than threatening, 'Friend, I beg you . . . you are toying with her.' Pause, a long look into his eyes. 'But I need her . . . I love her.' Chiari had just been through a bad case of melancholic love himself so he withdrew in good order, without causing a fuss."[2]

Paola accepted Welles's devotion. The courtship lasted three years, with all the attendant ups and downs, official announcements, and sud-

den cancellations. Meanwhile, the Mori home in Fregene became a creative refuge for Welles.

After Cannes, Welles continued to receive insults from the Italian
press. The latest came from an English journalist living in Italy, John
Francis Lane, who wrote an open letter to him in *Cinema* asking him
what all the camera movements in *Othello* were about and accusing him
of shallow psychological tricks: "It isn't cinema. It isn't William Shakespeare. It's only Orson Welles. . . . You have been wandering around
Europe for four years now. You probably consider Italy your spiritual
home. . . . You were outlawed from Hollywood, exiled. I imagine you cannot go back. Never mind. Why don't you try to make an American film
in Rome? Why don't you try to convince an intelligent Italian producer
(and they do exist) to let you do a film on the American way of life, its
culture and spiritual heritage?"[3]

It would not have been very original. What were *Citizen Kane, The
Magnificent Ambersons, The Stranger,* and *The Lady from Shanghai* if not
explorations of the power and contradictions of the American way of
life? After making numerous films of that kind, Welles had other ideas in
mind. In September 1951, he had announced *Capitan Noè* (Two by two)
would be produced independently by his film company. Not much remains of the film except its title and a storyline. It was to portray Noah as
a "nice old drunk" who enters into the graces of the Almighty in an epoch
rather like ours (Welles thought perhaps Noah's time was not so different from ours). According to Oberdan Troiani, the idea came from the
models made for *Othello:* "After *Othello,* he wanted to make a film based
entirely on models; he had already made all the miniatures for the great
deluge, in which he wanted to sweep away the famous buildings of antiq-
uity. The Ark would have been a kind of floating casino. Noah's children
were to have been black and white, equal only during the emergency,
and then immediately return to racism as soon as the danger was over."[4]

Salomé had been set aside after months of unsuccessfully looking
for the actress. During this period Welles turned down the direction
of a production of *Porgy and Bess* at the Metropolitan in New York and
two Verdi operas (most likely *Macbeth* and *Othello*) at Milan's La Scala.
According to the Rome edition of *The Daily American,* Welles received
these offers a short time before the Cannes Film Festival.[5]

In January, Welles first announced the forthcoming *Mr. Arkadin,* "a film that will tell the misadventures of an arms dealer along the lines of Basil Zaharoff."[6] In the spring and summer of 1952, Welles turned his mind back to Shakespeare and a film version of *Julius Caesar* (to be called *Caesar!*) to be set in present-day Rome; presumably the film would have been a transposition onto the screen of the famous 1937 stage production. On June 19, Oberdan Troiani found himself whisked away from a wedding reception (for which he was best man) and driven by Rocco Facchini, one of the directors of Orson Welles Productions, to the EUR district of Rome, where Welles was thinking of setting the film. He wanted Troiani to take photographs as he indicated, one by one; on those photos Welles drew characters and camera movements. Unfortunately, like so many things pertaining to Welles's work, this gigantic storyboard has been lost.

The press threw out some names for the cast: Welles as Mark Antony, Trevor Howard as Brutus, and Alida Valli as Brutus's wife. Perhaps reuniting the cast of *The Third Man* (with the exception of Joseph Cotten) would attract backers. Welles put more energy into this project than into many of his recent ideas. Who would play Caesar? Olivier? Another stumbling block was the competition from Joseph Mankiewicz, who was also planning to make a film based on the Shakespeare play. Troiani thought Welles already had a producer, one Friedman (probably a misspelling for Charles K. Feldman, executive producer of *Othello,* who was trying to make a film with De Sica and Zavattini),[7] who pulled out when Mankiewicz announced his own film. At this point Welles sent his screenplay to Mankiewicz's producers in Hollywood in the vain hope of persuading them to back his film instead. The envelope was returned unopened. In a few months the idea was dead and Welles began to turn his attention seriously to another Peter Brook suggestion: to take the lead role in a television production of *King Lear.*

In November 1952, *Hollywood* told its readers that the small production company Olympic Films of Rome had signed up Welles to produce, direct, and star in two films to be made in Italy in English and Italian. The article only cites one of them—*Benvenuto Cellini,* a biography of the Renaissance artist. The second might have been *Caesar!* or *Capitan Noè,* but it was more likely to have been *Operation Cinderella,* which was writ-

ten around that time. This film was to be about an American film crew
that arrives in a village near Naples to shoot a film set in Renaissance
Italy. The inhabitants are divided into those in favor and those against
the project and a kind of war breaks out between the two factions, with
guerrilla skirmishes of all kinds. The Cinderella in question is a sixteen-
year-old girl, Nanda, who is ensnared by Hollywood. Welles offered the
part to an actress he had met through Paola Mori, the young Marina
Vlady. She did a screen test in March 1952, and that evening received a
bouquet of flowers, the first of her career, with a note from Welles: "It
fits perfectly! O. W." The actress remembered, "He meant Cinderella's
shoe. That May was going to be my fourteenth birthday. I had the whole
of my adult life in front of me, and many, many films. But not *Cinderella*,
unfortunately, as often happens. Welles was unable to find a backer. He
married Paola Mori but didn't forget me. Fifteen years later, in 1967, he
used me in one of his masterpieces, *Falstaff*."[8]

Operation Cinderella was to have had a large cast of characters:
Nanda; her boyfriend (the actor Antonio Cifariello), who tries to persuade her not to leave; American star Gilda Gardner; starlet Tze Tze
Herzog; journalist Leila Parker (an evident caricature of Louella Parsons); a Communist mayor who secretly admires American films and
is in perpetual conflict with the parish priest; a miraculous statue of
the local saint; and a female Resistance fighter against Hollywood (perhaps a caricature of Pina in *Roma città aperta*—Welles certainly wanted
Anna Magnani for the role). There are evident references to *Don Camillo*
(which Welles had dubbed into English for the American market); *The
Unthinking Lobster*; *Pane, amore e fantasia*, with Lollobrigida; and *Due
soldi di speranza*, joint winner of the Cannes Film Festival. The tone
of the film is apparent from one of Gilda Gardner's lines: "Neorealism
means the stand-ins do the acting and nobody's allowed to take a bath!"[9]

Apart from Vlady's account, the only other memories of this unmade film are those of Piero Regnoli, a prolific screenwriter who was
on the 1951 Venice Film Festival jury. He and Welles wrote most of the
script in the Mori villa in Fregene. "We'd already done the screen tests,"
he says. "We had chosen Anna Magnani. Marina Vlady and Cifariello
did their first screen tests with us. The production company lost about
fifty million lire on the film, which they had already come up with. . . .

Most evenings in the villa in Fregene I ended up writing nothing at all. Instead, there were some spectacular shows. Welles had set up two floodlights in the garden which he could turn manually. He would put a glass of whisky in my hand and say: 'This evening we're not going to write. I'll act something for you . . .' One evening he played for me the entire third act of *King Lear,* doing all the characters. A born actor, just wonderful."[10]

Welles was particularly proud of *Operation Cinderella.* The best comic screenplay he ever wrote, he told Bogdanovich. And the only one.

Capitan Noè, Salomé, Mr. Arkadin, Julius Caeser, Benvenuto Cellini, and *Operation Cinderela:* between the end of 1951 and the beginning of 1953 Welles thought up six films, and appears to have written a script for each one. But he didn't shoot a single foot of film.

For his detractors this waste of creative energy was a symptom of a prolific but changeable temperament. It helped to consolidate his reputation as a volatile and unreliable, rather than protean, artist. Despite his victory in Cannes, he had enormous difficulty obtaining backing for his films, particularly in Italy, which had grudgingly accepted *Citizen Kane* and relegated *Macbeth* to a piece of footling experimentalism. Meanwhile, Scalera lost his battle with the authorities to obtain Italian nationality for *Othello,* in light of the crew and the funding, and the production company was soon forced to close.[11]

Other Italian producers feared that if they got involved with Welles they would follow Scalera into bankruptcy. The six films he had scripted remained without backers and Welles was forced, yet again, to turn to acting to fund his projects.

The role was in *L'uomo, la bestia e la virtù,* based on a play by Luigi Pirandello, which was in turn an adaptation of his novella *Richiamo all'ordine* (Call to order). Welles was interested in the author, whose *Enrico IV* had once occupied his mind. The film was to be directed by Steno, a gifted craftsman, but it was essentially a commercial product and vehicle for the great Neapolitan comic actor Totò. It is Welles's least-known film role and possibly his strangest, and certainly one he did not enjoy; in some respects, it became an analogue of his experience in Italy, playing second fiddle to a popular comedian in order to raise money for serious endeavors.

The story presents a series of paradoxes: Professor Paolino Lo Vico (the titular man, played by Totò) has just been informed by his lover, virtue (Viviane Romance) that she is pregnant with his child. It is the eve of the return of her husband—Captain Perella, the beast (Welles)—a brutal and unfaithful sailor who, on his rare returns to land, has always deserted the nuptial bed. Lo Vico tries to reconcile the couple sexually in order to justify his mistress's pregnancy; this obliges him to try to teach her how to seduce her husband, his rival. But she appears too virtuous and chaste to succeed in the enterprise. The last resort is a cake supposed to be a strong aphrodisiac.

The idea for the film seems to have been Carlo Ponti's. He saw the opportunity to cast two big names and score an international success with Pirandello. His co-producer was Dino De Laurentiis; the production vehicle was Rosa Film, which was generally used for their most commercial enterprises. Although the producers had artistic ambitions and wanted the film to be shown at Cannes, their main motivation was the box office: the titillating storyline, cast of ill-assorted but famous actors, and new Italian Gevacolor technique were sure to make the film a hit.

Totò, the chief draw, felt uncomfortable with Pirandello, whom he considered too great an artist for his abilities. He also disliked the strong lighting required for the new type of color film (which, in a few years, partially blinded him). Whatever his reservations, he was under contract to Ponti and De Laurentiis, who forced him to go ahead with the project. Viviane Romance, by then a retired French actress, arrived on set with her husband, Jean Josipovici, whose continuous interference earned him a credit as joint scriptwriter and the nickname Pallesecche ("Dry balls"), coined by Totò.

The comic was cajoled and encouraged by the usual set of extras and friends the producers provided, including Mario Castellani and Nino Vingelli. They also promised a small part to Totò's partner, Franca Faldini, with whom Welles had flirted while they were making *Black Magic*. The cast included some children, two of whom went on to become quite famous: Carlo Delle Piane, the character actor with the famously crooked nose, and Giancarlo Nicotra, a future director for television.

The script was no easy matter. The producers wanted to keep to Pirandello's original idea, while providing Totò with a comedy vehicle and appealing to an international audience; they also wanted to try out a new color film and dodge the censors, who had already murmured their disapproval. Writer Vitaliano Brancati, director Steno, and assistant Lucio Fulci worked hard on the script, even during shooting, but the copy they finally submitted to the censors had no finale; they did not know how to end the film without running into problems related to the titillating nature of the comedy (which had already been censored in the theater). The solution finally came in the form of a completely new character—a prostitute played by Franca Faldini, who marries Lo Vico and comforts him as he comes to terms with the newfound harmony in the Perella household.[12]

Welles's participation was uncertain to the last. On the work schedules the only names to appear are those of Totò and Viviane Romance. Until shooting began, there was a blank beside Captain Perella's name. Welles managed to secure a fee of three million lire a day, not enormous by American standards but a considerable sum for Italy (Totò usually worked for one million). Luigi De Laurentiis, the production manager, announced the deal to the scriptwriters: "We have found the beast, Orson Welles. He hasn't got a dime and no one in America wants him any more!"

The scriptwriters were more surprised than flattered and got ready to meet the American star. Apart from Vitaliano Brancati, who appeared with him in Irving Penn's famous photo at Caffè Greco, nobody on the set knew Welles personally; all they knew was that he was supposed to be some sort of a wild man. They asked Lea Padovani for advice; she told them to let him speak—roar if that's what he wanted to do—after which he would do as he was told: "He's a good man."

Welles arrived on schedule at the Hotel Hassler, accompanied by Paola Mori, some baskets of fruit, and a dozen or so photos of Totò. In the evening he called for the scriptwriters and told them he wanted to play the role in Italian. As he ate his way through a pile of oranges, he gave them twenty pages in English on Totò and the Lo Vico character. Welles's essay, sadly lost, spoke of "sinister comedy, a bleak Mediterranean tragedy and obscure treachery" and ended with the question: "Why are we making this film?"[13]

Steno, for one, was making the film because it was his trade and also because he had a family to feed. But Welles, why was he making it? Welles looked at Steno and said, "Because I'm in despair, I have no money. They don't want me any more. They say I'm a spendthrift!" "They" were the Hollywood majors.

Shooting began on January 12, 1953, in the Rome studios of Ponti–De Laurentiis, with the scenes inside the Perella home.

The producers, scriptwriters, and crew were worried that Welles would prove argumentative. In fact the only problems on set were caused by Viviane Romance's hogging the scenes and by her continually interfering husband, quizzing the scriptwriters about his wife's lines. Welles and Totò maintained a respectful distance. Welles was clearly fascinated by the Neapolitan comic and approved his contractual conditions: Totò was to be on set no earlier than 2:00 PM and was at the disposal of the director for five hours a day, no more. As a homage to Totò, who claimed to be heir of the emperors of Constantinople, Welles called it "Byzantine timekeeping." The Neapolitan comedian acted the perfect gentlemen and, with a gentleman's irony, referred to Welles as the "exiled genius." He read the translation of the twenty-page manuscript but was more curious to learn about Rita Hayworth.

The press was invited to visit the set. Lanocita, critic for *Corriere della Sera*, thought the three actors were well chosen, adding that Welles was perfect for the part of a beast, subjected to physical rather than psychological trials.[14] Italo Dragosei, the sparkling *Hollywood* journalist, watched them shooting the lunch scene, during which Welles managed to virtually clear the table. Totò's films were always made quickly, and Steno was a specialist in getting a film into the can, but it was surprising to see the normally tireless Welles worn down by the energy of the slender Roman director. "They work early in the morning," Dragosei wrote, "with Steno feverish—always on the point of retracting into his own body—and Orson Welles a tired giant. They seem to be competing. Steno is pushing the actors harder and harder. One evening at seven o'clock, after ten hours' shooting, he said they would press on to midnight. Welles protested, Steno insisted, and finally Welles caved in. In a corner, Totò was quietly smiling as the two battled it out. 'How many shots?' he asked. 'Thirty, but we need more . . .'"[15]

Of course the producers wanted the film finished in a hurry. Welles knew it and, at first, did not mess with Steno. The only discussions were about Welles's insistence that he deliver his lines in Italian (a lip-reader could confirm that he got his way in this, at least partly), whereas Totò wanted him to speak English and Fulci to tell him (Totò) when to reply.

Steno remembered Welles as "one of those directors who, when they act for another director, behave as a guest and not as the boss." Welles didn't interfere. If anything, it was Steno who asked his advice occasionally, and the opening sequence, with the schoolmaster Paolino seen from above or behind the bars of a gate, or the school headmaster seen from below, has the unmistakable visual style of the American filmmaker.

At the beginning of March, the set moved to Cetara on the Amalfi coast for the final scenes. Welles preferred to stay in Naples, where at least two days' shooting was scheduled in the port. He rented a flat for himself and Paola Mori, and worked hard on his own projects at night, eating his way through a mountain of oranges (Fulci counted forty-seven one evening; "Terrifying," he said).

The scene to be shot in the port of Naples was Perella returning home at the helm of his fishing boat. Steno suffered from seasickness and delegated the scene to someone else. Welles took advantage of the fact to ask De Laurentiis for a moment's respite. The experiment with Geva-color was proving more troublesome than expected (when developed the film had a pinkish color) and the crew had to stop shooting for five days. Welles told De Laurentiis he would forfeit his salary for the five days if he could use the crew for his own projects. De Laurentiis agreed and Fulci found himself caught up in Welles's plans. "Tomorrow you work for me," Welles said. He chose a junior assistant with a reputation for an iron grip over the extras to act as general manager. His name was Sergio Leone, and the film Welles wanted to work on was *Mr. Arkadin*.

Years later, Leone recounted,

> Welles told me to look for someone with the most terrifying face of a thief I could imagine. I found practically Mussolini's double, someone who also had smallpox scars on his face. When I showed him to Welles he immediately noticed the resemblance. "Perfect!" he said. "I'll take him for his similarity to the world's biggest thief." . . . He also wanted ten policemen to chase this thief and a real train. . . . We shot the first scene: the thief running away from the police and crossing a railway line just in front of a speeding train. It took us three evenings. Every time we repeated the scene Welles told the extra to get closer to the train, until he begged me to tell Welles he had agreed to be an extra in order to live, not to die![16]

That scene is one of the first in *Mr. Arkadin*.

It is understandable that Welles was taking part in Steno's film without the slightest enthusiasm. If Steno painted the portrait of a diligent and respectful actor, others saw him as nervous, uninterested, aloof. After shooting he went to his dressing room to write, and no one had the courage to disturb him.

On the set, Franca Faldini heard him say, "If you prostitute yourself out of need, you just close your eyes and get it over with."[17] The young Giancarlo Nicotra remembered two things in particular:

> [He was a] giant of a man, partly because I was so small, eight years old, but I had already made fifteen films, and he really was a huge, impressive figure. But he seemed out of sorts, sad, and kept to himself. When he sat in his chair, with "Orson Welles" written on the back, it looked like he was wondering what on earth he was doing there. Totò was very gracious, very proper, but Welles was sulky, introverted. Everyone treated him with the utmost respect, but there was always some tension on the set. The first day they sent a 1400 to pick him up. He refused to get in. Too small, they were told, so they sent an American car. On the set I remember one very complicated scene. In the film I had just gone to fetch him at the harbor; the "beast" was coming home and had me and a bunch of parcels in his arms. He enters the house and sees his wife all dressed up for him and breaks into roaring laughter. It was one of the first Italian color films, so it took a long time to get the lighting right. What's more, Steno wanted to do a long tracking shot, circling around Welles. Welles sat waiting as they fiddled with the lighting and the camera on the track, for hours on end. Welles picks me and the parcels up.—Silence. 325. Take 1. Action.—At that point, instead of saying his lines, Welles put me down, put the parcels down, and slow as you like took off his false beard and said, in Italian, "Tomorrow morning, fresh as daisies, we shoot the scene." And that's what we did. The crew was heartbroken.[18]

In point of fact, Welles was trying to increase his salary. He was tired of a film he neither understood nor cared for. And in his contract, there was a highly advantageous overtime clause. The longer the delays, the more he earned. So he began to take inordinate time for makeup, to get the beard just so; even the slightest alteration meant Steno had to call for the makeup artists once more, and everything ground to a halt. Beyond his standard day's pay, Welles received huge bonuses.

Steno began to ignore Welles's attempts to sabotage his beard, so shooting went ahead with the beard a little to the right one day and a little to the left the next, while Totò made up jokes about Welles's penalty clause ("Beard to the west, bonus at best"). The filmmaker's stay in Italy was becoming a farce.

At first Ponti paid the hefty penalties. Then he got wise to the trick and refused. The producer and the actor began to exchange threatening telegrams via their respective legal representatives. Ponti did not budge and, as the final days of shooting approached, Welles became increasingly irritated, until he finally made a drastic decision. As Fulci described it, "One evening he was furious. He ripped off his beard, picked up the phone and told the producers where they could put their film. There were three days to go to the end of shooting and Ponti had no intention of giving Welles any more money. He simply disappeared, leaving his bags at the Hotel Hassler. He left a letter thanking Steno, me, and Sergio Leone, followed by a series of 'Son of a Bitch' and 'Fuck you' to the producers. We finished the film with a stand-in."[19]

The film was finished in a few days, and Welles's bags were sold at auction. The musical score was given to Angelo Francesco Lavagnino, who used a lot of mandolin music and appeared to be parodying the funeral scene from *Othello* with a cello. This time Welles was not dubbed by Gino Cervi or Emilio Cigoli but by the more ordinary Mario Besesti. The result was a light comedy, perhaps altogether too light, here and there a little better than Totò's standard production.

Ponti wanted to present the film at Cannes, taking advantage of the fame of *Othello,* but the film was smacked down by the Italian critics. Lanocita led the way; on May 14, 1953, he wrote in *Corriere della Sera* that Steno had turned the film into a sexy romp.[20] Giulio Cesare Castello agreed with him, and blamed the scriptwriters. He added that the trivial and farcical film had upset Pirandello's heirs.[21]

The heirs were offended not least by the fact that they had received not a penny for the rights; they sued the producers. In the end they buried the film for forty years, after which it was released on VHS and broadcast on television. It then disappeared again due to changes in the law that gave the dead writer extended copyright. *L'uomo, la bestia e la virtù* is a film that few people have seen, and is often not listed in Welles's filmography.

The argument over pay with Carlo Ponti and the experience of making the film with Steno put the final nail into the coffin of Welles's love affair with Italy. He had spent six years being criticized for artistic exhibitionism and excessive formalism. Shocked by his vitality and methods, Italian producers refused to back him; the most they were prepared to do so was paste a beard on his face and give him a supporting role in a vehicle for Totò. Why carry on bashing his head against a brick wall?

Welles went first to France to play Benjamin Franklin in Sacha Guitry's *Versailles.* In August he was at the Edinburgh Festival, where he showed the final reel of *Macbeth* and the first of *Othello* and gave a lecture. He spoke at length about the relationship between Hollywood and Rome, the two cinema capitals of the world, on an equal footing for the first time. "It is old fashioned to blame Hollywood," he said, taking back some of the declarations of just a few years earlier. "We have seen Rome turn into a small Hollywood, and England try to do so and fall flat on its face. . . . The fact is that everything wrong with Hollywood is also there in Rome today. The Italian films, by the way, cost a great deal more than their publicity indicated. Rossellini is an extremely expensive director. The Italians did not make their films cheaply—it was simply that there was no way of their costing more. They should neither be praised nor blamed for this. Having always been a calligraphic people, they reacted against calligraphism after the war, and many of the results were called neorealism by one side and bad movie-making by the other."[22] It was a final criticism of neorealism and has the flavor of a good-bye to Italian cinema.

Welles had just accepted Peter Brook's offer to play King Lear in a CBS production, with his friend Micheál Mac Liammóir as Edgar. A few days later he returned to America.

Italian film critics gave no sign of repentance. Franco Dorigo, in *Cinema,* had recently returned to *Citizen Kane* only to dismiss it for its "overall questionable taste." *Macbeth,* he said, "spends its time in excessive attention to form and seeks visual effects with no inner justification." According to Dorigo, *Othello* was "the product of a bizarre, eccentric spirit" in which "the poetry is hard to find."[23]

The most violent and famous attack on Welles was launched by Umberto Barbaro in early 1954. He had already torn into *The Magnificent Ambersons.* Reviewing Mankiewicz's *Julius Caesar,* he took time out to define Welles's adaptations of Shakespeare "presumptuous, horrible, messy" and "poisoned baroque pies with an obtuse avant-garde style."[24] Not long afterward, Luigi Chiarini set out his ideas on the art of cinema, relegating Welles to a footnote: "Orson Welles's *Othello* shows how too much attention to cinema technique can ruin an otherwise high-level film."[25] Giovanni Calendoli wrote a short essay in which he said that *Macbeth* and *Othello* "are obfuscated by . . . an excessively romantic, barbaric vision" and are "frighteningly monotonous."[26]

In 1954, Ennio Flaiano published a novella in *il Mondo* entitled *Un marziano a Roma* (A Martian in Rome, later a theatrical flop featuring Vittorio Gassman), thought to be a caricature of Welles. In the story, the extraterrestrial visitor is welcomed with open arms into the society of Via Veneto, only to be brusquely discarded and ridiculed. The story ends with the Martian in Villa Borghese looking at the red planet with nostalgia and wishing to return, "provided he can get his spaceship out of the pound, after seizure following a protest by hotel owners."[27]

Todisco and Kezich believed the Martian was Welles. Others saw the real target as Farouk, the former king of Egypt, who arrived in Rome in 1952 and whiled away his days on Via Veneto. According to Maurice Bessy, the American filmmaker felt some affinity—almost a "secret brotherhood"—with King Farouk.[28] They knew each other and in February 1953, while Welles was shooting with Totò, Farouk suggested that Welles make a film of his life, a project that got nowhere fast.[29]

It hardly mattered whether Flaiano's real target was Welles or Farouk. His purpose was served by either.

On April 5, 1954, Rocco Facchini was appointed receiver of Orson Welles Productions. The minutes of the shareholders meeting to wind up the company were notarized by Angelo Angotti who for tax purposes, stated on February 11, 1955, that "they had no legal effect due to failure by the company to provide the necessary executive funds."[30]

15

Going, Going, Gone

Well now I am sorry to tell you that I've just received a signal
that the time has come to say, well . . . , not goodbye,
since we're in Italy the word is "ciao." It's a nice short word.
So, "ciao" for now. We'll be meeting soon again,
I hope, some place else in the world.
'Til then I'll remain, as always, obediently yours.

—Orson Welles, *Portrait of Gina*

It had been five years, since the hurried editing of *Macbeth,* that Welles
had set foot in his native country. McCarthyism was not yet over. The
hearings and terror went on. Dozens of filmmakers had been forced to
change profession or to work under assumed names. A few months earlier, on March 26, 1953, Dashiell Hammett had been recalled for a second
grilling by the HUAC, after invoking the Fifth Amendment and earning
himself jail time in 1951 for contempt of court. The second time around,
he was accused of dealing with "some social issues" in his detective stories.[1] His books were blacklisted and pulled from America's libraries;
the government revoked his royalties, claiming $100,000 in back taxes.
Along similar lines, Welles was allowed to make *King Lear* on American
soil only if he handed over his fee in partial payment of back taxes, less
minimal living expenses.

A virtual hostage in his hotel and the CBS studios in New York, despite the considerable interest in his imminent TV appearance, Welles
lost interest in the production during rehearsals. He received numerous
offers for new projects but none of them attracted him and the producers
in the same way.

A few weeks later, Welles returned to Europe to resume his exile. This time he didn't settle anywhere but kept roving, perhaps waiting for the right opportunity to return to the United States permanently. Several times he visited Italy, where there was a woman who loved him and a comfortable villa in Fregene, but generally he preferred Spain and France. The love affair with Italy was over. In spring 1953, when he had walked away from the location shooting in Cetara, he had abandoned not only a film.

In his former adopted country he was little more than an illustrious guest, enjoying the fine weather and food, and making a few cameos, and appearing in television advertisements. He came and went, and stayed briefly or lengthily, but no longer thought of Italy as his home or sought to engage the Italian public.

His transatlantic wanderings had the taste of a defeat. He hadn't succeeded in establishing himself as an auteur in Europe and couldn't stay in the United States without facing the taxman. In May 1954, he wrote an article for the Milanese weekly *Tempo* with the self-justifying title "I am not a refugee from Hollywood." In discussing the star system he tried to give the impression that he was not "an exiled genius" as he had been described since 1947. At the same time he denied any reconciliation with Hollywood producers. He called Tinseltown "the capital of a fantastic realm in the clouds" and regretted the passing of producers such as Sam Goldwyn. However, his second exile was the result of Hollywood's continued refusal to give him the artistic freedom he sought. He felt no bitterness about this, he claimed, adding, with a hint of pain, "almost none." He wrote,

A fine word, "studio," which doesn't come close to describing the desolating truth of one of those semi-deserted industrial plants where actors work half dazed and half asleep. It is one of the secrets of Hollywood that has yet to be revealed, and I challenge anyone to reveal it: neither a flood of words nor a collection of neorealist films could properly express the squalor. In any case, Dostoevsky is dead and Rossellini is married. . . . Why did I leave Hollywood? you will ask. Perhaps you will understand it better if I say why I went there in the first place. Not to become rich and famous or to get a nice California tan. . . . No, I wanted to make films. I thought it was an interesting thing to do. And, in fact, it is. The most interesting of things to do. So much so that I go on doing it. But I didn't want to act in the films, you see. I prefer being behind the camera. Hollywood wanted me in front of it. For every offer I received as a director

I got a hundred offers to act. Don't ask me why, ask Hollywood. Of course, I haven't made a hundred films, not even fifty, not ten. I dare say I've made fewer films than I could have. As soon as I could, I upped anchor and came over to your side of the Atlantic, hoping things would be different here. So don't think I was kicked out of Hollywood and a door slammed shut behind me. To be sure, no producer has a candle lit in his office in front on my picture, and I don't sleep with anyone's photo under my pillow. All things considered, I feel no bitter-ness—almost none.[2]

Back in Europe, Welles alternated between acting for other direc-tors and shooting his own *Mr. Arkadin,* the film he had begun in Naples using Steno's crew. He decided to give the leading female role to Paola Mori but first sent her to Ireland to study acting with Mac Liammóir and Edwards. He shot the film in Cannes, Madrid, Monaco, and Rome. Then one day in Spain he asked Paola Mori to accompany him to the station. As they got out of the taxi he asked her, somehow both point-blank and softly, "Would you be willing to marry me?"

In one of her rare published interviews she said,

I understand Orson and I know what people say about him. Irritable . . . unruly . . . difficult . . . wonderful . . . a genius. Try acting with him—they say—and you'll see. He's impossible. But I'm going to marry him. I know how to handle him . . . When he's working he's always tense. When something goes wrong he explodes. It lasts about five minutes. I leave the room until the explosion is over. Afterwards, he is perfectly calm. Or, if he is still seething, I sit down and knit and watch him closely . . . Orson and I understand each other so well that if we go to a restaurant we can sit and eat without uttering a word, perfectly happy . . . Of course, I want to go on acting. Perhaps with my husband. It will always be interesting, surprising, without a clue about what we are going to do next. It is not that Orson is abnormal; he is supernormal. The secret is finding out how normal he is underneath the super.[3]

"I take marriage seriously," Welles echoed. "I am sure I've found the right girl for me. She knows how to soften my rough edges, a gift more precious than gold. I intend to change, to improve."[4] On May 8, 1955, two months after the release of *Mr. Arkadin,* at the age of forty, Orson Welles married for the third and last time. The wedding ceremony took place in a Registry Office in Caxton Hall, Westminster.

The controversy accompanying *Othello* had not died down. The film had been released in Italy and France and was awaiting distribu-tion in England and America. Welles feared the American censor, who was unlikely to show deference to Shakespeare. In a French newspaper, he wrote,

> It is interesting to observe that under the present rules, it would be impossible to write *Othello*. The miscegenetic relationship of Othello the Moor, and Desdemona the Aryan, breaks the first and most important rule today. Shakespeare's daring, uncompromising language would not be allowed. Worse still, the murderer commits suicide, which today would be considered a way of "escaping justice." Prohibited. If Shakespeare were a Hollywood scriptwriter he would have to introduce into the nuptial chamber (with twin beds, naturally) a number of Cypriot policemen ready to arrest the tragic hero (... crime doesn't pay!).[5]

During the previous two years Welles had continued to work on the film, setting aside the much criticized Italo-French version for the one nearly shown at Cannes. Many of the changes were in the Venetian part of the film, where he gave the scenes a faster pace, almost at the expense of plot coherence. He cut the voiceover reciting the names of the cast (as in *The Magnificent Ambersons*) but added a commentary introducing Othello and Desdemona, taken from the novella by Gian Battista Giraldi Cintio, Shakespeare's source.

The soundtrack was reworked, due to the original recording problems. One-third of the dialogues were rerecorded. With a certain malicious satisfaction Welles eliminated the voice of Suzanne Cloutier, overdubbing her with the clearer diction and more forceful delivery of Gudrun Ure, the Desdemona of the stage production at the St. James's Theatre. He overdubbed about half of his own lines and also rerecorded some of the lines of Iago, Ludovico, and Roderigo (to whom, here and there, he had already given his own voice in the earlier version). The score and sound effects were also modified in line with the new editing and redubbing.

On September 15, 1955, *Othello* was finally released in the United States and was received with utter indifference. Some months later Welles returned to America under the pretext of proposing a *King Lear* to New York's City Center. He rented a villa in the Los Angeles hills, and as Paola was giving birth to Beatrice, he busied himself with theater, television, and film projects. He jumped at the chance to direct and act in *Touch of Evil*, which he hoped would be his ticket back to Hollywood. As a token of his willingness, he rewrote the entire script and agreed to be paid only for his acting. He got it wrong again; the producers didn't like what they saw, kept him away from the cutting room, and brought in other directors to shoot additional scenes.

An outcast once more, he went to Mexico to start his longest and most complicated work, *Don Quixote*, a repeat of the adventurous, fragmentary method of *Othello*, only more so. In the meantime the U.S. taxman was siphoning off his American earnings. Unable to return to the United States, he took refuge once more in his wife's country.

At the end of 1957, Welles took a transatlantic liner with his wife, Beatrice, and a dog called Colombina he had given to Paola for their anniversary. On his arrival in Genoa he told the press that he would be living and working in Italy, but

> without being part of it. In every foreign country I visit, I like to observe, taste, love it. I hope the Italians will understand my state of mind and my sincerity.... There should be no doubt that I like Italy. After all, I married an Italian and am very happy. One of the reasons I like Italy is that you never hear of a woman who has left the man she is with to go to see her psychoanalyst. There's always an old Aunt Rosalia she can confide her troubles to. In the United States that is quite impossible: the aunts live too far away, and they're busy with their clubs, their business affairs, their manias, and psychoanalysts. What fascinates, convinces and wins me over about Italy is the close-knit family. I've always admired it.[6]

The journalists continued to provoke him with questions about his perpetual returns to Italy. What was the reason? "It's a question of taste," he cut short. "Not a reason."[7]

The Welles family thought about settling in Tuscany or in eastern Sicily, but finally decided on the most comfortable and cheapest course: the Mori family villa in Fregene. Paola and Beatrice lived there for about five years while Welles travelled the world and shot footage for *Don Quixote*, accepting some roles here and there to pay the bills.

In addition to her beauty and amenable character, Paola had one huge gift: unlike his previous wives and lovers, she was able to accept his unruly artist's life and to protect him from everyday trials and tribulations so he could concentrate on his films. "I had a particular way of dealing with people who phoned Orson," she wrote. "Often they were angry. 'Orson has to act in this!' they would say. Or 'Orson has to go to such-and-such a place and do such-and-such a thing.' I knew that it would only make Orson mad to hear all these orders being thrown at him so I would say, 'I'm terribly sorry but Mr. Welles is currently taking a bath. He has just drowned himself'. . . . That usually shut them up and they didn't call back."[8]

One of the projects Welles worked on during this time was *Viva Italia!* better known as *Portrait of Gina*, a TV pilot dedicated to his old friend Gina Lollobrigida, now a formidable star. The program became a pretext to talk with admiration and irony about Italy, Rome, and Italian cinema. In many ways it was the forerunner of *F for Fake*. It featured Welles interviewing De Sica, Rossano Brazzi, Paola Mori, and a childhood friend of Lollobrigida's, Anna Gruber. As in *The Third Man*, the protagonist is not onscreen for the first half of the film. When she does appear, the actress chats about this and that, including her own problems with the taxman.

Shot in January 1958 and edited immediately, the film was made for ABC and cadenced for frequent commercial breaks. ABC didn't like the film, and Welles accidentally on purpose left the three cans of film in the Ritz in Paris, where they lay in storage for thirty years. After the film's discovery, it was shown at the Venice Film Festival in the presence of Lollobrigida, who had forgotten all about it.

She sat through it, left, and immediately ordered her lawyers to prevent its release. She recounted,

> It's a sorry story. I had met Orson much earlier, when I was working as an extra. At that time I was studying at the Academy of Fine Arts and sang for a little money, which always comes in handy. After ten years he wanted to interview me and came all the way out to Appia Antica to do so. "Why do you want to film an interview?" I asked him. It was all just an excuse to see me again and the film is the result. It is a sort of portrait, a homage to an actress he preferred to the new starlets of the day. He left it in a hotel. He wasn't very attentive, let's say. The man who found it—a waiter, who now has a production company—wanted to make money out of it. He waited for Orson to die to make his move. Orson never spoke to me about it, although I had seen him and photographed him in New York late in his life. I allowed the film to be shown in Venice because I was curious about it. The photography is truly wonderful and I promised Welles's daughter (because her mother, Paola Mori, is in the film) that I would sue the producers. The film is rightly hers and mine, not a Paris waiter's.[9]

Welles tried to make a documentary about another Italian actress, Elsa Martinelli, who also lived on the Appia Antica opposite Gina Lollobrigida. He walked into the garden, sent the keepers and gardeners packing, introduced himself, sat down next to her on the steps of her villa, and spoke to her for a full hour. But the actress had just had a baby and didn't want to go back to work so soon. "Elsa, I'm sorry to have disturbed you," he said, reading her mind. "You look tired out and not in the mood to make a film. Rest and I'll be back in a few months. We'll make a really interesting film together, mark my words."[10] And with that he took his leave.

To pay off an old debt to Zanuck (maybe for *Othello*) Welles agreed to take a small part in John Huston's *The Roots of Heaven*, for which he was paid an old Moviola which Twentieth Century Fox sent to him in Fregene. Shortly afterward he left for China to shoot his sequences for Lewis Gilbert's *Passage to Hong Kong*. In August 1959 he played King Saul in *David and Goliath*, jointly directed by Ferdinando Baldi and Richard Pottier. He insisted that his old friend Hilton Edwards be given a part, and he was allowed to write and direct his own scenes, which were shot after 5:00 PM. In the morning and afternoon he did some shooting for *Don Quixote* in the sunny Manziana countryside, near Rome. Audrey Stainton, his secretary at the time, remembers a breathless, almost sunstroked crew astonished by Welles's determination to reach the top of a small mountain, pulling Francisco Reiguera and Akim Tamiroff— Don Quixote and sidekick—along behind him. "Quite a vision he was," Stainton wrote, "sailing solidly upwards, that enormous man in a bright blue boiler suit, with a large straw hat planted on his head and a dainty Japanese sunshade in his hand. 'Orson Welles is about to get lost in a mountain,' Hilton Edwards remarked in his jovial way; and Paola added with a wistful sigh, 'If only he would get lost—for a month!'"[11]

Welles continued hopping around Europe, from Fregene to London, Madrid to Paris. In Italy he managed to put together a very skilled and patient crew, especially the editors and camera operators (Roberto Perpignani, Maurizio Lucidi, Giorgio Tonti, and Mauro Bonanni), whom he tried to keep together from one film to the next. He made new friends but left some old ones behind. Troiani had always answered his calls, but others were less inclined to self-sacrifice. But after *Julius Caesar* Welles seems to have dropped him. He called only once, when shooting with Steno in Naples. A woman's voice told him to join Welles there the next day. Troiani had just started a film in Jesi so he asked for details about Welles's film but received none. Troiani stayed put and Welles didn't call again. Troiani wrote,

> A few years later, I met his chauffeur, who I'd known since the days of *Cagliostro* and who had been with Welles everywhere and knew all there was to know about him. "You have no idea about Welles," he told me. "Waszynski went over to his villa one day and got him to take on a new cinematographer. I don't know what he said against you but that's the reason he dropped you."

Apparently, Troiani had angered Waszynski during the shooting of *Othello*. The two met again when Waszynski became director of special effects for the Hollywood studios in Rome. Troiani lost jobs on *Roman Holiday* and *Quo Vadis?* But he was more upset by losing Welles's friendship than the work:

> When I heard Welles had married Paola Mori, I remembered she had had a small part in *Febbre di vivere* (Fever for life) which I had shot. I went to the villa in Fregene and was greeted by her mother, who said, "The days of Welles doing things his own way are over. From now on, no one speaks to him unless I say so!" She wouldn't let me speak to him.
>
> Another time, they told me Welles was staying at the Hilton Hotel so I went and called his room from the lobby, although I knew generally he didn't come to the phone. That time he did. He was very kind. "I'm leaving for London," he said, "but I will call you as soon as I get back." That was the last time I heard the voice of Orson Welles.[12]

Welles could not help but provoke the Italians. In 1960 he met the actor Arnoldo Foà in Trieste during the shooting of *I tartari* and the teasing began. In his memoirs Foà wrote, "Welles said something I didn't like at all. "Italian isn't a theatrical language," he said. "That's why there are no good Italian actors." I pointed out that he couldn't pass such judgment given that he didn't speak Italian. As for Italian actors, apart from the world-famous actors of the past, what did he know of our theater actors? He replied that if an actor isn't well known he can't be any good. "Not true," I said. "You, after all, are very well known." He roared with laughter."[13]

In August and September 1960, Welles shot some more scenes for *Don Quixote* in Rome. As he had for *Othello*, he was willing to wait months for the right light; this time he wanted a bright summer day-light with puffy clouds in the sky.

The year 1961 was probably when he spent the most time in Fregene. Over a period of six months, in the Mori family villa, he wrote the script of *The Trial* and designed the sets. Both Arnoldo Foà and Elsa Martinelli were to act in the film.

The Trial was shot mostly in Paris and Yugoslavia, but one sequence was shot in Rome, in front of the Supreme Court of Appeal, affection-ately known as Palazzaccio (the ugly building), and another in the EUR area of Rome, with its skyscrapers. During shooting Oriana Fallaci interviewed Welles for *Europeo*. Welles spoke of his dual soul, divided between America and Italy, and of his increasing frustration with both countries: "In America I ruffle feathers because I do not conform: you shouldn't forget that America is like Russia in many ways, above all in its conformity. In Italy they don't like me because I don't match the cliché of the American. Italians think Americans are dumb and when they realize I'm not dumb they say I can't be American. I'm American to the bone and to say I'm not is like saying all Italians play the mandolin."[14]

The following year, *The Trial* was chosen by the Venice Film Festi-val. Despite the problems they had had with Welles (*Mr. Arkadin* had not been shown at the festival for technical and bureaucratic reasons), they still considered him an attraction. The screening was delayed pend-ing the final version of the film, and when that didn't arrive they filled the gap with the Italian premiere of *West Side Story*. Apart from a legal skirmish with the producers, the event went practically unnoticed: that year in Venice, Losey withdrew *Eve*, Pasolini was accused of obscenity for *Mamma Roma* and one of the selectors, Castello, resigned over cuts made in Godard's *Vivre sa vie*.

In 1963, Dino De Laurentiis persuaded Welles to direct the sacrifice of Isaac episode for the colossal *The Bible: In the Beginning. A New York Post* journalist asked him why he had agreed. Welles replied, "An Angel came unto me and said, 'Orson, get thee to De Laurentiis and sign for $200,000.'"[15] In Welles's version, Isaac was far from ready to be sacrificed, so De Laurentiis changed his mind and asked John Huston to direct the entire film. Welles promptly cashed the check and took his name off the credits.

His most important performance during this period was in Pasolini's "La ricotta," one of the shorts in the omnibus film *RoGoPaG* (the
others were by Rossellini, Godard, and Gregoretti). At the same time,
Welles was working in Paris, making the costume drama *La fabuleuse
aventure de Marco Polo* with Anthony Quinn, Tamiroff, Elsa Martinelli,
and Omar Sharif. His contribution took about a week, during which
he commuted between Italy and France. In "La ricotta," Welles plays a
Marxist making a film on the Passion of Christ, in which Stracci (Mario
Cipriani), a starving extra given the role of the good thief, is taunted by
the other actors and crew and ends up dying on the cross after stuff-
ing himself with ricotta cheese. Welles did not interfere with Pasolini,
who was fascinated by the ease with which Welles delivered his lines in
Italian. In the end, however, he had his voice overdubbed by Giorgio
Bassani, author of *Il giardino dei Finzi-Contini*. Welles commented on
Pasolini's tremendous intelligence and talent, but turned down every
one of the many subsequent offers he received to appear in another Pasolini film.

Of his Italian colleagues Welles had ever had good words only for
De Sica, director of *Sciuscià* and *L'oro di Napoli* ("For my money the pizza
scene in *Gold of Naples* is the funniest sequence ever made in talkies").[16]
He was less fond of *Bicycle Thieves*, which he considered "more commercial and slick, but less observed." He had originally wanted De Sica to act
in *Othello* but managed to include him only in *Portrait of Gina*.

Welles was dismissive of, if not insulting to, other Italian filmmakers—starting, of course, with Rossellini: "I've seen all his films: he's an
amateur. Rossellini's films simply prove that the Italians are born actors,
and that all you need to do in Italy to pass as a film director is get a camera
and put a few people in front of it."[17] About neorealism he was sarcastic,
as when he described *Una voce umana* (one of the episodes in Rossellini's
Amore), shown in Venice, as "a woman with tousled hair sitting *sur le siège
de toilette* and shouting 'Pronto! Pronto!' into a telephone!"[18]

As his fame grew, Michelangelo Antonioni became a new target.
"According to a young American critic, one of the great discoveries
of our age is the value of boredom as an artistic subject. If that is so,
Antonioni deserves to be counted as pioneer and founding father. His
movies are perfect backgrounds for fashion models. Maybe there aren't

backgrounds that good in *Vogue*, but there ought to be. They ought to get Antonioni to design them." He was appreciative of Fellini overall but had some reservations: "His limitation—which is also the source of his charm—is that he's fundamentally very provincial. His films are a small-town boy's dream of the big city. . . . But he shows dangerous signs of being a superlative artist with little to say."[19]

The only director who deigned to respond to Welles was Fellini, who thought over his words and then said, "He's right and it's no insult; adolescence is essential for a creative person." Of the three, Fellini was the only one who knew him to any degree. They bumped into each other occasionally in Fregene—where Fellini also had a villa—and at Cesarina's, a restaurant in Rome where they both dined regularly. As Fellini recalled,

> Welles was a huge black blob, larger than the table of six he was sitting at in Cesarina's in Rome. I went to say hello as if we had been friends for a lifetime. With the sign of a monk's benediction he invited me to sit down. They brought him four first courses, minestrone, fettuccine, cannelloni, and rigatoni. He deployed them all around himself, like a gambler with cards. He ate slowly, savoring every mouthful: a Henry VIII, a Jupiter as we had imagined him at high school. Another time, at 6:30 in the morning, in the fog of a winter's daybreak, from a great black jellyfish floating among the trees of Fregene his wonderful voice rang out: "Federico! I knew you lived here!" He was beginning to have health problems due to his intemperance and said, "Federico, let's take a swim, run a few miles, find a saw and cut down a couple of trees" . . . We had a coffee instead.[20]

Italy had consistently responded to Welles's barbed remarks about its cinema through its senior film critics. Reviewing Aldrich's *Autumn Leaves* (1956), Umberto Barbaro praised the film for its "renewed ability to use closeups properly, including the age-old effects of the iris, without the affectation and avant-garde winking of, say, an Orson Welles."[21]

Lavish in his compliments in the *History of Cinema* (published in 1949), two years later, Carl Vincent wrote an article for *La Rivista del Cinematografo* in which he compared Welles to "a meteor suddenly illuminating the sky with a strange energy and light, only to pass, leaving a few intermittent, pale sparks."[22]

In Italy, *Mr. Arkadin* was greeted with a shrug of the shoulders (Rondi: "the usual Wellesian hodgepodge of sophistication and Grand

Guignol"). Even *Touch of Evil* got short shrift: Morandini asked whether Welles's baroque was a mark of taste or the corruption of taste. When Italo Calvino saw Stalin in the morally corrupt Hank Quinlan, however, critics became less inclined to write the film off.[23]

As the established critics continued to reject Welles, a new generation of film lovers in Italy began to argue for a more balanced appreciation of his films. In 1956, Roberto Pariante published an article in *Bianco e Nero* that was by no means revolutionary but showed courage in challenging the assumptions and conclusions of the establishment critics. He reversed the view of *Citizen Kane* as a film of "empty technical virtuosity" and praised its formalism. He cited Aristarco's vision of the film as a "catalog of techniques and styles," an opinion he considered "if not entirely unjustified, at least exaggerated." Aristarco was criticized explicitly for trashing *The Lady from Shanghai,* and his opinions set against the benevolent criticism of Castello and Dino Risi. Pariante shared some of the old opinions about *Macbeth,* which he regarded as faithful to the barbaric spirit of the original tragedy but excessively stylish, and about *Othello,* where the expressive means, he said, are "unjustified, pointless, and counterproductive." He, too, accused Welles the actor of "narcissism," the sets of being "baroque," and the film "ugly and tedious." However, he concluded that Welles was "undeniably an important film director," a "free spirit" and the maker of six films, each of which is "a blow to Hollywood's anodyne production."[24]

Things changed radically in December 1963 when Goffredo Fofi, a literary, theater and film critic, published a monograph dedicated to Welles in *Il Nuovo Spettatore Cinematografico,* openly taking exception to Barbaro and friends: "If there is a director Italian critics, almost to a man, have consistently underestimated, it is Orson Welles," Fofi began.

He went on to analyze the reasons for the hostility to Welles in Italy and found four: "the disturbing techniques" challenging the beliefs and complacency of the so-called experts; "the historical situation of the Italian cinema," anxious only to return to realism after the war; "the influence on our intellectuals of Benedetto Croce," for whom the baroque was merely a synonym for bad taste; and "Socialist realism and its applications," unlike the original, sophisticated criticism of capitalism in Welles's films. Fofi spared none of the critics and exposed them to public scorn: "In 1952 Italian critics were outraged when *Othello* received joint recognition in Cannes with *Due soldi di speranza,* the so-called jewel of Italian neorealism and popular cinema. Today, in view of the fascinating contrast between instinct and grace, force and beauty, the splendor and sophistication of Venice and the uncouth Moor in Cyprus, the decision still appears scandalous, but for the opposite reason."

The monograph blew Italian film criticism out of the water. Finally, Welles was described as "one of the most important directors in the history of cinema," at last he began to receive his due as the heir of silent film and forerunner of a new cinema able to analyze the ambiguity and complexity of the human spirit, through the ambiguous and complex art of filmmaking. A few months later, in *Filmcritica,* Claudio Rispoli published a long essay on *Citizen Kane:* "[I]n his chaotic intuitions and his eclecticism," he wrote, "Welles has produced a film that is on par with the greatest works of modernity, whether literary, musical or whatever. ... [I]ts value is acknowledged everywhere."[25]

Just as Italy was belatedly coming to terms with Welles, the filmmaker had finally made up his mind to move on, this time to Spain, the other representative of the Latin and Mediterranean culture he so admired. He and his family first rented a villa in Malaga, then in Madrid. "I used to be an American émigré in Italy," he told Kenneth Tynan, "now I'm an Italian exile in Spain."

While making a Western, Lucio Fulci ran into Welles on a dirt road in Spain. He was dressed in costume and was swigging water from a terracotta pot. "Byzantine timekeeping!" shouted Welles, recognizing Fulci. Welles was making his third Shakespeare adaptation, *Falstaff,* with a Spanish backer. Once more he was with Alessandro Tasca, the man he had tried to fire from the set of *Black Magic* over the false noses. The cast included Marina Vlady, who was to have been Cinderella in *Operation Cinderella,* and Walter Chiari, his former rival for the love of Paola Mori, who had traveled a day and a half to play the small role of Master Silence. "I mortified myself," he told Tatti Sanguineti, "joyfully. I was happy to work for Orson Welles. Better a pig for Welles than an eagle for anyone else."

At the end of 1964, Italian state television broadcast *Nella terra di don Chisciotte* (In the land of Don Quixote) a documentary in nine episodes based on a series of films shot in 16 mm and featuring Paola Mori and tiny Beatrice—a notebook of images and sounds which Welles had edited himself without additional commentary, using his secondhand Moviola in the garage of the villa in Fregene. Executives at Italian state television viewed the footage with growing anxiety. The film needed a voiceover, they said. Tasca persuaded Welles to write a commentary, which he was to read himself in Italian. Again the executives were perplexed: Orson Welles speaking Italian with an evident American accent? They asked Gian Paolo Callegari to write the commentary, which was spoken by Arnoldo Foà.

Left-wing critics in Italy were fierce, and dismissed in the documentary for Welles's lack of engagement, his apparent indifference to Franco's Spain.[26] In fact, Welles had considered it appropriate to leave the images he had shot of Franco on the cutting room floor.[27] The following year, when the Venice Film Festival wanted to show *Falstaff*, Franco's regime vetoed the screening and the film ended up in Cannes, prompting Aristarco to wonder out loud, "Setting aside the political problems, is it worth sacrificing Resnais's *La guerre est finie*, dedicated to the anti-Franchist struggle, in order to show Orson Welles's latest work?"[28]

Meanwhile, a new version of *Citizen Kane* was released in Italy, entirely redubbed and with a new soundtrack, but still fifteen minutes shorter than the original.

Welles was happy in his new home in Spain. He went to bullfights and was pleased not to be pestered by journalists and filmgoers. Still, he had a hankering after America. One of the reasons he had stayed away—the anti-Communist purges—was now over and done with. It left him with some bitterness since he and others had left America, while the likes of Elia Kazan had denounced supposed communists in Hollywood with utter impunity. "What is so sad about the American Left," Welles declared in 1964, "is that it betrayed in order to save its swimming pools. There was no American Right in my generation. Intellectually, it didn't exist. There were only Leftists and they mutually betrayed each other. The Left was not destroyed by McCarthy; it demolished itself, ceding to the new generation of Nihilists."[29] However, the second obstacle to Welles's return to America remained: taxes. The old problems dating back to 1947 had not gone away. Whatever he earned in America would be garnished to pay off his debt. Better to remain in exile, accept some cameo roles, and carry on dreaming about his next projects!

Welles was obliged to accept whatever was offered, however beneath his dignity. Italian producer Pino Peserico asked him to advertise a liqueur only to discover that the company—Stock—had its reservations: "Who, pray, is Orson Welles?" they asked. Its executives demanded a screen test, which Welles dutifully subjected himself to, but he refused to appear in the final shot, in which a little man (believed by some to be Silvio Berlusconi) enthusiastically orders a brandy. Welles earned a million lire and "Berlusconi" eleven thousand. Stock took a look, did not like what they saw, and left the film to rot in the archives.[30] In May 1969, Welles was again in Rome, playing the superspy Bresnavich in John Huston's *The Kremlin Letter.* He told Ceretto of the *Corriere,* "There's a huge hole in the life of an actor forced to make a spectacle of himself." Ceretto asked why he didn't sign with a studio. "Because I sell my work, not myself," replied Welles, chewing on a cigar.[31]

Later that year, on location in northeastern Italy and Yugoslavia, Welles made several TV specials for CBS, including a *Merchant of Venice,* left unfinished after two reels of film were stolen from an office in Rome. The editing (and some shooting) was carried out in the Rome studios of Safa Palatino, where, in February 1970, Welles was seen entering a room with his young Yugoslavian assistant and then heard to lock the door. Welles was by now a familiar sight around town, not so his beautiful assistant; *Oggi* dutifully reported the new scandal.[32]

Welles met Oja Kodar in Zagreb during the shooting of *The Trial.* Slowly but surely, Oja had taken the place of Paola Mori in Welles's heart. In order to avoid gossip they left Rome, heading for Orvilliers, near Paris, where they started work on *F for Fake,* the dazzling display of truth and lies that included at least one sequence shot in Rome: the scene of the motorists admiring the beautiful pedestrian Kodar.

In 1974, Welles started work on *Filming Othello* (that *Intimate Diary of Othello,* which he had declared he wanted to make way back at the 1951 Venice Film Festival). It was a German production documenting the vicissitudes of the Italo-Franco-Moroccan film. For five days Welles returned to Venice and, at dawn, boarded a series of gondolas, pointing out to the cameraman—Gary Graver—the locations of the film he had made there nearly thirty years before. These reels also mysteriously disappeared—they were, perhaps, stolen—and the final footage of the program did not include the revisiting of the locations.

In 1975, the American Film Institute in Los Angeles gave Welles a lifetime achievement award, which he accepted graciously after the citation read by Ingrid Bergman on behalf of "all the mavericks." Behind the scenes lawyers were working to reduce his tax bill, and he was finally able to pay off his debt and resettle in America.

Back in Italy, numerous specialist journals and magazines (*Cinema e cinema, Filmcritica, Cult Movie*) dedicated monographs to his work, a conference was organized in Fiesole (1974) by the Union of Critics to discuss his place in world cinema, and Mereghetti (1977) edited a book of essays on his career. Salotti and Valentinetti published volumes on Welles. In 1975, Guido Fink wrote, "Today everyone is talking about Welles, perhaps because previously they had been stonily silent, an attitude the international film community ... appears to wish to maintain."[33]

Even Aristarco softened his views. In 1951, in his *Storia delle teoriche del cinema* (History of film theory) he had called Welles a "narcissistic barbarian,"[34] a judgment he had not changed when the book was reprinted in 1960. However, in his 1965 *Il dissolvimento della ragione* (The fading of reason), he wrote, "Welles's technique in *Othello*, in *Macbeth*, and, in general, throughout his production is far from simple."[35] In his final writings on Welles he managed to praise his artistic merits and admitted that *Citizen Kane* was a "masterpiece." The observations about the complex structures and baroque style of Welles's films remained, but this time he considered them to be in the service of "a new interpretation of the Bergsonian concept of time."[36]

In 1982 Welles edited the Christmas issue of the French edition of *Vogue*. It included drawings, articles, and memoirs. He attempted to defuse his paradoxical criticism of Italian acting: "Italy is a nation of born actors, the worst of whom you can find onstage." Welles cited Luigi Barzini's *The Italians*, where this opinion is attributed to Welles, who glossed, "I hope he is misremembering."[37] (Welles himself appears to have misremembered that the joke was first written in *The Unthinking Lobster*). The rest of the article is dedicated to Eduardo De Filippo, an actor Welles had never ceased to admire:

Italians are known for their eloquent gesticulation.... Eduardo is a pure
Neapolitan, yet no actor ever used his hands so little. He isn't content to merely
dominate the stage, he focuses the attention of the entire theater onto himself
... with an economy of movement that is simply extraordinary. There is no
one like him in screen acting, where actors are supposed to be inhibited by the
nearness of the camera. Eduardo projects his closeup onto every row of the
theater. He is the world's greatest actor.[38]

That year France gave Welles the Legion of Honor and Italy, more
modestly, a David di Donatello. Thirty-five years after mauling *Macbeth*
and *Othello* in print, Gian Luigi Rondi presented him with a special David, entitled the Luchino Visconti Award (Welles's reaction to the name
of the award is unknown). It was spring 1983 and Welles was trying to
raise money in France for one of his lifetime's ambitions, a *King Lear*. He
presented the awards at the Cannes Film Festival and talked to Aldo Tassone of *la Repubblica* about the adaptation of Pirandello with Totò: "[H]e
was good, I was lousy." He felt the urge to remind readers of the newspaper where the criticism of him as a baroque filmmaker came from: "The
first person to use the word about me was my friend Mondadori, may his
soul rest in peace, and when he said it he meant it as a compliment."[39]

The Davids were due to be awarded a month and a half later, but
given that Welles was close by, Rondi promised to send a car to Cannes
to pick him up and invited him to Rome University to meet the students
and give a seminar in the main lecture hall, to be introduced by Eduardo
De Filippo in person. The talk was to be called *Dreams and Optics* and
was to be filmed using three cameras controlled by Welles via monitors
on the desk. The footage would then be gifted to Welles.

Welles was awaited with great anxiety and then the visit was canceled, officially due to a knee injury sustained in Cannes (where he
leaped onto the stage in sprightly fashion to receive a standing ovation
from the audience of twenty-five hundred). Rondi rescheduled the seminar for July 2, when the Davids were due to be presented, but Welles once
more could not—or would not—make it.

Welles returned to the eternal *Don Quixote* and *The Other Side of
the Wind*, dogged by complicated production problems, and made TV
appearances, commercials, and rock video cameos.

He was due back in Rome in December 1984 to shoot the interiors
for one of his latest projects, *The Cradle Will Rock*, at Cinecittà when

the producers suddenly changed their minds and canceled the project. Around then Ettore Scola met him at Ma Maison, Welles's favorite Los Angeles restaurant, where the owner, a film lover, always failed to present the habitué with the bill. Scola recalled,

> Jack Lemmon introduced us . . . he asked us to sit with him. He beamed across his huge face and in Italian said that he found the opening sequence of *Una giornata particolare* [A special day] terrifying, by which he might have meant terrific, but his ironic look and good grasp of Italian made me wonder about his true intentions. . . . He added with a faraway look, "Italy is the best place in the world to work in, the country where you can run up the highest debts and where I got paid the most advances for films I never made.[40]

On October 9, 1985, Welles dined at the same restaurant with his biographer Barbara Leaming and producer Alessandro Tasca di Cutò, his first Italian friend. The following morning, around dawn, he suffered a fatal heart attack as he sat at his typewriter working on a new script.

Gian Luigi Rondi
"I have changed my mind only about Citizen Kane*"*

ROME, NOVEMBER 9, 2005

Gian Luigi Rondi was born in 1921 in Piedmont, northwest Italy, the son of an officer of the Royal Carabinieri. During World War II, Rondi took part in a number of actions with a group of Catholic Communists in support of the partisans. A law graduate, he began his career in journalism as a theater critic and then inherited the column of film criticism for the conservative newspaper *il Tempo* in 1947. The following year, he joined the Christian Democrat Party. In over sixty years he has written dozens of book, sat on film festival juries, instituted film awards, worked with filmmakers, and contributed articles to many newspapers and film journals.

Today, Rondi is the only anti-Wellesian film critic in Italy still writing (for the same newspaper). "I've never been a Welles fan," he told me over the phone when I asked for an interview. However, he graciously accepted, and we arranged to meet at the Davide di Donatello Institute, which he has headed since 1981.

GIAN LUIGI RONDI: I should warn you, I haven't changed my mind and am not about to now. However, I've found a review in which I praise *F for Fake*. I also wrote an obituary in which I spoke highly of him, admittedly as one tends to do on such occasions . . .

Let's start with Welles's arrival in Rome. You were there at the first press conference at the Excelsior Hotel. What do you remember?

GLR: In 1947, all we knew about Orson Welles was the *War of the Worlds* hoax and the fact that he was Rita Hayworth's husband. So when he arrived, we asked him about what we knew: his wife. He told us all that Hayworth's beauty was a risk and that he would show us in *The Lady from*

Shanghai how expressive, rather than just beautiful, she was. I also met him at the Quirinale when he was shooting *Black Magic* with Gregory Ratoff. Ratoff is a director I had always detested until Ingrid Bergman—of whom I was very fond and who made *Intermezzo* with him—told me one day, "You've got him all wrong. You think he's a big Russian bear but actually he's a person of delicacy, of sensibility." I dare say. I only met him on that one occasion, when he was arguing with Welles. They both had strong personalities. Otherwise, Ratoff wouldn't have argued with a famous filmmaker like Welles.

What do you know about his relationship with Lea Padovani?

GLR: I was a close friend of hers. And she was a close friend of Dmytryk's. They made *Cristo fra i muratori* (*Christ in concrete*) together in England. She told me a lot of tender and affectionate things about Welles. And I protested: but he's so cantankerous! And she would say that no, he wasn't, if you got to know him well . . . A woman in love, almost a wife.

But she dumped Welles.

GLR: That's what I heard, but not from her. I've never followed gossip . . .

The first of Welles's films to be shown in Italy was The Magnificent Ambersons, *in summer 1946. Did you review it?*

GLR: I started writing about the cinema on January 1, 1947. If the film came out in 1946 I couldn't have reviewed it. I was working as a theater critic with Silvio d'Amico.

When did you see Citizen Kane?

GLR: As soon as it was released in Italy . . . perhaps I was mistaken about it. I didn't like it . . . Probably I saw it just because I was so dumbfounded by Welles as a human being and because of everything they said about him. Or maybe I was just green and didn't understand it. I certainly saw it again much later when I was presenting a series of American films for Rai TV, when there was only one channel. This was at the end of the fifties or in the early sixties. In the meantime, I had learned how to be a film critic. When I watched it again, I saw that it was an extraordinarily important film. I liked it a great deal. When I presented it I told the audience that I hadn't understood it all those years ago. I was foolish and was sorry about getting it wrong.

I have been unable to find any of your original reviews of the film.

GLR: Now that you mention it, when I was collecting my reviews for a book I didn't find any . . . perhaps I actually didn't write about it. Perhaps I just remembered seeing it and not liking it. It was a time when I had to write a lot of articles, and I just can't remember . . . However, I haven't changed my mind about any of Welles's other films.

Only Citizen Kane?

GLR: Actually, it's also the only film of his I saw again. I'm like my friend René Clair, who said, "The screen is blank. Then they show a film and afterward the screen is blank again." I never go back to see a film, and I'm happy I don't. Sometimes, when I'm waiting for the driver to pick me up, I switch on the TV and see a film for a second time, and I really dislike it; it isn't a pleasant experience. The same would be true if I were to see any of Welles's other films again. All except *Citizen Kane,* which on TV I admitted to getting wrong.

The Venice Film Festival of 1948. Welles withdrew Macbeth from the competition and that caused quite a stir. Welles was with Elsa Maxwell . . .

GLR: A snake . . .

who said the jury was prejudiced and intended to give the top award to Olivier's Hamlet, which they did. Many Italian reviewers panned Macbeth. I have here your article . . .

GLR: Which wasn't so favorable. I remember using the word "barbaric," the film had made such an impression. But wasn't it Cannes?

No, that was Othello in Cannes.

GLR: Ah, right. "Barbaric" was the word I used for *Othello.*

And for Macbeth. And that's not all you said. Perhaps the toughest part of the review is this: "An overblown attempt to astound and confound, with editing involving one close-up after another, removing all solemnity and even the semblance of a tragic atmosphere. Not Wagner, Strauss. In Westminster Abbey Shakespeare's bones are turning in their grave. [sic]."[1]

GLR: Rather over the top.

There were also two press conferences that probably made things even worse. Do you remember the atmosphere of hostility?

GLR: Frankly, I don't. I remember liking Olivier and his film (in my newspaper I'd sung the praises of *Henry V* in *il Tempo*), and was pleased he won the Golden Lion. I remember that by a rare chance I was in Venice with my mentor Silvio d'Amico. After the film, he heard someone say, "That's not cinema" (I can tell you his name now, he's dead, poor fellow: Vinicio Marinucci; he wrote for *Momento Sera*). D'Amico said, "So much the worse for cinema." I remember the enthusiasm for Olivier, but not any rivalry between the two directors or the two Shakespeare adaptations.

For the 1951 Venice Film Festival you were on the jury. The copy of Othello *that arrived wasn't properly mixed. Were you at the press conference when Welles withdrew the film?*

GLR: No. I'm a film critic. I didn't and don't usually go to press conferences, where there are many journalists who follow gossip . . . not my thing. I don't think I wrote about Welles withdrawing the film.

The only press conference . . .

GLR: was in 1947 at the Excelsior. I did write about that.

And another in Cannes, in '52. You mention it in an article on the Grand Prix, shared by Welles and Castellani. You criticized Welles's behavior at the press conference and his condescension in relation to Italian filmmakers. You wrote, "Welles did not deserve any prize and his attempt to intimidate in the last press conference of the Festival increased in his admirers the displeasure of seeing him earn recognition for talents he does not possess. Asked by the journalists, he found a way to be discourteous about Italian actors and did not hesitate to opine that no Italian film is a complete success. His insults and boorishness were answered by the French jury which made the mistake of giving two prizes but made up for it to some extent by awarding the prize for best participation to Italy.'"[2]

GLR: Did I? I really don't recall.

You just don't like Welles's films.

GLR: Getting on a bit, I remember liking *F for Fake*. I wrote a positive obituary, which I've looked at again recently. I spoke well of him. But Welles's cinema is not one that I can have any sympathy for. I have always been very detached in relation to him.

Did you go to see Othello *after it was restored and rereleased in '92?*

GLR: No, I don't like film restorations and, as I say, I don't go back to films I have already written about. I only liked Welles's later films. I paid homage to his work after his death when I was director of the Venice Film Festival, showing *Portrait of Gina*. Which Oja Kodar had brought me.

Is it true that Gina Lollobrigida didn't like it?

GLR: She wasn't overly enthusiastic about the meeting with Welles or the film. She said she would come to see it if I wanted her to . . .

In 1962 you were one of the people who chose The Trial *for the Venice Film Festival.*

GLR: Yes, we saw the film in Paris. The festival director was Domenico Meccoli. Yes, we chose it. It may surprise you but I liked it.

But the definitive copy didn't arrive and The Trial *too was withdrawn. What happened?*

GLR: Meccoli said it was an act of spite against Welles. He was livid with him because he had withdrawn a film we'd selected (because we liked it) for reasons that were offensive regarding the festival, I seem to recall. Poor Meccoli is no longer with us, but I remember his irritation: a film that had been selected, announced, and then withdrawn.

In 1983 your citation for the special David di Donatello was as follows: "For your profound and innovative contribution to the evolution of cinematographic language, for your exploration of numerous forms of representation with powerful artistic originality and fierce independence." Had you changed your mind?

GLR: One moment. I was the president of the David, but the jury who gave the Award comprised Giulio Cesare Castello, Sergio Frosali—then the film critic of *la Nazione,* and quite a few others . . . After Luchino's death I inaugurated the Luchino Visconti Award and the jury chose Welles. I wasn't on the jury. I had no objection, I went along with it . . . but I don't recall Welles coming.

At the last minute he sent his apologies . . .

GLR: He didn't come.

What happened to the award?

GLR: Someone will have it for sure. Maybe we still have it here . . . One moment, I'll ask. No, we don't have it. Maybe one of the jurors gave it to him.

Apart from you, the critics who complained of the "baroque" in Welles, sometimes with genuine violence, were all Marxists: Aristarco, Casiraghi, Barbaro. This preference for content over form was part of the critical ideology of the time. Do you think the film criticism of the time was fundamentally ideological?

GLR: Film criticism in Italy has always been mostly left-wing. The jury of the Luchino Visconti David was no exception. It was decided unanimously. Barbaro was not a film critic as such. He was an intelligent essayist, open to new ideas, to the exploration of new expressive language in film... However, I'd say only Aristarco was really a Marxist. But I don't think his objection to Welles was ideological. As a follower of Croce, I have always been interested in form and maybe I was less interested in content than Aristarco and in ideology generally, to the extent that I liked films that did not reflect my own opinions at the time. My background was the movement of Catholic Communist partisans but I learned everything from d'Amico, Franco Rodano and Adriano Ossicini . . . Those were times in which politics had a great weight in people's minds when they came to evaluating others and certainly when they came to assessing a filmmaker's work. But I don't think the criticism was itself "political." Maybe I wasn't very interested in Welles so I didn't pay much attention to who was for or against him. I was against him because I found his films shoddy, thrown together: towels over the head in *Othello*, that kind of thing . . . I was also shocked by the rocks, the cliffs, the caves . . . and hence spoke of the barbaric.

Did you know Aristarco well?

GLR: I was very fond of him and his wife. He was a close friend. Of course, he was a Marxist with his theories about the cinema, which I never agreed with. I didn't agree with his opinions about several filmmakers at the time of *Cinema Nuovo*, the Marxist cinema journal he founded in 1952. Before that, when he was just an employee at *Cinema*, he was much more relaxed. I won't say he took orders; let's say he followed not an ideological but an aesthetic line, which was actually very balanced. When he wanted to make an ideological point or promote an aesthetic vision (his hero was Lukács), I parted company with him. But he was one of the most important and influential of all our film critics and intellectuals, indispensable. We were close. He invited me to lecture on the cinema at the University where he taught and asked me to speak on neorealism, where we had similar views.

Did you know Ugo Casiraghi?

GLR: Not well. He was the critic for *l'Unità* in Milan. I used to bump into him at festivals. In terms of ideology he was what today is called a maximalist, a tank, unstoppable. A nice man, however. I never had much to do with him because we lived in different cities.

Did you know Alberto Mondadori, another critic living in Milan and a friend of Welles's?

GLR: I met him during the war, up in the mountains, where he was on holiday convalescing after the African campaign—just imagine. That kind of brief acquaintanceship. I know nothing about him.

Didn't you meet him again in Venice?

GLR: No, never, just that one time. I remember he got amebiasis in Africa and complained about it often.

I would like to read you an extract from one of your books in which you talk about Welles's character. "His multifarious ideas, his genial flashes earned him no praise, but on the contrary, they were thought of as defects; therefore, throughout his relatively brief career, he attracted hostility, to which he contributed with his character and his wish to provoke and unsettle at all costs, as if it were a penchant of his, an instinct, and so he was always making a spectacle of himself, creating the legend of a wild, aggressive, untamed, and, above all, unpredictable personality. With all the consequences of that."[3]

GLR: I wrote those words just a few years ago. That is what I think now, too.

It sounds like a justification of the fact that you and others didn't understand him.

GLR: Certainly. Welles was contested, scorned, sometimes unjustly, at other times because his behavior warranted it. I put a great deal of thought into those sentences you read. However, I have changed my mind only about *Citizen Kane*. I'm not like John Paul II; I'm not going to apologize. But anyway, I said I was sorry . . .

16

Welles and Rossellini

Farewell the plumed troop, and the big wars
That makes ambition virtue! O, farewell!
Farewell the neighing steed and the shrill trump
The spirit-stirring drum, th'ear-pierced fire,
The royal banner, and all quality,
Pride, pomp and circumstance of glorious war!
And, O you mortal engines, whose rude throats
Th'immortal Jove's dread clamours counterfeit,
Farewell! Othello's occupation gone!

—Othello (Welles), *Othello*

Welles did not want to be buried in his homeland, from which he had been exiled for many years, nor in France which had denied him the backing for *King Lear.* In accordance with his last wishes, Beatrice buried Welles's ashes in Ronda, a small town not far from Seville, on the farm of the bullfighter Antonio Ordoñez, where the filmmaker had spent happy days in his youth.

The Italian technicians who had had the opportunity to learn from him continued their careers with a sense of loss and bewilderment. For many years film editor Mauro Bonanni, who resembled Welles so strikingly the filmmaker called him his "Sicilian son," kept hundreds of meters of footage for *Don Quixote,* saving them from attempts at commercial exploitation but risking the final deterioration of the film beyond any possible restoration. To the end of his days the cinematographer Oberdan Troiani continued to accuse Welles of ruining his career, not only by taking him away from better-paying jobs but also by insisting on a level of quality that was otherwise unheard of: "I worked for Visconti and others, but after Welles they all seemed mediocre."

Welles's reputation has been kept alive in Italy by the numerous releases of his films, in various versions, over the years. The integral *Citizen Kane* was released in Italy only in 2004, to the unanimous praise of the critics, but in a poor-quality DVD format. The original copy of *Macbeth*, with the Scottish burr and long takes, was found in 1980, and caused a number of critics to rethink their positions on Welles.

After many years Welles had managed to reacquire the rights to *Othello*. In 1992, Beatrice used a copy of the film similar, but not identical, to the one released in America in 1955 to redub some of the dialogue and make alterations to the score and sound effects.[1] This much criticized "restored" version was released in VHS and later in DVD format. That year in Essaouira (formerly Mogador), a square was named after Welles and the filmmaker was toasted by the mayor, Gina Lollobrigida, Dennis Hopper, King Hassan II of Morocco, and André Azoulay, one of the king's economic advisors (and, as a nine-year-old, he had been an extra in the film).

Othello was rereleased to unreserved praise in both America and Italy, where no one made mention of its original reception as a sterile pyrotechnical display by a megalomaniac. Instead it was called "one of the greatest films by one of the world's greatest directors" (Tornabuoni in *la Stampa*), "a masterpiece of modern cinema" (Ferzetti in *il Messaggero*), "immense" (Paolo Mereghetti in *Sette*) and "one of the most faithful adaptations of Shakespeare ever made" (Morandini in *Il Giorno*). Irene Bignardi in *la Repubblica* recommended the film to a new generation of film lovers "sick of today's plastic." There was no declaration of *mea culpa* by those who had given negative reviews earlier, of course.

This did not mean that Italy had come to accept Welles wholeheartedly, however. A new version of him—based variously on romanticism, psychoanalysis, or semiotics—began to circulate, one in which he was seen not as unable but unwilling to finish a film, intent on a sort of eternal *cupio dissolvi,* as supposedly demonstrated by the four years on *Othello* and many more on *Don Quixote.* This version rescued Welles from the accusations of profligacy, unruliness, and intolerance of producers only to damn him as a supreme egoist, endlessly dithering over work that was not intended for anyone else.

Alessandro Tasca di Cutò flew into a rage whenever he heard accusations of Welles's lack of professionalism. "Actually, Welles's career demonstrates the limitations of film production. Many producers were mediocre; others were out for a fast buck. At a Hollywood gathering, one of them trotted out the usual complaint about Welles's unreliability. I asked him how many films he had made, or tried to make, with Orson. None, of course. He had never met him. What I said to him is unprintable."[2]

Without the interference and unreliability of producers or co-producers like Scalera, time and time again, Welles had proved himself able to shoot on schedule and within budget. Ousted by RKO and replaced by Cohn for the editing of *The Lady from Shanghai,* Welles had not come to Italy to fall into another snake pit. But the less venomous animals he chose to deal with did not have the budgets, studio facilities, or advertising power of the majors. They may have interfered less with Welles artistically, but their lack of resources was an obstacle nevertheless.

The only element of truth in the "fear of completion" version of Welles is what Joseph McBride observed about Welles's "inability to work on an assembly line."[3] Like Chaplin and Rossellini, also rebels and so-called total auteurs, Welles was a perfectionist. If something was not right, he would keep the crew working until it was fixed. He had backing for *The Stranger, The Lady from Shanghai, Touch of Evil,* and *The Trial;* but the progress of *Othello* and *Don Quixote,* which he produced himself, was determined by the money he could raise from backers and from acting, as well as by the time he needed to dedicate to these things—that is, by objective circumstances rather than any inner promptings or impediments.

The new French reading of Welles was less psychoanalytical and followed the example of situationalists such as Deleuze and Debord. The praise was all a bit late and now came a little too easily.

In France, too, contrary to popular belief, Welles received a number of disappointments. In the first version of his essay on Welles (1950), Bazin says that "the most common criticism of Welles is that he instigated a huge bluff: himself."[4] This sentiment echoed the reservations about the filmmaker expressed in America, where they took the form of downgrading his contribution to *Citizen Kane,* shrugging at the loss of the full version of *The Magnificent Ambersons* and a nostalgic defense of the studio system.

To Bogdanovich he confessed, "I'm rock bottom in Italy.... Because I came and lived there. And, you don't know this, but in many countries you're only respected if you're not living there. They think there must be something wrong with you if you come and stay there. So I had a great week when I arrived for *Black Magic* with every intellectual in the world—and after that I became nobody because I lived there.—Who is he? Must be something wrong with him or he wouldn't be in Italy."[5]

The love affair between Welles and Italy was never consummated. He arrived at Ciampino Airport five hours late and left Steno's set in Naples three days early. He was seen as a director who was too far ahead of his times (*Macbeth*) and an actor who was too far behind them (*Black Magic*), a man who had procrastinated over *Othello* and finished *Mr. Arkadin* only years later, who would continually announce new projects he never completed and often never started (*Cyrano*)—a contradiction, a maverick, even a charlatan.

Offscreen he was larger than life and onscreen he was accused of similarly indulging himself with curious low, high, or wide-angle shots and camera movements, none of which satisfied the neorealist taste of the postwar period. Welles had the misfortune of arriving in the middle of a heated ideological, political, and artistic debate between Catholicism and Communism. After years of watching stately white telephone receivers being raised and lowered during the films of the Fascist era, the left wing wanted social commitment and realism, not the stylishness and formalism of *Macbeth* or *Othello.* Similarly, the Catholics (or at least the most proactive part of the Catholic movement) wanted realism, "far from the formalism that turns the cinema into a play of shadows, words, make-believe situations and complications for their own sake"[6]—in other words, far from the distorting, hallucinatory hall of mirrors of *The Lady from Shanghai* and the rest of Welles's cinema—and they hoped Rossellini would champion their cause and faith.

Perhaps Welles did not realize how his films alienated both sides of the neorealist debate, Catholics and Communists alike, unless he understood it only too well and was unrepentant. It is unlikely, however, that he fully understood what was at stake for him: not merely his art but his ability to live in Italy, his acceptance or rejection as a filmmaker, actor, and individual. Lanocita led the criticism from the left: "Welles's opinions about the Italian films in the school of realism are rather crude: just crowd six members of a family into a single room, the mother in the corner cooking on an oven and start shooting. The film ends a few hours later. Welles admits he doesn't have the lyricism of Chaplin or De Sica. 'I am interested not in victims,' he declares, 'but in heroes in the Greek sense of the term.'"[7]

Certainly he was brazen and direct, and lacked diplomacy. *Contriety,* as James Naremore has said, was part of his very nature;[8] he was a one-man opposition party, physically intimidating, ready for an argument, quick witted, intelligent, generous (as many colleagues remembered him), capable of both grand and petty gestures, and a man who could be stopped and made to listen only by a similar show of strength.

Italy's reaction to his provocations was to denigrate and ridicule him as an artist and a man, so that it was often difficult to understand whether it was his aesthetics, his ideology, or his manners that were considered objectionable. Orson Welles the illusionist, the drunk, the womanizer, the eccentric, the man with no dress sense who bellowed and laughed too loud, this man was also the maker of films that were exaggeratedly baroque, excessive, chaotic, and pyrotechnical. For Aristarco and his fellow critics the one was the natural result of the other. In 1948, after the poor reception of *Macbeth,* Alfredo Todisco saw it all coming: "In Italy we rather pride ourselves on our distinctive personalities. . . . Perhaps in no other country are personality clashes so common or so violent. And Welles undoubtedly has personality. Hence the gossip, the almost hidden antagonism—what I would find hard to call anything other than *professional jealousy.*"[9]

It is not surprising that in his six years in Italy Welles made *Othello,* a work about intrigue and jealousy. Welles's entire career can be seen as essentially about guilt and betrayal, and his life in Italy certainly gave him an acute sense of both. According to Valmarana, *Othello* is autobiographical, with the American Welles as strong, straightforward, brash Othello and complexly nuanced, multifaceted European culture in the role of

Iago. Welles/Othello is flattered, beguiled, and finally betrayed out of envy, and ends up smothering what he loves and destroying himself.

Welles was a free man and a free artist living in an Italy where there was little freedom from ideology and the critics were unable to shake off those shackles. Epithets such as "enfant terrible" and "wunderkind" were designed to diminish his reputation and freeze him into immobility, relegating his talents to those of a precocious child. He defended himself by saying that he considered only Chaplin and Griffith, not himself, geniuses of film—to no avail.[10] Driven out of America for his left-wing sympathies, in Italy he was criticized equally by the Marxist left and clerical right.

It took Welles six years to understand that in Italy he would get only cameos or roles that would reinforce his reputation as a buffoon. Having bumped into him on several occasions, film director Alberto Lattuada shook his head at what was happening to Welles: he was trapped in a spider's web and was about to be devoured. Lattuada chose to express this feeling in his description of another exile, Charlie Chaplin, who had understood quicker than Welles the way Rome and Italian society worked:

> Straight away he realized what it meant to be greeted by "Hi Chaplin, how are things?" accompanied by a slap on the back. He instinctively drew away from this false and fawning cordiality, this ritualistic benevolence towards someone who is, and always will be, an outsider. And he left Italy without ever setting foot here again. Chaplin saw what had happened to Orson Welles, who had been naïve enough to believe the welcome was sincere.[11]

The high society of Via Veneto in Rome was essentially provincial, and was unworthy of Welles. Probably it wouldn't be so different today if Quentin Tarantino decided to take up lodgings in Piazza di Spagna. A fortnight's praise, invitations, camaraderie, then a slow crescendo of murmuring about *Pulp Fiction:* Is it really all it's cracked up to be?

What became of Welles's ambition to work with Italian directors? At various times, he made attempts to collaborate with De Sica, Lattuada, and Rossellini (not to mention the gangster Lucky Luciano, who, as Welles told Leaming, met him hoping the American would write, direct, and play "the true story of his life.") but nothing ever came of these efforts. There is very little information about the abandoned projects. Between 1948 and 1950 he and Carol Reed tried to persuade De Sica to sell or give them "the ideal subject for a great film" (perhaps *Miracolo a Milano*, perhaps *Umberto D.*), a film De Sica then decided to make himself.[12] In 1951 Lattuada wanted him to act in a film he was preparing, perhaps *Il cappotto* (*The Overcoat*) or *Anna*. The two met in Rome when Welles was editing *Othello*: "Six days' work," Lattuada told him. "I would be truly honored." Orson readily agreed but the plan fell through.[13]

Apart from the idea of a *Life of Jesus*, which Welles might have merely thrown out as one of many possible projects, or which the French journalist reporting it in 1948 may have misconstrued or invented, there is little record of any attempts by Rossellini and Welles to work together. The two were in frequent proximity, between the Excelsior Hotel and the Veneto cafes, so they certainly ran into each other on numerous occasions. However, Welles's subsequent acrimony and Rossellini's wagging tongue suggest that something more than just a few words were exchanged now and then. Had one failed to keep a promise or stolen an idea from the other? Had they started working together and then, suddenly, stopped? The most plausible explanation is related to Rossellini's projects with Selznick, which included at least one biblical story, a *Mary Magdalene* to capitalize on the fame of Jennifer Jones, and a film about the circus. As chance would have it, a few years later Chaplin gifted Rossellini with a screenplay, *Shadow and Substance*, featuring a female lead similar to Nannina in Rossellini's *Il miracolo* (The miracle). In Chaplin's script the woman is taken advantage of by cruel monks. The English filmmaker suggested Welles for the role of the abbot.[14] The idea fell through. In 1975, Rossellini did make a life of Christ, *The Messiah*, but without Welles. As far back as 1941, Welles had written a script updating the Gospels to the modern day, but the closest he came to playing Christ was the dubbing into English of the crucifix in *Don Camillo*.

The two directors never worked together. Welles was made fun of, whereas Rossellini, whether he liked it or not, had become the champion of neorealism, and had a large following across the entire political spectrum. Perhaps this was the very reason Welles rapidly changed his mind about Rossellini. After initially praising him for *Roma città aperta* and *Paisà*, from 1948 onward Welles continually upbraided Rossellini and neorealist cinema, in the city in which it was produced and in the teeth of the evident pride of his hosts. In addition to the direct judgments of the filmmaker ("an amateur," "an extremely expensive director") or his films (of *Una voce umana* he said, "the shots change for no reason"), he used the Roman director to pour scorn on neorealism in general: by showing a willingness to give Anna Magnani the role of the head of the anti-Hollywood resistance movement in *Operation Cinderella* and by creating the parodic film director Alessandro Sporcacione in *The Unthinking Lobster*, defining neorealism as a woman with tousled hair shouting into a telephone. Interestingly, Elena Dagrada also sees a play on neorealism in *The Immortal Story* with its puppeteer "who believes only in real events and tries to turn a pure fiction into reality, seeking a sailor (as Rossellini himself had done in *Stromboli*) in Macao. Both men fail, Welles seems to say, because reality does not sit well onscreen. It kills directors (just as Mr. Clay is killed by his own production of the story)."[15]

Rossellini never responded to Welles's provocations. However, at times, the lives of the two filmmakers seem to rub up against each other, almost in rivalry: the donations from the receipts of the premiere of *Othello* were given to the victims of the flooding in Polesine, who were also the subject of a small film Rossellini was making at the time with Ingrid Bergman, the unfinished *S. Brigida;* Welles turned down the opportunity to direct at La Scala, while Rossellini agreed to direct Verdi's *Otello* at the San Carlo Theater in Naples; the parallel meetings with Totò, who was directed by Rossellini in *Dov'è la libertà . . . ?* (Where is freedom?) and a few months acted with Welles in *L'uomo, la bestia e la virtù;* and finally, the two men worked on *RoGoPaG*, in which *Ro* was Rossellini, and Welles had a role in the short film directed by *Pa*(solini), "La ricotta" (Welles's only appearance in a film with a top Italian director).

The two directors were poles apart. One was dedicated to realism and the collective consciousness; the other was intent on expanding, even exploding, reality within the framework of a very personal form of expressionism: an objective versus a subjective cinema. However, the two had a number of things in common: a dislike of Hollywood; a problematic relationship with film criticism; certain friends (including Marlene Dietrich) and enemies (including Howard Hughes); private lives that were considered scandalous, and—despite this—a certain inclination toward moralism; endless curiosity in relation to human experience;

and a pioneering interest in television. Fellini said as much: "Welles was an adventurer, a man like Cagliostro, Casanova, Rossellini."[16]

The two directors suffered at the hands of Italian film critics, who became increasingly irritated with Rossellini after *Germania anno zero*, as he took several steps away from neorealism and toward a more intimate, ascetic cinema in *L'amore* and *Stromboli*. It seems only the critics continued to believe in neorealism, even as one of its leading exponents was heading elsewhere, toward the sublime. They criticized Welles in the name of a neorealism one of its greatest practitioners was turning his back on.

Left-wing critics were confounded by both directors. Casiraghi and Aristarco wanted another *Paisà* or *Roma città aperta*, not the latest offerings, *Francesco giullare di Dio* and *Europa '51*. From *Citizen Kane*, with its criticism of capitalism and Hearst the tycoon, they had expected a revolutionary; but Welles then turned his attention to Shakespeare and an investigation of the human soul, using the most spectacular techniques of cinema, unlike anything by Rossellini, whose films tended toward monastic contemplation. As Rossellini became more meditative and seemed to turn his back on the world, Welles rummaged around in Pandora's box to see what he could find, unperturbed by whatever that might be; Rossellini saw life as Purgatory, Welles as a foretaste of Hell.

Neither of these visions pleased the film critics—neither Welles's anti-Americanism and anti-capitalism nor Rossellini's faith in a new social order born out of resistance. But by disappointing the critics and refusing to do what was demanded of them—preferring to grasp the thorns rather than smell the roses—Welles and Rossellini assured themselves a place in the history of cinema.

APPENDIX I
The Italian Version of *Othello*

The following data was taken from the copy of the film held by the Cineteca Nazionale (National Film Library), checked against and augmented by data from accounting documents, press articles, and eyewitness accounts.

The only uncertainty concerns the orchestra conductor, shown in this copy as Franco Ferrara, whereas the so-called original and the American version cite Willy Ferrero. A misprint? Ferrara worked with Lavagnino on the music for *Mambo* (1953); Willy Ferrero worked on *Ladri di biciclette* and *La terra trema*, in addition to working at La Scala in Milan (at the time Welles was finishing the film, Ferrero was tipped to direct an opera there).

This appendix also includes a translation of the original press release for the film.

CAST: Orson Welles (Othello), Micheál Mac Liammóir (Iago), Hilton Edwards (Brabantio), Suzanne Cloutier (Desdemona), Fay Compton (Emilia), Constance Dowling (Bianca), Robert Coote (Roderigo), Michael Laurence (Cassio), Nicholas Bruce (Lodovico), Jean Davis (Montano), Abdullah Ben Mohament (page), Lea Padovani and Betsy Blair (other Desdemonas), Riquette (Roderigo's dog).

DIRECTOR OF PHOTOGRAPHY: Anchise Brizzi, G. R. Aldo, George Fanto

CAMERAMEN: Alberto Fusi, Alvaro Mancori, Tonino Delli Colli

ASSISTANT CAMERAMEN: Oberdan Troiani, Domenico Cirillo, Nino Cristiani

EDITING: Jean Sacha, Renzo Lucidi, John Shepridge

ASSISTANT EDITOR: Rinaldo Boggio, Enza Boggio

SOUND EDITOR: Umberto Picistrelli, Carlo Stapler

SOUND ENGINEER: Silvio Santoloce

MICROPHONE TECHNICIAN: Benedetto Conversi

COSTUME DESIGN: Maria De Matteis

PRODUCTION MANAGER: Giorgio Papi

DIRECTOR OF PRODUCTION: Walter Bedogni

PRODUCTION SUPERVISOR: Rocco Facchini

ADMINISTRATION: Julien Derode

PRODUCTION ASSISTANT: Aldo Pace, Patrice Dally

ORIGINAL SCORE: Angelo Francesco Lavagnino, Alberto Barberis

ORCHESTRA CONDUCTOR: Franco Ferrara

SET PHOTOGRAPHER: Danilo Allegri

HAIRDRESSER: Vasco Reggiani

MAKEUP: Euclide Santoli, Camillo De Rossi

KEY GRIP: Mariano Sargenti, Augusto Sargenti

CHIEF ELECTRICIAN: Beniamino D'Alessandro

SECOND CHIEF ELECTRICIAN: Dario Altibrandi

ART DIRECTOR: Alexander Trauner, Luigi Scaccianoce

SECOND ART DIRECTOR: James Allen

ASSISTANT ART DIRECTOR: Auguste Capelier

SCRIPT DIRECTOR: Lee Kressel

SCRIPT GIRLS: Renée Gouzy, Ruth Hill

JOINT DIRECTOR: Michal Waszynski

ASSISTANT DIRECTOR: Carlo Lastricati, Hilton Edwards

COSTUMES: G. Peruzzi Florence House of Art, Cerratelli House of Art, M. Fortuny

FOOTWEAR: the Pompei Company, the Sacchi Company

ARMS AND ARMOR: the Rancati Company

WIGS: the Maggi Company

JEWELRY: Guattari Ltd.

DEVELOPMENT AND PRINTING: S.P.E.S.

Shot in the Scalera Studios in Rome and Venice

FILM: Ferrania

PRODUCER AND DIRECTOR: Orson Welles

DUBBING INTO ITALIAN:

ITALIAN DIALOGUE: Gian Gaspare Napolitano
Directed by Mario Almirante with the assistance of C.D.C.
OTHELLO: Gino Cervi
DESDEMONA: Rina Morelli
IAGO: Sandro Ruffini
CASSIO: Emilio Cigoli
RODERIGO: Carlo Romano
EMILIA: Giovanna Scotto
LUDOVICO: Giorgio Capecchi
BIANCA: Clelia Bernocchi
BRABANTIO: Mario Besesti
MONTANO: Manlio Busoni

DECLARED LENGTH: 2,850 m. (equivalent to 104', about 98' real playing time)
Censor's permit: no. 10864 dated November 6, 1951
PREMIERE: Rome's Barberini

APPENDIX 2
The Opinion of the Catholic Center for Cinematography

AESTHETIC JUDGMENT

The excellent and effective photography and the precious taste of the shots make the film often interesting, although the effort to render the Shakespearean drama in film does not seem to have succeeded.

MORAL JUDGMENT

Despite some crude expressions and the well-known story, the artistic treatment of this classic tale is suitable for viewing by adults in a public theater.

NOTES

TRANSLATOR'S PREFACE

1. Luigi Chiarini, "Il film è un'arte, il cinema è un'industria," *Bianco e Nero* 2, no. 7 (1938).

2. Lukacs's 1938 essay *Realism in the Balance* sought to debunk the claims of critics such as Ernst Bloch who defended literary expressionism. Lukacs called for a literary realism that reflected social reality—leading, for example, to a preference for Thomas Mann over Franz Kafka. This debate on aesthetics, which also involved Adorno and Bertolt Brecht, seems to have been reprised in relation to Welles by two Italian film critics—Aristarco in defense of neorealism, which he generally referred to as Italian realism, and Mondadori in defense of expressionism. For a more recent version, see David Levi Strauss, "The Documentary Debate: Aesthetic or Anaesthetic?" in *Between the Eyes: Essays on Photography and Politics* (New York: Aperture, 2005), 3–11.

3. Mark Shiel, *Italian Neorealism: Rebuilding the Cinematic City* (London: Wallflower, 2006), 89. This book includes an overview of film criticism in Italy in the neorealist period (88–91).

4. The film was scripted by Aristarco himself.

5. Guido Aristarco, *Il mestiere del critico, 1952–1958,* ed. Lorenzo Pellizzari (Alessandria: Falsopiano, 2007), 38–40.

6. G. L. Rondi, "La notte brava del cinema italiano" [Italian cinema's wild night out], in *il Tempo,* September 23, 1959.

7. James Naremore, *More than Night: Film Noir in Its Contexts* (Berkeley, Los Angeles, and London: University of California Press, 1998), 25.

8. André Bazin, *What Is Cinema?* trans. Hugh Gray (Berkeley: University of California Press, 2004), 1:60.

9. V. F. Perkins, *Film as Film: Understanding and Judging Movies,* new introduction by Foster Hirsch (New York: Da Capo Press, 1993), 38.

10. Bazin, *What Is Cinema?* trans. Hugh Gray (Berkeley: University of California Press, 2005), 2:27–28. Deleuze also noted the interpenetration of foreground, middle ground and background in Welles's deep focus, making each shot a dynamic space-in-depth, something he had observed in seventeenth-century painting. Deleuze, however, does not regard this as an attempt to make the scene more realistic. See Ronald Bogue, *Deleuze on Cinema* (New York: Routledge, 2003), 143.

11. Robert Sklar, *Movie-Made America: A Cultural History of American Movies*, rev. ed. (New York: Random House, 1994).

12. Raymond Borde and Etienne Chaumeton, *A Panorama of American Film Noir, 1941–1953*, trans. Paul Hammond (San Francisco: City Lights, 2002), 124–25.

13. Quoted in Mira Liehm, *Passion and Defiance: Film in Italy from 1942 to the Present* (Berkeley: University of California Press, 1984), 59.

14. De Sica to *Cinema nuovo* 2, no. 16 (August 1, 1953).

15. Quoted in Mario Guidorizzi, *Cinema italiano d'autore, Parte I: 1930–1965* (Verona: Cierre edizioni, 2006), 40.

16. Cesare Zavattini, *Opere*, ed. Valentina Fortichiari and Mino Argentieri (Milan: Bompiani, 2002), 705.

17. For a detailed discussion of neorealism, see, for example, Shiel, *Italian Neorealism;* and Gian Piero Brunetta, *Il cinema neorealista italiano, da* Roma città aperta *a* I soliti ignoti (Bari: Laterza, 2009). Italian film critics (particularly Chiarini and Aristarco) feature prominently in Brunetta's book, which also discusses the ideological underpinnings of neorealism (186–93). For a series of contemporary essays on neorealism, see Antonio Vitti, ed., *Ripensare il neorealismo: Cinema, letteratura, mondo* (Pesaro: Metauro, 2008).

18. Quoted in Antonio Costa, *Saper vedere il cinema* [How to watch films], 19th ed. (Milan: RCS Libri, Strumenti Bompiani, 2007), 105.

19. Naremore, *More than Night*, 26.

20. Interview with Oswald Stack in *Pasolini on Pasolini*, (Bloomington: Indiana University Press, 1970), 109.

21. There seems to have been a silent dialogue between Fellini and Welles, who had similar interests in the esoteric (magic), in the circus and in the satirical use of miracles in film (Fellini's screenplay for Rossellini's *Il miracolo*, Welles's *The Unthinking Lobster*, and Fellini's own *La dolce vita*). Both were accomplished sketch artists. Fellini's Toby Dammit comes to Rome to act in a life of Christ that was also a Western, an idea Welles had had back in the 1940s, and, as Jonathan Rosenbaum has pointed out, both *F for Fake* and *Filming Othello* are reminiscent of Fellini's film journals. The insistence on artifice in Welles's films, for example in *Mr. Arkadin* (where the makeup lines are left visible on the protagonist's face) is a characteristic of many late Fellini films, such as *E la nave va* (*And the Ship Sails On*), in which Fellini wanted one of the costumes to have clearly visible stitches. Both directors used what Michael Anderegg calls "a perceptible disjunction between sound and image" (interiorized monologues, bad lip-sync, for example, in Fellini's *Satyricon*, and countless examples in Welles). Their films appear to be pre- and postmodern at the same time. Welles made a film version of Kafka's *The Trial* and Fellini had a lifelong interest in Kafka's *Amerika*, which he is shown pretending to be about to film in *Intervista* (1987). In Pasolini's "La ricotta" (1962), the character played by Welles comments that Fellini "dances." Although they were neighbors for many years in the resort town of Fregene, there is no evidence that Welles and Fellini ever sought to work together. [Translator's note.]

22. Quoted in Roy Armes, *Patterns of Realism, a Study of Italian Neo-Realism* (Cranbury, N.J.: A. S. Barnes, 1971).

23. Catherine L. Benamou, *It's All True*, 207–208.

24. Cited in Michael Anderegg, *Orson Welles, Shakespeare and Popular Culture* (New York: Columbia University Press, 1999), 94.

25. Jonathan Rosenbaum, *Discovering Orson Welles* (Berkeley and Los Angeles: University of California Press, 2007), 236–37.

26. Robert Garis, *The Films of Orson Welles* (Cambridge: Cambridge University Press, 2004); Clinton Heylin, *Despite the System: Orson Welles versus the Hollywood Studios* (Edinburgh: Canongate, 2005); Peter Conrad, *Orson Welles, The Stories of His Life* (London: Faber and Faber, 2003); Irving Singer, *Three Philosophical Filmmakers: Hitchcock, Welles, Renoir* (Cambridge, Mass., and London: MIT Press, 2004).

27. Curiously, the two filmmakers had a few things in common: both had had their troubles in Hollywood, both had tried and failed to make a film in Latin America on a government-sponsored project. Both had had footage taken from them and had lost control over films they had been working on.

28. See Bazin, *What Is Cinema?* 1:23–40.

29. In June 1949, Tenney listed big names in Hollywood who had followed or appeased "the Communist party line over a long period of years." The names included the usual Charlie Chaplin and Humphrey Bogart, as well as Katherine Hepburn, Pearl S. Buck, Lillian Hellman, Lena Horne, John Huston, Gene Kelly, Myrna Loy, Fredric March, Dorothy Parker, Gregory Peck, Frank Sinatra, Donald Ogden Stewart and Orson Welles. (William J. Mann, *Kate: The Woman Who Was Katherine Hepburn* [London: Faber and Faber, 2007], 366.)

30. Peter William Evans, *Carol Reed* (Manchester and New York: Manchester University Press, 2005), 120.

31. Léon Grinberg and Rebecca Grinberg, "Psychoanalytic Perspectives on Migration," in David Bell, ed., *Psychoanalysis and Culture: A Kleinian Perspective*, 2nd ed. (London: Karnac, 1999), 154–69.

1. ARRIVAL

1. Mary Pacios, *Childhood Shadows: The Hidden Story of the Black Dahlia Murder*, (Bloomington: 1st Books, 1999). The author, a friend of the victim, correlates the way the crime was committed with some supposed clues as to the identity of the murderer, such as the mutilated female mannequin in the finale of *The Lady from Shanghai*, a shot cut by producer Harry Cohn. "I'm not saying Welles killed her," stated Pacios, "but that he should be considered a viable suspect" (n.p.). The heirs called the theory of Welles as the killer "a joke in the poorest taste" ("Orson Welles, spunta un delitto" [Orson Welles, up pops a crime], *la Repubblica*, August 20, 2000).

2. See Mariapaola Pierini, *Prima del cinema* (Rome: Bulzoni, 2005).

3. James Naremore, "The Trial: The FBI vs. Orson Welles," *Film Comment* 27, no. 1 (January–February 1991).

4. Orson Welles's column in the *New York Post*, 1945, quoted in James Naremore, *The Magic World of Orson Welles* (New York: Oxford University Press, 1978), 141.

5. Charles Higham, *Orson Welles, The Rise and Fall of an American Genius* (New York: St. Martin's Press, 1985), 308.

6. Charles Chaplin, quoted on the front page of *Espresso* (Rome), November 22, 1947, under the heading "Dichiaro guerra a Hollywood" [I declare war on Hollywood].

7. "È partito Tyrone Power, arriva Orson Welles" [Tyrone Power leaves, Orson Welles arrives], *Espresso*, November 10, 1947.

8. Gigi Cane, "Orson Welles: chi è" [Who is Orson Welles?], featuring a radio script written by Welles in 1942, *Columbus Day (Admiral of the Ocean Sea)*, translated into Italian by Gigi Cane. See *Dramma*, (September 1, 1947).

9. The Italian version of the film was given the go-ahead for screening on August 12, 1946. The censorship committee remarked on its excellent quality: "The narration proceeds with care under the watchful and attentive control of the director, who has paid the utmost attention to every detail and to the overall expressive effect of the film. The reconstruction of the period and the settings are extremely effective and interesting; good technique and excellent performances."

10. Review of *L'orgoglio degli Amberson* [*The Magnificent Ambersons*], *Corriere della sera* (Rome), August 27, 1946; Vice, "*L'orgoglio degli Amberson*," *il Messaggero* (Rome), August 22, 1946; Fabrizio Sarazani, *il Tempo* (Rome), August 22, 1946.

11. Amedeo Rivolta, "Ingresso libero: *L'orgoglio degli Amberson*" [Free entrance: *The Magnificent Ambersons*], *Hollywood* (Milan), July 12, 1947.

12. Umberto Barbaro, "Orson Welles e *L'orgoglio degli Amberson*" [Orson Welles and *The Magnificent Ambersons*], *l'Unità* (Rome), August 23, 1946, reprinted in *Servitù e grandezza del cinema* [Servitude and greatness of the cinema] (Rome: Riuniti, 1962), 498–99.

13. Arturo Lanocita, "Il festival cinematografico inaugurato a Venezia" (Venice Film Festival opens), *Corriere della Sera* (Milan), August 24, 1947; Guido Aristarco, "Cinema a Venezia," *Sipario* (Milan), October 1947; Adriano Baracco, "Venti giorni di cinema a Venezia" [Twenty days of films in Venice], *Hollywood*, September 1947.

14. Orson Welles, quoted in Luigi Barzini, Jr., "Finiva la benzina ma il pilota vide Roma" [The pilot ran out of fuel, but spotted Rome], *Europeo* (Milan), November 23, 1947.

15. Sergio Sollima, personal communication, May 27, 2006.

ORSON WELLES

1. The press conference was reconstructed from the following articles: Lancillotto, "Orson Welles all'Excelsior," *Espresso* (Rome), November 13 1947; Gian Luigi Rondi, "Orson Welles crede nel cinema italiano" [Orson Welles believes in Italian filmmaking], *il Tempo* (Rome), November 13, 1947; Sergio Sollima, "Il regista Orson Welles ama il cinema italiano" [Film director Orson Welles loves the Italian cinema], *l'Unità* (Rome), November 13, 1947; M. Cecchi, "Orson Welles, occhi da Cagliostro, sorriso da bimbo" [Orson Welles, Cagliostro's eyes, boyish smile], *Film* (Rome/Milan), November 22, 1947; Luigi Barzini, Jr., "Finiva la benzina ma il pilota vide Roma" [The pilot ran out of fuel, but spotted Rome], *Europeo* (Milan), November 23, 1947; Boezio, "Gazzettino Romano," *Momento Sera*, Rome, November 14, 1947; "'Conosceranno Rita quando sarà vecchia,' dice Orson Welles" ["They'll understand Rita when she is older," says Orson Welles], *Oggi* (Milan), November 23, 1947; Doriana Danton, "Linda Christian e Orson Welles," *Hollywood* (Milan), November 29, 1947.

2. PIZZA WITH TOGLIATTI

1. Mention of Welles's trips to Naples and Rome is made by Roberto Leydi in his article "L'uomo che volle diventare un genio" [The man who wanted to be a genius], *Europeo* (Milan), February 19, 1970.

2. Orson Welles and Peter Bogdanovich, *This Is Orson Welles*, ed. Jonathan Rosenbaum (London: Harper Collins, 1993), 39.

3. See Robert L. Carringer, *The Making of Citizen Kane* (Berkeley and Los Angeles: University of California Press, 1985; rev. ed. 1996). The scene was scrapped when the script was costed and Welles was forced to make cuts.

4. Barbara Leaming, *Orson Welles: A Biography* (New York: Viking, 1985), 429.

5. Luigi Barzini, Jr., *Finiva la benzina ma il pilota vide Roma* [The pilot ran out of fuel, but spotted Rome], *Europeo*, November 23, 1947.

6. Maurice Bessy, *Orson Welles* (Paris: Éditions Seghers, 1963), 29.

7. Indro Montanelli, *Addio, Wanda!* (Milan: Longanesi, 1956), 17–18.

8. Davide Ferrario, *Dissolvenza al nero* [Fade to black] (Milan: Longanesi, 1994). The writer—a film director and passionate Welles fan—adapts some of the episodes of Welles's life in Rome to create an international political intrigue. One of the virtues of the novel is the reconstruction of the Italian film industry and politics of the day, of late all too often seen through rose-colored glasses. Ferrario restores the blood and sweat, hypocrisy, and jockeying for position of those years, when America, the Catholic Church, the Mafia, and political parties were all trying to establish their power in an Italy still bloody from war. In 2006, the novel was made into a movie directed by Oliver Parker, which was not successful.

9. See Giorgio Bocca, *Palmiro Togliatti* (Bari: Laterza, 1973), 380.

10. Palmiro Togliatti, "Sumner Welles conferma di essere un calunniatore" [Sumner Welles repeats his slander], *l'Unità* (Rome), May 20, 1947.

11. Emanuele Rocco, "Il pranzo della pace" [Peace meal], *Tempo* (Milan), December 20, 1947; Luigi Barzini, Jr., "Togliatti a tavola" [Togliatti at dinner], *Europeo*, December 21, 1947.

12. Another version of the story exists—as told, or embellished, by Welles. Roosevelt was due to address a political rally and was temporarily blinded by the spotlights. "Which way do I have to go, left or right?" he asked, and Welles assured him that moving to the left had never done him any harm. See the notes of Maurice Bessy, published as "Orson Welles par Orson Welles" in *Écran* 33 (February 1975). See also Barbara Leaming, *Orson Welles: A Biography* (New York: Viking, 1985), 294.

13. James Naremore, "The Trial: The FBI vs. Orson Welles," *Film Comment* 27, no. 1 (January–February 1991).

3. BLACK MAGIC

1. Quoted in Moraldo Rossi and Tatti Sanguineti, *Fellini & Rossi: Il sesto vitellone* (Bologna: Cineteca di Bologna; Recco: Le Mani, 2001), 7.

2. Application made by Edward Small Productions to the prime minister's office, September 1947; copy held in the State Archives, Rome.

3. Frank Brady, *Citizen Welles* (New York: Charles Scribner's Sons, 1989), 419.

4. This and the previous quotation are from a note made by the head of Ufficio Centrale per la Cinematografia for the under-secretary of state, dated September 23, 1947; State Archives, Rome.

5. Giberto Severi, *Pittura e avventura* [Painting and adventure] (Rome: Carlo Bestetti Edizioni d'Arte, 1975), 180.

6. Alessandro Tasca di Cutò, *Un principe in America* [A prince in America] (Palermo: Sellerio, 2004), 253.

7. Orson Welles, "Out of a Trance," *New York Times,* April 17, 1949. "Each man kills the thing he loves," is a quotation from Oscar Wilde's *The Ballad of Reading Gaol.*

8. Maurice Bessy, *Orson Welles* (Paris: Éditions Seghers, 1963), 43.

9. Carlo Laurenzi, "Roma caput cinema," *Tempo* (Milan), 25 December 1947.

10. Georges Annenkov, *Vestendo le dive* [Dressing the divas] (Rome: Bocca, 1955), 67.

11. Laurenzi, "Roma caput cinema."

12. Annenkov, *Vestendo le dive,* 69, quoted in Franca Faldini and Goffredo Fofi, *L'avventurosa storia del cinema italiano, 1935–1959* [The adventurous history of Italian cinema] (Milan: Feltrinelli, 1979), 132.

13. Franca Faldini, *Roma Hollywood Roma* (Milan: Baldini & Castoldi, 1997), 35.

14. Emanuele Rocco, "Il pranzo della pace," *Tempo,* December 20–27, 1947.

15. Brady, *Citizen Welles,* 421.

16. Osvaldo Civirani, *Un fotografo a Cinecittà* (Rome: Gremese, 1995), 64.

17. Francesco Càllari, "Vengano pure a 'girare' in Italia ma con garbo e discrezione" [Let them by all means come and shoot in Italy, provided it's with suavity and discretion], *Hollywood* (Milan), December 20, 1947.

18. Il cronista, "Era già Cagliostro prima di diventarlo" [He was already Cagliostro before he played him], *Film* (Rome/Milan), March 27, 1949.

19. Quoted in Franca Faldini and Goffredo Fofi, *L'avventurosa storia del cinema italiano,* 131.

20. Gian Luigi Rondi, *Un lungo viaggio 2: Gli stranieri* [A long journey 2: The foreigners] (Florence: Le Monnier, 2001), 278.

21. See Augusto Borselli, "Il Quirinale conteso fra Repubblica e registi" [The Quirinale Palace battled over by the state and film directors], *Momento Sera* (Rome), January 4, 1948.

22. Annenkov, *Vestendo le dive,* 66–67.

23. Quoted in Alberto Farina, "Tutto genio e sregolatezza" [Bizarre genius], *Film Cronache* (January/February 1993). There are no models of military camps in the film; Troiani was remembering the scene in which Macbeth first appears with the crown, and the woman Welles wanted to minimize was Lady Macbeth.

24. *Filming Othello* (dir. Orson Welles, 1978).

25. Alberto and Francesco Fratellini, "3 Fratellini" [The three Fratellinis], *Cinema Nuovo,* July 15, 1954. French circus performers of Italian origin, the trio initially comprised Paul (who died in 1940), Albert, and François Fratellini—whose stage names were August, Footit, and Chocolat. The interview with the two surviving members was certainly from several years before the publication date.

26. Tasca di Cutò, *Un principe in America,* 258.

27. Quoted in Alberto Farina, "Tutto genio e sregolatezza."

28. The incident was reported in *Corriere della Sera* (Milan), January 25, 1948.

29. In his May 23, 1945, column for the *New York Post* Welles reviewed Eisenstein's *Ivan the Terrible* and spoke of the Russian filmmaker as "supremely the master of film rhetoric," adding, "Eisenstein's uninhibited preoccupation with pictorial effect sometimes leads him, as it has led others of us who work with the camera, into sterile exercises, empty demonstrations of the merely picturesque." These accusations were to be leveled by the world's film critics—particularly in Italy—against Welles himself.

30. In a sketch Welles places himself at the end of a line beginning with the great patriarchs Méliès and Griffith and continuing through Eisenstein. He distinguished between four categories of filmmaker at the origin of the art form: the entertainers, poets, narrators, and realists. He placed Chaplin in the first three categories; Sennet and Sturges in the first; Murnau, Renoir, Flaherty, and De Sica in the second; Feyder and Lubitsch in the third; and Stroheim and Italian filmmakers in the fourth—as far from himself as it was possible to be, in this scheme of things. See Bessy, *Orson Welles*, 105.

31. Luigi Barzini, Jr., "Roma può diventare la capitale cinematografica d'Europa" [Rome may become the capital of European filmmaking], *Il Corriere di Milano*, January 11, 1948.

32. Orson Welles and Peter Bogdanovich, *This Is Orson Welles*, ed. Jonathan Rosenbaum (London: Harper Collins, 1993), 106.

4. DOLCE VITA

1. Ennio Flaiano, review of *Gli anni migliori* [The best Yyears of our lives], *Bis* (Milan), April 27, 1948; reprinted in *Lettere d'amore al cinema* [Love letters to the cinema] (Milan: Rizzoli, 1978), n.p.

2. Michel Sander, "Mister Welles, c'est le diable s'exclament les Romains," *L'Écran français*, April 27, 1948.

3. Giberto Severi, "Jennifer Jones si riposa a Roma" [Jennifer Jones is resting in Rome], *Fotogrammi* (Rome), January 13, 1948.

4. Doriana Danton, "Jennifer Jones è a Roma" [Jennifer Jones is in Rome], *Hollywood* (Milan), January 24, 1948.

5. C. A. Felice, "Bluffa, questo W" [W is a bluff], a review of *The Stranger*, *Film* (Rome/Milan), January 3, 1948.

6. Mario Gromo, "Lo straniero" [The stranger], *la Stampa*; reprinted in *Film visti* [Films I've seen] (Rome: Edizioni di Bianco e Nero, 1957).

7. Augusto Errante, "Orson Welles si sposa" [Orson Welles is getting married], *Oggi* (Milan), April 25, 1948.

8. Doriana Danton, "Tamiroff e René Clair," *Hollywood*, April 3, 1948.

9. Paola Ojetti, "Ma ti calmi si o no? Un po' di discrezione Orson!" [Will you please quiet Orson!) *Film*, February 21, 1948.

10. Transit, "Cronache dei 4 venti" [Chronicles of the four winds], *Film*, April 10, 1948.

11. Sergio Sollima, personal communication, May 27, 2006.

12. Luciana Peverelli, "Donnina da 2 soldi" [Wretched wench], *Cine Illustrato* (Rome), May 9, 1948.

13. Zeta, "Lea Padovani al bivio: Serato o Welles?" [Lea Padovani must decide: Serato or Welles?], *Film*, May 1, 1948.

14. See Sander, "Mister Welles, c'est le diable." I am grateful to François Thomas for drawing my attention to this article. In 1941 Welles had written *The Life of Christ*, set in the modern day; Rossellini made *Il messia* in 1975. By the time of this meeting between Welles and Rossellini, the neorealist filmmaker had been trying for several years to make a film about Italian emigrants to America. It was made a year later by

Edward Dmytryk, with the title *Christ in Concrete* starring, coincidentally or not, Lea Padovani.

15. Roberto De Paolis, "Un solo Welles non basta" [One Welles is not enough], *Bis,* April 6, 1948.

FRANCA FALDINI

1. Franca Faldini, *Roma Hollywood Roma* (Milan: Baldini & Castoldi, 1997), 36.
2. Faldini, *Roma Hollywood Roma*, n.p.

5. *CITIZEN KANE*

1. An Italianate pronunciation of the name "Kane" effectively changes the title to *Il cittadino cane,* or "Citizen dog."

2. The Fourth Review Commission of the Ufficio Centrale per la Cinematografia issued the following statement after its review of the film: "A man may obtain everything from life but he may also lose everything. This is the message of a noteworthy film featuring the superb acting of Orson Welles and a series of magnificent sets. The Commission has no objections to the morals of the film and has therefore approved it for dubbing into Italian and for public screening."

3. Roberto De Paolis, "Un solo Welles non basta" [One Welles is not enough], *Bis* (Milan), April 6, 1948.

4. Ugo Casiraghi, "Kane è arrivato in ritardo su Orson" [Kane arrives after Orson], *l'Unità* (Milan), May 13, 1948.

5. Lan (Arturo Lanocita), "Cittadino Kane," *Corriere della Sera* (Milan), May 13, 1948.

6. Alfredo Panicucci, "Tanto rumore per Orson" [Much ado about Orson], *Avanti!* (Milan), May 13, 1948.

7. Guido Aristarco, "Festival internazionale: Il cittadino Kane" *Bis,* May 25, 1948.

8. Aristarco, "Festival internazionale."

9. See Guido Aristarco, "Cinema a Venezia," *Sipario* (Milan), October 1947.

10. Alberto Mondadori, "Il cittadino Kane," *Tempo* (Milan), May 22, 1948.

11. Literary critic Cesare Garboli, co-founder with Mondadori of the Saggiatore publishing group, wrote, "Alberto truly loved a film that I have always considered, to a chorus of disapproval from my intellectual friends, rather mediocre: *Citizen Kane* by Orson Welles. I think he saw part of himself in the film. He was moved whenever he talked about it; he identified with it, identified himself in it" ("Citizen Mondadori," *Panorama,* May 2, 1993).

12. Giulio Cesare Castello, "10 anni di cinema" [Ten years of films], *Sipario,* June 1948.

13. g. v. (Glauco Viazzi), "*Citizen Kane (Quarto potere),*" *Bianco e Nero,* July 1948.

14. Jean George Auriol, "Diario Romano" [Roman diary], *La critica cinematografica,* June–July 1948.

15. The American version of the film, reviewed in March 1948, measured 3,126 meters.

16. Goffredo Fofi, "Un regista maledetto" [A damned director], *Il Nuovo Spettatore Cinematografico,* December 1963.

17. Guido Fink, "Rapporto confidenziale su Orson Welles e la critica italiana" [Confidential report on Orson Welles and Italian film criticism], *Bianco e Nero*, January–March 1986.

18. In 1963, Ultra Film bought the distribution rights to *Citizen Kane* in Italy, Libya, Eritrea, and Italian Somalia. They made a completely new soundtrack, replacing some of Bernard Herrmann's music with standard pieces. The film was relicensed and released in May 1966. This is the version available for rental in Italy and the one most Italians know. Welles was given the warm voice of Emilio Cigoli (as he was in *The Third Man* and *The Lady from Shanghai*) and Gino Cervi is the narrator of *News on the March*.

19. Guido Aristarco, "Il cittadino Orson Welles e il mito del potere" [Citizen Welles and the myth of power], *Cinema Nuovo*, July–August 1966.

20. M. C., "Orson e il Quarto potere" [Orson and the Fourth Estate], *Film* (Milan/Rome), November 20, 1948.

21. Callisto Cosulich, "Il magnifico istrione" (The magnificent ham), *Paese Sera* (Rome), October 12, 1985.

22. Callisto Cosulich, "*Quarto potere*" *Giornale di Trieste*, February 19, 1949; reprinted in C. Cosulich, *Il cinema secondo Cosulich* (Gorizia: Transmedia, 2005), 61–62.

23. "Quarto potere" (Citizen Kane), *Corriere della Sera*, July 14, 1949.

24. Vice, "Quarto potere," *Cinema*, July 31, 1949.

25. G. A. (Guido Aristarco), "*Quarto potere*," *Sipario*, August–September 1949.

26. Volpone (Pietro Bianchi), review of *Citizen Kane*, *Bertoldo*, August 7, 1949; reprinted in P. Bianchi, *L'occhio di vetro: Il cinema degli anni 1945–1950* [The glass eye: Films from 1945 to 1950] (Milan: Il formichiere, 1979), 232–33.

27. Ennio Flaiano, "Cagliostro," *il Mondo*, Rome, June 4, 1949; reprinted in Flaiano, *Ombre fatte a macchina* [Machine-made shadows] (Milan: Bompiani, 1996), 136.

6. LIFE AFTER RITA

1. Anita Colby, "Filo diretto" [Direct line], *Hollywood* (Milan), June 18, 1949. *Hollywood* also translated an article by Hedda Hopper recounting numerous anecdotes about the shooting of *The Lady from Shanghai*, with the title "Quando il marito è un genio" [When your husband's a genius], July 12, 1947.

2. J. Heyn, "Rita divorzia ma risposerà" [Rita is divorcing to remarry], *Espresso* (Rome), November 19, 1947.

3. In Mario Gilardon, "Rita Hayworth e i suoi brevi amori" [Rita Hayworth and her brief love affairs], *il Messaggero* (Rome), February 16, 1948.

4. Doriana Danton, "Lea Padovani rivale di Rita Hayworth," *Hollywood*, June 5, 1948.

5. Joe Morella, Edward Z. Epstein, *Rita: The Life of Rita Hayworth* (London: Comet, 1983), 126.

6. Orson Welles and Peter Bogdanovich, *This Is Orson Welles*, ed. Jonathan Rosenbaum (London: Harper Collins, 1993), 108.

7. G. L. R. (Gian Luigi Rondi), "Il cinema nelle scuole e nei caffè" [Cinema at school and in the cafés], *il Tempo* (Rome), June 5, 1948.

8. Welles and Bogdanovich, *This Is Orson Welles*, 402.

9. Bret Wood, *Orson Welles: A Bio-bibliography* (Westport, Conn.: Greenwood Press, 1990), 218.

10. See Samuel Blumenfeld, *L'homme qui voulait être prince* (Paris: Grasset, 2006).

11. Jean Malin, "Rita schiaffeggiò il principe" [Rita slaps prince], *Cine Illustrato* (Rome), August 22, 1948. See also John Staff, "Il principe azzurro di Rita Hayworth" [Rita Hayworth's fairytale prince], *Cine Illustrato,* January 2, 1949.

12. "Rita Hayworth e Welles si sono incontrati in Riviera" (Rita Hayworth and Welles meet on the Riviera), *Corriere della Sera* (Milan), July 25, 1948.

13. In Barbara Leaming, *Orson Welles: A Biography* (New York and London: Penguin, 1986), 452.

14. Rondone, "Notti Bianche" [Sleepless nights], *Fotogrammi* (Rome), August 17, 1948.

15. Reported by Rondone, "Notti Bianche" [Sleepless nights], in *Fotogrammi,* October 19, 1948.

16. Bruno Ventavoli, "Roma 1948: Welles indaga" [Rome 1948: Welles investigates], *la Stampa* (Turin), September 3, 1994.

17. Gianpiero Mughini reconstructs the event, attributing the source to Penn himself, in *Che belle le ragazze di via Margutta* [How beautiful were the girls in Via Margutta] (Milan: Mondadori, 2004), 127.

7. THE FALL OF MACBETH

1. Alfredo Todisco, "Incontro con Orson Welles" [Meeting with Orson Welles], in *Ultimissime* (Trieste), August 31, 1948.

2. *Combat,* August 29, 1948.

3. Jean Cocteau, foreword to André Bazin, *Orson Welles* (Paris: Chavane, 1950); published in English as "Profile of Orson Welles," in André Bazin, *Orson Welles: A Critical View,* trans. Gilbert Adair (Los Angeles: Acrobat, 1991), 31–32.

4. Cocteau, "Profile of Orson Welles," 29.

5. "Piangevano o stavano per piangere Anna Magnani e Orson Welles" [Anna Magnani and Orson Welles were about to burst into tears], *Europeo* (Milan), September 13, 1948.

6. "Orson Welles contro il realismo cinematografico" [Orson Welles against cinematic realism], *Europeo,* October 15, 1950.

7. André Bazin and Jean Jacques Tacchella, "Les secrets d'Orson Welles," *L'Écran français,* September 21, 1948.

8. Renzo Renzi, "Sullo schermo per una volta" [Screened once only], *Cinema* (Milan), February 15, 1949.

9. Bazin and Tacchella, "Les secrets d'Orson Welles."

10. Jean Desternes, "Le realisme ne m'interesse pas," *La Revue du cinéma,* September 1948. The first part of the interview was translated by Michelangelo Antonioni, then a journalist, and included in his "Breviario del cinema" [Notes on the cinema], published in *Cinema,* October 15, 1949.

11. Todisco, "Incontro con Orson Welles."

12. Giulio Cesare Castello, "A Orson Welles piacciono Eduardo De Filippo e De Sica" [Orson Welles likes Eduardo and De Sica], *Il mattino del popolo* (Venice), September 4, 1948.

13. James Naremore, *The Magic World of Orson Welles* (New York: Oxford University Press, 1978), 170.

14. Rudolf Kurtz, *Espressionismus und Film* (Berlin: Verlag der Lichtbildbuhne, 1926).

15. Claude Daire, "Une interview exclusive d'Orson Welles," *L'Écran français,* June 26, 1950.

16. Alfredo Todisco, "Uomini e film sulla laguna" [Men and films on the lagoon], *Ultimissime,* August 31, 1948.

17. Alberto Mondadori, "Gioia dell'anima mia, se le tempeste...," *Epoca* (Milan), September 8, 1951.

18. The other jurors were Alberto Consiglio, Vinicio Marinucci, Mario Melloni, and Giorgio Prosperi.

19. Ugo Casiraghi, "Macbeth è il film che non vi fa dormire" [Macbeth murders our sleep], *l'Unità* (Milan), September 4, 1948.

20. Bazin and Tacchella, "Les secrets d'Orson Welles."

21. Castello, "A Orson Welles piacciono Eduardo De Filippo e De Sica."

22. Alfredo Panicucci, "Buona volontà e ambizione di Orson Welles" [Orson Welles: good intentions and ambition], *Avanti!* (Milan), September 4, 1948.

23. Castello, "A Orson Welles piacciono Eduardo De Filippo e De Sica."

24. Alfredo Todisco, "Orson Welles 'riabilitato' dalla stampa italiana" [Orson Welles "rehabilitated" by the Italian press], *Ultimissime,* September 18, 1948.

25. Todisco, "Orson Welles 'riabilitato' dalla stampa italiana."

26. "Piangevano o stavano per piangere Orson Welles e Anna Magnani."

27. Desternes, "Le realisme ne m'interesse pas."

28. Leone Comini, "Soldati lascia perplessi, Orson Welles sconcerta" [Perplexing Soldati, disconcerting Orson Welles], *Giornale di Trieste,* September 4, 1948.

29. Quoted in Leone Comini, "L'astrattismo non si addice a *Macbeth*," [Abstraction doesn't suit *Macbeth*], *il Gazzettino-Sera* (Venice), September 4–5, 1948.

30. Panicucci, "Buona volontà e ambizione di Orson Welles."

31. Bazin and Tacchella, "Les secrets d'Orson Welles."

32. Desternes, "Le realisme ne m'interesse pas."

33. Gian Battista Cavallaro, review of *Macbeth, L'Avvenire d'Italia* (Rome), September 4, 1948.

34. Alberto Mondadori, "I due scandali del festival" [The festival's two scandals], *Tempo* (Milan), September 11, 1948.

35. Translated by Giuseppe Prezzolini for inclusion in his article "Cinematografai [*sic*] americani scontenti dell'Italia" [American filmmakers displeased with Italy], *la Nazione* (Florence), September 29, 1948. The original remarks by Elsa Maxwell and Orson Welles appeared in *Daily Variety* on September 8 and 15, 1948.

36. Alberto Mondadori, "Conclusioni sul festival" [Summing up the festival], *Tempo,* September 18, 1948.

37. Augusto Borselli, "Guerra tra pubblico e giuria" [The public and jury at odds], *Oggi* (Milan), September 19, 1948.

38. Gian Luigi Rondi, "Orson Welles alle prese con Shakespeare fa del teatro roboante e wagneriano" [Orson Welles's Shakespeare is bombastic, Wagnerian theater], *la Nazione,* September 4, 1948. The article, in a slightly abridged form, appeared the same day in *il Tempo* (Rome) under the title "La tragedia di Macbeth insuccesso di Orson Welles" [Macbeth's tragedy, Orson Welles's failure].

39. Leonardo Mitri, "Welles con Macbeth ci ha voluto macbeffare" [Welles mocks us with his Scottish Macbeth], *Espresso* (Rome), September 4, 1948.

40. Arturo Lanocita, "*Fuga in Francia* di Mario Soldati," *Corriere della Sera* (Milan), September 4, 1948.

41. Panicucci, "Buona volontà e ambizione di Orson Welles."

42. Guido Aristarco, "Molte buone occasioni perdute alla mostra veneziana del cinema" [Many missed opportunities at the Venice Film Festival], *Sipario* (Milan), September 1948.

43. Casiraghi, "*Macbeth.*"

44. Ennio Flaiano, review of *Cagliostro, il Mondo* (Rome), June 4, 1949; reprinted in Flaiano, *Ombre fatte a macchina* [Machine-made shadows], (Milan: Bompiani, 1996), 136.

45. Mondadori, "Conclusioni sul festival." A week later Mondadori wrote, "*Macbeth* is the kind of film that should be called art, pure and simple." ("Postille a Venezia" [Venetian postscript], *Tempo*, September 25, 1948). Welles replied with a letter in English: "Dear Alberto, I want to feel sure, and I do, that you expressed your honest opinion about *Macbeth*, that none of the good things you wrote about it were meant merely as a favour to me." The undated letter was typed on letterhead from the Excelsior Hotel in Rome and signed, "your devoted friend. Orson" (archives of the Arnoldo and Alberto Mondadori Foundation, Milan, Saggiatore historical archive, in a folder titled "Welles").

46. Actually, $800,000 was the figure quoted in "Servizio segreto" (Secret service) in *Fotogrammi* (Rome), February 10, 1948. The film had had a budget of $885,000.

47. Mario Gromo, "Hollywood contro Venezia: Una risposta" [Hollywood versus Venice: A rebuttal], *la Stampa* (Turin), September 29, 1948.

48. Giorgio Prosperi, "Risposta ad Elsa Maxwell e ad Orson Welles" (Reply to Elsa Maxwell and Orson Welles), *Cinema*, October 25, 1948.

49. Gian Francesco Luzi, "Critici" [Critics], *La Critica Cinematografica*, November 1948.

50. Jean Bourgeois, "Le sujet et l'expression au cinéma, à propos d'*Hamlet* et de *Macbeth*," *La Revue du cinéma*, September 1948.

51. Cocteau, "Profile of Orson Welles," 29.

52. Claude Mauriac, "Le cinéma est-il un art complet?" *Filmcritica*, October 1951.

53. Gherardo Casale, *L'incantesimo è compiuto: Shakespeare secondo Welles* [The charm's wound up: Welles's Shakespeare] (Turin: Lindau, 2001).

ALFREDO TODISCO

1. Alfredo Todisco, "Incontro con Orson Welles" [Meeting Orson Welles], in *Ultimissime* (Trieste), August, 31 1948.

2. Todisco, "Incontro con Orson Welles."

3. From act 1, scene 1. The exchange is actually between Brabantio and Iago, and takes place in front of Roderigo.

4. Luigi Einaudi was an economist and president of Italy from 1948 to 1955.

8. *OTHELLO* BEGINS SHOOTING

1. Micheál Mac Liammóir, *Put Money in Thy Purse* (London: Methuen, 1952), 25.

2. Scalera Film, "Promemoria sul film *Otello*" [Memorandum on the film *Othello*], Rome, December 28, 1951; held in the State Archives, Rome.

3. *Il Sindacato Giornalisti Cinematografici* (The Italian Union of Film Journalists) presented Zanuck with an award for the John Ford–directed *My Darling Clementine*, considered the best foreign film of the 1947–48 season (the film was released in America in 1946).

4. Quoted in Francesco Savio, *Cinecittà anni Trenta* [Cinecittà in the Thirties] (Rome: Bulzoni, 1979), 354.

5. Nino Bo, "Ty combatte a San Marino" [Tyrone is fighting in San Marino], *Cine Illustrato* (Rome), September 26, 1948.

6. Amy Ravagnan, "Orson e Lea gireranno *Otello*" [Orson and Lea will make *Othello*], *Fotogrammi* (Rome), November 9, 1948.

7. Gian Gaspare Napolitano, "Al terzo uomo piace il bloody marriage" [The third man likes a bloody marriage], *Europeo* (Milan), January 14, 1951.

8. Alessandro Tasca di Cutò, *Un principe in America*, 259.

9. Maurice Bessy, *Orson Welles* (Paris: Éditions Seghers, 1963), 68–69.

10. Harriet White Medin, "Othello, Desdemona and Me" *Video Watchdog* 23 (May–July 1994).

11. This and other anecdotes about the making of the film are featured in *Shadowing the Third Man* (dir. Frederick Baker, 2004).

12. Mac Liammóir, *Put Money in Thy Purse*, 11.

13. Mac Liammóir believed an Italian actor (not Everett Sloane) had originally played Iago: "Name, though he was found unsuitable, escapes me (Freud? Probably.)" (Mac Liammóir, *Put Money in Thy Purse*, 11).

14. *il Gazzettino-Sera* (Venice), November 5–6, 1948.

15. *il Gazzettino-Sera*, November 10–11, 1948.

16. Orson Welles and Peter Bogdanovich, *This Is Orson Welles*, ed. Jonathan Rosenbaum (London: Harper Collins, 1993), 222.

17. Alfredo Todisco, "Una martellata nel bagno" [Hammering in the bathroom], *Europeo*, October 29, 1950.

18. Lea Padovani, interviewed by P. Porro on December 14, 1973, in Franca Faldini and Goffredo Fofi, *L'avventurosa storia del cinema italiano, 1935–1959* [The adventurous history of Italian cinema] (Milan: Feltrinelli, 1979), 303.

19. Matilde Amorosi, "Lea Padovani: 'Ero bellissima e Massimo Serato lasciò la Magnani per amor mio'" [Lea Padovani: "I was beautiful and Massimo Serato left Anna Magnani for me"], *Gente* (Milan), February 1, 1990.

20. Bessy, *Orson Welles*, 69.

21. Mariella Parker, "Cinecittà e dintorni" [In and around Cinecittà], *Film* (Rome/Milan), April 17, 1949.

22. Barbara Leaming, *Orson Welles: A Biography* (New York and London: Penguin, 1986), 360.

9. SCALERA GETS COLD FEET

1. Alfredo Panicucci, "Passo doppio" [Paso doble], *Tempo* (Milan), March 12–13, 1949.

2. Silvana Pampanini, *Scandalosamente perbene* [Indecently respectable] (Rome: Gremese, 1996), 161–62.

3. Luigi Barzini, Jr., "I tavolini di via Veneto" [The tables in Via Veneto], *Oggi* (Milan), February 12, 1949. See also Luigi Barzini, Jr., "Almanacco dei sette giorni: Febbraio 21 lunedì" [Almanac of the Week: Monday, February 21], *La Settimana Incom* (Rome), February 26, 1949.

4. Orson Welles to Alberto Mondadori, Paris, February 25, 1949 (typewritten); in the archives of the Arnoldo and Alberto Mondadori Foundation, Milan, Saggiatore Historical Archive, Orson Welles file.

5. Here is Welles's imperfect, but witty, Italian:

Caro Alberto,

Era un vero piacere di ricevere la Sua lettera, ma sfortunatamente non esiste una copia di *Macbeth* in Europa. Quella mandata a Venezia fu rimandata in Inghilterra dove i dragoni dei Republic Pictures la salvaguardano contra chi sa cosa nel più profondo nascondiglio delle Isole Britanniche.

Peggio ancora, ora stanno considerando a Hollywood un progetto per rimontare il film secondo il loro squisito gusto—nella speranza, assumo, che il giudizio dei Dogi di Venezia possa essere cambiato attraverso un rimeschiare della celluloide. Non posso, né voglio pensare quale potrà essere il risultato.

... Che cosa faranno con *Macbeth* dopo avere finito di rovinarlo non posso dire. Nel fratempo sto lavorando duramente su *Othello* che completerò parte in Italia, parte in Francia.

Intendo passare la maggiore parte di marzo, e forse anche aprile, a Roma. Se Lei si troverà da quelle parti mi farà molto piacere rivederla. Lei è un vero amico e voglio che

Lei sappia che io questo lo so e che io sono il Suo.

Frattanto l'invio i miei più cordiali ed affettuosi saluti,

Suo Orson

6. Welles makes this comment in *Filming Othello* (dir. Orson Welles, 1978), in response to a question from the member of an audience as to whether Roderigo's dog is a terrier [translator's note].

7. Micheál Mac Liammóir, *Put Money in Thy Purse* (London: Methuen, 1952), 12.

8. Mac Liammóir, *Put Money in Thy Purse*, 19.

9. Mac Liammóir, *Put Money in Thy Purse*, 39. [Translator's note: In his diary Mac Liammóir often referred to Welles by his first initial—meaning both Orson and Othello.]

10. "Ty con turbante ed Orson conturbato" [Ty with turban, Orson perturbed], *Cine Illustrato* (Rome), July 17, 1949.

11. Società Scalera Film, application for permission to begin shooting *Othello*, May 22, 1949; State Archives, Rome.

12. Annibale Scicluna, judgment in favor of censorship, June 3, 1949.

13. Quoted in Barbara Leaming, *Orson Welles: A Biography* (New York: Viking 1985), 453.

14. Betsy Blair, *The Memory of All That* (New York: Alfred A. Knopf, 2003), 176.

15. Blair, *The Memory of All That*, 177.

16. Michele Scalera, letter to Direzione Generale per la Cinematografia, dated June 21, 1949; State Archives, Rome.

17. Mac Liammóir, *Put Money in Thy Purse*, 98.

18. Simone Mougin, "A grand renfort de coups de guele et d'éclats de rire Orson Welles fait d'Othello un Maure de Mogador," *L'Écran français*, Paris, July 25, 1949.

19. Blair, *The Memory of All That*, 162–63.

20. Mac Liammóir, *Put Money in Thy Purse*, 116–18.

21. Thomas Brady, "Welles plans film on *Iliad, Odyssey*," *New York Times*, July 25, 1949.

22. Italo Dragosei, "Settimana Romana: Comincia l'euforia pellicolare" [The week in Rome: Film frenzy begins], *Hollywood* (Milan), July 30, 1949.

23. Mac Liammóir, *Put Money in Thy Purse*, 119.

10. THE LAST DESDEMONA

1. Zorro, "I dimenticati" [The forgotten], *Hollywood* (Milan), November 27, 1948.

2. "Settegiorni: Orson è tornato" [Seven days: Orson is back], *Oggi* (Milan), March 10, 1949.

3. Hedda Hopper, "Quelli che credono al proprio mito" [People who fall for their own myth], *Hollywood*, July 23, 1949.

4. Alberto Mondadori, "Ancora di Welles" [Welles again], *Tempo* (Milan), October 2, 1948.

5. Guido Aristarco, "La signora di Shangai" [*The Lady from Shanghai*], *Cinema*, October 25, 1948.

6. Dino Risi, "Morte della sequenza" [Death of the take], *Cinema*, November 25, 1948.

7. Callisto Cosulich, "La signora di Sciangai" [*The Lady from Shanghai*], *Giornale di Trieste*, September 19, 1948; reprinted in C. Cosulich, *Il cinema secondo Cosulich* (Gorizia: Transmedia, 2005), 32.

8. Volpone (Pietro Bianchi), in *Bertoldo* (Milan), September 26, 1948; reprinted in Pietro Bianchi, *L'occhio di vetro. Il cinema degli anni 1945–1950* [The glass eye: Films from 1945 to 1950] (Milan: Il formichiere, 1979), 203.

9. Giulio Cesare Castello, "The Magnificent Orson Welles," *Bianco e Nero*, January 1949.

10. Lan (Arturo Lanocita), "Cagliostro," *Corriere della Sera*, (Rome), May 19, 1949.

11. Dino Falconi, "Due righe in fretta" [A few hurried lines], *Film* (Rome/Milan), July 17, 1949.

12. Ennio Flaiano, "Cagliostro," *il Mondo* (Rome), June 4, 1949; reprinted in Flaiano, *Ombre fatte a macchina* [Machine-made shadows], (Milan: Bompiani, 1996), 136.

13. Mario Luporini, application to the Ministry of Foreign Trade, April 28, 1949; in the State Archives.

14. Giorgio Papi, letter to the Ministry of Foreign Trade, July 28, 1949; in the State Archives.

15. As photographed in *il Gazzettino-Sera* (Venice), August 6, 1949.

16. "Orson Welles nuovamente in città" [Orson Welles back in town], *il Gazzettino di Venezia*, August 4, 1949.

17. Barbara Leaming, *Orson Welles: A Biography* (New York: Viking, 1985), 455.

18. Reported by Fabio Galvani in "Orwell, grande fratello per le spie inglesi" [Orwell, Big Brother for English spies], *la Stampa*, June 23, 1998.

19. James Naremore, "The Trial: The FBI vs. Orson Welles," *Film Comment* 27, no. 1 (January–February 1991).

20. Micheál Mac Liammóir, *Put Money in Thy Purse* (London: Methuen, 1952), 126.

21. Quoted in Franca Faldini and Goffredo Fofi, *L'avventurosa storia del cinema italiano, 1935–1959*, [The adventurous history of Italian cinema] (Milan: Feltrinelli, 1979), 303.

22. Oberdan Troiani in *Memorie a 15 ASA* (Memoirs in 15 ASA), a documentary by Massimiliano Troiani produced by La grande opera in 2006. The previous quotation is from another documentary by Massimiliano Troiani that is still in production.

23. Ennio Flaiano, "L'attesa del capolavoro" [Waiting for the masterpiece], *il Mondo*, August 27, 1949; reprinted in *Lettere d'amore al cinema* (Milan: Rizzoli, 1978), 135–36.

24. André Bazin, *Orson Welles* (Paris: Chavanne, 1950), 70–71.

25. Carlo Martini, "Orson Welles e i gatti" [Orson Welles and cats], *Film*, September 11, 1949.

26. "Cartoni animati: l'Otello di Orson" [Cartoons: Orson's *Othello*], *Cine Illustrato* (Rome), September 18, 1949.

27. Francesco Càllari, "La crisi del cinema americano" [The crisis of the American film industry], *Cinema*, September 15, 1949.

28. Quoted in Alberto Farina, *Tutto genio e sregolatezza* [Bizarre genius], *Film cronache*, January/February 1993.

29. Oberdan Troiani, from a documentary by Massimiliano Troiani still in production.

30. Mac Liammóir, *Put Money in Thy Purse*, 159.

31. The scene was probably shot in one of the Scalera Studios and was to be accompanied by a long tracking shot from the circular ceiling window to Othello and the body of Desdemona, only rapid fragments of which seem to have survived in the film (according to Alvaro Mancori [see Mancori interview, pp. 175–84, this book]). The model of the peephole may have been used immediately afterward for the reverse shot, but the illusion is not evident and it is not clear from any printed version of the film whether the miniature peephole device was actually used.

32. Orson Welles, preface to Maurice Bessy, *Les Trucquages Au Cinema*, (Paris: Éditions prisma), 1951.

33. Mac Liammóir, *Put Money in Thy Purse*, 183.

34. Mac Liammóir, *Put Money in Thy Purse*, 180.

35. Mac Liammóir, *Put Money in Thy Purse*, 191.

36. "A Orson costano fiato le ultime scene di Otello" [Orson breathless over the final scenes of *Othello*], *il Gazzettino-Sera*, November 3, 1949.

37. "Nel cortile della Ca' d'Oro Desdemona piangeva sul serio" [Desdemona bursts into real tears], *il Gazzettino-Sera*, November 5, 1949.

38. Mario Gromo, "Il terzo uomo" [*The Third Man*], *la Stampa*, n.d., 1949; reprinted in *Film visti*, [Films I've seen] (Rome: Edizioni di Bianco e nero, 1957), 332–33.

39. Vice, review of *The Third Man*, *Cinema*, February 15, 1950.

40. Luigi Barzini, Jr., "Almanacco dei sette giorni" [Almanac of the week], *La Settimana Incom*, (Rome), January 28, 1950.

41. Angelo Ratti, "Lea non pubblicherà le lettere di Orson" [Lea won't publish Orson's letters], *La Settimana Incom*, issue 51, Rome, December 17, 1949.

11. BLESSED AND DAMNED

1. Micheál Mac Liammóir, *Put Money in Thy Purse* (London: Methuen, 1952), 226.

2. Quoted in Alberto Farina, "Tutto genio e sregolatezza" [Bizarre genius], *Film cronache*, January/February 1993.

3. André Bazin and Charles Bitsch, "Entretien avec Orson Welles," *Cahiers du cinéma* 84 (1958); reprinted in André Bazin, *Orson Welles*, (Paris: Chavanne, 1950), 109.

4. This was Welles's almost unaccented, imperfect but technically savvy Italian: "Cannoni che sparano dalle mura come gia stabilito. . . . Questa scena dovra essere di effetto alba e tramonto. Si capisce che alba puo andare per tramonto e vice versa. Pero suggerisco girarlo la mattina e anche il pomeriggio tardi. . . . La seconda scena è una inquadratura a piombo dalla torre. Questo lo faremo con un 40 se questo era l'obiettivo usato per fare le fotografie che ho marcato e che inchiudo qui dentro. . . . l'erba che cresce sul mura dev'essere strapato e li bisogna mettere nove o dieci soldati ben vestiti dei quali uno o due devono passeggiare su e giu lentamente ma non in modo troppo evidente. . . . Se è un giorno senza vento levare le bandiere dagli stendardi e usate soltanto i stendardi perche sarebbe ridicolo avere le bandiere ferme. . . . La macchina non si muove da Otello al castello ma dal casello atraverso il muro a Otello: contrario a quello che sembra logico. . . . La macchina dev'essere tenuta in mano e deve seguire i movimenti dei gabbiani per dare l'illusione di delirio. . . . l'inquadratura dei cannoni che sparano e l'alzata di Otello dopo l'epilessia debbono essere girate con pellicola inglese. . . . NON DIMENTICATE I CANNONI. NON DIMENTICATE I CANNONI" (Orson Welles, "Altre riprese da fare a Mogador," typescript for Oberdan Troiani; reprinted courtesy of Massimiliano Troiani).

5. Giorgio Papi, letter to Direzione Generale della Cinematografia, April 5, 1950; in the State Archives.

6. Nicola de Pirro, letter to Luigi Attilio Jaschi, June 13, 1950; in the State Archives.

7. Nicola de Pirro, letter to Luigi Attilio Jaschi, June 17, 1950; in the State Archives.

8. The Ministry of Foreign Trade to the Banca d'America e d'Italia, June 22, 1950; copy in the State Archives.

9. Pier Luigi Carli, "Sarà Ulisse e, con la barba, il moro di Venezia" [He will play Ulysses and the bearded Moor of Venice], *La Gazzetta di Livorno*, April 22, 1950. The article was published in various newspapers.

10. Peter Noble, *The Fabulous Orson Welles* (London: Hutchinson, 1956), 194–201, 217. Dino De Laurentiis remembered nothing about such a remote episode.

11. Orson Welles, "An Introductory Letter to the Author," preface to Kenneth Tynan, *He That Plays The King, A View of the Theatre* (London: Longmans, Green & Co., 1950), 13.

12. "Alla commedia di Welles in prima fila Rita Hayworth" [Rita Hayworth in the front row at Welles's play], *Corriere d'Informazione* (Milan), June 20, 1950.

13. Lorenzo Bocchi, "Stravaganza di Orson Welles" [Orson Welles's extravagant play], *La Settimana Incom* (Rome), June 24, 1950.

14. Marco Ramperti, "Cronache dei 4 venti" [Chronicle of the four winds], *Film d'oggi*, November 15, 1950.

15. Giuseppe Grieco, "I santi si vendono meglio dei cowboys" [Saints sell more easily than Cowboys and Indians], *Cinema Nuovo*, July 15, 1953.

16. Gulliver, "Resti fra noi: Orson Welles" [Between you and me: Orson Welles], *L'elefante* (Rome), July 19, 1950.

17. The five articles were published in Italy by *Corriere d'Informazione* on December 20, 21, 22, 23, and 27, 1950. They were entitled "Ma che cos'è questa Germania?" [What is a Germany like this?]; "Berlino Est Berlino Ovest" [East and West Berlin]; "Le do a un

nazi le prendo da una antinazi" [I hit a Nazi and am hit by an anti-Nazi woman]; "Musica del 'Terzo Uomo' fra i ruderi di Berchtesgaden" [*The Third Man* theme among the ruins of Berchtesgaden]; and "I Tedeschi mi insultano perchè la penso come Nietzsche" [The Germans insult me because I agree with Nietzsche].

18. Welles, "Ma che cos'è questa Germania?"

19. Welles, "Le do a un nazi le prendo da una antinazi."

20. Welles, "Le do a un nazi le prendo da una antinazi."

21. Welles, "Musica del 'Terzo Uomo' fra I ruderi di Berchtesgarden."

22. "Contro Orson Welles finimondo dei tedeschi" [Germans ostracize Orson Welles], *il Gazzettino-Sera* (Venice), November 6, 1950.

23. "Orson Welles contro il realismo cinematografico" [Orson Welles against film realism], *Europeo* (Milan), October 15, 1950.

24. "Servizio segreto: Anche lui" (Secret service: Him, too), *Film* (Rome/Milan), October 28, 1950.

25. Lan (Arturo Lanocita), "Orson Welles il ribelle" [Orson Welles the rebel], *Corriere d'Informazione*, May 27, 1950.

26. Francis Koval, "Interview with Welles," *Sight & Sound*, December 1950; reprinted in Orson Welles, *Interviews*, ed. Mark W. Estrin (Jackson: University Press of Mississippi, 2002), 34. The interview took place around July, during the performances of *The Blessed and the Damned*.

27. Quoted in Arturo Lanocita, "Qualcuno ricorda Petrolini e altri evoca Shakespeare" (Reminders of Petrolini, evocations of Shakespeare), *Corriere della Sera* (Milan), November 29, 1950.

28. Gian Gaspare Napolitano, "Al terzo uomo piace il bloody marriage" [The third man likes a bloody marriage], *Europeo*, January 14, 1951.

29. The episode is mentioned in *Too Brief a Treat: The Letters of Truman Capote*, ed. Gerald Clark (New York: Random House, 2004), 141–42, 144.

30. Quoted in Ludovica Ripa di Meana, "Un decaduto in attesa di giudizio" [A fallen man awaiting judgment], *Europeo*, December 10, 1983.

31. Lanocita, "Qualcuno ricorda Petrolini, altri evoca Shakespeare."

32. F. R. (Franco Rispoli), "Orson 'il diavolo' non è brutto come si dipinge" [Welles is less devilish than he would have you believe], *Film*, November 11, 1950.

33. "Oggi parla Orson Welles dell'Otello e di altre cose" [Today Orson Welles will speak about *Othello* and other things], *Araldo dello Spettacolo* (Rome), November 13, 1950.

34. For these and other details about the making of *Othello*, see Jean-Pierre Berthomé, "Les labyrinthes d'Othello," *Positif*, July–August 1998.

35. Giuliano Doge, "Con una risata Orson respinge i marziani" [Orson laughs away the Martians], *il Gazzettino-Sera*, November 21, 1950.

36. Quoted in Alberto Farina, *Tutto genio e sregolatezza*, 23.

12. WAITING FOR *OTHELLO*

1. "Orson Welles morso da un cane idrofobo" [Orson Welles bitten by a rabid dog], *Corriere d'Informazione* (Milan), January 16, 1951, front page; "Morso da un cagnolino l'attore Orson Welles" [Orson Welles the actor bitten by a dog], *Momento Sera* (Rome), January 17, 1951.

2. Oberdan Troiani in Alberto Farina, "Tutto genio e sregolatezza" [Bizarre genius], *Film cronache*, January/February 1993.

3. Jack J. Jorgens, *Shakespeare on Film* (Bloomington: Indiana University Press, 1977), 177.

4. Gian Gaspare Napolitano, "Al terzo uomo piace il bloody marriage" [The third man likes a bloody marriage], *Europeo* (Milan), January 14, 1951.

5. Harriet White Medin, "Othello, Desdemona and Me" *Video Watchdog* 23 (May–July 1994).

6. Jean Jacques Tacchella, "Sans commentaire," *L'Écran français*, March 14, 1951.

7. Giorgio Berti, "Il Tevere ha parlato con la erre moscia" [The Tiber speaks with an aristocratic accent], *La Settimana Incom* (Rome), February 3, 1951.

8. Giorgio Berti, "Una ragazza di sangue blu sarà la Wandissima di domani" [A blue-blooded girl tomorrow's Wanda Osiris], *La Settimana Incom*, March 31, 1951.

9. Gisella Sofio, personal communication, November 19, 2004.

10. Alberto Mondadori, "Orson Welles e Shakespeare," *Epoca* (Milan), December 2, 1950.

11. Ennio Flaiano, "La macchina di Welles" [Welles's machinery], *il Mondo* (Rome), March 24, 1951; reprinted in Flaiano, *Lettere d'amore al cinema* [Love letters to the cinema] (Milan: Rizzoli, 1978), 203–204.

12. Guido Aristarco, "Film di questi giorni" [New releases], *Cinema* (Milan), February 15, 1951.

13. Mario Gromo, *Film visti* [Films I've seen] (Rome: Edizioni di Bianco e Nero, 1957), 372–73.

14. Callisto Cosulich, "Macbeth," *Giornale di Trieste*, June 5, 1951; reprinted in *Il cinema secondo Cosulich* (Gorizia: Transmedia, 2005), 192.

15. G. L. R. (Gian Luigi Rondi), "Macbeth," *il Tempo* (Rome), March 10, 1951.

16. Fernaldo Di Giammatteo, "Macbeth," *Bianco e Nero*, April 1951.

17. Alberto Moravia, "Macbeth con le convulsioni" [Macbeth with convulsions], *Europeo*, March 25, 1951.

18. Frank Brady, *Citizen Welles*, (New York: Charles Scribner's Sons, 1989), 440.

19. Anita, "Filo diretto: Mascherate di Welles" [Direct line: Welles masquerades], *Hollywood* (Milan), March 17, 1951.

20. Brady, *Citizen Welles*, 434. Brady's biography contains invaluable information about Welles's years in Italy, but numerous inaccuracies. Many Italian names are incorrect (most notably he wrote of one Montatori Scalera, a misspelling of Commendatore Scalera, later repeated in various books and articles by others) and some of the locations and events are incorrectly reported. Brady did not cite his source for the cost of *Othello* and says the contract with Zanuck was for $75,000. In fact the correct amount was 195,000,000 lire ($312,000 at the exchange rate of the time).

21. Unsigned and undated note, Direzione Generale dello Spettacolo; in the State Archives.

22. Unsigned and undated note, Direzione Generale dello Spettacolo; in the State Archives.

23. The letter from Patrice Dally to George Fanto, dated April 14, 1950, is among George Fanto's papers in the Lilly Library, Indiana University. According to the letter it would seem that the producers had already received 18,100,000 francs from Tenoudji on

March 18, 1950, and 9,600,000 were expected shortly. Jean-Pierre Berthomé, personal communication, 19 February 2006.

24. Sacha, Lucidi, and Shepridge are credited as editors of the Italian version of the film, distributed by Scalera. In the slightly different American version, William Morton was added to the credits.

25. "Orson Welles," *Cento Stelle* 2, no. 76 (September 3, 1951).

26. "Otello, il Moro di Venezia," *L'Eco del Cinema e dello Spettacolo,* special issue for the Venice Film Festival, August 1951.

27. Ugo Casiraghi, "È cominciato a Venezia il carnevale della mondanità" [High society moves to Venice], *l'Unità* (Milan), September 1, 1951.

28. From an article in *Ce soir* (Paris), September 6, 1951; quoted in Jean-Pierre Berthomé, "Les labyrinthes d'Othello," *Positif,* July–August 1998.

29. Luigi Fossati, "Ritirato all'ultima ora l'Otello di Orson Welles" [Orson Welles's *Othello* withdrawn at the last minute], *Avanti!* (Rome), September 1, 1951. The other members of the jury were Antonio Baldini, Ermanno Contini, Fabrizio Dentice, Piero Gadda Conti, Vinicio Marinucci, and Giorgio Vigolo.

30. Callisto Cosulich, "Neppure quest'anno Welles ha voluto smentirse se stesso" [Welles lives up to his reputation yet again], *Giornale di Trieste,* September 2, 1951; reprinted in *Il cinema secondo Cosulich,* 280.

31. Oreste Tesei, "Orson vestito di bianco ha sedotto i giornalisti" [In a white suit, Orson wins over the journalists, *Oggi* (Milan), September 13, 1951.

32. Vittorio Bonicelli, "Il colpo di scena di Orson Welles" [Orson Welles pulls a surprise], *Tempo* (Milan), September 15, 1951.

33. Paolo Valmarana, "Il caso Orson Welles" [The Orson Welles affair], *L'Eco del Cinema e dello Spettacolo,* September 1951.

34. Tesei, "Orson vestito di bianco ha sedotto i giornalisti."

35. Bonicelli, "Il colpo di scena di Orson Welles."

36. Adriano Baracco, "Venezia, primo tempo" [Venice, first half], *Hollywood,* September 15, 1951.

37. Arturo Lanocita, "Orson Welles ha agitato le acque chete del Festival" [Orson Welles upsets an unsuspecting Venice], *Corriere della Sera* (Milan), September 2, 1951.

38. Valmarana, "Il caso Orson Welles."

39. Gian Gaspare Napolitano, "Churchill a Venezia si sente ancora giovane" [Churchill in Venice feeling young again], *Europeo,* September 9, 1951.

40. Joseph Cotten, *Vanity Will Get You Somewhere* (San Francisco: Mercury House, 1987), 106.

41. Orson Welles and Peter Bogdanovich, *This Is Orson Welles,* ed. Jonathan Rosenbaum (London: Harper Collins, 1993), 227. Cotten's version seems more plausible than Welles's account, although he misplaces the event in 1949 during his previous visit to Venice.

42. On the relationship between Welles and Louise de Vilmorin, see Giuseppe Scaraffia, "Nota," in Louise di Vilmorin, *La lettera in un taxi* [Letter in a taxi] (Palermo: Sellerio, 2000); Giuseppe Scaraffia, "Ti amerò per sempre: Stasera" [I will always love you: This evening], *Amica* (Milan), August 30, 2000.

43. Orson Welles, "La lunga notte di Don Carlos" [Don Carlos's long night], *Epoca,* September 15, 1951, 62–67.

13. REVIEWING *OTHELLO*

1. Alberto Mondadori, "Gioia dell'anima mia, se le tempeste . . . ," *Epoca* (Milan), September 8, 1951.

2. Paolo Valmarana, "Il caso Orson Welles" [The Orson Welles affair], *L'Eco del Cinema e dello Spettacolo,* September 1951.

3. Luigi Chiarini, "Pane al pane" [Telling it like it is], *Cinema* (Milan), October 15, 1951. Roberto Paolella joined the discussion by mocking the so-called purists who considered this or that good or bad cinema (rather like Cocteau in his profile of Welles in Bazin's biography), "Questo è cinema, questo non è cinema" [This is cinema, this ain't], *Cinema,* December 1, 1950.

4. Alberto Mondadori, letter to Luigi Chiarini, October 31, 1951; quoted in A. Mondadori, *Lettere di una vita, 1922–1975* [Letters of a lifetime, 1922–1975] (Milan: Fondazione Arnoldo e Alberto Mondadori, 1996), 392–93.

5. "Orson Welles querela ma poi non si presenta" [Orson Welles sues but isn't in court], *Corriere d'Informazione* (Milan), November 5, 1951, last edition.

6. Angelo Maccario, "Orson Welles e Pagnol," *Teatro scenario* (Milan), December 1, 1951.

7. Lan (Arturo Lanocita), "Otello," *Corriere della Sera* (Rome), December 1, 1951.

8. Vittorio Bonicelli, "L'inquieto Otello di Orson Welles" [Orson Welles's restless Othello], *Tempo* (Milan), December 15, 1951.

9. Angelo Solmi, "Il geometrico Otello di Welles" [Welles's geometrical Othello], *Oggi* (Milan), December 13, 1951.

10. Ermanno Contini, "Otello," *il Messaggero* (Rome), December 6, 1951.

11. Alberto Moravia, "Un Otello forte ma senza cervello" [A strong but mindless Othello], *Europeo* (Milan), December 12, 1951.

12. G. L. R. (Gian Luigi Rondi), "Otello," *il Tempo* (Rome), December 6, 1951.

13. Giorgio Santarelli, "Prima visione: Otello" [New releases: *Othello*], *La Rivista del Cinematografo,* January 1952.

14. fo. (Luigi Fossati), "Otello," *Avanti!* (Milan), December 1, 1951.

15. This word refers to the rapes committed in Italy by French soldiers immediately after liberation [translator's note].

16. u. c. (Ugo Casiraghi), "Otello," *l'Unità* (Milan), December 1, 1951.

17. Guido Aristarco, "Otello," *Cinema,* December 15, 1951.

18. Luigi Chiarini, "Pane al pane . . . Noticina sull'Otello" [Telling it like it is: Note on Othello], *Cinema,* December 31, 1951.

19. Franco Berutti, "I film del mese" [Films of the month], *Sipario* (Milan), December 1951.

20. f. d. g. (Fernaldo Di Giammatteo), "Otello e Umberto D.," *Rassegna del film,* Turin, February 1952.

21. f. d. g., "Otello e Umberto D."

22. Maurizio Del Ministro misses this similarity but finds others with Olivier's film, believing Welles had been influenced by the camera's discovery of the bridal chamber and of the seascape (at the beginning of the "To be or not to be" soliloquy) in *Hamlet.* Maurizio Del Ministro, *Othello di Welles* (Rome: Bulzoni Editore, 2000), 91, 93.

23. Jack J. Jorgens, *Shakespeare on Film* (Bloomington: Indiana University Press, 1977), 176. See also Antonio Tuzzi, "Welles e Shakespeare," *Cinemasessanta,* November–December 1985.

24. André Bazin, *Orson Welles* (Paris: Chavanne, 1950), 162.

25. Michael Anderegg, *Orson Welles, Shakespeare and Popular Culture* (New York: Columbia University Press, 1999), 104–111.

26. Joseph McBride, *Orson Welles,* rev. ed. (New York: Da Capo Press, 1996), 126.

27. James Naremore, *The Magic World of Orson Welles* (New York: Oxford University Press, 1978), 212–19.

28. Micheál Mac Liammóir, *Put Money in Thy Purse* (London: Methuen, 1952), 28.

29. Quoted in Peter Noble, *The Fabulous Orson Welles* (London: Hutchinson, 1956), 180.

30. Orson Welles and Peter Bogdanovich, *This Is Orson Welles,* ed. Jonathan Rosenbaum (London: Harper Collins, 1993), 242.

31. Welles and Bogdanovich, *This Is Orson Welles,* 242.

32. Gian Luigi Rondi, "Primato del cinema italiano" [Italy gets first prize], *il Tempo,* May 13, 1952 (see also Rondi's article in *la Nazione* of Florence the same day); Arturo Lanocita, "Due soldi di speranza e Otello vincono il Gran premio a Cannes" [*Due soldi di speranza* and *Othello* share the Grand Prix at Cannes], *Corriere della Sera,* May 11, 1952; Ugo Casiraghi, "Né la flotta né McCarthy hanno fatto vincere i film di Hollywood" [Neither the fleet nor McCarthy manage to obtain a prize for Hollywood), *l'Unità,* May 13, 1952; Alfredo Di Lauro, "V festival di Cannes," *La Rivista del Cinematografo,* 1952.

33. Casiraghi, "Né la flotta né McCarthy."

34. Jean-Jacques Gautier, "En couronnant Othello, le jury n'a-t-il pas rendu homage aux qualités de *Citizen Kane?*" *Le Figaro* (Paris), May 13, 1952.

35. Henry Magnan, "Deux sous d'ésperance (Renato Castellani) et Othello (Orson Welles) Grand Prix ex aequo du Ve Festival de Cannes," *Le Monde* (Paris), May 13, 1952.

14. BYZANTINE TIMEKEEPING

1. Patrizia Mori, personal communication, June 2, 2006.

2. Tatti Sanguineti, personal communication, April 21, 2006.

3. John Francis Lane, open letter to Orson Welles, *Cinema* (Milan), February 1, 1952.

4. Quoted in Alberto Farina, *Tutto genio e sregolatezza,* [Bizarre genius], *Film cronache,* January/February 1993.

5. Leonard Lyons, "The Lyons Den," *The Rome Daily American,* April 16, 1952.

6. Jean Jacques Tacchella, "Sans commentaire," *L'Écran français,* Paris, January 30, 1952.

7. Quoted in Farina, *Tutto genio e sregolatezza,* 25.

8. Marina Vlady, *24 images/second* (Paris: Fayard, 2005), 18.

9. Daniel Kothenschulte, "Attendez que je sois mort: Tout sera vendable!" in *The Other Side of the Wind,* ed. Giorgio Gosetti and Stefan Drössler (Paris: Cahiers du cinéma; Locarno: Locarno International Film Festival, 2005), 93–95.

10. Quoted in Franca Faldini and Goffredo Fofi, *L'avventurosa storia del cinema italiano, 1935–1959* [The adventurous history of Italian cinema] (Milan: Feltrinelli, 1979), 303–304.

11. In a letter dated January 8, 1952, Eitel Monaco, President of ANICA, asked Direzione Generale dello Spettacolo to grant the film Italian status, given "the financial straits of the production company." On July 15, 1954, in another letter also in the State Archives, Annibale Scicluna informed the SIAE that "Othello must not be considered Italian."

12. For a more detailed analysis of the effect of censorship on this film, see Alberto Anile, *Totò proibito* [Forbidden Totò] (Turin: Lindau, 2005), 70–75.

13. See Lucio Fulci, "Totò e Orson Welles, l'impossibile coppia" [Totò and Orson Welles, the impossible couple], *L'Italia* (Rome), March 24, 1993. Enrico and Carlo Vanzina, Steno's sons, looked for the twenty pages among their father's papers but found nothing. Welles's essay on Totò and Pirandello has probably been lost forever.

14. Arturo Lanocita, "Totò rivale di Orson Welles in un film tratto da Pirandello" [Totò, Welles's rival, in a film adaptation of Pirandello], *Corriere della Sera* (Milan), January 20, 1953.

15. Italo Dragosei, "Tra l'uomo e la bestia in pericolo la virtù" [Virtue, endangered between man and beast], *Festival* (Milan), February 28, 1953.

16. Quoted in Marcello Garofalo, *Tutto il cinema di Sergio Leone* (Milan: Baldini & Castoldi, 1999), 56.

17. Franca Faldini, *Roma Hollywood Roma*, (Milan: Baldini & Castoldi, 1997), 35.

18. Giancarlo Nicotra, personal communication, February 22, 2006.

19. Lucio Fulci in Marcello Garofalo, "Uno, nessuno, centofulci," *Segnocinema*, November–December 1993.

20. Arturo Lanocita, "L'uomo, la bestia e la virtù," *Corriere della Sera*, May 14, 1953.

21. Giulio Cesare Castello, "L'uomo, la bestia e la virtù," *Cinema*, April 30, 1953.

22. Orson Welles, "The Third Audience," *Sight & Sound*, January–March 1954.

23. Franco Dorigo, "Orson Welles," *Cinema*, February 15, 1953.

24. Umberto Barbaro, "Giulio Cesare," *Vie Nuove* (Rome), January 17, 1954; reprinted in Barbaro, *Servitù e grandezza del cinema* [The servility and greatness of the cinema] (Rome: Editori riuniti, 1962), 460.

25. Luigi Chiarini, *Il film nella battaglia delle idee* [Film in the battle of ideas] (Milan and Rome: Fratelli Bocca, 1954), 258.

26. Giovanni Calendoli, "A Shakespeare si addice la dimensione fantastica" [Shakespeare the phantasmagorical], *L'Eco del Cinema e dello Spettacolo*, November 30, 1954.

27. Ennio Flaiano, *Diario notturno* [Nocturnal diary] (Milan: Adelphi, 1994), 165–85.

28. Maurice Bessy, *Orson Welles*, (Paris: Éditions Seghers, 1963), 76.

29. "Orson Welles impersonerà l'ex re d'Egitto Farouk" [Orson Welles will play Farouk, former king of Egypt], *Corriere d'Informazione* (Milan), February 13, 1953, front page. According to the announcement, the film was to be an Italo-French production starring Welles, Micheline Presle, and Eric von Stroheim. Bogdanovich says Farouk offered to finance *Caesar!*

30. Declaration by notary public Angelo Angotti dated February 11, 1955; in the State Archives. Chamber of commerce records still bear traces of the Orson Welles Productions company, with erroneous references to connections in Argentina. The records may have been lost or deteriorated over time, but generally the disappearance of documents of this kind is considered an attempt to conceal debts and insolvency.

15. GOING, GOING, GONE

1. The accusation was made during the hearing of March 26, 1953.

2. Orson Welles, "Non sono un profugo di Hollywood" [I'm not a refugee from Hollywood], *Tempo* (Milan), May 13, 1954.

3. Paola Mori, "L'uomo che sposo" [The man I'm marrying], *Tempo*, May 19, 1955.

4. R. S., "È morta l'attrice Paola Mori, ultima moglie di Orson Welles" [Death of the actress Paola Mori, Orson Welles's last wife], *la Stampa* (Turin), August 14, 1986.

5. Orson Welles, "Il n'y a pas d'art apprivoisé," *La Démocratie combattante*, April–May 1953; reprinted in Maurice Bessy, *Orson Welles*(Paris: Éditions Seghers, 1963), 104.

6. Giorgio Salvioni, "È venuto in Italia per sposare sua moglie" [He has come to Italy to marry his wife], *Epoca* (Milan), January 19, 1958.

7. Enrico Roda, "34 domande a Orson Welles" [Thirty-four questions to Orson Welles], *Tempo,* January 30, 1958.

8. Mori, "L'uomo che sposo."

9. Gina Lollobrigida, personal communication, April 15, 2002.

10. Elsa Martinelli, *Sono come sono* [I am what I am] (Milan: Rusconi, 1995), 206.

11. Audrey Stainton, "Don Quixote: Orson Welles's secret," *Sight & Sound,* Fall 1988.

12. Oberdan Troiani in the documentary *Memorie a 15 ASA,* by Massimiliano Troiani, produced by La grande opera, 2006, and a more recent uncompleted documentary by Massimiliano Troiani.

13. Arnoldo Foà, *Recitare* [Acting], (Rome: Gremese, 1998), 52.

14. Oriana Fallaci, "L'uomo che sarà presidente" [The man who will be president], *Europeo* (Milan), February 4, 1962.

15. Quoted in Leonard Lyons, "The Lyons Den," *New York Post,* April 2, 1963.

16. Orson Welles and Peter Bogdanovich, *This Is Orson Welles,* ed. Jonathan Rosenbaum (London: Harper Collins, 1993), 141.

17. Orson Welles, interview by André Bazin, Charles Bitsch, and Jean Domarchi, *Cahiers du cinéma,* September 1958; translated and reprinted in Orson Welles, *Interviews,* ed. Mark W. Estrin (Jackson: University Press of Mississippi, 2002), 76.

18. C. Quarantotto, "La moda del neorealismo conquista produttori e registi" [The vogue of neorealism wins over producers and directors], *Rome* (Naples), March 1, 1960.

19. Orson Welles, interview by Kenneth Tynan, *Playboy,* March 1967; reprinted in Orson Welles, *Interviews,* 135.

20. Quoted in Lietta Tornabuoni, "Fellini, il barocco di Orson Welles," *la Stampa* (Turin), October 12, 1985.

21. Umberto Barbaro, "Foglie d'autunno" [Autumn leaves], *Vie Nuove* (Rome), February 2, 1957; reprinted in Umberto Barbaro, *Servitù e grandezza del cinema* [The servility and greatness of the cinema] (Rome: Editori riuniti, 1962), 396.

22. Carl Vincent, "Orson Welles ovvero l'ingegno dello sbalordimento" [Orson Welles, engineering dismay], *La Rivista del Cinematografo,* April 1958.

23. Italo Calvino, "Due film e Stalin" [Two films and Stalin], *Cinema Nuovo,* January–February 1959.

24. Roberto Pariante, "Orson Welles da Citizen Kane a Othello," *Bianco e Nero,* March 1956.

25. Claudio Rispoli, "Introduzione a Citizen Kane," *Filmcritica,* July–August 1964.

26. See Maurizio Ponzi, "Welles à la TV," *Cahiers du cinéma,* April 1965.

27. See Alessandro Tasca di Cutò, *Un principe in America,* [A prince in America] (Palermo: Sellerio, 2004), 296.

28. Guido Aristarco, "Il cittadino Orson Welles e il mito del potere" [Citizen Orson Welles and the myth of power], *Cinema Nuovo,* July–August 1966.

29. Juan Cobos, Miguel Rubio, and J. A. Pruneda, "A Trip to Don Quixoteland: Conversations with Orson Welles" [1964], in *Cahiers du cinéma in English* 5 (1966); reprinted in Ronald Gottesman, *Focus on Citizen Kane* (Englewood Cliffs, N.J.: Prentice-Hall, 1971), 17.

30. See Marco Giusti, "Silvio rimembri ancor quel carosello?" [Silvio, do you recall that fairground roundabout?], *il Manifesto,* Rome, July 2, 1996.

31. Alberto Ceretto, "Welles a Roma fa la superspia" [Welles a super-spy in Rome], *Corriere della Sera* (Rome), May 13, 1969.

32. Mila Murzi, "Moglie via, Orson se la spassa con Oja" [Welles enjoys Oja's company in his wife's absence], *Oggi* (Milan), February 17, 1970.

33. Guido Fink, "L'accostamento a Welles" [Approaching Welles], *Cinema e cinema,* April–June 1975.

34. See Guido Aristarco, *Storia delle teoriche del cinema* [History of film theory] (Turin: Einaudi, 1951). The few comments dedicated to Welles (and practically only to *Macbeth*) were reprinted, unchanged, in the 1960 edition.

35. Guido Aristarco, *Il dissolvimento della ragione: Discorso sul cinema* [The fading of reason: An essay on film] (Milan: Feltrinelli, 1965), 379.

36. See Guido Aristarco, "Rosebud," in *L'utopia cinematografica* (Palermo: Sellerio, 1984), 150–55. The book is a selection of essays and reviews from the 1960s and 1970s.

37. "Orson Welles once acutely observed that Italy is full of actors, fifty million of them, in fact, and they are almost all good; there are only a few bad ones, and they are on the stage and in the films" (Luigi Barzini, Jr., *The Italians* [London: Penguin, 1968]), 81.

38. Orson Welles, "Eduardo," *Vogue* (French edition), Christmas 1982.

39. Aldo Tassone, "Welles: Chi ha paura di quel Falstaff?" [Welles: Who's afraid of Falstaff?], *la Repubblica* (Rome), June 30, 1983.

40. Ettore Scola, "Cosa vi ricorda quella 'Giornata particolare?'" [What does that special day remind you of?], *l'Unità* (Rome), February 18, 1995.

GIAN LUIGI RONDI

1. Gian Luigi Rondi, "Orson Welles alle prese con Shakespeare fa del teatro roboante e wagneriano" [Welles's Shakespeare is bombastic, Wagnerian theater], *la Nazione* (Florence), September 4, 1948. A slightly modified, shorter article titled "La tragedia di Macbeth, insuccesso di Orson Welles" [Macbeth's tragedy, Orson Welles's failure] was published in *il Tempo* (Rome), the same day.

2. Gian Luigi Rondi, "Primato del cinema italiano" [Italian cinema given first prize], *il Tempo,* May 13, 1952. The article was also published in *la Nazione* the same day.

3. Gian Luigi Rondi, *Un lungo viaggio 2: Gli stranieri* [A long journey 2: The foreigners] (Florence: Le Monnier, 2001), 275–76.

16. WELLES AND ROSSELLINI

1. Studies of the "restored" 1992 version of Othello include François Thomas, "La tragédie d'Othello," *Positif* 424 (June 1996); and Michael Anderegg, *Orson Welles, Shakespeare and Popular Culture* (New York: Columbia University Press, 1999).

2. Alessandro Tasca di Cutò, *Un principe in America*, [A prince in America] (Palermo: Sellerio, 2004), 301–302.

3. Joseph McBride, *Orson Welles* (Cambridge: Da Capo Press, 1996), 6–7.

4. André Bazin, *Orson Welles* (Paris: Chavanne), 1950.

5. Orson Welles and Peter Bogdanovich, *This Is Orson Welles*, ed. Jonathan Rosenbaum (London: Harper Collins, 1993), 76–77.

6. Félix Morlion, "Le basi filosofiche del neorealismo cinematografico italiano" [The philosophical basis of Italian neorealist cinema], *Bianco e Nero*, June 1948; quoted in Elena Dagrada and Tomaso Subini, "Félix Morlion e Roberto Rossellini," in *Cinema italiano e chiesa: Una storia culturale* [Italian cinema and the Church: A cultural history], ed. Ruggero Eugeni and Elena Mosconi (Rome: Ente dello Spettacolo, 2006), n.p.—an illuminating essay on the role of Dominican Padre Morlion, who worked on *Stromboli, Francesco giullare di Dio*, and *Europa '51*, and the attempts by the Catholic Church to annex neorealism.

7. Lan (Arturo Lanocita), "Orson Welles il ribelle," [Orson Welles the rebel], *Corriere d'Informazione*, May 27, 1950.

8. James Naremore, *The Magic World of Orson Welles* (New York: Oxford University Press, 1978).

9. Alfredo Todisco, "Orson Welles 'riabilitato' dalla stampa italiana" [Orson Welles "rehabilitated" by the Italian press], *Ultimissime*, September 18, 1948.

10. "Orson Welles," *Cento Stelle* 2, no. 76 (September 3, 1951).

11. Alberto Lattuada in Franca Faldini and Goffredo Fofi, *L'avventurosa storia del cinema italiano, 1935–1959*, [The adventurous history of Italian cinema] (Milan: Feltrinelli, 1979), 287.

12. See Francis Koval, "Interview with Welles," reprinted in Orson Welles, *Interviews*, ed. Mark W. Estrin (Jackson: University Press of Mississippi, 2002), 33.

13. Gian Gaspare Napolitano, "Al terzo uomo piace il bloody marriage" [The third man likes a bloody marriage], *Europeo* (Milan), January 14, 1951.

14. Tag Gallagher, *The Adventures of Roberto Rossellini* (New York: De Capo Press, 1998), 390.

15. Elena Dagrada, "Conta di più una bella voce o un buon microfono? Orson Welles, la tecnica" [What matters more, a beautiful voice or a good microphone? The technique of Orson Welles], *La Valle dell'Eden*, January–June 2005. Dagrada dedicates several pages to André Bazin who "not accidentally" loved both filmmakers and, "together with Renoir, placed them at the center of his thoughts about the cinema, far from the extremes of the *politiques des auteurs*, to reaffirm the importance of the work of art over its creator (a statement Welles was later to make his own)."

16. Quoted in Lietta Tornabuoni, "Fellini, il barocco di Orson Welles," *la Stampa* (Turin), October 12, 1985.

INDEX

ALBERTO ANILE is an Italian film critic and journalist. He is author of several books and essays about director Roberto Rossellini and comedy actor Totò. *Orson Welles in Italia* first appeared in Italy in 2006. His most recent book (co-authored with Maria Gabriella Giannice) concerns Luchino Visconti's *The Leopard.*

MARCUS PERRYMAN graduated from Sidney Sussex College, Cambridge, in 1977 and has lived in Italy ever since. He is editor and translator, with distinguished British poet Peter Robinson, of *The Selected Poetry and Prose of Vittorio Sereni* and author and translator of *The Journey of G. Mastorna, the Film Fellini Didn't Make.*

CPSIA information can be obtained
at www.ICGtesting.com
Printed in the USA
LVOW04s1354071215

465773LV00028B/1042/P